MINORITY GROUP POLITICS
a reader

Minority Group Politics

a reader

STEPHEN J. HERZOG

Moorpark College

HOLT, RINEHART AND WINSTON, INC.

NEW YORK   CHICAGO   SAN FRANCISCO   ATLANTA

DALLAS   MONTREAL   TORONTO

Preface

The subject of this volume is, quite simply, the politics of three minority groups—blacks, Mexican-Americans (or Chicanos), and American Indians. The general framework is problem oriented; that is, the reading selections are arranged according to the major problems faced by these groups in their search for the "good life" as it is defined by American society: a good education, a respectable job, and the material possessions that result from these achievements—a nice home (preferably in the suburbs), a reasonably new car, and the ability to borrow enough to "keep up with the Joneses." (The major assumption made by the author has been that this is the primary goal of the vast majority of blacks, Mexican-Americans, and American Indians, despite the statements made by a minority of these groups. However, this goal, admittedly, has been very vaguely stated, and no attempt has been made by the author to find a more exact description of the goals of Americans because this point is really peripheral to the thrust of the text.)

Minority Group Politics differs from the other works on the general subject in several ways. First, it is the result of an effort to bring together material on the three *major* minority groups in American society. The greater portion of the collections now available focus only on the blacks. In no case has there been a systematic effort to present materials relating to the other two groups. This failure is understandable in light of the history of

v

the civil rights movement, where the blacks have been the most active group. The other two groups are just beginning to become more active, but as the selections indicate, they have far fewer major leaders and formalized organizations than do the blacks. This lack of activity is no excuse for overemphasizing the black groups; there simply has been a failure to study all three, a fault this volume attempts to remedy by providing the necessary information.

The second difference is that this is a study of the *politics* of minority groups. Most previously published works have focused on either sociological-anthropological or historical studies. There are some collections of Supreme Court decisions dealing with race relations (that is, on black-white relations), but there has been no single volume that brings together legal and political materials. No doubt this is in part due to the absence of a formal field of minority group politics at the graduate level in political science departments. Without training in the field it is unlikely that a scholar will investigate and publish materials relating to it.

The third difference is more subtle and philosophical. Although the orientation of *Minority Group Politics* is to the problems of minority groups and the methods they use to solve them, the author takes the point of view articulated by Gunnar Myrdal in *The American Dream* (New York: McGraw-Hill, 1964) that these are not the problems of the minority community, but problems for the total society. In every case at least 90 percent of the population has control over the resources necessary to solve these problems; it is the responsibility of the majority to allocate these resources to solve the problems. To say that blacks, Mexican-Americans, and American Indians can solve their own problems is not only unrealistic in terms of modern society, but denies the fact that most of the power lies in the hands of the white Anglo majority.

The heavy emphasis on legal materials is another factor that differentiates this reader from the majority of collections. There are two reasons for this emphasis. First, the author's extensive training in constitutional law has resulted in a strong orientation toward legal materials. Second, the law plays a very important role in the politics of this society (as evidenced by the effect on race relations of the school desegregation decision in *Brown* v. *Board of Education*), and thus a thorough review of minority group politics must include these materials.

The uses to which this volume can be put in teaching are quite diverse. For the introductory course in American government or sociology it would serve as an effective supplement to a basic text. It is also desirable as a basic text or one of several books for a course in minority groups or race relations in the sociology, history, or anthropology department. Finally, it is a core book around which to build a course in minority group politics.

There is a crying need for more reasoned discourse on the problems of human relations in America. *Minority Group Politics* is dedicated to two men who gave their lives to the cause of brotherhood between the races, Dr. Martin Luther King, Jr., and Senator Robert Kennedy. Their commitment to an integrated American society achieved by nonviolent means is also the position taken by the author. To achieve this goal, however, requires patience and understanding—patience to meet the complex problems of human relations and overcome them one by one, and understanding that there are still people whose racist attitudes prevent a more complete realization of intergroup harmony. One way in which the goal will be reached is by careful and responsible examination of the record that is available. This book is offered to such an examination.

The author wishes to express his gratitude to the administration of Moorpark College for their support of this task; to a number of students, too numerous to list, who aided in collecting the materials; to Nicki Crowe, Pat Palmer, and Sharon Hoshida, who acted as secretary, girl Friday, and frequent critic; and to his wife, Elaine, who bore up admirably under the trauma of a nocturnal writer. The author is responsible for all errors of omission and commission.

S. J. H.

Moorpark, Illinois
April 1971

Contents

MINORITY GROUP POLITICS
a reader

INTRODUCTION

Minority group relations has become the most pressing
issue of American politics, especially in the last fifteen
years. Names such as Martin Luther King, Jr., Stokely
Carmichael, Malcolm X, Cesar Chavez, and Reies
Tijerina are familiar to most Americans. Ghetto names
such as Watts, Hough, and Harlem similarly have
assumed a central place in the political vocabulary; and
cities such as Newark, Chicago, and Los Angeles have
received a new form of publicity.

The beginning of this dramatic series of events is
usually identified with the decision by the Unites States
Supreme Court on May 17, 1954, in *Brown* v. *Board of
Education,* that racial discrimination in public education
was a violation of the Constitution. However, the real
beginning of the major court rulings in favor of blacks
were in 1944 when, in *Smith* v. *Allwright,* the Court
declared the white primary unconstitutional and
dramatically increased the protection of the Constitution
for black voters, and in 1948 when, in *Shelley* v. *Kraemer,*
the Court rejected the judicial enforcement of restrictive
covenants in housing as state action in violation of the
Fourteenth Amendment. Nevertheless, it was the Brown
decision that signaled a massive drive by civil rights
groups to extend the benefits of American society to all
blacks. The period since 1954 has not been easy for

blacks, however; whites, especially in the South, have used every method to prevent school desegregation, and almost twenty years later, there is still a massive lack of enforcement of the 1954 decision. Whites have used police dogs, water hoses, and cattle prods to break up demonstrations by blacks against school, political, and economic discrimination.

At the same time that the rights of blacks were being increased, Mexican-Americans and American Indians remained in conditions essentially similar to the pre-1954 period. While sit-ins and demonstrations produced changes in the treatment of black customers in restaurants, hotels, and stores, and open-housing laws provided opportunities for blacks to move into previously segregated neighborhoods, Mexican-Americans and American Indians remained in low-paying agricultural jobs, received the poorest education in the United States, and lived in the worst ghettoes of the country. The "sleeping giant of the Southwest," the Mexican-American, began to awaken only in the last few years, and the American Indian has yet to organize effectively on the national level and to press for changes in his life.

Many reasons might be given for the importance of the Brown decision. Basically what was involved was the increased recognition of the importance of education for success in an industrial society on the one hand, and the immense difference between educational opportunities for blacks and whites on the other. Yet it seems more relevant to the intensity of reactions to note that the individuals involved were children. Children are not born to hate, and white southerners must have recognized that their children would be presented with living denials of the white southern stereotype of the black man. How could southerners hope to maintain a segregated society if their children did not share their prejudices?

Thus the revolution began. From the legal decisions of 1954 and 1955 to the bus boycott in Montgomery, Alabama, in 1957, the sit-ins and picketing of the late 1950s and early 1960s, the Selma marches of 1964, the Delano grape strike, the violence in Watts in 1965, to violence since then, the movement for minority equality has developed. There have been many problems, but they can be classified into six areas: education, housing, employment, relations with law-enforcement personnel, voting and political power, and psychological self-esteem. Similarly, the responses have been varied, but can be classified in five areas: legalism and appeal through the courts, employment opportunities through negotiation, integration through nonviolent demonstration, separation, and minority power. Broadly, the question now being asked is, Does the solution lie within the existing system (integration), or is the system so corrupt that physical separation is the only solution? The answer to this question may not only decide the future of relations in America, but also the future of American society as a whole.

In reviewing the historical evolution of the efforts by blacks, Mexican-Americans, and American Indians to achieve a more equal position in American society, several trends emerge, including:

1. The shift in focus from one area of the country—the South—to the nation as a whole

2. The growing militancy of members of minority groups

3. The changing character of the problems and the responses with increased urbanization

4. The increasing factionalization of the groups, with divisions occurring over both the goals to be achieved and the methods for achieving them

5. The shift in general emphasis from integration into the white Anglo society to at least temporary separation and the desire for cultural pride

6. The increasing concern over the relationship between the groups and government agents, particularly police

7. The continuing emphasis on education as a central factor in the improvement of the lives of the group members, with a changing emphasis on level and type of education

8. Greater participation in the political process both as voters and as candidates for public office, especially among the blacks.

Let us consider these factors individually. In the late 1950s and early 1960s, during the heyday of the black civil rights movement, most of the public attention was focused on the South. People outside of the South felt quite free to criticize the racial bigots of that region, and tacitly to assume that they lived in a different world. This belief was rudely shaken by the series of black revolts in urban centers of the North beginning in Watts in 1965. The warning signs should have been clear. The rejection of open housing in California in the 1964 election by the overwhelming majority of whites was only the most publicized of a series of such actions by communities in the North. The segregation in housing produced large-scale *de facto* school segregation. Job opportunities were limited and increasingly poor as more education and skills were required. At the same time, the Mexican-Americans and American Indians were awakening. They began to borrow the methods of confrontation from the civil rights groups and became more articulate. Geographically, Mexican-Americans are concentrated in the Southwest, but the Indians are distributed throughout the nation. As a result, today the arena of conflict extends from Alaska to Florida and from southern California to New England. Certainly, the belief of northerners and westerners that "it can't happen here" has been shown to have been naïve.

The second factor to note is the growing militancy of minority groups. If we look at the types of organizations and at the changes in the positions of some, it is clear that there is an increasing willingness to be aggressive in demanding changes in the social, economic, and political position of the group members. At first groups such as the National Association for the Advancement of Colored People (NAACP), the Urban League, and the Congress of Racial Equality (CORE) emphasized negotiation and legal processes to achieve change. The victory in the Brown decision was a product of the NAACP's legal and political efforts. As the 1950s progressed, legal techniques were replaced by more active demonstrations such as the Birmingham bus boycott in 1957, the freedom riders of 1960, and the march from Selma to Montgomery in 1964. The tactics were still based on the goal of integration and the nonviolent methods of the pre-1954 period. The groups that emerged in this period were the Student National Coordinating Committee (SNCC) [1] and the Southern Christian Leadership Council (SCLC). As the 1960s progressed, groups such as the Black Muslims, the Black Panthers, the Brown Berets, and the Red Muslims developed.[2] They rejected both the goals and methods of the past, and talked of violence as a tactic for change. They pressed the traditional groups, which responded by taking a more militant stance. SNCC became a vehicle for the leading Black Power spokesman, Stokely Carmichael, and even the oldest groups, such as CORE, NAACP, and MAPA,[3] were affected. At the present time, the trend still appears to be in the direction of increasing militancy, tied to the growing sense that

[1] Formerly called the Student Nonviolent Coordinating Committee.

[2] The Brown Berets and the Red Muslims originated in the Los Angeles area and have since spread throughout the Southwest. The members of the former wear berets, as symbols of militancy. Both groups use the vocabulary of confrontation and violence to describe the methods they feel are necessary to win their goals.

[3] MAPA (Mexican-American Political Association) is one of the oldest Mexican-American organizations, and one of the few that have been specially committed to political activity. It is the most involved in political party activities, working closest with the Democratic party.

the exploitation of blacks, Mexican-Americans, and American Indians is similar to the exploitation of Vietnamese, Cubans, or Africans. The result of this feeling has brought the two factions of the New Left together, so that the efforts of the antiwar movement are tied to ending prejudice and racism in the United States, and the racial militants oppose the war in Vietnam.

One of the main reasons for the increasing militancy is that more and more blacks, Mexican-Americans, and American Indians are living in the largest urban areas of the country. For minority groups, urbanization has aggravated the problems of education, housing, law enforcement, and employment while improving their political influence. The reason for the impact of urbanization is that most minority groups, especially the blacks, have only recently migrated to the cities from the rural South, where frequently they were denied the opportunity to obtain the education necessary to compete in the urban job market. Most blacks, Mexican-Americans, and American Indians therefore, are able to get only poor-paying jobs with little prospect for personal betterment. Most came to the cities of the North and the West during or after World War II: They came during the war because there were jobs available in defense industries as a result of large numbers of men drafted for the service, or they themselves were drafted and were processed through the cities on their way overseas. After the war, the job opportunities disappeared as the white servicemen returned, but the blacks continued to migrate. They settled in the old ghettoes of the European immigrants who had come sixty years before, which by now were extremely dilapidated; the chances for escape were negligible. Conditions have changed very little. The migration of the white middle class to the suburbs has left the cities with a withering tax base from which to improve the schools and housing of the central city, and the states have been unable to generate the tax revenues to support improvement. The federal government has been the only level to provide any relief, and the commitment of large sums of money to the war in Vietnam seems to preclude any massive injection of funds into the cities.

With the advance of technology there is a proportionate advance in the demand for greater skills in jobs; but with the lack of improvement in education, the minority groups, especially the blacks, are actually regressing. The problems of relations between the blacks and the police have been aggravated by the ghettoization of the blacks and their contact with the police as the only whites they see. The policeman is not seen as a protector, but as the agent of "the man," whose job it is to keep the black man in his place. One result of the breakdown in relations between minority groups and the police is the use of violence by militants such as the Black Panthers. The recent alleged murders of Panthers by the police has tended to reduce further the confidence of blacks in particular.

In relation to its effect on the political role of the minority groups, urbanization has been associated with the opportunity to vote and with the fact that minority groups are "swing blocs" in gubernatorial and presidential elections. For the latter reason they are courted by candidates for those offices and have tended to enjoy greater access to executive officials at both levels than other groups. In a few cases, such as Cleveland, Ohio, and Gary, Indiana, minority groups have been able to elect one of their own to the office of mayor. The recent defeat of Thomas Bradley in the race for mayor of Los Angeles and the appeal of "law and order" as an issue in local, state, and federal elections may signal at least a temporary hiatus in black political influence, although these developments must be weighed against the victories of liberals in Detroit and New York.

Even though the general direction in change of attitude among the three groups is toward a more militant stance, there are still many individuals who support more traditional goals and methods. In fact, there is probably more diversity today than ever before, simply because there are more groups and leaders attempting to identify their own positions. The spectrum is widest for the blacks because of their longer history of activity. From the NAACP and the Urban League on the "right" to "US" and the Black Panthers on the "left," there are presently ten national organizations claiming to speak for the black community. In the Mexican-American group there are at least six groups, ranging from the more conservative League of United Latin-American Citizens (LULAC) and the Community Service Organization (CSO) to the militant Brown Berets. At the bottom of the ladder in terms of development are the American Indians, whose activism has emerged most recently. There is only one national organization at present, the National Congress of American Indians (NCAI), but other organizations are growing, such as the American Indian Movement (AIM) in Minnesota and American Indians United (AIU) in Los Angeles, and promise to bring a more aggressive voice to the debate over Indian needs.

If one major trend can be identified in the political activities of all three groups, it is the replacement of integration at all costs with greater emphasis on equality of status in the society. The motivation behind the Black Power movement was to build the economic and political resources of the black community so that blacks could negotiate with whites on an equal level instead of begging for acceptance into what was tacitly seen by both as the superior white society. The increasing emphasis on cultural identification is another manifestation of the rejection of integration. All three groups assert that they have cultural roots that are being destroyed by the pressure to become like white Anglos. The cry "Black is beautiful" and the demand for ethnic studies programs are overt manifestations of this attitude. It is interesting to note the relationship between this attitude and the theory of pluralism upon which the United States presumably has been built. The theory is that America is a great nation because so many cultures have been integrated in a melting pot out of which has come a distinctive amalgamation of all the different ethnic, religious, and racial groups. In fact, for most of American history the pressure of the society on new immigrants has been to force them to lose their attachment with their roots and to become "Americans" in accordance with the Protestant middle-class model. Until recently blacks, Indians, and Mexican-Americans have followed this pattern. Now the youth of these groups are calling for the first real test of the efficacy of a truly pluralistic society. There is no way of determining how successful the present effort will be. The validity of the original theory of pluralism hangs in the balance.

A sixth general trend has been the increasing attention toward the relations between the members of the minority groups and government personnel, particularly policemen. The problem of conflict between the police and blacks or Mexican-Americans has been before the courts many times in the past, but the series of riots and revolts beginning in 1965 has forced an intensive review of training programs for police, community relations campaigns, and procedures for reviewing police conduct. In many states the training program now includes courses in the problems of minority groups and police-community relations. The courses are required primarily at the preservice level, and greater effort is necessary to include more in-service training. The debate over review procedures still continues, with most police opposed to some form of civilian review board. At present review is an internal matter in most departments. Other government officials who have been subjected to minority criticism are social workers and welfare and employment agents. Greater effort is now being made to recruit personnel from the minority groups to hold these positions, especially where a different language is spoken. Finally, much criticism has been leveled against whites working in the "war on poverty," both by members of the minority groups and by general society. The former have condemned the poverty workers as "do-gooder liberals" who are working out their guilt by patronizing the poor. The latter sees the workers receiving inordinantly high salaries in a wasteful social experiment. Neither view is completely correct, but through the combined efforts of both groups, the programs have been almost completely eliminated.

Education is the one area of need that has continued to receive the most attention, although the focus has varied in terms of level and type of interest. During the early 1950s, attention was directed to legal segregation at the college level, as a review of Supreme Court decisions will reveal. With the landmark 1954 decision outlawing segregation in public education the focus shifted to the elementary- and secondary-school levels where it remained for the rest of the decade and for the greater part of the 1960s, although there was a shift in geographic *de facto* segregation. Programs of bussing students were developed to overcome this northern variant, although northern whites frequently withdrew their children from public schools rather than have them in integrated classrooms. The problems in the South remained, forcing compliance with the Brown decision. Massive resistance by southerners included mob action, closing of schools, and creating private schools; integration occurred at the rate of about 1 percent per year. Although the Department of Health, Education, and Welfare has tried to force change by denying money to schools, this is in reality a punishment for black children, because white school officials cut off funds to black schools. At present, the progress in desegregation has been very poor. In the North, massive opposition to bussing to end *de facto* segregation has surfaced and been legitimized by national leaders. The opposition to bussing is clearly a code for racism and endangers the future of school desegregation. The opponents of desegregation use the militant support for community control to justify resistance to a serious effort at change. As the 1960s drew to a close, there was a renewed interest in higher education, which included not only provision of more opportunity for minority group students to attend college, but also concern over the content of the curriculum. On numerous campuses minority group students have organized themselves and have pressured the administration into developing ethnic study programs. Courses in black history or Mexican-American literature are appearing on high-school campuses also. A further development in the general area of education has been the application of research done by anthropologists on cultural bias in IQ and placement tests to demonstrate that minority group students are discriminated against in the determination of their basic abilities. One recent administration of an IQ test to Mexican-American students in Spanish produced an average increase in IQ of 28 points. Finally, there has been a shift from support for integrated schools to community control of separate schools. The most publicized example of this has been in the New York City schools, although the issue has also been raised in cities in other states.

The final trend to be identified is the increasing politicalization of all three groups, but especially of the blacks. Despite the rejection of political activity by many of the militants such as the Black Muslims, more candidates from the minority groups are running for office, and more members of the groups are voting. In addition, the minority groups, which in the past have been virtually the captives of the Democratic party, are becoming more sophisticated in their negotiation with the two major parties. Unfortunately, the Republican party has not provided the benefits that would force the Democratic party to provide more meaningful recognition of the needs of the minority groups.

The prognosis for the future depends on whether the perspective is short or long range. The immediate future seems rather bleak. The Nixon administration does not appear committed to any massive action that would substantially improve the lives of any of the three groups. The pressure of the Vietnam War on the economy seems to be forcing increased consideration of reductions in domestic spending, and the programs that will probably be cut first are those which benefit these groups. There is a great deal of concern among businessmen in the Detroit area, for instance, that the jobs created for 40,000 ghetto blacks will be lost as a result of the pressure for economic caution; as a result the men will be returning to the ghetto streets even more alienated than before. The proposed program of black capitalism has yet to get off the ground, and its first director, a black, resigned shortly after being appointed. The general societal support for the theme of "law and order" suggests a growing acceptance of more repressive responses to violent or nonviolent demonstrations by the groups.

The prospects of the long-range picture appear less bleak.

Even though the lines of antagonism seem to be hardening and the stance of many minority individuals is becoming more militant, the general conditions of minority groups are improving. More members are obtaining the education necessary to compete in the job market; more are exercising their political rights; and at least there is a recognition by society that discrimination in education, employment, housing, voting, and the administration of justice is in violation of the values of the community. The difficulty is that patience is a luxury that usually only those living in basic comfort can enjoy. Thus, the key question seems to be, Can America survive the next few years of intensified antagonisms so that in the long run ameliorative forces can work?

I areas of conflict

chapter one

THE CURRENT SETTING

1 / Black Militancy and Pride

ELDRIDGE CLEAVER

As the 1960s drew to a close, the character of black leadership continued to change. From the integration-oriented, nonviolent leadership of Dr. Martin Luther King, Jr., Roy Wilkins, and Whitney Young, the movement has turned to such leaders as Stokeley Carmichael, H. Rap Brown, Floyd McKissick, and Malcolm X. The most militant leaders have come from a group known as the Black Panthers. The trend has been toward greater and greater militancy and, in the minds of many whites, increasing acceptance of violence as a method. The trial of Huey Newton, a Panther leader, for murdering an Oakland police officer, tended to focus on the fears of many whites. Another Panther leader who has received much of the spotlight is George Murray, who while lecturing at San Francisco State College precipitated a crisis on that campus. The third of the leaders, Eldridge Cleaver, was in jail, and has been a fugitive recently for breaking his parole. In this selection from his book *Soul on Ice* one can see the influence of Malcolm X on his thinking and the willingness to have a nonviolent society if the whites support it.

America's penology does not take this into account. Malcolm X did, and black convicts know that the ascension to power of Malcolm X or a man

SOURCE: From *Soul on Ice* by Eldridge Cleaver, pp. 59–61, 80–83. Copyright © 1968 by Eldridge Cleaver. Used with permission of McGraw-Hill Book Company.

13

like him would eventually have revolutionized penology in America. Malcolm delivered a merciless and damning indictment of prevailing penology. It is only a matter of time until the question of the prisoner's debt to society versus society's debt to the prisoner is injected forcefully into national and state politics, into the civil and human rights struggle, and into the consciousness of the body politic. It is an explosive issue which goes to the very root of America's system of justice, the structure of criminal law, the prevailing beliefs and attitudes toward the convicted felon. While it is easier to make out a case for black convicts, the same principles apply to white and Mexican-American convicts as well. They too are victimized, albeit a little more subtly, by "society." When black convicts start demanding a new dispensation and definition of justice, naturally the white and Mexican-American convicts will demand equality of treatment. Malcolm X was a focus for these aspirations.

The Black Muslim movement was destroyed the moment Elijah cracked the whip over Malcolm's head, because it was not the Black Muslim movement itself that was so irresistibly appealing to the true believers. It was the awakening into self-consciousness of twenty million Negroes which was so compelling. Malcolm X articulated their aspirations better than any other man of our time. When he spoke under the banner of Elijah Muhammad he was irresistible. When he spoke under his own banner he was still irresistible. If he had become a Quaker, a Catholic, or a Seventh-Day Adventist, or a Sammy Davis-style Jew, and if he had continued to give voice to the mute ambitions in the black man's soul, his message would still have been triumphant: because what was great was not Malcolm X but the truth he uttered.

The truth which Malcolm uttered had vanquished the whole passle of so-called Negro leaders and spokesmen who trifle and compromise with the truth in order to curry favor with the white power structure. He was stopped in the only way such a man can be stopped, in the same way that the enemies of the Congolese people had to stop Lumumba, by the same method that exploiters, tyrants, and parasitical oppressors have always crushed the legitimate strivings of people for freedom, justice, and equality —by murder, assassination, and mad-dog butchery.

What provoked the assassins to murder? Did it bother them that Malcolm was elevating our struggle into the international arena through his campaign to carry it before the United Nations? Well, by murdering him they only hastened the process, because we certainly are going to take our cause before a sympathetic world. Did it bother the assassins that Malcolm denounced the racist strait-jacket demonology of Elijah Muhammad? Well, we certainly do denounce it and will continue to do so. Did it bother the assassins that Malcolm taught us to defend ourselves? We shall not remain a defenseless prey to the murderer, to the sniper and the bomber. Insofar as Malcolm spoke the truth, the truth will triumph and prevail and his name shall live; and insofar as those who opposed him lied, to that extent will their names become curses. Because "truth crushed to earth shall rise again."

So now Malcolm is no more. The bootlickers, Uncle Toms, lackeys, and stooges of the white power structure have done their best to denigrate Malcolm, to root him out of his people's heart, to tarnish his memory. But their million-worded lies fall on deaf ears. As Ossie Davis so eloquently expressed it in his immortal eulogy of Malcolm:

> If you knew him you would know why we must honor him: —Malcolm was our manhood, our living, black manhood! This was his meaning to his people. And, in honoring him, we honor the best in ourselves. . . . However much we may have differed with him—or with each other about him and his value as a man, let his going from us serve only to bring us together, now. Consigning these mortal remains to earth, the common mother of all, secure in the knowledge that what we place in the ground is no more now a man—but a seed—which, after the winter of our discontent will come forth again to meet us. And we will know him then for what he was and is—a Prince—our own black shining Prince!—who didn't hesitate to die, because he loved us so.

We shall have our manhood. We shall have it or the earth will be leveled by our attempts to gain it. . . .

The Negro revolution at home and national liberation movements abroad have unceremoniously shattered the world of fantasy in which the whites have been living. It is painful that many do not yet see that their fantasy world has been rendered uninhabitable in the last half of the twentieth century. But it is away from this world that the white youth of today are turning. The "paper tiger" hero, James Bond, offering the whites a triumphant image of themselves, is saying what many whites want desperately to hear reaffirmed: *I am still the White Man, lord of the land, licensed to kill, and the world is still an empire at my feet.* James Bond feeds on that secret little anxiety, the psychological white backlash, felt in some degree by most whites alive. It is exasperating to see little brown men and little yellow men from the mysterious Orient, and the opaque black men of Africa (to say nothing of these impudent American Negroes!) who come to the UN and talk smart to us, who are scurrying all over *our* globe in their strange modes of dress—much as if they were new, unpleasant arrivals from another planet. Many whites believe in their ulcers that it is only a matter of time before the Marines get the signal to round up these truants and put them back securely in their cages. But it is away from this fantasy world that the white youth of today are turning.

In the world revolution now under way, the initiative rests with people of color. That growing numbers of white youth are repudiating their heritage of blood and taking people of color as their heroes and models is a tribute not only to their insight but to the resilience of the human spirit. For today the heroes of the initiative are people not usually thought of as white: Fidel Castro, Che Guevara, Kwame Nkrumah, Mao Tse-tung, Gamal Abdel Nasser, Robert F. Williams, Malcolm X, Ben Bella, John Lewis, Martin Luther King, Jr., Robert Parris Moses, Ho Chi Minh, Stokeley Carmichael, W. E. B. DuBois, James Forman, Chou En-lai.

The white youth of today have begun to react to the fact that the "American Way of Life" is a fossil of history. What do they care if their old baldheaded and crew-cut elders don't dig their caveman mops? They couldn't care less about the old, stiffassed honkies who don't like their new dances: Frug, Monkey, Jerk, Swim, Watusi. All they know is that it feels good to swing to way-out body-rhythms instead of dragassing across the dance floor like zombies to the dead beat of mind-smothered Mickey Mouse music. Is it any wonder that the youth have lost all respect for their elders, for law and order, when for as long as they can remember all they've witnessed is a monumental bickering over the Negro's place in American society and the right of people around the world to be left alone by outside powers? They have witnessed the law, both domestic and international, being spat upon by those who do not like its terms. Is it any wonder, then, that they feel justified, by sitting-in and freedom riding, in breaking laws made by lawless men? Old funny-styled, zipper-mouthed political night riders know nothing but to haul out an investigating committee *to look into the disturbance* to find the cause of the unrest among the youth. Look into a mirror! The cause is you, Mr. and Mrs. Yesterday, you with your forked tongues.

A young white today cannot help but recoil from the base deeds of his people. On every side, on every continent, he sees racial arrogance, savage brutality toward the conquered and subjugated people, genocide; he sees the human cargo of the slave trade; he sees the systematic extermination of American Indians; he sees the civilized nations of Europe fighting in imperial depravity over the lands of other people—and over possession of the very people themselves. There seems to be no end to the ghastly deeds of which his people are guilty. *GUILTY*. The slaughter of the Jews by the Germans, the dropping of atomic bombs on the Japanese people— these deeds weigh heavily upon the prostrate souls and tumultuous consciences of the white youth. The white heroes, their hands dripping with blood, are dead.

The young whites know that the colored people of the world, Afro-Americans included, do not seek revenge for their suffering. They seek the same things the white rebel wants: an end to war and exploitation. Black and white, the young rebels are free people, free in a way that Americans have never been before in the history of their country. And they are outraged.

There is in America today a generation of white youth that is truly worthy of a black man's respect, and this is a rare event in the foul annals of American history. From the beginning of the contact between blacks and whites, there has been very little reason for a black man to respect a white, with such exceptions as John Brown and others lesser known. But respect commands itself and it can neither be given nor withheld when it is due. If a man like Malcolm X could change and repudiate racism, if I myself and other former Muslims can change, if young whites can change, then there is hope for America. It was certainly strange to find myself, while steeped in the doctrine that all whites were devils by nature, commanded by the heart to applaud and acknowledge respect for these young whites—despite the fact that they are descendants of the masters and I the descendant of slave. The sins of the fathers are visited upon the heads of the children—but only if the children continue in the evil deeds of the fathers.

2 / I Am Joaquin

RODOLFO GONZALES

The most important recent development for Mexican-Americans is their growing political activity. The phrase used in the Southwest to describe this is "the sleeping giant; and the giant is beginning to awaken." Beginning with the presidential campaign in 1960 for John F. Kennedy and the accompanying "Viva" Kennedy groups, a new wave of organized effort has occurred. In the late 1960s this wave grew larger and the participants become more militant. Leaders such as Reies Tijerina (see Selection 47) and Cesar Chavez (Selection 40) typify the changing character of the movement. "Viva la Raza," or "Long Live the Race" has become the battle cry, and even more aggressive groups, such as the Brown Berets, are now talking of violence in a fashion similar to that of the Black Panthers. One of the key factors is cultural identity and with it the revitalization of Spanish as a living tongue. A major spokesman for this effort at cultural rebirth is Rodolfo Gonzales, whose epic poem, "I Am Joaquin," is reprinted here.

I am Joaquin,
Lost in a world of confusion,
Caught up in a whirl of an
        Anglo society,

SOURCE: Rodolfo Gonzales, *I Am Joaquin,* An Epic Poem. Copyright 1967.

Confused by the rules,
Scorned by attitudes,
Suppressed by manipulations,
And destroyed by modern society.
My fathers
   have lost the economic battle
and won
   the struggle of cultural survival.
And now!
   I must choose
           Between
   the paradox of
Victory of the spirit,
despite physical hunger
         Or
   to exist in the grasp
of American social neurosis,
sterilization of the soul
   and a full stomach.

Yes,
I have come a long way to nowhere,
Unwillingly dragged by that
   monstrous, technical
   industrial giant called
         Progress
and Anglo success . . .
   I look at myself.
     I watch my brothers.
       I shed tears of sorrow.
       I sow seeds of hate.
   I withdraw to the safety within the
Circle of life . . .
            MY OWN PEOPLE

I am Cuahtemoc,
Proud and Noble
       Leader of men,
King of an empire,
civilized beyond the dreams
   of the Gauchupin Cortez,
Who also is the blood,
   the image of myself.
I am the Maya Prince.

I am Nezahualcoyotl,
Great leader of the Chichimecas.
I am the sword and flame of Cortez
                    the despot.
                        And
I am the Eagle and Serpent of
                the Aztec civilization.

I owned the land as far as the eye
could see under the crown of Spain,
and I toiled on my earth
and gave my Indian sweat and blood
            for the Spanish master,
Who ruled with tyranny over man and
beast and all that he could trample
                    But . . .
        THE GROUND WAS MINE . . .
I was both tyrant and slave.

As Christian church took its place
    in God's good name,
to take and use my Virgin strength and
                        Trusting faith,
The priests
        both good and bad,
                    took
But
    gave a lasting truth that
            Spaniard,
                Indian,
                    Mestizo
Were all God's children
And
    from these words grew men
                who prayed and fought
                        for
    their own worth as human beings,
                for
                that
        GOLDEN MOMENT
                of
        FREEDOM.

I was part in blood and spirit
    of that

courageous village priest
                    Hidalgo
in the year eighteen hundred and ten
who rang the bell of independence
and gave out that lasting cry:
    "El Grito de Dolores, Que mueran
    los Gauchupines y que viva
la Virgin de Guadalupe" . . .
I sentenced him
                who was me.
I excommunicated him my blood.
I drove him from the pulpit to lead
    a bloody revolution for him and me . . .
                    I killed him.
His head,
    which is mine and all of those
    who have come this way,
I placed on that fortress wall
    to wait for Independence.
Morelo!
        Matamoros!
            Guerrero!
All Companeros in the act,
STOOD AGAINST THAT WALL OF
                    INFAMY
    to feel the hot gouge of lead
    which my hands made.
I died with them . . .
    I lived with them
        I lived to see our country free.
Free
    from Spanish rule in
    eighteen-hundred-twenty-one.
                Mexico was Free ? ?

The crown was gone
                but
all his parasites remained
                and ruled
                and taught
    with gun and flame and mystic power.
I worked,
I sweated,
I bled,

I prayed
      and
waited silently for life to again
                      commence.

I fought and died
                  for
        Don Benito Juarez
Guardian of the Constitution.
I was him
        on dusty roads
                on barren land
as he protected his archives
   as Moses did his sacraments.
He held his Mexico
          in his hand
          on
       the most desolate
         and remote ground
         which was his country,
And this Giant
        Little Zapotec
           gave
   not one palm's breadth
of his country's land to
   Kings or Monarchs or Presidents
of foreign powers.

I am Joaquin.
I rode with Pancho Villa,
   crude and warm.
A tornado at full strength,
nourished and inspired
   by the passion and the fire
   of all his earthy people.
I am Emiliano Zapata.
   "This land
       This Earth
        is
            OURS"
The Villages
   The Mountains
   The Streams

belong to Zapatistas.
Our life
Or yours
is the only trade for soft brown earth
and maize.
All of which is our reward,
A creed that formed a constitution
for all who dare live free!
"This land is ours . . .
Father, I give it back to you.
Mexico must be free . . ."

I ride with Revolutionists
against myself.
I am Rural
Course and brutal,
I am the mountain Indian,
superior over all.
The thundering hoof beats are my horses.
The chattering of machine guns
are death to all of me:
Yaqui
Tarahumara
Chamula
Zapotec
Mestizo
Español
I have been the Bloody Revolution,
The Victor,
The Vanquished,
I have killed
and been killed.
I am despots Diaz
and Huerta
and the apostle of democracy
Francisco Madero.
I am
the black shawled
faithful women
who die with me
or live
depending on the time and place.
I am

faithful,
   humble,
      Juan Diego
      the Virgen de Guadalupe,
      Tonatzin, Aztec Goddess too.

I rode the mountains of San Joaquin.
I rode as far East and North
   as the Rocky Mountains
      and
all men feared the guns of
         Joaquin Murrietta.
I killed those men who dared
  to steal my mine,
    who raped and Killed
           my Love
           my Wife
Then
I Killed to stay alive.
I was Alfego Baca,
  living my nine lives fully.
I was the Espinoza brothers
  of the Valle de San Luis.
All,
were added to the number of heads
that
  in the name of civilization
were placed on the wall of independence.
Heads of brave men
who died for cause or principle.
Good or Bad.
      Hidalgo! Zapata!
       Murrietta! Espinozas!
are but a few.
They
dared to face
The force of tyranny
      of men
    who rule
      By farce and hypocrisy
I stand here looking back,
and now I see
     the present

and still
  I am the campesino
  I am the fat political coyote
        I,
of the same name,
      Joaquin.
In a country that has wiped out
all my history,
      stiffled all my pride.
In a country that has placed a
different weight of indignity upon
      my
       age
      old
        burdened back.
     Inferiority
is the new load . . .
  The Indian has endured and still
emerged the winner,
  The Mestizo must yet overcome,
   And the Gauchupin will just ignore.
  I look at myself
  and see part of me
who rejects my father and my mother
and dissolves into the melting pot
  to disappear in shame.
  I sometimes
   sell my brother out
  and reclaim him
for my own when society gives me
  token leadership
    in society's own name.

I am Joaquin,
who bleeds in many ways.
The altars of Montezuma
    I stained a bloody red.
  My back of Indian Slavery
     was stripped crimson
   from the whips of masters
   who would lose their blood so pure
   when Revolution made them pay
Standing against the walls of

Retribution,
   Blood . . .
  Has flowed from
    me
on every battlefield
    between
Campesino, Hacendado
  Slave and Master
   and
   Revolution.
I jumped from the tower of Chapultepec
  into the sea of fame;
My country's flag
   my burial shroud;
With Los Ninos,
   whose pride and courage
could not surrender
   with indignity
    their country's flag
To strangers . . . in their land.
Now
 I bleed in some smelly cell
 from club.
 or gun.
 or tyranny.
I bleed as the vicious gloves of hunger
 cut my face and eyes,
as I fight my way from stinking Barrios
 to the glamour of the Ring
  and lights of fame
  or mutilated sorrow.
My blood runs pure on the ice caked
hills of the Alaskan Isles,
on the corpse strewn beach of Normandy,
the foreign land of Korea
    and now
     Viet Nam.

Here I stand
   before the Court of Justice
    Guilty
for all the glory of my Raza
   to be sentenced to despair.

Here I stand
　　Poor in money
　　Arrogant with pride
　　　　　　Bold with Machismo
　　　　　　Rich in courage
　　　　　　and
　　　　　　Wealthy in spirit and faith.
My knees are caked with mud.
My hands calloused from the hoe.
I have made the Anglo rich
　　　　　　yet
　　Equality is but a word,
　　　　the Treaty of Hidalgo has been broken
　　and is but another treacherous promise.
My land is lost
　　　　　　and stolen,
My culture has been raped,
　　　　　　I lengthen
　　　　the line at the welfare door
and fill the jails with crime.
　　　　　　These then
are the rewards
　　　　　　this society has
For sons of Chiefs
　　　　　　and Kings
　　　　　　and bloody Revolutionists.
Who
gave a foreign people
　　　　all their skills and ingenuity
to pave the way with Brains and Blood
for
those hordes of Gold starved
　　　　　　　　　　Strangers
Who
changed our language
and plagiarized our deeds
　　　　　　　as feats of valor
　　　　　　　of their own.
They frowned upon our way of life
　　and took what they could use.
　　　　　　Our Art
　　　　　　Our Literature
　　　　　　Our music, they ignored

so they left the real things of value
and grabbed at their own destruction
                    by their Greed and Avarice

They overlooked that cleansing fountain of
                    nature and brotherhood
        Which is Joaquin.
                The art of our great señors
                        Diego Rivera
                        Sequieros
                        Orozco is but
another act of revolution for
            the Salvation of mankind.
            Mariachi music, the
            heart and soul
            of the people of the earth,
            the life of child,
            and the happiness of love.
            The Corridos tell the tales
            of life and death,
                    of tradition,
            Legends old and new,
            of Joy
              of passion and sorrow
            of the people: who I am.
I am in the eyes of woman,
                sheltered beneath
her shawl of black,
                deep and sorrowful
                eyes,
That bear the pain of sons long buried
                or dying,
                Dead
on the battlefield or on the barbwire
                of social strife.
Her rosary she prays and fingers
endlessly
                like the family
working down a row of beets
                to turn around
                and work
                and work
                There is no end.

Her eyes a mirror of all the warmth
        and all the love for me,
And I am her
And she is me.
      We face life together in sorrow.
      anger, joy faith and wishful
      thoughts.

I shed tears of anguish
as I see my children disappear
behind the shroud of mediocrity
never to look back to remember me.
I am Joaquin.
      I must fight
        And win this struggle
        for my sons, and they
        must know from me
        Who I am.
Part of the blood that runs deep in me
Could not be vanquished by the Moors
I defeated them after five hundred years,
and I endured.
      The part of blood that is mine
      has labored endlessly five-hundred
      years under the heel of lustful
         Europeans
         I am still here!
I have endured in the rugged mountains
   of our country
I have survived the toils and slavery
   of the fields.
      I have existed
in the barrios of the city,
in the suburbs of bigotry,
in the mines of social snobbery,
in the prisons of dejection,
in the muck of exploitation
and
in the fierce heat of racial hatred.

And now the trumpet sounds,
The music of the people stirs the
      Revolution,
Like a sleeping giant it slowly

rears its head
to the sound of

Tramping feet

Clamouring voices

Mariachi strains

Fiery tequila explosions

The smell of chile verde and

Soft brown eyes of expectation for a

better life.

And in all the fertile farm lands,
the barren plains,
the mountain villages,
smoke smeared cities
We start to MOVE.

La Raza!
Mejicano!
Español!
Latino!
Hispano!
Chicano!
or whatever I call myself,
I look the same
I feel the same
I cry
and
Sing the same

I am the masses of my people and
I refuse to be absorbed.
I am Joaquin
The odds are great
but my spirit is strong
My faith unbreakable
My blood is pure
I am Aztec Prince and Christian Christ
I SHALL ENDURE!
I WILL ENDURE!

3 / Navahos Chart Their Own Education Path

LINDA MATHEWS

After almost twenty years of relative disinterest, the minority groups are again focusing their concern about the educational opportunities for their children upon the colleges and universities. Not since the series of court decisions of the late 1940s and early 1950s has higher education been forced to consider seriously its politics toward minority-group students. The issues today are: (1) revision of admission policies to permit more Negro and Mexican-American students to attend colleges; (2) creation of more relevant courses in the history, literature and language fields; (3) recruitment of more faculty from the minority groups; (4) provision of greater financial assistance for minority group students; and (5) creation of ethnic studies programs. At many schools, the faculty, the administration, and the trustees have rejected these proposals, or "nonnegotiable demands" as the students have called them, and violence has ensued. At others change has occurred without violence. Perhaps the most extreme technique is the creation of an all-minority group college, as described in this selection on a new Indian Junior College.

Source: Linda Mathews, "Navahos Chart Own Education Path," *Los Angeles Times,* June 1, 1969, Section C, pp. 1–3. Copyright, 1969, by the Los Angeles Times. Reprinted by permission.

31

Robert A. Roessel Jr. may be the only college president in the country who wears cowboy boots to the office.

His apparel is entirely appropriate, for the school he commands— 5-month-old Navaho Community College in the far sandy reaches of northeastern Arizona—is as unusual as its president.

It is the first institution of higher learning on an Indian reservation, the first college in fact established and controlled by Indians and, some educators think, the first sign that the Navahos and other tribes are charting a course of self-determinism that may lift them out of their 100-year-old cycle of poverty and illiteracy.

Because the college is a "community college," open to any Navaho adult over the age of 18 whether or not he has ever spent a day in school, the students who appeared from all parts of the far-flung Navaho reservation for the first day of classes last January did not represent the typical picture of an apple-cheeked matriculating class.

There were modishly dressed coeds and youths, of course, there to learn a trade or earn credits that can be transferred to a four-year university.

But they brushed up against middle-aged women in velveteen skirts and turquoise bracelets, many of them eager for handicraft training and driver education; tribal elders in crumpled felt hats who came to learn— and maybe teach—a little Navaho history, and a raggle-taggle bunch of lean, hard-eyed dropouts whose presence attested to the failure of the kind of education the Indians have had before.

NAVAHO CHEATED BADLY

"Education has cheated the Navaho, cheated them badly," says Roessel, who came to teach on the reservation 20 years ago, and stayed to marry a Navaho girl—daughter of a noted medicine man—and father five children.

> For years, the white man's schools—and that's what the Indians call them—have educated the Indianness out of these people, taught the young people that the hogan is dirty, that their parents were ignorant.
> The result is a group of bleached Indian youth, who are miserable on the reservation but rarely learn to adjust when they leave for the big city. They are neither Anglo nor Indian, but just full of self-hatred.

Top students in each graduating class at the high schools run by the Bureau of Indian Affairs have for years been awarded college scholarships by the tribe, Roessel points out, and every year, 90% of these students— "90% of the cream of the crop"—have flunked out of college.

They return, directionless, unskilled, to a reservation where most jobs are held by Anglos imported by the federal government, and they end up drunk in the honky-tonks of nearby Gallup, N.M.

The contempt Navahos feel for the schools that dot their reservation is clearly expressed by the names they give them.

Bureau of Indian Affairs schools—which required children to board, taking them away from their families—are called Washington beolta; the mission schools are eeneishoodi beolta (for "those who drag their skirts behind them," meaning the first Catholic priests), and the public day schools, staffed and run largely by Anglos, are belagona beolta, politely translated as "white man's schools."

Navaho Community College, on the other hand, is dine beolta ("the people's school") and everywhere on its temporary campus outside the tiny community of Many Farms, in buildings leased from the BIA, there is a pioneer, do-it-yourself spirit.

"Here you find a group of people who are by all standards of misery on the bottom of the totem pole," Roessel explains. "Their average income is less than $700 a year, their illiteracy rate is the highest in the country, 40% of them are unemployed.

TRY TO HELP SELVES

"And yet they have not been content to sit down and cry for themselves or to destroy. They are trying to help themselves and the reservation they love."

The college was founded with Navaho tribal money and continues to count on that support as the basis of its budget, which now also includes funds from the Office of Economic Opportunity and several "aid to higher education" programs.

Land for the college's permanent site—on a woody plateau overlooking a lake 20 miles from Many Farms—was contributed by several "chapters"—subdivisions—of the tribal government.

NAVAHOS ON STAFF

What is more important, the college has become the mecca for Navaho talent. Its faculty includes the first Navaho Ph.D., who teaches courses in agriculture and soil chemistry, as well as several Navaho language teachers, a Northern Cheyenne Indian who is dean of students, a renowned Navaho silversmith, a young Navaho artist and the 73-year-old former tribal chief (himself educated off the reservation) who holds the seat as "distinguished professor of Navaho culture and history."

Although this semester's enrollment of 330 students (almost all of them Navaho though there is a policy of open enrollment) was made up largely of students who had nowhere else to go in January, next year some of the best high school graduates are expected to choose the college rather than off-reservation schooling. By 1971, when the school moves to its permanent campus, enrollment will hit 1500.

SECRETARIAL CORPS

For the moment, the borrowed quarters are maintained and staffed by students who earn their board and room under the federal work-study program and by slightly older Navaho women, who form as trim and efficient a secretarial corps as exists at major universities.

("Like everywhere else, the secretaries actually run the school," a teacher quips.)

The students themselves collect the equipment and specimens needed for their science and art classes and for the sessions on Navaho lore. To compile a backlog of historical materials for the library, they often spend their evenings in the traditional hogans nearby, interviewing parents and tribal leaders who remember snatches of Navaho history and legend.

"One summer I went to one of those push-button colleges where everything is done for the students," says Annie Kahn, a thirtyish Navaho mother of six who says she may take up high school counseling when she gets her degree.

"Here, everything is different. We do things for ourselves and we're better for it."

BOARD OF REGENTS

Overseeing this entire operation is a 10-man Navaho board of regents, elected from all parts of the reservation. The regents' education is disparate: one completed two years of college, another still signs his name with a thumbprint, a third is a respected judge, others run successful business.

As was visualized by Raymond Nakai, the Navaho tribal chairman who persisted with his dream of a college while Arizona educators scoffed, the regents rule with a firm hand, doing all the hiring and firing and directing the search for a permanent source of income. A student is a voting member of the board.

The college they run tries to be all things to all people; administrators are fond of calling it an "educational supermarket."

AWARE OF NEEDS

Courses run day and night, for the regents are aware of the need on their reservation for adult education. Lights in the auto shop, the typing room and the arts and crafts studios sometimes are not turned off until 11 P.M.

Study of Navaho history, culture and language is particularly popular with all age groups at the college. Roessel sees such courses as a means of combatting the indoctrination of the white man's schools.

But the greatest emphasis is on what is usable, whether it is vocational training (which two-thirds of the students have chosen) or solid academic subjects that will provide transfer credit for Navahos aiming for professional positions.

DEMAND SKILLS

"This is no ivory tower," says Jerold Judd, the young teacher of biology and driver education who grew up on the reservation with his parents, white traders.

"Talk about the cry for relevant education! Our students demand the relevant. They want skills that will pay off, because they've seen educated Indians before who were still jobless despite their education."

Roessel and Nakai remain confident that the vocational training offered at the school will create a trained labor force and attract industry to the reservation.

"Thousands of jobs already exist on the reservation, but they are held by Anglos," Roessel says. Only a handful of teachers in the elementary and secondary schools are Navaho, and other jobs are to be had in two electronics plants, a sawmill and a new power plant in the area.

ACADEMIC STANDING

In addition, the tribe has been negotiating for grants to develop tribal parks on its bleakly beautiful land, which would create openings for park rangers, tour guides, archeologists and historians and hotel and restaurant workers.

Besides the very real necessity of assuring Navaho youths that they are being trained for something, that jobs are available, the college, like any other, is forced to pay attention to its academic standing.

The college has secured correspondent status from the North Central Assn. of Secondary Schools and Colleges, the first step toward full accreditation. And Arizona's state universities have agreed to accept transfer credit from the Navaho institution.

And yet, for all its promise and all the promises it has made its students, this college has its problems—bringing its educationally deprived students up to standard after years of neglect, retaining teachers whose wives may resent hardship conditions, finding permanent funding for an enterprise that is literally located in the middle of nowhere.

HARD WORKERS

"Typing is difficult for these students," says Robert Westover, the typing teacher, "especially for the dropouts. They work hard—I don't mean to question their motivation. But to be able to type, you have to be able to read."

Westover, like several other teachers, has had to use unorthodox methods and some remedial devices to compensate for his students' language problems. Next term, he says, he has prepared typing exercises that are related to tribal business and coordinate reading practice with typing.

Not far away from Westover's classroom, in the biology lab, Jerold Judd has found that his students are sometimes stumped by written tests. Fully aware that they know the material, he has tested them orally, using tape recorders.

What happens to such students when they transfer to schools where professors do not make allowances for them? No one knows.

"I'd match my students' knowledge against those from any college in the state," Judd says. "But I don't know if, at the moment, they could prove what they know on traditional tests."

Realizing the degree of this problem, the faculty has agreed that there will be no pressure on students to meet a rigid two-year junior college timetable. "We tell them, 'take your time,' " Roessel says. " 'Take three or four years, if you need them.' "

Roessel recruited his faculty from such far-flung institutions as the University of Arizona, UCLA, Iowa, Harvard and MIT. They give the impression of being zealots about Indian education, launching themselves on 18-hour working day regimens.

600 APPLICATIONS

As word has spread throughout the world of education, the college has received 600 applications for employment in the past six months. One ad in a library journal brought 121 applications.

Holding faculty members, many of whom have wives and small children, is another matter. Six staff members (of 40) will leave this year, in many cases because the women—not as committed to the project as their husbands—develop "desert fever," a wild desire to be any place in the world except Many Farms.

Some teachers express vague uneasiness about forthcoming operating funds, since next year's $1 million budget is tied very firmly to federal financing and it is feared the Nixon Administration will cut social welfare funds.

Roessel brushes aside such protestations. "I don't worry about our funding under Nixon because I don't believe there is any partisanship with regard to Indian matters."

ALSO FUND-RAISER

"And besides," he adds, grinning wickedly, "being against Indian self-help is like being against motherhood and God."

Despite his cowboy boots, his silver belt buckle and turquoise tie clasp and his wide-as-the-mesas expansiveness, Roessel—who holds a Ph.D. but is never called "doctor"—spends much of his time doing what every college president does, meeting with his constituents and raising funds.

On a typical day, he will greet a visiting senator or a delegation from another Indian tribe interested in establishing its own college (52 have made inquiries), drive two hours over dusty roads to confer with the tribal chairman in Window Rock and eat fried bread and mutton stew at a chapter meeting.

In his travels, he has learned to anticipate the criticism from Anglos who see Navaho Community College as part of a dangerous separatist or red power movement.

"By teaching our students Navaho history, we are not trying to build walls up, we are trying to tear walls down," he retorts. "We want our students to have some self-confidence, some identity, so they can succeed at what they try to do."

Neither, he says, is "ours a back-to-the-blanket movement. We teach Navaho basket-weaving—which provides an income for many Navaho people—but we do not teach anyone how to shoot buffalo. Indians want to live in the 20th Century like everyone else."

There is no conflict, as Roessel sees it, between teaching Indian legends and the latest auto mechanics courses; between searching out jobs on the reservation and preparing students to leave.

"This is not an either-or situation," he insists. "We're not urging students either to leave the reservation or to stay. We're just educating them to make an intelligent choice, which is something they've never been offered."

TRIFLE UNEASY

Feeling as strongly as he does about Navaho self-determinism, Roessel is a trifle uneasy about his position—as an Anglo leading a Navaho college. And so, true to his word, he is stepping down July 1, turning over direction of the school to Ned Hatathli, the dapper Navaho vice president. Roessel will continue to teach and run development programs.

His students seem uniformly to respect Roessel for what he has done —and for his decision to step aside for a Navaho. His message of self-pride and self-rule has gotten through.

Albert Laughter, a shy 20-year-old business education major, speaks for other students when he says:

"Someday, I may sit behind a big desk, with a big job. But no matter how many degrees I have, I want to be able to wear my knot (the traditional Navaho hairstyle) with pride. I don't want to forget my great-grandfathers, as other tribes have, and I don't want people to forget that Albert Laughter is a Navaho."

chapter two

EDUCATION

4 / *Brown* v. *Board of Education*

The case of *Brown* v. *Board of Education* (1954) has been described by Anthony Lewis as the beginning of the "Second
American Revolution" (*Portrait of a Decade: The Second
American Revolution* [New York: Random House, 1964]). In
this landmark decision the Supreme Court declared that discrimination in education based on race was a violation of the
constitutional prohibition (in the Fourteenth Amendment)
against denial of equal protection of the law. The case was
the culmination of a series of cases beginning in 1938 that un-
dermined the Supreme Court's earlier support of segregation
in the 1896 case of *Plessy* v. *Ferguson.* The rejection of the
doctrine of separate but equal in the Plessy decision makes
the Brown decision a landmark; in addition, the reference in
footnote 1 in Brown to several major sociological and psychological studies stamps this as a decision that will be studied
for many years.

Mr. Chief Justice Warren delivered the opinion of the Court.

These cases come to us from the States of Kansas, South Carolina,
Virginia, and Delaware. They are premised on different facts and different

SOURCE: *Brown* v. *Board of Education,* 347 U.S. 483 (1954).

local conditions, but a common legal question justifies their consideration together in this consolidated opinion.

In each of the cases, minors of the Negro race, through their legal representatives, seek the aid of the courts in obtaining admission to the public schools of their community on a nonsegregated basis. In each instance, they had been denied admission to schools attended by white children under laws requiring or permitting segregation according to race. This segregation was alleged to deprive the plaintiffs of the equal protection of the laws under the Fourteenth Amendment. In each of the cases other than the Delaware case, a three-judge federal district court denied relief to the plaintiffs on the so-called "separate but equal" doctrine announced by this Court in *Plessy* v. *Ferguson*. . . . Under that doctrine, equality of treatment is accorded when the races are provided substantially equal facilities, even though these facilities be separate. In the Delaware case, the Supreme Court of Delaware adhered to that doctrine, but ordered that the plaintiffs be admitted to the white schools because of their superiority to the Negro schools.

The plaintiffs contend that segregated public schools are not "equal" and cannot be made "equal," and that hence they are deprived of the equal protection of the laws. Because of the obvious importance of the question presented, the Court took jurisdiction. Argument was heard in the 1952 Term, and reargument was heard this Term on certain questions propounded by the Court.

Reargument was largely devoted to the circumstances surrounding the adoption of the Fourteenth Amendment in 1868. It covered exhaustively consideration of the Amendment in Congress, ratification by the states, then existing practices in racial segregation, and the views of proponents and opponents of the Amendment. This discussion and our own investigation convince us that, although these sources cast some light, it is not enough to resolve the problem with which we are faced. At best, they are inconclusive. The most avid proponents of the post-War Amendments undoubtedly intended them to remove all legal distinctions among "all persons born or naturalized in the United States." Their opponents, just as certainly, were antagonistic to both the letter and the spirit of the Amendments and wished them to have the most limited effect. What others in Congress and the state legislatures had in mind cannot be determined with any degree of certainty.

An additional reason for the inconclusive nature of the Amendment's history, with respect to segregated schools, is the status of public education at that time. In the South, the movement toward free common schools, supported by general taxation, had not yet taken hold. Education of white children was largely in the hands of private groups. Education of Negroes was almost non-existent, and practically all of the race were illiterate. In fact, any education of Negroes was forbidden by law in some states. Today, in contrast, many Negroes have achieved outstanding success in the arts and sciences as well as in the business and professional world. It is true that public school education at the time of the Amendment had advanced further in the North, but the effect of the Amendment on Northern States was generally ignored in the congressional debates. Even in the North, the conditions of public education did not approximate those existing today. The curriculum was usually rudimentary; ungraded schools were common in rural areas; the school term was but three months a year in many states; and compulsory school attendance was virtually unknown. As a consequence, it is not surprising that there should be so little in the history of the Fourteenth Amendment relating to its intended effect on public education.

In the first cases in this Court construing the Fourteenth Amendment, decided shortly after its adoption, the Court interpreted it as proscribing all state-imposed discriminations against the Negro race. The doctrine of "separate but equal" did not make its appearance in this Court until 1896 in the case of *Plessy* v. *Ferguson* . . . involving not education but transportation. American courts have since labored with the doctrine for over half a century. In this Court, there have been six cases involving the "separate but equal" doctrine in the field of public education. In *Cumming* v. *County Board of Education* . . . and *Gong Lum* v. *Rice* . . . the validity of the doctrine itself was not challenged. In more recent cases, all on the graduate school level, inequality was found in that specific benefits enjoyed by white students were denied to Negro students of the same educational qualifications. . . . In none of these cases was it necessary to re-examine the doctrine to grant relief to the Negro plaintiff. And in *Sweatt* v. *Painter* . . . the Court expressly reserved decision on the question whether *Plessy* v. *Ferguson* should be held inapplicable to public education.

In the instant cases, that question is directly presented. Here, unlike *Sweatt* v. *Painter,* there are findings below that the Negro and white schools involved have been equalized, or are being equalized, with respect to buildings, curricula, qualifications and salaries of teachers, and other "tangible" factors. Our decision, therefore, cannot turn on merely a comparison of these tangible factors in the Negro and white schools involved in each of the cases. We must look instead to the effect of segregation itself on public education.

In approaching this problem, we cannot turn the clock back to 1868 when the Amendment was adopted, or even to 1896 when *Plessy* v. *Ferguson* was written. We must consider public education in the light of its full development and its present place in American life throughout the Nation. Only in this way can it be determined if segregation in public schools deprives these plaintiffs of the equal protection of the laws.

Today, education is perhaps the most important function of state and local governments. Compulsory school attendance laws and the great expenditures for education both demonstrate our recognition of the importance of education to our democratic society. It is required in the performance of our most basic public responsibilities, even service in the armed forces. It is the very foundation of good citizenship. Today it is a principal instrument in awakening the child to cultural values, in preparing him for later professional training, and in helping him to adjust normally to his environment. In these days, it is doubtful that any child may reasonably be expected to succeed in life if he is denied the opportunity of an education. Such an opportunity, where the state has undertaken to provide it, is a right which must be made available to all on equal terms.

We come then to the question presented: Does segregation of children in public schools solely on the basis of race, even though the physical facilities and other "tangible" factors may be equal, deprive the children of the minority group of equal educational opportunities? We believe that it does.

In *Sweatt* v. *Painter* . . . in finding that a segregated law school for Negroes could not provide them equal educational opportunities, this Court relied in large part on "those qualities which are incapable of objective measurement but which make for greatness in a law school." In *McLaurin* v. *Oklahoma State Regents* . . . the Court, in requiring that a Negro admitted to a white graduate school be treated like all other students, again resorted to intangible considerations: ". . . his ability to study, to engage in discussions and exchange views with other students, and, in general, to learn his profession." Such considerations apply with added force to children in grade and high schools. To separate them from others of similar age and qualifications solely because of their race generates a feeling of inferiority as to their status in the community that may affect their hearts and minds in a way unlikely ever to be undone. The effect of this separation on their educational opportunities was well stated by a finding in the Kansas case by a court which nevertheless felt compelled to rule against the Negro plaintiffs:

> Segregation of white and colored children in public schools has a detrimental effect upon the colored children. The impact is greater when it has the sanction of the law; for the policy of separating the races is usually interpreted as denoting the inferiority of the negro group. A sense of inferiority affects the motivation of a child to learn. Segregation with the sanction of law, therefore, has a tendency to [retard] the educational and mental development of negro children and to deprive them of some of the benefits they would receive in a racial [ly] integrated school system.

Whatever may have been the extent of psychological knowledge at the time of *Plessy* v. *Ferguson,* this finding is amply supported by modern authority.[1] Any language in *Plessy* v. *Ferguson* contrary to this finding is rejected.

We conclude that in the field of public education the doctrine of "separate but equal" has no place. Separate educational facilities are inherently unequal. Therefore, we hold that the plaintiffs and others similarly situated for whom the actions have been brought are, by reason of the segregation complained of, deprived of the equal protection of the laws guaranteed by the Fourteenth Amendment. This disposition makes unnecessary any discussion whether such segregation also violates the Due Process Clause of the Fourteenth Amendment.

Because these are class actions, because of the wide applicability of this decision, and because of the great variety of local conditions, the formulation of decrees in these cases presents problems of considerable complexity. On reargument, the consideration of appropriate relief was necessarily subordinated to the primary question—the constitutionality of segregation in public education. We have now announced that such segregation is a denial of the equal protection of the laws. In order that we may have the full assistance of the parties in formulating decrees, the cases will be restored to the docket, and the parties are requested to present further argument on Questions 4 and 5 previously propounded by the Court for the reargument this Term. The Attorney General of the United States is again invited to participate. The Attorneys General of the states requiring or permitting segregation in public education will also be permitted to appear as *amici curiae* upon request to do so by September 15, 1954, and submission of briefs by October 1, 1954.

[1] [In the original opinion this footnote was number 11; this note and its references to social science research was the target of much criticism.—Ed.] K. B. Clark, *Effect of Prejudice and Discrimination on Personality Development* . . . ; Witmer and Kotinsky, *Personality in the Making* (1952), chap. VI; Deutscher and Chein, "The Psychological Effects of Enforced Segregation: A Survey of Social Science Opinion," 26 *J. Psychol.* 259 (1948); Chein, "What are the Psychological Effects of Segregation . . . ?" 3 *Int. J. Opinion and Attitude Res.* 229 (1949); Brameld, "Educational Costs," in *Discrimination and National Welfare* (MacIver, ed., 1949), 44–48; Frazier, *The Negro in the United States* (1949), 674–681. And see generally Myrdal, *An American Dilemma* (1944).

5 / *De Facto* Segregation

CARL J. DOLCE
ALAN K. CAMPBELL
ALBERT SHANKER

The issue of integration versus segregation has been less relevant in the North than in the South. Rather, the issue in the
North has been what to do about the *de facto* segregation
caused by such problems as discrimination in housing and
employment. As a result of these conditions, blacks,
Mexican-Americans, and Indians have been forced to move
into the ghetto areas previously occupied by immigrant
groups. They are faced with an environment that produces a
low level of motivation and with education that holds little
promise. Schools in the ghetto areas tend to be the oldest in
the cities; the staffs are composed of the young, the nonten-
ured or the older, more authoritarian teachers; and the textbooks are out of date. Response to these conditions has
been of two types. First, there have been proposals to integrate the schools by bussing students from ghetto schools to
other areas and vice versa. Second, there have been plans for

SOURCE: Carl J. Dolce, "The Inner City—A Superintendent's View," *Saturday
Review,* January 11, 1969, p. 36; Alan K. Campbell, "Inequities of School Finance,"
Saturday Review, January 11, 1969, pp. 44–48; Albert Shanker, "What's Wrong with
Compensatory Education," *Saturday Review,* January 11, 1969, pp. 56–58. Pub-
lished in cooperation with the Committee for Economic Development. Copyright
1969 Saturday Review, Inc.

improvement. This selection is a general survey of *de facto* segregation in the North and West.

THE INNER CITY—A SUPERINTENDENT'S VIEW

—Carl J. Dolce

A victim of his environment, the ghetto child begins his school career psychologically, socially, and physically disadvantaged. He is oriented to the present rather than the future, to immediate needs rather than delayed gratification, to the concrete rather than the abstract. He is often handicapped by limited verbal skills, low self-esteem, and a stunted drive toward achievement; by sight, hearing, and dental deficiencies; by hernias, malnutrition, and anemia.

Education in the ghetto, for the most part, has failed to come to grips with these predicaments. The ghetto child's failure to achieve according to middle-class standards is often reinforced by low expectations on the part of his teachers—and these constitute a form of self-fulfilling prophecy. A common notion among ghetto teachers is: "These children aren't prepared for learning in a formal setting; their achievement levels are low compared to middle-class children, so why expect them to achieve very much?"

Other factors aggravate conditions for learning in the ghetto. Schools tend to be older because ghettos generally form in older areas of the cities. They tend to be overcrowded because of the higher population density and greater proportion of children per family in the ghetto. Moreover, the flight to the suburbs by the middle class has eroded the tax base, and this has been largely responsible for the meager financial resources available to ghetto schools when compared to schools in the surrounding suburbs.

It is often assumed that recent progress in civil rights has established a framework for eventually resolving ghetto problems and that with future progress education in the ghetto will receive a new lease on life. These are faulty assumptions. There have been some legislative and judicial reforms—even some modification in public attitudes—but these have benefited the Negro middle class primarily. The ghetto poor are becoming poorer, and most educational institutions are failing to provide their children with instruction that relates to their present condition. The result is that demands have heightened for community control of ghetto schools as a means of providing parents with the power to determine what their children will learn and how they will learn it.

Paradoxically, education in the ghetto cannot be improved merely by intervention through the school. The many variables of the ghetto subculture will also have to be substantially modified. A public commitment is needed—a coordinated effort to provide jobs, eliminate crime, improve housing and transportation, health and welfare, as well as education. Such an effort will require creative adaptations from locality to locality because ghettos are not alike. Statistics may make them appear the same, but are misleading because they tend to have a non-human connotation, and those of us who don't live in the ghetto can never fully understand its problems.

Nonetheless, certain ghetto conditions and responses to them occur frequently enough to permit certain generalizations. Two basic aspects of ghetto life have overpowering effects upon the psychology of ghetto dwellers:

1. Ghettos are inhabited by people who live there because they have no alternative. Their lack of alternatives tends to create feelings of entrapment and powerlessness. Such feelings are difficult to simulate among persons who might live in a slum area by choice, but who have an escape whenever such escape is necessary or desirable. For most, the modern-day ghetto is not open-ended; rather it is closed and restrictive. The effect of television on the poor remains to be defined and measured. I suspect that it has served to heighten feelings of entrapment and powerlessness by emphasizing that there are alternative conditions which are enjoyed by the majority of Americans, but which are not open to the poor.

2. Ghetto areas, particularly black ghetto areas, are occupied by people who have a heritage of deprivation, frustration, maltreatment, and discrimination, and this heritage has a profound impact on their lives. The quality of life must be significantly different, in my judgment, for the inhabitants who, of necessity, live in the ghetto but whose style of living at one time was richer and more optimistic.

While these generalizations will not serve as valid bases for action in specific situations, they are important for analysis and understanding of ghetto conditions. But it should be recognized that all ghetto residents do not react to these two factors in the same manner. Neither do all ghetto residents live under the identical conditions or manifest the same characteristics.

By absolute standards, improvements are being made in the quality of life of ghetto residents even in education. But by relative standards, compared to non-ghetto residents, the differences are widening. Our individual and national consciences must not allow such conditions to continue.

INEQUITIES OF SCHOOL FINANCE

—Alan K. Campbell

Throughout its history this nation has stressed education as the primary means of guaranteeing every citizen an equal chance at obtaining the rewards of an open society. If educational opportunities are unequal, then the American experiment in equality of opportunity must fail. The evidence indicates that we are indeed failing. Nor is there any strong indication that we are about to correct this failure.

It is possible, of course, to read the evidence differently. The proportion of national income devoted to education is increasing, as is the proportion of total public expenditure for education. But these favorable trends do not overcome one of the fundamental weaknesses of our educational system—the basic mismatch between inadequate educational resources and great educational needs. This inequality is the result of an allocation system which provides more resources for educating the suburban child than the city child. Such differences would make sense, if it were easier to educate the city child than the suburban child. Just the opposite, of course, is the case.

The problem of matching resources to needs in education was created by a redistribution of population in the United States. The result has been that poor, less educated, non-white Americans are staying in the central cities, while higher-income, white families, and a substantial part of the industrial sector are moving to the suburbs and taking their tax base with them. This phenomenon varies with the size of the metropolitan area and the region of the country, but it applies with force to most large metropolitan areas.

While this shift in population was occurring, research studies were demonstrating that the single best indicator of educational achievement is the family background of the pupil. Thus, it was made clear that a lower-income city student was at a significant educational disadvantage when compared to a more affluent student in a suburban community. Further, it became apparent that educational programs were essentially designed by middle-income people for middle-income students. Educational materials are full of examples and illustrations drawn from the life of the suburban middle class. Teachers are recruited largely from the middle-income stratum and are trained in schools of education and liberal arts colleges by faculty members who come from this same background.

All of this demonstrates that present personnel and educational practices are not equal to the needs of the city child. Curricula must be revised, teacher-training changed, and teaching methods adjusted to his needs. To do all these things will require new and massive resources. Small incremental differences will not do the job.

Despite the obvious need for more resources in city schools, we are spending less—any way you measure it—in the cities than in the suburbs. For the thirty-seven largest U.S. metropolitan areas, the average per capita expenditure for education in the central cities is $82; the same expenditure in the suburbs is $113. On a per student basis, the comparable figures are $449 for the cities and $573 for the suburbs. These figures would not be so startling if the gap between city and suburb appeared to be closing. It is widening however. To compete with the suburbs, central cities must have a resource advantage. Yet, the present system of resource allocation clearly discriminates against the city. Why?

Because of educational difficulties in many central-city schools, experienced teachers seek assignments in the so-called "better" schools within the city system; many abandon the central city entirely for more attractive suburban districts. Schools are older, and site costs for new buildings are higher in the city than in the suburbs. Moreover, the pressure for other public services—police protection, welfare, and the like—is greater in the city.

To a large extent, it is the available income which influences the ability of a governmental unit to meet the service requirements of its population. Central cities are losing ground in this respect, while their functional needs are increasing simultaneously. As part of the metropolitan pattern, economic activities are becoming decentralized, moving from the core city to the surrounding areas and weakening the central-city tax base in the process. An examination of the central cities of twelve large metropolitan areas demonstrates that the proportion of manufacturing compared to that of suburban areas has clearly declined over the past three decades, especially in the post-World War II period. In 1929, these twelve cities accounted, on the average, for 66 per cent of manufacturing employment. This percentage decreased to 61 per cent by 1947, dropped to 49 per cent by 1958, and has since declined even further.

As industries continue to move outward, taxable assessed valuation—the source of local property taxes—has barely held its own in many localities and has actually declined in several large cities. For example, in a recent five-year period, the percentage changes in taxable assessed valuation for seven cities were: Baltimore, −11 per cent; Boston, −1 per cent; Buffalo, −1 per cent; Detroit, −2 per cent; St. Louis, +1 per cent; Philadelphia, +3 per cent; and Cleveland, −3 per cent.

Translated into educational terms, the tax base in large cities has not kept pace with the recent growth and changing nature of the school population in these cities. Indeed, an examination of the per pupil taxable assessed valuation over a five-year period shows that ten large cities out of fourteen experienced a decrease in this source of revenue. Since local property taxes are the major source of local educational revenues, large city schools can barely meet ordinary education needs, let alone resolve problems resulting from shifting population patterns. Complicating the picture is the burden which non-educational services place on the tax bases of central cities. Non-educational expenditures constitute 68 per cent of total public expenditures in the central cities of the thirty-seven largest metropolitan areas. The comparable percentage for the suburbs is only 47 per cent. Accordingly, the distribution of needs and resources creates heavier total local tax burdens in cities than in suburbs. Measured against personal income, local taxes constitute 8 per cent of that income in cities and only 6 per cent in suburbs, or a one-third greater burden on city taxpayers.

WHAT'S WRONG WITH COMPENSATORY EDUCATION
—Albert Shanker

There has been much controversy and uncertainty about how educational disadvantage can be overcome. But one thing is clear, it cannot be done cheaply. Whether the answer is integration, compensatory education, community control, more private schools, or some combination of these and other approaches, the cost will be high. To substitute educational experimentation and innovation for increased resources is to sentence those experiments to failure.

Further, the educational problems now found in cities are becoming increasingly apparent in some suburban areas. As more and more people move to suburbia, communities are being created with many central-city characteristics. Tax burdens are high, educational disadvantage is growing, and political resistance to applying increased local resources to education is on the rise. Unless major breakthroughs in central city education are made soon, the same problems will spread throughout metropolitan areas.

The present allocation of resources may match the distribution of political power in American society; but it does not match the distribution of need. If we are to make breakthroughs, it must.

Compensatory education, which was once thought the answer to our educational problems, is now under heavy attack for a number of reasons. First, it has been used in various parts of this country as a substitute for school integration. When civil rights proponents demanded integration, they were offered improved segregated facilities instead. This is one of the reasons why compensatory education has earned a poor reputation.

There is a second reason. The concept of compensation brought with it an implication that somehow something was wrong with the child, not with the schools, teachers, or our educational institutions. It was the child who was deprived; therefore, we had to do something to compensate for the deprivation of the child. Thus, the theory behind compensatory education, it is charged, is one-sided in placing the blame for educational failure.

Third, the child is subjected to large classes, inadequately trained teachers, and a poor curriculum. School systems try to undo the damage done during the school day after school hours, or in a summer school program, or an evening school. We put the child in a setting where he is likely to fail, and then attempt remediation, or to undo what we did to him in the first place.

There are a number of reasons why this remediation approach has been used. In the first place, it is relatively inexpensive. If we were to talk about reducing class size, not by one, or two, or three, but bringing it down from a maximum of thirty-five or forty to a maximum of ten, fifteen, or twenty, we would be talking about a doubling of the educational budget at the very least. But to hire a teacher after school for as much as $8 an hour to work with a group of children is very inexpensive compared to doing something about what goes on in the classroom with teachers and children throughout the day.

The second reason for the popularity of remediation in our school systems is that it is visible. If you reduce class size by two, three, four, or five, when the public takes a look inside they see a teacher and children in a room, and books, and it doesn't look as if anything has changed. But when several teachers work after school, the public can see that the school is open a little longer. There is a great push in the education world for public credit and acceptance, and that often results in programs which may have doubtful educational validity, but which add to the public relations impact of the school system.

Compensatory programs throughout the country, as they have been evaluated, show consistently poor results. In addition, they create great disappointments because practically all remedial and compensatory programs are launched with great fanfare. Impressive results are publicized for several years—how children have made three to five years' reading progress in the first two weeks of the program, for instance—when the program really isn't working. The Higher Horizons Program in New York City was privately abandoned by the Board of Education, but the favorable publicity on it kept coming out for another three years. School systems all over the country were adopting this "excellent" program, while it was being phased out in the city of New York.

Equality of Educational Opportunity, a Government study headed by Professor James S. Coleman of Johns Hopkins University, has been used unfairly to show that differences in the type of school building, the size of classes, and the amount of money spent have very little effect on educational output. The Coleman report doesn't show that at all; it shows that given the variations which Professor Coleman was able to measure— which were not that great—it doesn't make much difference if you have a class size of thirty-seven or twenty-seven. It does not show that if children were able to go to school, especially at an early age, in classes with six, eight, ten, or twelve, there would be no difference. Professor Coleman obviously was not able to tell us what would happen in such cases because there was no place where he could evaluate the impact of conditions which do not yet exist.

The gloom which emanates from evaluation of compensatory programs has led to a series of alternative approaches. For example, we now hear the great shout that money is not the answer, that we have to look in some other direction. One approach stems from the view that somehow the fault with our school systems is that our schools are a Government monopoly, that there is no competition, and that we ought to provide some form of private alternative.

Some experimentation with this approach might be very worthwhile, but we should be wary of it. There is no evidence to show that private business does not suffer from the same organizational diseases that large or small public systems suffer from. The arguments about centralization and decentralization have gone on in the world of business and industry for a very long time, just as they are now going on in the educational world.

If we move toward private schools for the poor, we will have to have strong governmental agencies to regulate them. There has to be some way of evaluating and regulating a private system of education. Otherwise, the poor will be cheated in the educational field, as they are in the local commercial enterprises.

6 / Notes from a Mini-School

JACK BECK

The debate over education for minority groups has shifted
from the goal of integration of minority-group children into majority-group schools to the establishment of quality schools in
the ghettoes, *barrios,* or reservations under the control of the
people in that area. The recent conflict in the New York City
schools over community control is a reflection of the desire of
blacks for their own school system. In California, Mexican-
Americans are pressing for similar goals, particularly in the
elementary grades. This article describes the motivations
leading all three groups to press for locally controlled schools.
First, they see their children failing in the majority-group
schools at a rate far greater than their white Anglo counterparts.
Second, they see the schools teaching history and literature
that either distort or omit any reference to their history and
contributions to America. And third, they find that a testing
and counseling system in which acculturation is tested for is
dead-ended as far as giving nonwhites a chance for college.
One example of an attempt to increase community involvement is the "mini-school" in Philadelphia's predominantly
black Mantua-Powelton district. It is a small-scale experimental school with an enrollment of 120, which is housed in a

SOURCE: Jack Beck, "Notes from a Mini-School," *Rockefeller Foundation Quarterly* 2 (1969), pp. 30–36. Reprinted by permission.

converted cookie factory. The school, which receives financial support through the Rockefeller Foundation Equal Opportunity Program, is a working example of parent participation in the planning and operation of a school.

School began. No bells rang, nobody stood in line.

Through doorways without doors, I saw groups of six and eight children sitting with their teachers, sometimes only one child with a teacher.

In the library, two boys were playing checkers. Examining the board closely, I saw that pieces of paper had been pasted over the black squares, and that they contained handwritten words. The one I noticed was "soul."

I was in the Mantua-Powelton ghetto of Philadelphia, and the little red schoolhouse was a renovated factory.

In 1968 the factory was to be demolished. The plumbing and electricity were already ripped out when the concept of the neighborhood mini-school made it back into a factory, a child factory.

When it was a factory, no machinery had made as much noise as the children did the morning I walked into the school. It was early, and the decibel count was high.

I had expected to find children playing outside the building, waiting for school to open. There were none. Inside, because the interior space is open and uncluttered, the boys were playing handball and the girls were playing jacks. Uncluttered with objects, but visually overstuffed—walls painted brilliant colors—purple, yellow, green, red—and covered with elephants, giraffes, flowers, printed words.

The kids had been at work decorating their own place.

The building is three stories high and the street entrance is up an exterior stair to the second floor. The schoolroom on the first floor opens out to the back of the building through factory-type doors, creating a classroom on the verge of being outdoors.

The second floor is taken over by the administrative staff (in one small corner), the kids in classrooms, and a menagerie of monkeys, chickens, rabbits, fish, and exotic and neighborhood plants.

The animals run in a large area which is screened from floor to ceiling, suggesting a zoo more than a school; and of course the children are in with the animals.

Up a steel and concrete factory stairwell is the third floor: more classrooms, a photographic darkroom, a drama room, and a science room.

Back on the main floor I became aware of the teachers moving into the groups. One was playing handball with the boys, another was listening patiently while a little girl wearing thick glasses described the sore throat that had kept her out of school.

And then I met Forrest Adams, the director, the man responsible for the mini-school. An architect-engineer-city planner, working hard at this.

He is tall and thin and appears even taller because he is always surrounded by little people who tug at his pants for attention.

He wears round metal-rimmed glasses, has a number of short hairs on his chin, and continually rubs, pushes, and pulls his nose, as if it itched, when in high excitement he talks about education.

I followed him through the school's rooms. "How much is 27 and 67?" he asked, as if thinking aloud. He got back an enthusiastic chorus of answers—86, 72, 300, laughter.

Two girls stopped him in the hall and said Alvin had taken their jacks. "Tell Alvin I want to see him." Alvin appeared, grinning, not at all scared; he seemed to like the attention he was getting. "Alvin, give back the jacks." Alvin gave back two. The girls said he had more. Alvin said no.

"Alvin, if you say you don't have any more jacks, I'll believe you. But if you do have more jacks, I'll never be able to believe you again."

Alvin submitted willingly to inspection by Adams.

"Now, girls, I want you to apologize to Alvin for calling him a liar." They solemnly apologized, and shook hands. Then they all ran off down the hall.

I asked Adams to have lunch with me. He said he only ate supper, but suggested we go to his apartment for coffee and talk.

First he went to his small, cluttered office, which he shares with another teacher, stepped around a child studying on the floor, and gathered some papers; then we left the mini-school-in-a-factory-experiment-in-the-ghetto.

A few blocks from the school we entered a ground-floor apartment. Rambling rooms, large enough to hold Forrest Adams. Plum-colored mohair stuffed couches, an oriental rug on the floor, some of the kids' sculpture, sunlight filtering through shuttered windows.

Adams apologized for the bad coffee. I agreed. He fell into a chair, lit a pipe, and pulled his nose.

For the next hour I heard about the mini-school, education, society, philosophy, money, and future plans. In between, people dropped in to join the conversation and drift out again. A white girl complained about plans falling through on a health center she was involved with—they had an option on a building, but no funds to proceed. A bearded white architect sat dejectedly, and bitterly denounced the city fathers for reneging on a neighborhood development program. He was going to California to work professionally, "earn a lot of money," and try to get over his disappointment.

Adams kept on talking.

The original plan had been to construct a middle school for 1500 students, on an area of about five square blocks. It would have meant displacing many hundreds of families. Naturally this plan met with great dissatisfaction from the community; and in any case the land was owned by a utility company not overly eager to give it up.

At this point, Mark R. Shedd, Philadelphia's superintendent of schools (who has attracted nationwide attention for his insistence on major reforms in the school system), urged the school board to experiment with a new teaching program that would involve the ghetto community.

He proposed decentralized schools—mini-schools that wouldn't force families to move, within the ghetto or outside it.

This new kind of school would be compatible with the established school system.

When the idea was approved by the school board last July, Adams had to find a building, a teaching staff, and students for a September opening.

First Adams gathered his staff, some of them dedicated teachers and teacher's aids from within the school system. Then he sent them into the neighborhood to recruit students by knocking on doors and telling parents about the new school coming to their community. He also placed ads about the school in local newspapers.

Local people participated in all stages of the planning, and in discussions of the curriculum with the teachers.

In the early months, interior school construction went on around the children, and was considered not an inconvenience but an actual teaching device. The children saw plumbing being installed, electricity turned on.

From an original budget estimate of $127,000, which included salaries, the factory was rented and $50,000 was required for minimal reconstruction.

The school board has given $89,000. The Rockefeller Foundation has given $150,000. But expenditures have crept up over $230,000, and Adams hesitates to answer the phone.

"Once our teachers went a month without salaries," he informed me.

By April, operating expenses had depleted all funds, and Adams borrowed $6000 from the school board to get through June.

The school has a teaching staff of 18. Three are accredited teachers and nine "have degrees from somewhere." Adams says even the school bus driver doubles as a counselor.

Teachers come in at 8:00. Classes begin at 9:00 for the 120 children from the surrounding neighborhood, many of them "problem children," enrolled with the parents' consent and hopefully with their participation.

The school goes from fifth to seventh grade. Next year it will include eighth grade. Students who decide to drop out can move into other grammar schools at equivalent grades.

"We are creating a 'ghetto being' on the third floor," Adams said. "It's 16 feet square, and duplicates our neighborhood ghetto. The kids are building it from exploring our area, drawing maps, and then putting in models of each building.

"They should be able to define a ghetto, tell what's wrong with it, what they would like to change and correct; and then they will go ahead and do that in the 'ghetto being,' whether it's trees, swimming pools, or new homes. I got a call the other day from another school—eight of my kids were there, wanted to interview the principal with a tape recorder!

"Kids should not be told no. Kids should fly—or at least they shouldn't be told they can't. If they try and fail, then they'll learn what a compound fracture is.

"We have no tests or report cards so far."

I had read the students' mimeographed newspaper on the bulletin board, which complained that they didn't get report cards like other schools.

"In our science program we have explored not only rockets and space, but the idea of claiming areas on the moon, what's good and bad about it, and then back to earth and its boundaries between countries.

"Two boys sat down with our whole staff and explained their embarrassment when they didn't understand the subject being taught. Taught the teachers something. In our close relationship we can obtain detailed knowledge about each student.

"Yes, we will be trying to integrate this program so students can plug into the Parkway High School." An answer to my question about how a student will fit into high school after he leaves the mini. Philadelphia's Parkway program will eventually be a learning environment for 2400 students, using existing cultural centers as "classrooms," with shuttle buses between the various buildings.

"There's no reason for schools to be just schools. We will be using our school buildings for night courses for adults—for movies. Why can't schools have a movie house attached to them, or a museum?

"Kids that can't read, can read when they view old silent films! We use TV as homework to enlarge their vocabulary."

Forrest Adams hopes to have five more mini-schools by 1971–1972. And then he wants them to proliferate five at a time until there are 45 of them functioning in 1976.

At the end of our conversation, I felt that Adams recognized that he was in the midst of a whole new educational process for the black ghetto child, but that the talk about the future depressed him, because he was aware that today's adventure would inevitably become an accepted part of the school system.

He asked me if I wanted to interview the mother of one of the school children whose brother had been killed standing on a street corner. Gang fight. He said it happens from time to time. I declined.

Then I visited other parents. They approved of the school, felt it belonged to them, appreciated the liaison they had with it. "We don't get report cards marked A or D. I never knew what to do about those letters. Now the teachers tell us if our children need help in a certain subject, and tell us how we can help." . . . "My boy wants to go to school every day."

The absence rate is down. The working mothers seemed to be especially relieved.

One mother suggested they be given a day's pay so they could visit the classroom during the week. She wanted her other children to attend the mini-school too. She felt put off by the larger schools, and, I gathered, so did her children.

She said the teachers at the larger schools had criticized her unfairly, through her children. "One teacher told my son I should have bought him clothes instead of toys at Christmas."

Another woman, mother of 13: "A teacher asked my son if I was in the hospital having another baby. I wasn't, and it was none of her business . . . Embarrassed my boy."

So the parents in the Mantua-Powelton area of Philadelphia feel they have helped create a community school that comes closer to providing what their children need.

I read in *The New York Times* that a school bond issue was defeated (for the first time in the modern history of Philadelphia). I called Adams, who was not discouraged. "Now they won't have the money to build big new schools."

Later Forrest Adams notified me that the Philadelphia school board had approved his $146,000 budget for next year.

7 / The Schooling Gap and Signs of Progress

LEO GREBLER

For the Mexican-American, education problems are worse than they are for blacks. For example, in California the educational achievement of Mexican-Americans is lower than that of blacks by an average of one full school year. They suffer from the difference in languages used in the home (Spanish) and in school (English). They come predominantly from homes where the entire family is involved in farm labor or unskilled physical labor in an urban setting, and are encouraged to drop out of school as soon as possible to join their fathers (and often their mothers) in this type of employment. There is an increased awareness of these problems, and efforts are being made (1) to develop less culture-bound testing and placement policies and (2) to provide financial assistance to more Mexican-American students so they can go to college. Recently, testing in several schools in California has shown that when Mexican-American children take an IQ test in Spanish, the overall IQ increase can be as much as 30 points. This selection indicates some of the problems discovered by a study of Los Angeles schools and proposals for reform.

SOURCE: Leo Grebler, *The Schooling Gap and Signs of Progress* (Mexican-American Study Project, *Advance Report 7,* UCLA, March 1967), pp. 3–5, 7–10, 33–34. These materials are analyzed in broader context in Leo Grebler, Joan W. Moore, and Ralph C. Guzman, *The Mexican-American People: The Nation's Second Largest Minority* (New York: The Free Press, 1970).

Our analysis starts with a set of data that is widely cited by Mexican-American spokesmen, as well as others, to indicate the educational deficiency: the years of schooling completed by persons 25 years and over. . . . Unfortunately, as will be shown shortly, this is a somewhat deceptive measure of the gap.

The differences between the adult Spanish-surname population and the two reference populations are indeed enormous. In 1960, in the Southwest, adult Mexican-Americans had, on the average, 7.1 years of schooling as against 12.1 for Anglos and 9.0 for nonwhites. If the Anglo record is taken as a norm, the gap was 5 years or 41 percent for Mexican-Americans and 3.1 years or 26 percent for nonwhites. And the picture repeats itself in every state, though with some significant variations. The median attainment of the Spanish-surname group in 1960 ranged from 8.6 years in California to a dismal 4.8 years in Texas—the latter being barely above the level of 4 years, which is generally considered the demarcation line for functional illiteracy. Characteristically, this range was far greater than the range for Anglos (from 12.2 years in California and Colorado to 10.3 in Texas), and so was the variation for nonwhites (11.2 years in Colorado to 7.0 in Arizona).

California and Colorado, which have the highest general educational attainment record, show also the lowest schooling gaps for both Mexican-Americans and nonwhites. Texas, which ranks lowest in general and Anglo attainment, showed the largest gap for the Spanish-surname group though not for nonwhites. In three of the five states, the 1960 record was notably better for nonwhites than for Mexican-Americans. The reverse was true for New Mexico, and the standing of the two minority groups was equally low in Arizona. Again, one must remember that nonwhites in these two states include a fairly large admixture of American Indians, whose schooling generally is far poorer than that of Negroes. In contrast, the inclusion of Orientals in the nonwhite category tends to raise the nonwhite average in California.

Nevertheless, there has been progress even for the adult population. Average education attainment of Spanish-surname persons of 25 years or over increased between 1950 and 1960 from 5.4 to 7.1 years of schooling (and that of nonwhites improved as well). It increased more than Anglo attainment, with the result that the education gap was somewhat reduced from 52 percent in 1950 to 41 percent in 1960. This trend is repeated in each of the states. . . .

There is nothing wrong, conceptually or otherwise, with measuring the educational accomplishment of the adult population. The underlying notion that the age of 25, when even elaborate schooling is usually completed, is a good cut-off point for measurement is unassailable. Yet, the yardstick produces a somewhat biased view of the attainment of groups whose average age is markedly lower than that of the general population. Both the Mexican-American and, to a lesser extent, the nonwhite minority is younger than the Anglos. When one adopts another often used cut-off point for educational statistics, 14 years and over, it turns out that the adult groups (25 years and more) represent 70.0 percent of the Spanish-surname persons in the Southwest, 75.8 percent of the nonwhites, and 79.3 percent of Anglos—all figured as percentages of the persons 14 years and over in each subpopulation.

Therefore, one obtains a broader and more meaningful perspective by pushing the measure of educational attainment back to the age of 14. Also, by distinguishing between persons aged 14 to 24 and the persons of 25 years and more, one can detect the presence or absence of progress from the older to the younger generation. The drawback here is the undeniable fact that the record for the age group of 14 to 24 years is incomplete, and it is surely differentially incomplete when the two minorities are compared with the white Anglo population which represents the American "norm."

The picture presented on the basis of a wider age range is indeed much more favorable than the record for the adult population alone. . . . It shows gains in the younger age group for both minorities. While Anglos of 25 years and over have a higher educational attainment than those of 14 to 24 years, the reverse is true for the Spanish-surname and the nonwhite populations. In these two cases, the younger age groups have already shown substantially more years of schooling to their credit than do the adult groups, despite the fact that their education may as yet be unfinished. In the Southwest the younger Mexican-Americans had completed, in 1960, 9.2 median years of formal education as against 7.1 years for the adults. The figures for nonwhites were 10.6 and 9.0 years, respectively. The schooling gap between the Spanish-surname group and Anglos was 2.1 years or 19 percent in the 14–24 age class, as against 5 years or 41 percent for the population 25 years and over. When the two age groups are merged as "14 years and over" the schooling gap is also lower than that for adults alone.

This condition applies to every one of the five states, and the rank order of states in terms of the schooling gap is about the same for the younger generation as it is for the adult population. In California, the "best" of the five states, the schooling gap between Mexican-Americans and Anglos of 14 to 24 years was only 10 percent, or one-third of the gap for the adult group. Even in Texas, the "worst" state, the gap is reduced from the staggering 58 percent for the adult population to 27 percent for the age group of 14 to 24 years.

Contrary to conventional notions about the role and upbringing of females in traditional Mexican culture, the average schooling of Spanish-surname females was about the same as for males. . . . This is true for both the adults and the younger generation. The differentials in the several states are minor and not in the same direction. (As is well known, the picture is somewhat different in the nonwhite population, especially for Negroes. Here, the average educational attainment of females is usually greater than that of males).

A word is in order on the relative standing of the several states. Because of internal migrations, the figures do not necessarily measure precisely the current attainment, for instance, in Arizona versus Texas. Data on the educational level were obtained by the Census at the 1960 place of residence. If Mexican-Americans or, for that matter, others who received their schooling in Texas had moved to Arizona before the Census date, the latter state would be credited or debited with schooling that occurred in the former. If those who moved had an above-average education, Arizona's record may be raised and the record of Texas lowered. This observation has particular relevance to the data for the adult population. At the same time, it will be seen that inter-state differences in respect to education are highly consistent no matter what yardsticks are used—the schooling of adults or of young people, 1960 school enrollment, or the number of school years completed. Consequently, the marked variations from state to state cannot be explained away by internal migrations.

Rural to urban migration may also be a factor in the schooling progress of Mexican-Americans between 1950 and 1960. Part of the improvement is attributable to the rapidly increasing urbanization of this minority population. Educational attainment is generally better in the cities and suburbs than in the country. School facilities and the enforcement of compulsory education laws are usually superior. Also, when parents shift from agricultural to urban jobs the impediments to the children's schooling that come from migrant farm work or seasonal child labor are removed or diminished. [Table 3] shows, indeed, that the educational attainment of Spanish-surname persons conforms to the "normal" rank order of urban, rural-nonfarm, and rural-farm areas, for all major age groups. But the migration from the country to the cities and towns is just one factor contributing to progress. The *urban* Mexican-Americans had also more schooling by 1960 than did the *urban* segment of the group in 1950. . . . This is true despite the fact that the migrants to cities come from areas with lower average levels of education. Those who migrate may have above-average schooling and may be more motivated to seek better opportunities in urban environments. . . .

Our analysis has detailed the well-known gap in formal schooling of Mexican-Americans by comparison with Anglos as well as with non-whites. An extraordinary differential existed in 1960 in school years completed, especially for the adult population. The gap was much smaller when the educational attainment of the younger generation or its school enrollment were used as yardsticks. Even by these criteria, however, deficiencies appeared in the relatively late beginning of formal education, the widening enrollment differentials as children reached the high school level, and in the low percentage of Mexican-American youngsters who completed high school or college. Also, we found appalling state and local differences in the educational gap. The differences in attainment were far greater for the Spanish-surname group (and nonwhites) than for Anglos.

The gap is attributable in part to intergroup variations in rural-urban background, to immigrant status, and poverty and other aspects of the home environment. The extreme disparities in different locales suggest an hypothesis concerning a strategic determinant in the larger society: the extent to which the local social systems and, through these, the school systems have held the Mexican-American population in a subordinate position. This hypothesis will engage our attention in other publications of the Mexican-American Study Project.

But the thrust of our analysis was directed at the frequently neglected or ignored evidence of moderate progress. Progress was visible in the 1950–1960 comparisons which showed that the schooling gap relative to Anglos had been narrowed. This progress became readily apparent when the educational attainment of the younger generation was contrasted with the schooling of higher age groups. It manifested itself in still another intergenerational advance; from extremely low educational levels of the foreign born to far better performance by the native born, though further improvement between the second and the subsequent generation was evident only in school enrollment.

Progress seems to have contained since 1960, but no data are available to document this impression. In any event, it is encouraging to note that the educational standing of this disadvantaged minority improved, even though slowly, in a period when the current arsenal of federal aids to education and anti-poverty programs was not available and when neither the ethnic community nor the larger society was fully geared to the task. The present efforts, then, have started from a basis of dynamic changes in favor of better schooling.

There is no room for complacency, however. The educational gaps in most of the Southwest are still so great that their removal will take much time and energy, and much reorientation of school philosophy, curriculum, teachers, and teaching techniques, in addition to large sums of money. Nevertheless, the evidence of recent, and largely unaided progress is sufficient to indicate that the schooling of Mexican-Americans is in a "take-off" stage—a stage in which massive improvement becomes possible if financial assistance is matched with better knowledge and with greater willingness of our society to face the job that needs to be done.

8 / Indian Schools

DANIEL HENNINGER
NANCY ESPOSITO

Indians are confronted with a different set of problems than those of either the blacks or the Mexican-Americans. Because of the peculiar legal status of the Indian (to be discussed further in Chaps. 4 and 5), most of them are segregated from society on reservations. Schooling is provided in a variety of ways, from schools on the reservations to boarding schools off the reservation. In one important way the Indian shares a problem with the other minority groups: he has a deep fear of the consequences of Indian youth receiving a higher education. He sees such youth failing to return to help other Indians (or blacks or Mexican-Americans) and therefore being lost to the tribe, or returning and then ridiculing the uneducated (and frequently nonwesternized) members, very often including his parents. The Indian is perhaps especially suspicious of government programs for sending Indian youth to universities because of the way they have been misled and exploited in the past. This selection describes very clearly the fears of older members of all three minority groups, fears that must be overcome if the older members are to support needed higher education for their youth.

Source: Daniel Henninger and Nancy Esposito, "Indian Schools," *The New Republic,* February 15, 1969, pp. 18–21. Reprinted by permission of *The New Republic,* © 1969, Harrison-Blaine of New Jersey, Inc.

Senator Edward Kennedy has taken over the chairmanship of his late brother's Indian Education Subcommittee, which is soon to release a report recommending basic changes in the ways we educate Indian children. It's about time. The Bureau of Indian Affairs spent $86 million of its $241 million budget in 1968 on the education of 55,000 Indian children, and there's little to show for it.

Nearly 60 percent of these youngsters must attend BIA boarding schools, either because there's no public or federal day school near their home or because they are "social referrals" (BIA jargon for anything from a bilingual difficulty to serious emotional disorders and juvenile delinquency). One percent finish college. In Alaska there is only one federal high school, so two-thirds of the Alaskan Indians are sent to a boarding school in Oregon; 267 others go to school in Chilocco, Oklahoma. The Navajo nation comprises one-third of the BIA's responsibility, and 92 percent of its children are in boarding schools. The schools have a 60 percent dropout rate, compared to a national average of 23 percent.

Assimilation has been the aim of the Bureau of Indian Affairs since the early 1800s. But it no longer expresses that purpose in the embarassing language of a World War II House subcommittee: "The final solution of the Indian problem [is] to work toward the liquidation of the Indian problem rather than toward merely perpetuating a federal Indian Service working with a steadily increasing Indian population." From the BIA's "Curriculum Needs of Navajo Pupils" we learn that the Navajo child "needs to begin to develop knowledge of how the dominant culture is pluralistic and how these people worked to become the culture which influences the American mainstream of life . . ."; "needs to understand that every man is free to rise as high as he is able and willing . . ."; "needs assistance with accepting either the role of leader or follower . . ."; "needs to understand that a mastery of the English language is imperative to compete in the world today . . ."; "needs to understand that work is necessary to exist and succeed. . . ."

Often the government places children in federal boarding schools at the age of six or seven; over 9000 under the age of nine are so placed. That quite a few parents resist having their young taken from home for a year is indicated by a 1966 HEW survey: 16,000 Indian children between the ages of eight and 16 were not in school.

The Indian school curriculum is standard: ancient history, European history, American history, geography, arithmetic, art, music (an Indian "needs training in proper tone production in order to properly and effectively sing Western music"). Not much about *their* history. The Interior Department investigated Indian schools in Alaska last spring and found that "education which gives the Indian, Eskimo and Aleut knowledge of —and therefore pride in—their historic and cultural heritage is almost nonexistent. . . . In the very few places where such an attempt is made, it is poorly conceived and inadequate." Most of the boarding school teachers are aware of the variations in language, dress and customs of their students, but their sensitivity to the less obvious differences in Indian values, beliefs and attitudes is peripheral and by the way. Most Indian children speak English poorly or not at all; communication between teacher and pupil is difficult or impossible. Yet Bureau schools conduct *all* classes in English.

It doesn't take long to discourage young, dedicated teachers: "Most of the teachers came to Chilocco because of humanitarian reasons," said a former teacher at the Oklahoma boarding school. "They saw the pitiful situation and truly wanted to help, but after months of rejection and failure, they either quit or they began looking at it as an eight to five job with no obligation to their students." A teacher at an Arizona school wrote the BIA last year, suggesting that the inclusion of courses in agriculture and native crafts might arouse his habitually unresponsive students. "This idea [didn't] set well with many of the 'old hands' among the administrators," he later said. "The only thing that came out of it were some dark days for me, and a label as a trouble-maker." The turnover rate among teachers is double the national average. To an Indian child, the teacher is a stranger passing through. An obvious remedy is to enlist more Indian teachers. At present only 16 percent of the Bureau's teachers are Indian, and with only one percent of the Indians graduating yearly from college, there is little chance that the percentage will rise.

Estranged from his family, confronted with an alien culture and unable to talk to his teachers, the Indian's academic performance is predictably poor. What is harder to explain is the "crossover phenomenon." For the first few years of school, Indian achievement parallels that of white children and then slowly but persistently regresses. An Indian starts to fall behind between the sixth and eighth grades, and if he doesn't drop out finishes high school with a 9.5 grade education. Despite this regression, a boarding school student is never held back for academic failure; at the end of each year, he is promoted to the next grade whatever his performance. Summer school programs are scarce. Bureau teachers are contracted by the year, and one-third go on educational leave during the summer while the rest clean up the schools, take inventory and so on. As a result the typical high school class contains highly intelligent students as well as many who should still be in grade school. The teacher tries to compensate by aiming his instruction somewhere between the two extremes, so much of the class drops off to sleep or stares blankly at books.

One would think that after school the children could find some release from this dreariness, in the dorms or in some extracurricular activity.

Life at a federal boarding school, though, is regimented and arbitrary. Seen from the air, many of the schools look like military installations—complexes of one-color, one-texture buildings set in the middle of otherwise barren areas. The impression of physical isolation mirrors the cultural isolation in the classroom. The building-complex usually includes dormitories (boys and girls), classroom buildings and housing for the staff. Many of the buildings are in disrepair. In a number of places (Tuba City, Arizona, for example) condemned buildings are still in use. The Fort Wingate Elementary Boarding School in New Mexico uses old Fort Wingate, once commanded by Douglas MacArthur's father. Forty years ago, the Brookings Institution's Merriam Report declared this plant unsuitable.

Even the new buildings are designed to reinforce the numbing sterility. Long, narrow, lifeless dormitories house row upon row of double-deckered iron beds and little else. Windows are sometimes barred. Floors are bare; the vivid personal decorations that are so much a part of many Indian communities are discouraged. Dress, too, is strictly regulated. The system makes individualizing one's appearance or environment fairly impossible. Beneath all the regulation is the Bureau's implicit concept of the children: all Indians are alike. In reality some children are at boarding schools because there is no alternative schooling available, while an increasing number, the "social referrals," come to the schools with serious emotional problems. Dr. Anthony Elite of the Public Health Service's Indian Health office in Phoenix has said that "with this great change in the profile of the student body, there has not been a concomitant change in staffing skilled workers or training existing personnel to cope with these problems."

Each hour of a child's day is planned by the clock, with strict schedules posted in the dorms. Classes, meals, study periods, chores, free time, bed—the routine never varies. Frequent headcounts are taken to quickly identify runaways or "AWOLS" as the Bureau calls them. Demerits are handed out for breaking the rules. The demerits can be removed by performing extra chores or by sacrificing privileges like TV, a school movie or snacks. At the Chinle Elementary Boarding School each child has a punchcard fastened to the end of his bed with punched holes representing demerits on one side and merits on the other. A little boy proudly displayed his card to a visitor. He was especially proud of the large number of holes he had accumulated. Most of the holes were on the demerit side. He didn't know the difference. At another school two small boys were seen sitting on the floor, tearing up old textbooks as a punishment.

Dr. Robert Bergman, a PHS psychiatrist on the Navajo Reservation said, "the somewhat limited social opportunities of the boarding high school give the adolescent students few protected ways of exploring boy-girl relationships. The sexes are pretty well kept separate most of the time, and even casual contact between them is looked on with some suspicion by school officials anxious about possible scandal. A hostile rebellious attitude develops in the students, and they make their own opportunities away from the potential help of adults. Many students make a very abrupt transition from no dating at all to sneaking out to drink and make love." The administration's response to such behavior is more repression and school officials at a number of boarding schools cite discipline as their most important problem. Asked what he would do if given more money, the superintendent at Chilocco said he would build a jail and hire more guards.

To maintain discipline, the schools eliminate as many outside or uncontrollable influences as possible. A visitor is discouraged from talking to the children. A child "caught" talking to a visitor gets a sharp warning glance from a school official. Authorities address the children in English and discourage using native language in both the classroom and dorms. Dr. Bergman relates the rather bizarre results of this policy: "I often encounter [dorm attendants] who pretend not to speak Navajo. They have become so convinced that speaking Navajo is a bad thing to do that they often won't admit that they can. [Most attendants are themselves products of boarding schools.] The children learn that what they say in Navajo is effectively kept secret from the authorities even if one of the Navajo-speaking members of the staff hears them, because the Navajo staff member will be too ashamed of having understood to tell anyone."

School authorities in effect dictate when children may go home for weekends and when parents may visit the schools. The Bureau has a *de facto* policy of discouraging such visits, because the children are noticeably upset and troublesome afterwards, and the number of runaways invariably increases. To reach the school, parents must travel long distances over roads that are impassable most of the year. The schools afford them neither accommodations nor transportation. At the easily accessible Fort Wingate school, signs on the dormitory doors announced that no child would be permitted home for two weekends prior to Thanksgiving. A teacher at the Tuba City Boarding School wrote of the problem last year to Sen. Robert Kennedy, then chairman of the subcommittee on Indian Education: "Most children on the reservation starting at age six only see their parents on occasional weekends, if that often. At these times parents are usually allowed to check out their children—if the child's conduct in school warrants it, in the opinion of the school administration. If he has been a 'problem' (e.g., has run away) parents are often not allowed to take him until he has 'learned his lesson.'" The students' most visible emotional problem is boredom—the deadening routine of marching in line to meals and class, the lack of recreation or an interesting diversion. The letter to Sen. Kennedy summarized the emptiness of life at a boarding school: "The children search everywhere for something—they grasp most hungrily at any attention shown them, or to any straw that might offer some escape from boredom. You can't help but see it in their faces when you visit the dorms of the younger children. At the older boys' dormitories, they are used to the conditions—you can see that, too. They no longer expect anything meaningful from anyone."

Their reaction to this gradual dehumanization is extreme. Recently on the Navajo Reservation, two young runaways froze to death trying to make it to their homes 50 miles away. Escape through glue-, paint- and gasoline-sniffing is as common as chronic drunkenness at the boarding schools. On Easter morning two years ago, authorities at the Chilocco school found a Crow boy who had apparently drunk himself to death. More recently a runaway at the Albuquerque Boarding School was found frozen to death after an alcoholic binge.

Suicide among young Indians is over three times the national average and an even greater problem at the boarding schools. Yet the Superintendent of the Albuquerque school said he had never seen an Indian suicide in any school in his 28 years of experience. Testifying before Sen. Kennedy's subcommittee, Dr. Daniel O'Connell found evidence to the contrary: "The situation as far as suicide is concerned is especially acute among the boarding school children, particularly in high school. . . . In the Busby School in the Northern Cheyenne Reservation, for example, with fewer than 250 students, there were 12 attempted suicides during the past 18 months."

The closest thing the child has to a surrogate parent is the so-called instructional aide or dormitory attendant. Aides are responsible for the children in the dorms and supervise their routine activities—dressing and washing the smaller children, housecleaning and free time. Psychologically, the instructional aide is the most important member of the staff since the dorm is the closest thing the children have to a home life. But he is the lowest paid and has the lowest status in the school hierarchy. Each aide is expected to care for 60 to 80 children. At a conference with Dr. Bergman, an aide asked for help in getting her 75 first-graders to put their shoes by their beds at night. Every morning is mass hysteria as seven-year-olds scramble for a missing right or left shoe. Night attendants are responsible for 180 to 260 children, so there is rarely someone to comfort a youngster having a normal childhood nightmare.

The instructional aides are not encouraged to take a personal interest in the children. An aide was severely reprimanded for inviting some girls to her room to make Navajo fry-bread. The authorities would prefer that the system's few professional guidance counselors handle the children's problems. The present ratio of students to counselors is 690 to one. One counselor complained that 30 to 40 percent of his time is spent retrieving runaways, another 30 percent supervising housekeeping, leaving little time for serious counseling.

For its more serious problems—the suicide-prone, the alcoholics, the psychotics—the BIA employed one full-time psychologist last year for the entire federal school system. A rebellious or uncooperative student gains a reputation as a "troublemaker" and is expelled from one school after another until he is old enough to drop out. A Fort Hall boy who has attempted suicide six times was sent to Chilocco last fall for lack of anywhere else to send him. Among the Indians, Chilocco is considered the end of the line.

The Rough Rock Demonstration School in northeastern Arizona is a welcome anomaly in this chain of dead-end desert schools. Jointly funded by the Office of Economic Opportunity and the BIA, the Navajo boarding school is innovative in that it is run by Indians. The seven Indians who comprise the school board set school policy, hire and fire teachers and manage the school's $700,000 budget. The curriculum includes daily instruction in Navajo culture, history and language, and the school's Cultural Identification Center attracts talented Navajo artists and translators to produce meaningful texts for Indian children. Nor is the built-in bleakness of dorm life found at Rough Rock. The school has 10 counselors, and parents are invited to live in the dorms for eight-week periods (reducing the child-adult ratio to 10 to one). The parents work as dorm aides, with pay and attend adult education programs, since many are less-educated than their children. Students are encouraged to go home on weekends and the school provides transportation for those who would otherwise have to stay at school. The school's teachers make periodic visits to the children's homes to let the parents know how their children are doing. (The parents of many children at other schools haven't the slightest idea of what grade their children are in.) Of the school's 82 full-time employees, 62 are Indians, and for many it is their first permanent job. It is too early to say whether Rough Rock's community-involvement approach is *the* answer to Indian education. The experiment is expensive ($2500 per student) and the school will have to look elsewhere for support after OEO funding expires in June. What the Indians at Rough Rock have proved is that given effective control of the immediate forces that shape their lives, they can be a success, qualified in measurable achievement, total in terms of self-respect.

chapter three

HOUSING

9 / *Shelley* v. *Kraemer*

The process historically used to prevent black integration of
white neighborhoods is known as the "restrictive covenant."
For many years, these covenants, or agreements, among
homeowners not to sell to specific racial, religious, or ethnic
groups were part of local or state legislation. In 1917, in *Buchanan* v. *Warley,* the Supreme Court declared such state laws
to be unconstitutional; however, the state courts continued to
uphold private covenants in contracts as binding. The case of
Shelley v. *Kraemer* (1948) ended that form of state support for
segregated housing by declaring such court decisions to be
state action as defined in the Fourteenth Amendment, and
therefore in violation of the equal protection clause of that
amendment. This case broke the last legal barrier to integrated housing.

Mr. Chief Justice Vinson delivered the opinion of the Court.

These cases present for our consideration questions relating to the
validity of court enforcement of private agreements, generally described
as restrictive covenants, which have as their purpose the exclusion of per-

SOURCE: *Shelley* v. *Kraemer,* 334 U.S. 1 (1948).

sons of designated race or color from the ownership or occupancy of real property. Basic constitutional issues of obvious importance have been raised.

The first of these cases comes to this Court on certiorari to the Supreme Court of Missouri. On February 16, 1911, thirty out of a total of thirty-nine owners of property fronting both sides of Labadie Avenue between Taylor Avenue and Cora Avenue in the city of St. Louis, signed an agreement, which was subsequently recorded, providing in part:

> . . . the said property is hereby restricted to the use and occupancy for the term of Fifty (50) years from this date, so that it shall be a condition all the time and whether recited and referred to as [sic] not in subsequent conveyances and shall attach to the land as a condition precedent to the sale of the same, that hereafter no part of said property or any portion thereof shall be, for said term of Fifty-years, occupied by any person not of the Caucasian race, it being intended hereby to restrict the use of said property for said period of time against the occupancy as owners or tenants of any portion of said property for resident or other purpose by people of the Negro or Mongolian Race.

The entire district described in the agreement included fifty-seven parcels of land. The thirty owners who signed the agreement held title to forty-seven parcels, including the particular parcel involved in this case. At the time the agreement was signed, five of the parcels in the district were owned by Negroes. One of those had been occupied by Negro families since 1882, nearly thirty years before the restrictive agreement was executed. The trial court found that owners of seven out of nine homes on the south side of Labadie Avenue, within the restricted district and "in the immediate vicinity" of the premises in question, had failed to sign the restrictive agreement in 1911. At the time this action was brought, four of the premises were occupied by Negroes, and had been so occupied for periods ranging from twenty-three to sixty-three years. A fifth parcel had been occupied by Negroes until a year before this suit was instituted.

On August 11, 1945, pursuant to a contract of sale, petitioners Shelley, who are Negroes, for valuable consideration received from one Fitzgerald a warranty deed to the parcel in question. The trial court found that petitioners had no actual knowledge of the restrictive agreement at the time of the purchase.

On October 9, 1945, respondents, as owners of other property subject to the terms of the restrictive covenant, brought suit in the Circuit Court of the city of St. Louis praying that petitioners Shelley be restrained from taking possession of the property and that judgment be entered divesting title out of petitioners Shelley and revesting title in the immediate grantor or in such other person as the court should direct. The trial court denied the requested relief on the ground that the restrictive agreement, upon which respondents based their action, had never become final and complete because it was the intention of the parties to that agreement that it was not to become effective until signed by all property owners in the district, and signatures of all the owners had never been obtained.

The Supreme Court of Missouri sitting *en banc* reversed and directed the trial court to grant the relief for which respondents had prayed. That court held the agreement effective and concluded that enforcement of its provisions violated no rights guaranteed to petitioners by the Federal Constitution. At the time the court rendered its decision, petitioners were occupying the property in question.

The second of the cases under consideration comes to this Court from the Supreme Court of Michigan. The circumstances presented do not differ materially from the Missouri case. In June, 1934, one Ferguson and his wife, who then owned the property located in the city of Detroit which is involved in this case, executed a contract providing in part:

> This property shall not be used or occupied by any person or persons except those of the Caucasian race.
> "It is further agreed that this restriction shall not be effective unless at least eighty percent of the property fronting on both sides of the street in the block where our land is located is subjected to this or a similar restriction.

The agreement provided that the restrictions were to remain in effect until January 1, 1960. The contract was subsequently recorded; and similar agreements were executed with respect to eighty percent of the lots in the block in which the property in question is situated.

By deed dated November 30, 1944, petitioners, who were found by the trial court to be Negroes, acquired title to the property and thereupon entered into its occupancy. On January 30, 1945, respondents, as owners of property subject to the terms of the restrictive agreement, brought suit against petitioners in the Circuit Court of Wayne County. After a hearing, the court entered a decree directing petitioners to move from the property within ninety days. Petitioners were further enjoined and restrained from using or occupying the premises in the future. On appeal, the Supreme Court of Michigan affirmed, deciding adversely to petitioners' contentions that they had been denied rights protected by the Fourteenth Amendment.

Petitioners have placed primary reliance on their contentions, first raised in the state courts, that judicial enforcement of the restrictive agreements in these cases has violated rights guaranteed to petitioners by the Fourteenth Amendment of the Federal Constitution and Acts of Congress passed pursuant to that Amendment. Specifically, petitioners urge that they have been denied the equal protection of the laws, deprived of property without due process of law, and have been denied privileges and immunities of citizens of the United States. We pass to a consideration of those issues.

I

Whether the equal protection clause of the Fourteenth Amendment inhibits judicial enforcement by state courts of restrictive covenants based on race or color is a question which this Court has not heretofore been called upon to consider. Only two cases have been decided by this Court which in any way have involved the enforcement of such agreements. The first of these was the case of *Corrigan* v. *Buckley*. There, suit was brought in the courts of the District of Columbia to enjoin a threatened violation of certain restrictive covenants relating to lands situated in the city of Washington. Relief was granted, and the case was brought here on appeal. It is apparent that that case, which had originated in the federal courts and involved the enforcement of covenants on land located in the District of Columbia, could present no issues under the Fourteenth Amendment; for that Amendment by its terms applies only to the States. Nor was the question of the validity of court enforcement of the restrictive covenants under the Fifth Amendment properly before the Court, as the opinion of this Court specifically recognizes. The only constitutional issue which the appellants had raised in the lower courts, and hence the only constitutional issue before this Court on appeal, was the validity of the covenant agreements as such. This Court concluded that since the inhibitions of the constitutional provisions invoked apply only to governmental action, as contrasted to action of private individuals, there was no showing that the covenants, which were simply agreements between private property owners, were invalid. Accordingly, the appeal was dismissed for want of a substantial question. Nothing in the opinion of this Court, therefore, may properly be regarded as an adjudication on the merits of the constitutional issues presented by these cases, which raise the question of the validity, not of the private agreements as such, but of the judicial enforcement of those agreements.

The second of the cases involving racial restrictive covenants was *Hansberry* v. *Lee*. In that case, petitioners, white property owners, were enjoined by the state courts from violating the terms of a restrictive agreement. The state Supreme Court had held petitioners bound by an earlier judicial determination, in litigation in which petitioners were not parties, upholding the validity of the restrictive agreement, although, in fact, the agreement had not been signed by the number of owners necessary to make it effective under state law. This Court reversed the judgment of the state Supreme Court upon the ground that petitioners had been denied due process of law in being held estopped to challenge the validity of the agreement on the theory, accepted by the state court, that the earlier litigation, in which petitioners did not participate, was in the nature of a class suit. In arriving at its result, this Court did not reach the issues presented by the cases now under consideration. . . . .

We hold that in granting judicial enforcement of the restrictive agreements in these cases, the States have denied petitioners the equal protection of the laws and that, therefore, the action of the state courts cannot stand. We have noted that freedom from discrimination by the States in the enjoyment of property rights was among the basic objectives sought to be effectuated by the framers of the Fourteenth Amendment. That such discrimination has occurred in these cases is clear. Because of the race or color of these petitioners, they have been denied rights of ownership or occupancy enjoyed as a matter of course by other citizens of different race or color. The Fourteenth Amendment declares "that all persons, whether colored or white, shall stand equal before the laws of the States, and, in regard to the colored race, for whose protection the amendment was primarily designed, that no discrimination shall be made against them by law because of their color." Only recently this Court had occasion to declare that a state law which denied equal enjoyment of property rights to a designated class of citizens of specified race and ancestry, was not a legitimate exercise of the state's police power but violated the guaranty of the equal protection of the laws. Nor may the discriminations imposed by the state courts in these cases be justified as proper exertions of state police power.

Respondents urge, however, that since the state courts stand ready to enforce restrictive covenants excluding white persons from the ownership or occupancy of property covered by such agreements, enforcement of covenants excluding colored persons may not be deemed a denial of equal protection of the laws to the colored persons who are thereby affected. This contention does not bear scrutiny. The parties have directed our attention to no case in which a court, state or federal, has been called upon to enforce a covenant excluding members of the white majority from ownership or occupancy of real property on grounds of race or color. But there are more fundamental considerations. The rights created by the first section of the Fourteenth Amendment are, by its terms, guaranteed to the individual. The rights established are personal rights. It is, therefore, no answer to these petitioners to say that the courts may also be induced to deny white persons rights of ownership and occupancy on grounds of race or color. Equal protection of the laws is not achieved through indiscriminate imposition of inequalities.

Nor do we find merit in the suggestion that property owners who are parties to these agreements are denied equal protection of the laws if denied access to the courts to enforce the terms of restrictive covenants and to assert property rights which the state courts have held to be created by such agreements. The Constitution confers upon no individual the right to demand action by the State which results in the denial of equal protection of the laws to other individuals. And it would appear beyond question that the power of the State to create and enforce property interests must be exercised within the boundaries defined by the Fourteenth Amendment.

The problem of defining the scope of the restrictions which the Federal Constitution imposes upon exertions of power by the States has given rise to many of the most persistent and fundamental issues which this Court has been called upon to consider. That problem was foremost in the minds of the framers of the Constitution, and, since that early day, has arisen in a multitude of forms. The task of determining whether the action of a State offends constitutional provisions is one which may not be undertaken lightly. Where, however, it is clear that the action of the State violates the terms of the fundamental charter, it is the obligation of this Court so to declare.

The historical context in which the Fourteenth Amendment became a part of the Constitution should not be forgotten. Whatever else the framers sought to achieve, it is clear that the matter of primary concern was the establishment of equality in the enjoyment of basic civil and political rights and the preservation of those rights from discriminatory action on the part of the States based on considerations of race or color. Seventy-five years ago this Court announced that the provisions of the Amendment are to be construed with this fundamental purpose in mind. Upon full consideration, we have concluded that in these cases the States have acted to deny petitioners the equal protection of the laws guaranteed by the Fourteenth Amendment. Having so decided, we find it unnecessary to consider whether petitioners have also been deprived of property without due process of law or denied privileges and immunities of citizens of the United States.

For the reasons stated, the judgment of the Supreme Court of Missouri and the judgment of the Supreme Court of Michigan must be reversed.

Mr. Justice Reed, Mr. Justice Jackson, and Mr. Justice Rutledge took no part in the consideration or decision of these cases.

10 / Poverty in America—The Role of Urban Renewal

ROBERT C. WEAVER

While upper- and middle-class blacks and Mexican-Americans have been attempting to obtain housing in previously all-white neighborhoods, the ghetto dwellers have had a much different problem. They have had to try to survive in the inferior housing of the central cities. In many of the metropolitan areas, such as Chicago, New York, Cleveland, Detroit, Newark, Boston, and Los Angeles, over 90 percent of ghetto housing units are either substandard or unfit for human habitation. Rents are exorbitant, and absentee landlords refuse to improve the properties because they know that (1) there is no other place for the people to live and (2) the penalties for failure to correct deficiencies are small enough to be paid and not make the improvements. The solution attempted in the majority of cities is urban renewal, or the replacement of slums with new public housing projects. These have more often than not been failures, primarily because they are sterile in design. The author of this review of efforts at urban renewal was the first black member of a President's cabinet and headed the office of Housing and Urban Development.

SOURCE: Weaver, Robert C., "Poverty in America—The Role of Urban Renewal," pp. 329–334, in Margaret C. Gordon (ed.), *Poverty in America* (San Francisco: Chandler Publishing Company, 1965).

Just as better housing is not the whole answer to rooting out poverty, neither are civil rights. Freedom to stay poor is no freedom at all. Or, as a young Harlem man put it, "What does it mean to be integrated into poverty?"

And so we must have better housing, we must eliminate slum living. And we must have equality for all citizens before the law. But that is still not the whole story on poverty. The most critical need remains: the need to maximize human opportunities. Or, sticking to urban renewal terms, the need to restore fully the city's primary function: the fullest opportunities for the civilization of man.

THE GRAY AREAS PROGRAM

Just about the time that the federal urban renewal program was entering its second decade, several cities deeply involved in the program began to devise the means for expanding opportunities. In Oakland, California, New Haven, Connecticut, and a few other cities, perceptive men began to dig away at the root causes of poverty and slum living. These were men who had worked hard in urban renewal, and learned well its strengths and weaknesses. For financial aid, they turned to a great nonprofit institution, the Ford Foundation. Other benefits aside, this threw a powerful new force into the battle against slums and poverty.

The Gray Areas program of the Ford Foundation set the pattern for what is called today the war against poverty. It called for all the institutional forces of the city—private and public alike—to rally together in that conflict. The ultimate objective: to break the deadly poverty cycle.

Not surprisingly, the program gave priority to young people. Job clinics were established to find work for those under 25 or so, and to train them. In the case of many dropouts, they were encouraged to finish high school, while still holding jobs. The key to success was quickly found to rest with developing aspirations—give a young person a meaningful, realizable goal to shoot for, and watch him (or her) succeed. These young people were not trained in skills alone. They were made to realize their value to the larger community.

While programs of job opportunities, schooling, and training proceeded with young men and women, other programs were engineered for the very young. Educators had learned that many dropouts suffer primarily from a low learning capacity. By second or third grade, it was already obvious that some children simply were not going to learn very much. Most tragically, in the overcrowded classrooms characteristic of impoverished neighborhoods, many overworked teachers simply gave up on such children.

The new approach aimed to solve this problem by catching the child when he or she is very young, well before kindergarten age. Three- and four-year-olds were placed on an experimental basis, into "learning situations." Tots, not long out of crib and cradle, were read to and permitted a wide variety of self-expression in art, music, and speaking. Much of what happens in these sessions seems shockingly rudimentary. But for many of these children, the book in teacher's hands is the first one they have ever seen in use. Out of these classrooms, hundreds of small children are already taking the first uncertain steps away from the poverty cycle.

There is another aspect of the pre-kindergarten schooling I should mention. In New Haven, Boston, and other cities, the parents are very much a part of this approach. Teachers and parents meet weekly, discuss the children or just general problems. Many teachers serve coffee and cookies. The atmosphere is relaxed. The child sees its parent and its teacher talking together, enjoying the chance. It is the sort of thing, the psychologists tell us, that children long remember.

Moreover, the parents learn, too. For some of them, it is the first time in a school since *they* dropped out. The lesson of the role education plays in shaking off the chains of impoverishment is not usually lost on them.

There are many other aspects to the Gray Areas approach—special aids to fight juvenile delinquency, providing legal assistance to the poor, promoting special activities for the elderly and handicapped. These programs are, at the local level, usually engineered and operated by existing social service agencies. In some cases, new agencies have been established.

The Gray Areas approach pointed squarely at erasing the causes of poverty. It established the pattern for the federal program which followed. Last year, the Congress passed the Economic Opportunity Act, which threw the weight of the Federal Government into the war against poverty on a much broader scale than ever before. Not only were new programs enacted to attack the causes of poverty, but the new Office of Economic Opportunity became a rallying point around which many other programs—of several federal departments and agencies—could form up for a concerted assault.

With the establishment of OEO, the Federal Government announced its purpose to deal comprehensively with the total urban environment. The social as well as the physical fabric of cities would be repaired—and, indeed, must be repaired—if cities are to function at the highest level.

Last year, our housing programs reflected the impact of the anti-poverty approach. For one thing, relocation payments were increased and, perhaps even more important, a new element was introduced into the whole notion of relocation aids. For the first time, the Federal Government provided supplemental rent payments for up to one year for relocated families or individuals in need. Also, special urban renewal demonstration programs in Pittsburgh and New York are helping identify the problems and potential solutions for families to be relocated in large areas of those two cities.

URBAN REHABILITATION

Another important feature of the "new look" in renewal is the increased emphasis on rehabilitation, with a new program of special, low-interest loans for homeowners and renters alike. Although funds were not authorized for the administration of this program last year, President Johnson has requested that Congress provide appropriations for the rest of this year as well as 1966.

Rehabilitation in the most impoverished areas of large cities continues to be a major difficulty. Now, with community action programs being initiated in those areas, we shall have to bend our efforts—federal and local, public and private—to provide higher housing quality. The new programs will help. And some other approaches, which I shall mention in a moment, should also get us closer to our goal of providing decent housing to *every* American family and individual, regardless of income.

In this regard, I think a slight digression on the workings of the housing market is in order. Recently, we have been pressing for more low and moderate-income housing on urban renewal sites. In this regard, the program of below-market interest rate loans, called Section 221(d)(3), has been markedly successful. At interest rates of 3⅞ per cent and 40-year mortgages, this housing is built to rent for $15 to $20 per month less than corresponding homes built with typical FHA financing.

This housing is obviously still above the economic reach of the very poor or the lower moderate-income sector of the market. But we have recently had some insights into the workings of the housing market which lead us to believe that such housing can be of decided help to poor families. This is not to say that the old filter-down theory, in its pure form, works. The unqualified premise that any new housing can, after sufficient depreciation, serve as decent housing for the poor has been discredited by experience. By the time this housing is "depreciated" enough to get its cost down to where the poor can afford it, it is pretty terrible housing.

But if new output is priced fairly close to what the poor are paying for their bad housing, then you are likely to get some families moving out to the newer supply and consequently loosening up the older supply. This process involves a relatively brief period of time and is quite different from the old-fashioned filter-down theory. It seems to be working.

NEW DIRECTIONS

Today, urban renewal and other housing and community development programs are working with anti-poverty programs to provide a comprehensive approach to the problems of the poor. I think I can best illustrate the comprehensiveness of the approach by telling you something about the new directions we contemplate in federal programs for housing and urban development.

In the first place, we do not intend to stop repairing the city's physical condition just because we have learned that such action alone will not solve all our problems. The fact is that we must prosecute the physical rebuilding of our cities more vigorously than ever. But we must be more careful about what we build and where we build it. Obviously the market for high-priced apartments is not unlimited. And certainly such housing does not provide for the poor.

But there must be much more new housing production in our cities, and we shall propose programs to accomplish this. There must also be a higher order of rehabilitation—more production, as well as more realistic standards. We must make a more pronounced effort at code enforcement, as a means of upgrading the quality of the housing stock. Now, under urban renewal, cities can declare large areas to be code enforcement areas, and receive federal aid for their upgrading.

For new housing aimed at moderate- and low-income families, we shall develop a new program of rent supplements. We also propose to step up the public housing program and make much more use of existing units for low-income families. This will ameliorate the problems of finding large sites for new construction and also provide a more flexible supply of subsidized housing. It will also provide low-rent housing more quickly than can new construction.

Public housing can serve the poor in ways other than simply giving them a roof over their heads. We have initiated a program, on an experimental basis, of concerted social services in public housing projects. Through this program, we have brought badly needed social services to poor families, the elderly, and the handicapped. And we intend to expand these efforts.

Largely through our urban renewal experience, we have learned the vital role that sound neighborhood facilities can play in the redevelopment of old sections. One of the earliest such projects was in the Wooster Square of New Haven, where a community center was established in an urban renewal area stressing rehabilitation. I might remind you again that this pioneering project occurred in a city with a long renewal history—and the same city which was among the first to realize the need for a broad-gauge attack on social as well as physical problems.

So we shall propose direct capital grants for neighborhood facilities to serve the gray areas and districts where the antipoverty programs are operating.

Other new programs will be recommended by President Johnson to improve the physical condition and enhance the beauty of neighborhoods in our cities. Obviously, such activities mean little without coincident attention to expanding job opportunities and educational training, but now we are proceeding on all these fronts.

CONCLUSION

There can be no Great Society if any significant portion of our population continues to suffer want and impoverishment. The expansion of opportunities which will lead us to the goal of a Great Society can only come through a concerted attack upon the social as well as the physical disorder which blight our cities. Such an attack is now being mounted, and the urban renewal program plays a key role.

I shall not, in closing, have the temerity to predict the utter abolition of poverty in this nation in the foreseeable future. Earlier seers are still choking on such high-flown predictions as "No slums in ten years."

These objectives which we have set for ourselves will take unremitting effort. They shall have to be prosecuted just as we prosecute war. The analogy is apt.

And Oliver Wendell Holmes has provided us with some guidelines for war, which are particularly appropriate:

> To fight out a war, you must believe something and want something with all your might. . . . More than that, you must be willing to commit yourself to a course, perhaps a long and hard one, without being able to foresee exactly where you will come out.

11 / *Mulkey* v. *Reitman*

One of the techniques used for correcting the problem of segregated housing has been the passage of open-housing legislation. In some states the laws were passed by state legislatures; in others, individual cities created open-housing
ordinances. Not until 1968 was there federal legislation, and
the law passed by Congress in April of that year was cata-
lyzed by the death of Martin Luther King, Jr., rather than as an
expression of belief in the principle. In California the open-
housing law is known as the Rumford Act, and it has been the
center of debate ever since it was adopted in 1963. In 1964, a
proposition appeared on the California ballot to repeal the
Rumford Act and was approved by a margin of two to one. A
legal battle ensued to determine the constitutionality of the repeal proposition, and eventually the United States Supreme
Court declared the repeal proposition unconstitutional, thus
leaving the Rumford Act in force.

In 1959, the State Legislature took the first major steps toward eliminating
racial discrimination in housing. The Unruh Civil Rights Act (Civ. Code,
sections 51–52) prohibited discrimination on grounds of "race, color, reli-

SOURCE: *Mulkey* v. *Reitman*, 413 P. 2d 825 (1966).

gion, ancestry, or national origin" by "business establishments of every kind." On its face, this measure encompassed the activities of real estate brokers and all businesses selling or leasing residential housing. . . .

At the same session the Legislature passed the Hawkins Act (formerly Health and Saf. Code, sections 35700–35741) that prohibited racial discrimination in publicly assisted housing accommodations. In 1961 the Legislature broadened its attempt to discourage segregated housing by enacting proscriptions against discriminatory restrictive covenants affecting real property interests (Civ. Code, section 53) and racially restricted conditions in deeds of real property (Civ. Code, section 782.)

Finally in 1963 the State Legislature superseded the Hawkins Act by passing the Rumford Fair Housing Act. (Health and Saf. Code, sections 35700–35744.) The Rumford Act provided that "The practice of discrimination because of race, color, religion, national origin, or ancestry is declared to be against public policy" and prohibited such discrimination in the sale or rental of any private dwelling containing more than four units. The State Fair Employment Practice Commission was empowered to prevent violations.

Proposition 14 was enacted against the foregoing historical background with the clear intent to overturn state laws that bore on the right of private sellers and lessors to discriminate, and to forestall future state action that might circumscribe this right. In short, Proposition 14 generally nullifies both the Rumford and Unruh Acts as they apply to the housing market.

Prior to its enactment the unconstitutionality of Proposition 14 was urged to this court in *Lewis* v. *Jordan,* Sac. 7549 (June 3, 1964). In rejecting the petition for mandamus to keep that proposition off the ballot we stated in our minute order "that it would be more appropriate to pass on those questions after the election . . . than to interfere with the power of the people to propose laws and amendments to the Constitution and to adopt or reject the same at the polls. . . . " But we further noted in the order that "there are grave questions whether the proposed amendment to the California Constitution is valid under the Fourteenth Amendment to the United States Constitution. . . ." We are now confronted with those questions. . . .

It is now beyond dispute that ". . . among the civil rights intended to be protected from discriminatory state action by the Fourteenth Amendment are the rights to acquire, enjoy, own and dispose of property. Equality in the enjoyment of property rights was regarded by the framers of that Amendment as an essential pre-condition to the realization of other basic civil rights and liberties which the Amendment was intended to guarantee." (*Shelley* v. *Kraemer,* 334 U.S. 1, 10; see also *Buchanan* v. *Warley* [1917] 245 U.S. 60, 62; *Brown* v. *Board of Education* [1954] 347 U.S. 483; *Barrows* v. *Jackson* [1953] 346 U.S. 249; *Jackson* v. *Pasadena City*

School Dist. [1963] supra, 59 Cal. 2d 876; *Sei Fujii* v. *State of California* [1952] 38 Cal. 2d 718).

The question of the fact of discrimination, by whatever hand, should give us little pause. The very nature of the instant action and the specific contentions urged by the defendants must be deemed to constitute concessions on their part that article I, section 26, provides for nothing more than a purported constitutional right to *privately* discriminate on grounds which admittedly would be unavailable under the Fourteenth Amendment *should state action* be involved. Thus, as a complete and only answer to plaintiffs' allegations which irrefutably establish a discriminatory act, defendants urge that section 26 accords them the right as private citizens to so discriminate. The only real question thus remaining is whether the discrimination results solely from the claimed private action or instead results at least in part from state action which is sufficiently involved to bring the matter within the proscription of the Fourteenth Amendment. For reasons stated below we have concluded that state action is sufficiently involved to fall within the reach of the Constitutional prohibition. . . .

However subtle may be the state conduct which is deemed "significant," it must nevertheless constitute action rather than inaction. The equal protection clause and, in fact, the whole of the Fourteenth Amendment, is prohibitory in nature and we are not prepared to hold, as has been urged, that it has been or should be construed to impose upon the state an obligation to take positive action in an area where it is not otherwise committed to act. . . .

To conclude that there is state action in the instant circumstances we are not limited to action by one who, cloaked with the authority of the state, acts as its designated representative. In the broad sense, state action has been consistently found where the state, in any meaningful way, has lent its processes to the achievement of discrimination even though that goal was not within the state's purpose. . . .

Shelley, and the cases which follow it, stand for the proposition that when one who seeks to discriminate solicits and obtains the aid of the court in the accomplishment of that discrimination, significant state action, within the proscription of the equal protection clause, is involved. The instant case may be distinguished from the *Shelley* and the *Abstract* cases only in that those who would discriminate here are *not seeking* the aid of the court to that end. Instead they are in court only because they have been summoned there by those against whom they seek to discriminate. The court is not asked to enforce a covenant nor to eject a tenant, but only to render judgment denying the relief sought in accordance with the law of the state. Thus, it is contended by defendants that the isolated act of rendering such a judgment does not significantly involve the state in the prior act of discrimination.

It must be recognized that the application of *Shelley* is not limited to state involvement only through court proceedings. In the broader sense the prohibition extends to any racially discriminatory act accomplished through the significant aid of any state agency, even where the actor is a private citizen motivated by purely personal interests. (See *Burton* v. *Wilmington Pkg. Auth.,* supra, 365 U.S. 715, 722.) Thus, in *Marsh* v. *State of Alabama,* 326 U.S. 501, an entire town was owned by a purely private company, the agents of which caused the arrest for trespass of persons engaged in exercising their constitutional freedom of speech. Although no government officials or agents were involved, the Supreme Court found sufficient state action to invoke the Fourteenth Amendment. This was based on the view that the company managers were performing a governmental function of managing and controlling a town wherein persons resided who were entitled to Fourteenth Amendment protections: ". . . In our view the circumstances that the property rights to the premises where the deprivation of liberty, here involved, took place, where held by others than the public, is not sufficient to justify the State's permitting a corporation to govern a community of citizens so as to restrict their fundamental liberties. . . ." (*Marsh* v. *State of Alabama,* supra, at p. 509.) There, as contended by defendants in the instant case, the state did not participate except to condone private action.

Even more applicable in the instant circumstances are the so-called "white primary cases." (*Smith* v. *Allwright,* 321 U.S. 649; *Terry* v. *Adams,* 345 U.S. 461; *Nixon* v. *Condon,* 286 U.S. 73; *Baskin* v. *Brown,* 174 F. 2d 391; *Rice* v. *Elmore,* 165 F. 2d 387.) In those cases private action infringing the right to vote was held to be the equivalent of state action where accomplished with the culpable permission of the state. In *Nixon* v. *Condon,* supra, 286 U.S. 73, for instance, a state statute which forbade voting by Negroes in primaries was declared to be unconstitutional. It was thereupon repealed and a substitute measure enacted which was wholly permissive, that is, political parties were allowed to prescribe the qualifications for membership and voting rights in the party's primaries. A local political party thereafter barred Negroes from voting in its primaries and it was held that the permissive private action was chargeable as action. (See also *Baskin* v. *Brown,* supra, 174 F. 2d 391, 394.)

A similar abdication of a traditional governmental function for the obvious purpose of condoning its performance under color of private action has recently been struck down by the Supreme Court in *Evans* v. *Newton,* supra, 382 U.S. 296. There, a park for the enjoyment of white persons was owned, managed and maintained by the City of Macon, Georgia, as trustee under the 1911 will of Senator August Bacon. When a question was raised whether the city could continue to maintain the segregated park consistent with the Equal Protection Clause, it purported to transfer the park to private trustees with the intent that it would continue to be maintained for the enjoyment of white persons only. The foregoing conduct on the part of the municipality was held to be proscribed by the Fourteenth Amendment.

It is contended by defendants, however, that the foregoing cases, in the main, involved some recognized governmental function which, although undertaken by private persons, nevertheless was required to be performed in the same non-discriminatory manner as would be required in the case of performance by the state. Such contention fails to recognize the basic issue involved. Those cases are concerned not so much with the *nature* of the function involved as they are with *who* is responsible for conduct in performance of that function. If the function is traditionally governmental in nature unquestionably the state is responsible. But this cannot be the only instance wherein the state assumes responsibility—it is also responsible when, as we have stated, it becomes significantly involved in *any* discriminatory conduct. (See *Burton* v. *Wilmington Pkg. Auth.,* supra, 365 U.S. 715, 722.)

Going to the question of what constitutes significant involvement, it is established that even where the state can be charged with only encouraging discriminatory conduct, the color of state action nevertheless attaches. Justice Black, in writing for the majority on *Robinson* v. *State of Florida,* 378 U.S. 153, 156, and for the dissenters in *Bell* v. *State of Maryland,* 378 U.S. 226, 334, asserted that private racial discrimination violated the Fourteenth Amendment once the state in any way discourages integration or instigates or encourages segregation. In *Barrows* v. *Jackson,* supra, 346 U.S. 249, in holding that a racially restrictive convenant could not constitutionally support a suit for damages, the court explained at page 254: "The result of that sanction by the State would be to encourage the use of restrictive convenants. To that extent, the State would act to put its sanction behind the convenants. If the State may thus punish respondent for her failure to carry out her covenant, she is coerced to continue to use her property in a discriminatory manner, which in essence is the purpose of the covenant. Thus it becomes not respondent's voluntary choice but the State's choice that she observe her convenant or suffer damages."

Proscribed governmental encouragement of private discrimination has not been confined to the courts. *Anderson* v. *Martin,* 375 U.S. 399, involved racial labelling of candidates on ballots. Although the state practice did not *require* discrimination on the part of individual voters, it was struck down because it *encouraged* and assisted in discrimination. (See also *Baldwin* v. *Morgan,* 287 F. 2d 750.) Similarly, as early as 1914, in *McCabe* v. *Atchison, T. and S. F. Ry.,* 235 U.S. 151, it was stated at page 162 that the denial of equal railroad facilities to Negroes by a private railroad was unconstitutional state action on the ground that the right to discriminate was authorized by a local statute and that should the carrier perpetuate such discrimination, it would be acting under "the authority of a state law." The court reasoned that the state *authorization* to discriminate was no less state action than state *imposed* discrimination. (See also *Boman* v. *Birmingham Transit Company,* 280 F. 2d 531.)

The Supreme Court has recently spoken out against state action which only authorizes "private" discrimination. In *Burton* v. *Wilmington Pkg. Auth.,* supra, 365 U.S. 715, the court had before it the question of whether the State of Delaware discriminated against a Negro who was excluded from a privately operated restaurant leased from a public agency of that state. The court stated at page 725, that the state "not only made itself a party to the refusal of service, but has elected to place its power, property and prestige behind the admitted discrimination. The State has so far insinuated itself into a position of interdependence . . . that it must be recognized as a joint participant in the challenged activity. . . ." In a concurring opinion Justice Stewart, concluding that the state enactment involved, as construed by the state court, *authorized discrimination,* stated at page 727: "I think, therefore, that the appeal was properly taken and that the statute, as authoritatively construed by the Supreme Court of Delaware, is constitutionally invalid." Even the dissenting justices agreed that if the state court had construed the state enactment as authorizing racial discrimination, there was a denial by the state of equal protection of the laws, Justice Frankfurter stating at page 727: "For a State to place its authority behind discriminatory treatment based solely on color is indubitably a denial by a State of the equal protection of the laws in violation of the Fourteenth Amendment."

In a case involving a fact situation similar to *Burton,* and clearly pertinent to our present inquiry, a Tennessee statute renounced the state's common law cause of action for exclusion from hotels and other public places and declared that operators of such establishments were free to exclude persons for any reason whatever. In the particular circumstances of that case the statute was deemed to bear on the issues "only insofar as" it "expressed an affirmative state policy fostering segregation." The court stated that: "our decisions have foreclosed any possible contention that such a statute . . . may stand consistently with the Fourteenth Amendment." (*Turner* v. *City of Memphis* [1962] 369 U.S. 350, 353.)

The instant case presents an undeniably analogous situation wherein the state, recognizing that it could not perform a direct act of discrimination, nevertheless has taken affirmative action of a legislative nature designed to make possible private discriminatory practices which previously were legally restricted. We cannot realistically conclude that, because the final act of discrimination is undertaken by a private party motivated only by personal economic or social considerations, we must close our eyes and ears to the events which purport to make the final act legally possible.

Here the state has affirmatively acted to change its existing laws from a situation wherein the discrimination practiced was legally restricted to one wherein it is encouraged, within the meaning of the cited decisions. Certainly the act of which complaint is made is as much, if not more, the legislative action which authorized private discrimination as it is the final, private act of discrimination itself. Where the state can be said to act, as it does of course, through the laws approved by legislators elected by the popular vote, it must also be held to act through a law adopted directly by the popular vote. When the electorate assumes to exercise the law-making function, then the electorate is as much a state agency as any of its elected officials. It is thus apparent that while state action may take many forms, the test is not the novelty of the form but rather the ultimate result which is achieved through the aid of state processes. And if discrimination is thus accomplished, the nature of proscribed state action must not be limited by the ingenuity of those who would seek to conceal it by subtleties and claims of neutrality.

Contrary to defendant's claims, the state's abstinence from making the decision to discriminate in a particular instance does not confer upon it the status of neutrality in these circumstances. Justice Byron R. White's view of the facts in *Evans* v. *Newton,* supra, 382 U.S. 296, poses an almost identical issue to that here presented. In his view the majority in *Evans* was not justified on the record in concluding that the City of Mason was continuing to operate and maintain the park there involved after transfer to private trustees, and he grounded his conclusion of proscribed state action on 1905 legislation which did not compel but would nevertheless make it possible for the maintenance of segregated private parks for either white or colored persons. His reasoning and resolution of the issue are stated at page 306 in the following language: "As this legislation does not compel a trust to condition his grant upon use only by a racially designated class, the State cannot be said to have directly coerced private discrimination. Nevertheless, if the validity of that racial condition in Senator Bacon's trust would have been in doubt but for the 1905 statute and if the statute removed such doubt only for racial restrictions, leaving the validity of nonracial restrictions still in question, the absence of coercive language in the legislation would not prevent application of the Fourteenth Amendment. For such a statute would depart from a policy of strict neutrality in matters of private discrimination by enlisting the State's assistance only in aid of racial discrimination and would so involve the State in the private choice as to convert the infected private discrimination into state action subject to the Fourteenth Amendment."

From the foregoing it is apparent that the state is at least a partner in the instant act of discrimination and that its conduct is not beyond the reach of the Fourteenth Amendment.

The question remains whether section 26 in whole or in part must be struck down. . . .

It is immediately apparent from the operative portion of the instant constitutional amendment that it is mechanically impossible to differentiate between those portions or applications of the amendment which would preserve the right to discriminate on the basis of race, color or creed, as distinguished from a proper basis for discrimination. The purported preservation of the right to discriminate on whatever basis is fully integrated and under the rule of *Blaney,* not severable. Moreover, while we can conceive of no other purpose for an application of section 26 aside from authorizing the perpetration of a purported private discrimination where such authorization or right to discriminate does not otherwise exist, any such other purpose clearly "entails the danger of an uncertain or vague future application of the [enactment]" and would thus require that it be struck down. (*Franklin Life Ins. Co.* v. *State Board of Equalization* [1965] 63 A. C. 221, 227.)

For the foregoing reasons the severability clause is ineffective in the instant case, and the whole of the constitutional amendment must be struck down.

Article I, section 26, of the California Constitution thus denied to plaintiffs and all those similarly situated the equal protection of the laws as guaranteed by the Fourteenth Amendment to the federal Constitution, and is void in its general application.

The judgment is reversed. Peek, J.

Traynor, C. J., and Peters, J., Tobriner, J., and Burke, J., concur.

White, J., and McComb, J., dissent. . . .

12 / Indians in Rural Reservation Areas

**CALIFORNIA STATE ADVISORY COMMISSION
ON INDIAN AFFAIRS**

Housing conditions among the American Indians are worse than those endured by either blacks or Mexican-Americans. As this selection indicates, almost 90 percent of Indian housing units are substandard or condemned. For the Indian inferior housing means a lack of protection from cold and other natural dangers. The Indians live in what can easily be described as squalor. In reservation after reservation, there is no running water or electricity, and toilet facilities are not of the caliber enjoyed by the rest of America. Tepid streams or lakes serve as the source of drinking and cooking water, often resulting in epidemics of communicable diseases.

The principal reason for these incredible conditions seems to be that the Indian has been isolated from the rest of the society on reservations and left to exist in housing similar to that of the preindustrial era. There have been few attempts to correct the housing problems, and in at least one case, in South Dakota, the federal government constructed housing so foreign to the culture and way of life of the Indian that it has remained virtually unoccupied.

Source: *Progress Report to the Governor and the Legislature by the California State Advisory Committee on Indian Affairs, on Indians in Rural Reservation Areas* (Senate Bill 1007). (Sacramento: California Office of State Printing, February 1966), pp. 26–32.

LIVING CONDITIONS

Spokesmen for the division of Indian health, Public Health Service, U.S. Department of Health, Education, and Welfare, have stated that 9 of 10 Indian families in the United States live in housing that is far below the minimum standards of comfort, safety, and decency. Additionally they state that:

> More than half of the American Indians and Alaska natives live in one- or two-room dwellings, the majority constructed by themselves from indigenous materials. The average occupancy is 5.4 persons. Many are subject to serve climatic conditions for which their dwellings are illsuited or inadequate. More than 70 percent of the water comes from potentially contaminated sources. More than 80 percent of the Indians must haul or carry all the water for their household use and have inadequate waste disposal facilities—12 percent have no facilities at all.[1]

In contrast to this view of the low level of American Indian living conditions are a number of reports which purport that California Indians are at the end of the continuum which is closer to the standards considered adequate for the average U.S. citizen. According to these studies, California Indians have better homes, are better clothed, educated, nourished, live longer, and have a higher income than other American Indians.[2] This has been one of the arguments utilized in rationalizing the policy of termination of federal responsibility for Indians in California. Regretfully, it is also one of the arguments which has often been used to explain the lack of services by the Bureau of Indian Affairs in California. To argue that the poverty of California Indians is better than the poverty of Indians or minority groups in other areas of the country constitutes a defeatist attitude and one which prevents initiating programs to remedy existing conditions. There is substantial evidence available which indicates that the socio-economic condition of the Indian in California is lower in most areas than that of any other minority group. It is worthwhile to discuss some of these sources at this point.

The Bureau of Contract Services Survey

In 1960 a survey of the use of public health and medical resources by American Indians was undertaken by the California State Department of

---

[1] Wagner, Carruth J., and Erwin S. Rabeau, Indian Poverty and Indian Health. Health, Education, and Welfare Indicators, March 1964.

[2] U.S. Department of Health, Education, and Welfare, Health Services for American Indians. 1957.

Public Health through its Bureau of Contract Services.[3] The survey included the 10 counties which contract for health services, namely: Alpine, Amador, Calaveras, El Dorado, Mariposa, Modoc, Mono, Nevada, Sierra, and Trinity. The survey was chiefly concerned with health facilities usage. Of relevance to this section was the extension of the survey to include the conditions of housing and sanitation facilities on all federal Indian land in Modoc County.[4] The conclusions were as follows:

> Of the 65 homes surveyed for sanitation . . . only two had properly functioning sewage disposal systems. Two had systems that were failing, 10 were on a common pipe system, and 51 dwellings were served by privies that were substandard. It was felt that all of the shallow wells should be discontinued and that the deep drill wells in existence should be altered so that protection would be given to the source. Poor housing was found to be one of the biggest problems on the Indian properties. Many of the dwellings offered practically no protection against the elements. Faulty wiring and structural deficiencies constituted health hazards.

Elsewhere the study concluded that:

> The Indians themselves do not usually perceive poor housing and unsanitary living conditions as being detrimental to their health.

The Indian households, in a sample representing 79 percent of the Indians in the area, tended to have a higher occupancy rate than white households. The average size of household was 4.7 persons per Indian household compared to 2.9 persons per household in the non-Indian sample. Only 4 of 67 Indian households had telephones compared with 35 of 58 white households.

The Indian Sanitation Facilities Survey

Late in 1963 the division of Indian health of the U.S. Public Health Service, Phoenix area office, conducted an environmental sanitation survey of 75 nonterminal reservations in California (those not named in Public Law 85–671, the termination bill). The purpose of the survey was to evaluate existing conditions and to develop information for selecting priorities and

---

[3] California State Department of Public Health, "Use of Public Health and Medical Resources by American Indians in 10 California Counties." In California Health, Vol. 20, No. 10 (Nov. 15, 1962). Other information relating to living conditions was taken from field notes furnished by Dr. Loyd Bond, Chief of the Bureau of Contract Services.

[4] The following federal properties in Modoc County were surveyed: Fort Bidwell, Cedarville, XL Ranch, Alturas Rancheria, and Lookout.

methods of construction of projects under the Indian Sanitation Facilities Act (Public Law 86–121). . . . The general conclusions were that existing sanitation facilities are not adequate. They found that 38 percent of the people use a potentially contaminated water supply, 48 percent must haul their water, and 73 percent of the families have unsatisfactory excreta disposal facilities. Community water supply systems serve approximately 46 percent, individual systems 38 percent of the Indian homes, and the remaining 16 percent have no source of water at the homesite. . . .

The Bureau of Indian Affairs Housing Survey

The field technical office of the Bureau of Indian Affairs conducted a housing survey on 41 nonterminal California Indian reservations in cooperation with the U.S. Public Health Service at the time they were conducting their sanitation facilities survey. Estimations were made on 16 other reservations to bring the total reservations surveyed to 57. Of 1129 occupied housing units, 14 percent are considered adequate (compared to approximately 10 percent of all U.S. Indians), 58 percent require renovations, and 28 percent require complete replacement. . . .

The California Commission's Reservation Survey

During 1964 a special survey was made of the living conditions on some reservations in California by the commission staff. Preliminary visits were made by Thomas Weaver and Jack A. Tobin to Alexander Valley, Alpine County, Auburn, Barona, Fort Yuma, Geyserville, Graton, Lytton, Middleton, Modoc County, Morongo, San Pasqual, and Susanville. A survey form was devised from the information gathered on these trips. Subsequently, in May, June, and July 1964, Jack A. Tobin surveyed the following 10 reservations using this form: Auberry (Big Sandy), Baron Long (Viejas), Big Valley, Hopland, Pala, Rincon, Robinson, Santa Ysabel, Stewart's Point, and Tule River. . . . The survey included 794 persons living in 146 households on 10 reservations. This sample represents 11.3 percent of an estimated 7000 reservation Indians.

The social characteristics of the sample population investigated in the commission survey include type and composition of household, sex of household head, birthplace, present address of family members, religious affiliation, and military service.

Household type and composition can tell much about the social relationships which exist in any community, such as the economic relationships a member has with relatives outside of the primary family. Is the check a man brings into the house expended on obligations outside of his primary family (or nuclear family: a man, woman, and their children)? The survey provides some answers to this question.

Seventy percent of the 146 households in our sample of 10 reservations are nuclear family households; and the remaining are extended or joint families—that is, other relatives live under the same roof with the primary family. These outside members are most frequently grandchildren (21 households), a married child with spouse and their children (7 households), nieces or nephews (5 households), and the remaining 22 households contained brothers or sisters of the husband or wife (7 households) and other more distantly related kin. Sixty-one percent of the persons listed as household heads are male. The larger number of female heads of household are women who are widowed, separated, or divorced, and represent a serious dependency problem.

Although the persons interviewed listed only 794 persons as living on the reservation, an additional 104 were listed as family members away from home. These are almost exclusively "sons" and "daughters" and actually do not go far from home. Sixty-five (62.5 percent) of these live in the same or an adjacent county, twenty-five (25 percent) in other California cities, six (6 percent) in other states and two (1.9 percent) in a foreign country (Germany and Mexico). The address of six persons was either unknown or the information was withheld from the interviewer.

Place of birth is given for 92 percent of the resident and nonresident reservation family members. Thirty percent of the total population give their place of birth as the reservation where they are now living, 41 percent were born in the same county, 13 percent in adjacent counties, and 4.5 percent in other California cities. Only 3.2 percent of the resident and nonresident family members were born in other states, and only one-third of one percent (three persons) were born in a foreign country (Mexico). One of the significant facts emphasized by these figures is support for the statement made in the section on population of rural county areas, that approximately 84 percent of the Indian population of the reservation surveyed in our sample derive from the reservation itself or from the immediately surrounding region.

Two additional interesting social characteristics which pertain to our sample population are the high incidence of membership in the Roman Catholic Church and the number of persons with military service. With regard to the first factor, religious affiliation, 68 percent list Roman Catholic, 15 percent Protestant, 2.6 percent Pentecostal, and 4.3 percent Dreamer (a native Indian religious group found in the north, mostly at Stewart's Point). Roman Catholicism occurred more frequently in the southern area of the state where the early Spanish priests were most active. Pentecostalism was found only at Stewart's Point and Tule River Reservations in our sample. The second of these two factors—military service—provides a surprising fact in that 42 percent of the resident and nonresident male members 18 years of age and older of these 10 reservations have had some type of military service: 2 are veterans of World War I, 44 of World War II, 15 of the Korean conflict and 33 have had peacetime military service.

An average of 5.4 persons were found living in each household with a reservation range of 2.7 persons (Hopland and Rincon) to 7.6 persons (Tule River) per household. The average number of 5.4 persons per home corresponds to the average for all American Indians. The average household contained 4.9 rooms, but this is misleading in that the rooms are usually very small. A factor which would increase the occupancy rate per household is that during this time of the year many persons are seasonally employed away from the reservation.

A rating scale for the structural condition of each home was utilized with the following categories: *excellent, very good* included homes which were equal to or better than comparable homes in a middle-class suburban non-Indian area, that is, homes with permanent, substantial walls, foundation, and roof; *good* and *fair* were utilized to designate homes which seemed to provide a moderate degree of protection from extreme climatic variations but which needed some improvements; and *poor* and *very poor* designated houses which were substandard in construction, i.e., poor or nonexistent foundations, apparently unsafe electrical wiring, no insulation or wall covering, poor roof, etc. Utilizing this rating scale 6.8 percent are judged to be adequate homes, 39.0 percent need improvement, and 50.7 percent of the homes provide inadequate protection in extreme climates, are unsafe and unsanitary, and should be replaced.

One means of assuring economic advancement is the facilitation of the Indian's ability to acquire loans for improving housing, for establishing small businesses, and for improving livestock, water supplies or land resources. There have been a sufficient number of complaints to the commission to indicate that Indians have difficulty in getting loans under the G.I. Bill, or under provisions of the Small Business Act, Federal Housing Authority, or other local lending agencies. Some reasons for denying loans to Indians are that they live on trust lands and do not have title to their lands, or that Indians are allegedly poor credit risks. Several Indians reported being unable to qualify for G.I. loans even though they were veterans. Another Indian indicated denial of local loans because "Indians are poor pay." This was done despite the subjects' good credit standing in the community. A federal lending firm with headquarters in San Francisco told the executive secretary in 1964 that Indians would be denied loans on the basis of not being sufficiently needy. He added that "Indians are richer than you and I."

Moreover, the revolving loan fund available to Indians in other areas is not available to California Indians. Bureau of Indian Affairs officials have erroneously assumed that loans are readily available to Indians in

California. For this reason they have withheld the revolving loan program from this state.

Discussions with officials of the Bureau of Indian Affairs and the Public Housing Administration in California have helped to delineate what these two organizations consider to be some of the obstacles to the initiation of public housing programs in California.

1. *Difficulties in clearing titles* and in long-term leasing of Indian trust and allotment lands.

2. *Density of population.* Many believe that Indians are not found in sufficient numbers to make public housing programs feasible. This idea ignores two facts: (a) 30 percent of all California reservations and rancherias have at least 80 persons on them, a number which is certainly large enough to favor institution of these programs, and (b) a much greater density of Indian population is to be found in the vicinity of rancherias and reservations, although not living on actual Indian lands. The addition of these two populations makes the institution of public housing highly feasible and desirable.

3. *Unemployment.* Two kinds of arguments are offered here. First, Indians are not sufficiently *unemployed* to have the necessary free time to contribute labor to some of these programs. Second, Indians are employed away from the immediate areas and, therefore, cannot contribute labor to these programs. Both of these arguments have been found to be false by the work of the commission staff.

4. *Insufficient staff facilities* in the BIA for implementation is another obstacle to establishing public housing in California for Indians. Some Bureau of Indian Affairs officials felt that they needed additional staff in order to explore the feasibility of these programs for California Indians. They argue that the general congressional attitude in Washington is for termination in California and against budgeting additional moneys for new programs.

5. Another type of obstacle concerns the ability of tribal councils to form a *local housing authority*. The formation of such organizations is limited to Indian tribes with constitutions which enable the delegation of broad authority to the council in contract and police matters. A review of tribal charters and organizational structures by the Bureau of Indian Affairs and Public Housing Administration attorneys indicates that many reservations and rancherias in California do not have the power to create housing authorities.

13 / Residential Segregation in the Urban Southwest

JOAN W. MOORE
FRANK G. MITTELBACH

Discrimination in the sale and rental of housing is not limited
to white treatment of blacks. Mexican-Americans have also
been the victims of illegal practices in their attempt to live
wherever they desire. For at least three reasons their plight
has not received as much attention as that of the blacks. First,
it is only in the last several years that Mexican-Americans
have become urban residents in large numbers, because generally they worked in the rural areas of the state. Second, because they have been less well-organized, they lacked national organizations such as the NAACP that could have
brought the legal issue to the national level. Third, because
they are a minority it has been difficult to focus attention on
their situation. This selection is one of the first efforts to document housing segregation of the Mexican-American.

SOURCE: Joan W. Moore and Frank G. Mittelbach, *Residential Segregation in
the Urban Southwest* (Mexican-American Study Project, Advance Report 4, UCLA,
June 1966), pp. 98–101. These materials are analyzed in broader context in Leo
Grebler, Joan W. Moore, and Ralph C. Guzman, *The Mexican-American People:
The Nation's Second Largest Minority* (New York: The Free Press, 1970).

This study was undertaken because understanding of the residential segregation of Mexican-Americans in the urban Southwest is one of the important building blocks toward an understanding of this minority's overall social and economic position. Mexican-Americans are differentiated from the larger society in many respects, such as income, occupations, educational attainment, political participation and power, culture, and language. The various kinds of differentiation are in all probability highly interrelated. Differentiation in terms of urban residence location reflects not only physical distance from the majority population but the more pervasive social distance as well.

Besides, the study of the residential segregation of Mexican-Americans affords additional insights into one of the most enduring characteristics of American cities, the concentration of ethnic or racial minorities in ghettoes. First considered a threat to American values, the ethnic ghetto came later to be viewed as an adaptive and transitional device that would help immigrant groups in the "inevitable" assimilation to American society. This optimistic view was punctured as Negro ghettoes developed or expanded in Northern and Midwestern and finally in Western cities and appeared to become permanent fixtures of the urban scene.

Segregation patterns in the urban Southwest are of special significance because this region includes two large population groups generally recognized as disadvantaged minorities: Mexican-Americans and Negroes. There are also significant numbers of Orientals and Indians in many cities. This constellation makes it possible to examine not only the residential separation of each minority from the members of the dominant society but also the segregation of the two subordinate groups from each other.

While all of the three principal population segments considered in this study—white Anglos, Mexican-Americans, and Negroes—are now about equally urbanized, with roughly four-fifths of each living in cities, their patterns of urbanization have varied a great deal. A large percentage of Mexican-Americans continue to reside in the outlying portions of metropolitan areas. Negroes are highly concentrated in central city districts. Anglos have become increasingly suburban. The different urbanization patterns of Mexican-Americans and Negroes reflect in part the origin of the ghettoes now occupied by each minority. Many of today's *barrios* once were labor camps or agricultural settlements and became only later engulfed in urban expansion. Hence, they are today still outside the central cities. The Negro ghetto is typically in the core of urban areas—and so are, of course, some of the Mexican-American neighborhoods.

Analysis of residential segregation in 35 Southwest cities yields one clear-cut finding. Mexican-Americans are substantially less segregated from the dominant group than are Negroes, without exception, but the level of segregation for both groups has remained high. The results show the following general rank order: the most severe segregation exists between Negroes and white Anglos; the next highest degree of segregation is observed between Mexican-Americans and Negroes; and the lowest of the three types of segregation applies to Mexican-Americans versus Anglos. Within the Mexican-American group there is also some segregation between native born and foreign born.

However, the degree of segregation varies greatly from city to city as well as between the three population groups in each city. It seems difficult at first to detect any order in the chaos of the "indexes of dissimilarity" that are used to measure residential segregation. Cities can, however, be classified by patterns of segregation affecting the minority groups. There are basically two types of cities. In most cities, segregation of Negroes from Anglos is the highest; segregation of Mexican-Americans from Negroes is next highest, and segregation of Mexican-Americans from Anglos is lowest. But in some cities a different pattern emerges in which the order of the last two types of segregation is reversed. There seems to be some indication that varying degrees of segregation might have different overall concomitants in cities of the two types.

Common observation tells us that residential segregation may be determined by a great variety of factors including but not limited to discrimination in housing markets. The scholarly literature on the subject offers a number of hypotheses on this point; the unusual admixture of minority groups in Southwest cities provides an opportunity to test the general validity of existing "explanations" and to develop new insights as well. But the scientific tools available for this kind of analysis are still so imperfect that the results show "correlates" of residential segregation rather than truly causal explanations.

Some of the factors suggested by previous research have been confirmed as being significantly related to residential segregation. Others have not. Among those which proved to be relatively unimportant as "explanatory" variables were the absolute income of the minority group, vacancies in the supply of housing, the population density of the city, and the concentration of the minority in the central city as contrasted with outlying areas. We found the following factors important in accounting for segregation:

- The larger the city, the greater the intensity of segregation in all of its three principal types: Mexican-Americans versus white Anglos, Negroes versus white Anglos, and Mexican-Americans versus Negroes.
- The greater the proportion of large households in the two minorities, the more severe is the residential separation of all three types. The proportion of large households among minorities, in turn, can be interpreted as an indicator of their acculturation.
- While residential segregation does not seem to be systematically related

to low minority incomes as such, it is associated with income *differentials* between the two minorities and the white Anglos. However, the income factor does little if anything to "explain" the segregation between Mexican-Americans and Negroes.

The intensity of residential segregation is also a function of the ethnic composition of the total minority population. The separation of either minority from the dominant group is more pronounced in cities with a large nonwhite population relative to their Mexican-American population, and vice versa. And these numerical relationships do not seem to influence in any significant measure the segregation of the two minorities from each other.

The strength of the relationships differs from case to case, as it always does in correlation analysis. Some of the factors enumerated above are more clearly associated with the severe forms of residential segregation than others. And there are remaining variances of different magnitudes that are left "unexplained" by the factors isolated. Several factors that were intuitively believed to be of importance failed to show significant statistical relationships to segregation. Perhaps the most important among these is discrimination of various kinds.

Of course, the conceptual scheme underlying this analysis included what has come to be called the "taste for discrimination." But it turned out to be extremely difficult to find a statistical proxy for discrimination—as one must in multiple regression analysis. The statistical measure selected for this purpose failed to show any significant relationships to both intercity and intergroup segregation. This outcome does not negate or diminish the significance of discrimination. It merely demonstrates the problem of expressing some facts of life in such form that they lend themselves to quantitative analysis.

Under these circumstances, one must conclude that some of the influence of discrimination on the varying extent of residential segregation is buried in the variance left unaccounted for by the analysis. But we know that, once established, the ghetto becomes a "way of life" affecting all perceptions of the larger system. It becomes a way of life in that it provides defenses, to be sure, but there is little doubt that it is highly meaningful and valuable to many of its residents. Though we have been equally handicapped in coping with this kind of factor in our analysis, there is little doubt that it persists. Despite such questions of value, which are particularly salient in the study of Mexican-Americans, the American society is committed to an overall ideal of full participation and freedom of choice for all of its members. As long as there is any suspicion that freedom of choice is being abrogated and that full participation is being denied, the problem of residential segregation must be of concern to us all.

chapter four

EMPLOYMENT

14 / Discrimination in Employment

U.S. COMMISSION ON CIVIL RIGHTS

In the area of employment and economic opportunities, the United States Supreme Court has not spoken with the clarity that characterizes the other problem areas. There is no case that stands out in a fashion similar to the *Brown* . . . decision in education or the *Smith* . . . decision in voting. The principal reason for the relative silence of the Court is that in these other areas government agencies were practicing discrimination, whereas in the field of employment, private individuals have exercised the bulk of the control. The Fourteenth Amendment, which has been measured, restricts only public bodies, not private individuals.

The absence of court decisions does not mean that there has not been discrimination. The data published by the Department of Labor on employment have consistently shown that minority group members have a much higher rate of unemployment than the white majority. The familiar description, "Last hired, first fired," is unfortunately accurate for minority group members. The hearings of the U.S. Civil Rights Commission in 1963 uncovered discrimination in virtually every area of employment and found it practiced not only by management, but also by the labor unions as well.

Source: U.S. Commission on Civil Rights, *Report,* Book 3, "Employment" (Washington, D.C.: U.S. Government Printing Office, 1961), pp. 153–161.

Although their occupational levels have risen considerably during the past 20 years, Negro workers continue to be concentrated in the less skilled jobs. And it is largely because of this concentration in the ranks of the unskilled and semiskilled, the groups most severely affected by both economic layoffs and technological changes, that Negroes are also disproportionately represented among the unemployed. The recent recession made this all too clear. But even now Negroes continue to swell the ranks of the unemployed as technological changes eliminate the unskilled or semiskilled tasks they once performed. Many will be permanently or chronically unemployed unless some provision is made for retraining them in the skills required by today's economy. The depressed economic status of Negroes is the product of many forces, including the following:

• Discrimination against Negroes in vocational as well as academic training
• Discrimination against Negroes in apprenticeship training programs
• Discrimination against Negroes by labor organizations—particularly in the construction and machinists' crafts
• Discrimination against Negroes in referral services rendered by State employment offices
• Discrimination against Negroes in the training and "employment" opportunities offered by the armed services, including the "civilian components"
• Discrimination by employers, including Government contractors and even the Federal Government

Related to all of these is a basic problem that contributes to the limited extent and type of Negro employment—the lack of motivation on the part of many Negroes to improve their educational and occupational status. Generally, of course, lack of motivation is itself the product of long-suffered discrimination.

Throughout the Commission study, the vicious circle of discrimination in employment opportunities was clear: The Negro is denied, or fails to apply for, training for jobs in which employment opportunities have traditionally been denied him; when jobs do become available, there are consequently few, if any, qualified Negroes available to fill them; and often, because of lack of knowledge of such newly opened opportunities, even the few who are qualified fail to apply.

Perpetuation of discriminatory training and employment practices is often supported by State employment offices. Present methods of determining Federal financial contributions to State offices encourage the referral of those applicants who are easiest to place and discourage the "selling" of merit employment. Some public employment offices openly base referrals on traditional employment practices in the community; the Commission survey revealed several instances of complaints from employers that no Negroes were ever referred for employment unless they were specifically requested. Moreover, except in States with enforceable fair employment legislation, Federal policy has permitted the acceptance and processing of discriminatory job orders from all employers other than Government contractors and Federal agencies. In practice, some employment offices have accepted and processed discriminatory job orders from the latter as well. The Commission survey revealed that, at least in Atlanta, Baltimore, and Detroit, Government contractors relied primarily on State employment offices as a recruitment source for most production employees and to a lesser degree for office clerical employees. Many companies utilize the services of these offices for testing applicants for employment or for admission into apprenticeship training programs.

In the building and construction trades, the craft unions are the main source of recruitment and also largely determine admission into apprenticeship training programs. Here, too, there is a vicious circle of discrimination. Many craft unions formerly denied membership to Negroes; some still do; others admit only a few Negroes. The paucity of Negro members may be based on several factors—the generally restrictive membership policies of the craft unions; the fact that Negroes have not obtained the training to qualify for membership; and lack of applicants. The last two factors are largely the product of past discrimination. A glaring example of the almost ineradicable effects of years of denial is the minimal participation of Negroes in apprenticeship training programs in the construction crafts. Many Negroes do not have the educational background—generally a high school education—to qualify for apprenticeship training; others feel it is futile to apply for the limited number of openings which have traditionally been denied to them because of their race. Yet without training, Negroes cannot hope to qualify for membership in the unions and, without such membership, the chances of obtaining employment in construction crafts—where job opportunities will soon far exceed the number of qualified applicants—are slight indeed.

It is clear, then, that even if employment opportunities were made equally available to Negroes, their occupational status would not be greatly improved. Discrimination in education, training, and referral, whether by employment offices or by labor organizations, must first be overcome.

But the goal of equal employment opportunity is still far from achievement. Efforts of the Federal Government to promote nondiscriminatory employment by Government contractors and Federal agencies have not generally been effective in overcoming resistance to hiring Negroes in any but the lowest categories. Although opportunities for employment by the Federal Government have increased in recent years, the Commission's nine-city survey disclosed a disproportionate number of Negroes in the lower Classification Act positions and a concentration of Negroes in the unskilled Wage Board jobs. Similarly, Commission investigations in Atlanta, Baltimore, and Detroit revealed examples of racial discrimination in the form of "underemployment," outright refusal to employ, and exclusion from company-sponsored training programs by Government contractors.

The limitations on employment opportunities available to Negroes are reflected in their earnings. Thus, where the heads of the families have received the same amount of formal education, the median income of Negro families is considerably less than that of white families. A study by the State of Connecticut Commission on Civil Rights revealed that the average income of Negro families whose members had completed high school or college was roughly equivalent to that of white families whose members had not gone beyond grade school. It is little wonder, then—in view of the limited job opportunities and the lack of any demonstrable reward for completing their education—that Negroes tend to leave school earlier and in much greater proportions than do white students. Although the educational level attained by Negroes has increased considerably during the past 20 years, it is still much lower than the level of education attained by whites. The Negro school dropout suffers the worst employment handicaps; the rate of unemployment among this group is four times the average unemployment rate.

Some progress has been made in providing increased training and employment opportunities for Negroes. Through the efforts of the former Committee on Government Contracts, opportunities were made available to Negroes—even if sometimes only on a "token" basis—in nontraditional jobs, including office clerical, technical, and professional positions. One large automobile manufacturer now employs Negroes in management and administrative positions. Companies that had refused to hire any Negroes have finally employed them. Even one of the most restrictive of the construction craft unions eventually agreed to refer a Negro for work on a Government project. Educational programs undertaken by this Committee and by the former Committee on Government Employment Policy focused attention on the problem of motivation of minority group members and resulted in increased training and counseling services in some communities. The desegregation of the Armed Forces initiated by Executive Order 9981 in 1948 resulted in increased "employment" opportunities for Negroes and, even more important, enabled many Negroes to obtain technical training which would not otherwise have been available to them.

Indications are that the establishment in 1961 of the President's Committee on Equal Employment Opportunity, with its prestige and broad authority, will bring considerably more progress. The requirement of "affirmative action" by Government contractors in adopting a nondiscriminatory employment policy, for example, should do much to overcome lack of motivation on the part of minority group members and should eventually elicit from them more applications for "nontraditional" jobs. The Civil Service Commission's current educational program should accomplish similar results in Federal employment. The new Committee's efforts to work with other Federal agencies in the fields of training and recruitment are also hopeful signs.

But much remains to be done that may well be beyond the new agency's jurisdiction. The Government-contract nondiscrimination clause has not been applied to employment created by Federal grant-in-aid and loan programs. With few exceptions these programs are administered without a nondiscrimination requirement. Yet Federal funds are used to create these employment opportunities in much the same manner as employment by Government contractors. The "civilian components" of our Military Establishment—the National Guard and reserve units attached to educational institutions—are beyond the scope of Executive Order 9981, and in some States Federal funds are being used to subsidize the discriminatory exclusion from, or segregation of Negroes in, these units.

Perhaps the greatest need for future Federal action, however, lies in the area of training. The Commission survey revealed that without adequate training opportunities, the goal of equal employment opportunity can never be achieved. Unless the Federal Government takes an active role in providing vocational education and apprenticeship training on a nondiscriminatory basis, Negroes will continue to suffer the economic and legal deprivations of the past.

The need for training and retraining has been further emphasized by the demands of today's economy. Even during the recent recession with its high rates of unemployment, jobs were going begging for lack of *skilled* workers to fill them. As technological changes and the replacement of old industries with new ones have been largely responsible for swelling the ranks of the unemployed, they have also increased the demand for skilled craftsmen and technicians. The demand will continue to increase. It is estimated that for every 100 skilled workers that the Nation had in 1955, it will need 122 in 1965, and 145 in 1975. Yet today our vocational education and apprenticeship training programs are not training even enough skilled workers to replace those who retire. Discrimination in such programs is a waste of human resources which this Nation can ill afford, particularly during an era when it is being challenged to develop to the utmost all the human and material resources at its command.

FINDINGS

General

1. Although the occupational levels attained by Negroes have risen sharply during the past 20 years, Negro workers are still disproportionately concentrated in the ranks of the unskilled and semiskilled in both private and public employment. They are also disproportionately represented among the unemployed because of their concentration in unskilled and semiskilled jobs—those most severely affected by both cyclical and structural unemployment—and because Negro workers often have relatively low seniority. These difficulties are due in some degree to present or past discrimination in employment practices, in educational and training opportunities, or both.

2. Directly or indirectly, Federal funds create employment opportunities for millions in the civilian and military establishments of the Federal Government and in employment by Government contractors and grant-in-aid recipients. In addition, Federal funds provide training opportunities and placement services that directly affect employment opportunities. A policy of equal opportunity for all regardless of race, color, religion, or national origin has been declared with respect to some programs in each of these areas of Federal involvement in employment, but that policy has yet to be made consistent or thoroughly effective.

Enforcement of Federal Policy of Equal Employment Opportunity

3. The principal enforcement agency for Federal policy in this field is the President's Committee on Equal Employment Opportunity. This Committee has already taken steps to overcome obstacles encountered by the former Committee on Government Employment Policy and the Committee on Government Contracts in administering past programs of nondiscriminatory employment. Among projects which could contribute substantially to the effectuation of the Federal nondiscrimination program are the following:

a. Regular surveys of all Federal employment, in both the civilian and military establishments (including members of reserve components), to show current patterns of minority group employment, participation in training programs, and methods used to recruit for, and fill, jobs;

b. Appointment of full-time employment policy officers in all executive departments and major agencies, and the appointment of full-time contracts compliance officers in the principal contracting agencies, all to be thoroughly trained, by or under the supervision of the President's Committee, in the objectives, problems, and techniques for effectuating the Federal policy of nondiscriminatory employment. (In the largest agencies with substantial field establishments, the appointment of specially trained regional deputy employment policy officers and deputy contracts compliance officers may also be required.)

c. Expansion of the program of the former Committee on Government Employment Policy of conducting conferences in various locations with local administrators, deputy employment policy officers, and line supervisors to explain the Federal program of nondiscriminatory employment and discuss the problems involved and the techniques for overcoming them;

d. Establishing and maintaining a centralized list of current Government contractors and circulating it regularly to State employment offices;

e. Reaffirming that, when Government contractors completely delegate to labor organizations the power of hiring, or of determining admission to apprenticeship training programs or other terms and conditions of employment, they will be held responsible for the discriminatory acts of the unions;

f. Requesting the Secretary of Labor to require State employment offices to report to the Committee all discriminatory job orders placed by Federal agencies and Government contractors.

4. The Committee's potential effectiveness is, however, limited. Established only by executive action, it is necessarily limited in budget and legal authority. Its jurisdiction over labor unions is indirect and tenuous. Its authority over employment created by grants-in-aid and over federally assisted training programs and recruitment services is not clearly defined.

15 / Peonage in Florida

ROBERT COLES
HARRY HUGE

The problems of minority group members finding employment
are not limited to urban dwellers. Until recently the large number who remained in the rural areas of America were able to
obtain employment even if at very low wages. In the South, the
traditional system of sharecropping—an arrangement where
the black family worked the land and "shared" the income of
the crop with the landlord—meant that blacks had moderate
job security, even if bought at the price of virtual serfdom. In
the West, the Mexican-American farm worker lacked even this
minimal amount of security.

Changes in agricultural methods, however, especially the
mechanization of crop harvesting, have produced dramatic effects on the lives of rural minority group members. The rapid
mechanization of more and more farms in the South is driving
blacks off the land and into the cities, where they are unskilled for industrial jobs and unprepared for the urban way of
life. Similarly, the development of new harvesting techniques
is threatening the precarious position of farm workers in the
West.

SOURCE: Robert Cole and Harry Huge, "Peonage in Florida," *The New Republic*, July 26, 1969, pp. 17–21. Reprinted by permission of *The New Republic*, ©
1969, Harrison-Blaine of New Jersey, Inc.

Around October, cold spells begin to reach up North and into the Mid-west, and thousands of Americans remind themselves that in a nation as large as ours, spread out over so many latitudes, a willing traveller can find summer anytime. So the trek to Florida begins. The southern part of the state begins to bulge with the rich and the not-so-rich, the owners of winter homes and the one-week guests who fill up thousands of hotels, mo-tels and rooming houses.

Others also manage a return to Florida in October, though to get there they don't use jets or toll roads. Often they even shun our new and free interstate roads, and if asked why, they demur, or quickly assert their wish to move quietly, to attract nobody's attention. Yet, they do get atten-tion. When they arrive at a state line, they may be met by the police and told to go right through, fast and with no stops at all; if they should try to pause here and there, to use a rest-room or enter a restaurant, they are quickly singled out and shouted at and pushed away. The owner of one gas station in Collier County, Florida, told us who these other winter visitors are: "They're dirty, the migrants. They'll come by, and I tell them to scram. They'll ruin your restrooms for good, inside an hour. Sure, we need them here, to pick the crops, but that's all they're good for, if you ask me, and I've lived here all my life and seen them come and go each year. I'll tell you—I don't even want to sell them gas. You know why? We're a first-class station, and if tourists or the regular people here drove up and saw those migrants around, they'd go somewhere else with their business, and I wouldn't blame them. You don't come from up North all the way to Collier County, only to find yourself standing next to—the likes of them."

What *are* they like? Where do they come from and how do they live, the some one-hundred-thousand migrant farmers who each year harvest Florida's vegetables and fruit, worth millions of dollars?

Actually we don't know all there is to know, because the migrants commonly slip by census-takers or local officials charged with recording births and deaths. Nomads, itinerants, wanderers, they live everywhere and nowhere. Each county of each state calls them someone else's responsibil-ity, though in all places the terribly hard and demanding work they do is considered essential. Nor has the federal government ever seen fit to step in and say, yes they will in a sense belong to all of us, for whose benefit, after all, so much of that travelling and stopping and cutting and picking is done. On the contrary, migrant farmers are denied just about every benefit that 30 years of struggle achieved for other workers—such as the right to organize into labor unions without harassment and bargain collectively with employers, and the right to get unemployment insurance or a degree of compensation for injuries sustained at work. Most migrants can't vote, are ineligible for any kind of welfare or other advantages and services that towns or counties offer their residents.

Here is how one migrant worker talked to us about his life as a virtual peon:

Well sir, I was born in Louisiana, I was; my daddy worked there on shares, and before him my granddaddy, and I guess it goes back to slavery. (My granddaddy, he'd tell us about all the slaves he used to know, and how one by one they died, and when the last slave died—I mean that was a slave before they was all set free— well my granddaddy, he said his mother said she hated to see him die, but it was just as well we tried to forget about slavery.) I guess I thought I was going to stay there, in Louisiana, but I sure didn't, I'll tell you. I was thirteen or fourteen, I think it was, and my daddy was telling us that we were in real bad trouble, because the government up in Washington was giving the bossman a lot of money, and in return he wasn't doing as much planting as before; and what he was planting, he was going to do it all by machine and he didn't need us anymore to pick the crops. So, he told us we could stay there in the cabins, but that was all, and the sooner we went up to Chicago the better, he said, and my daddy was all set to go with us, but we got the message that his sister up there had died all of a sudden, and he got scared to go.

I remember him saying that if we went up there, we'd all die like his sister, and if we stayed down on that plantation, we'd not last long, and so there wasn't anything to choose—except that one day a man came along, and he was going from door to door, he said, and signing people up for work, to pick the crops he said, over in Florida. And he told us, I remember, that all our worries was over, and all we had to do was go on over there with him and the others and do what we knew to do, pick some beans and some tomatoes and like that, and it wasn't any different from working on cotton, and maybe easier, he said. So daddy told us he thought we should go, and there was, I think, five or six families he got, just from our bossman's place; and of course he got others. And would you believe it that they had these buses, four of them I recall, and they put us on them, and they looked like the school buses, only they were older, much older, and soon we were on the road, yes sir; and I'll tell you, it's been a lot of that ever since, moving here and there and everywhere, until you don't know where you're at and how you'll ever stop. Believe me, sir, we wants to stop and find us a place to live, all year round, like other folks do. But if you're trying to eat, and you owe them all that money, and you have to eat while you try to get even and not be owing them, well then, you just have to go up North and come back, or else they'll have you in jail, I'll tell you that, or worse than that, much worse, they'll just go and pull the trigger, I believe some of them might, if you tried to run free of them. And I'd like to know where you could go even if they let you, and they didn't try to stop you, and they didn't call the sheriff, and they even drove you where you wanted to go. We wouldn't know where to go, because the people, they just don't want us, to use their restrooms or even buy from them. They'll tell you to 'git,' and they sure mean it, you can tell on their face by the way they looks down on you.

His story is not unusual. Thousands of sharecroppers and tenant farmers have gone North to our cities, where they frequently found no work and went on welfare. Thousands of other field hands have given their lives to constant travel and the hardest, most menial jobs, for which they are called "lazy" and "shiftless" and paid the lowest possible wages. (Only recently did farm workers come under the protection of the minimum-wage law, and their minimum wage just moved up from $1.15 to $1.30 per hour, whereas other workers are guaranteed $1.60 per hour.) Worse, migrants like the man just quoted fall victim to a kind of peonage that seals not only their fate but that of their children. They are brought to Florida, whole families or single men or single women or groups of teen-aged children. The men who bring them are called "contractors" or "crew leaders," and are paid, say, "50 dollars a head," (their words) by growers. The frightened, confused former sharecroppers and their children are housed in camps and put to work, but soon they discover that in return for long hours on their knees out in the fields they will get very little cash. For one thing, in the course of a year there are days, even weeks, when there is no work to be had. The migrants move from one camp to another, and become part of a world few outsiders know anything about. The camps have their own stores and vendors, and are often guarded by "camp boys" who walk around with guns. Migrants are told they cannot leave unless all their debts are paid; the ledgers are tallied by the men who own and run the camps.

"There's always something you owe them," we kept on hearing as we talked with one migrant after another. From Rodolfo Juarez, a new and young leader of Mexican-American migrants in Florida (they make up about half the state's agricultural workers), we heard it spelled out:

I was born in South Texas, in San Benito, and when I was about fifteen I was sold, that's right. They came and got a whole group of us and told us there was a lot of money to make up North and over in Florida, if we just went along with them, and they'll take us and even feed us. I now know they got so much money from the growers for each body they brought up from Texas. Well, we were living like animals where we were, and getting practically nothing for doing crop work in south Texas, so we thought: why not? why not? I was taken up to Indiana and Ohio, to work on farms there, and then we tried to break out, but it's hard. They tell you that you owe them for the food and the transportation and the mattress on the floor you use for sleeping, and they tell you that if you try to leave, they'll get you thrown in jail and you'll never get out until you pay your bills. How else can you pay them but by going back to work for them, and when you do that, you have to eat and you have to sleep somewhere and a lot of the time there's no work, until it's time to harvest, and so you're their property, that's what it amounts to with some of those contractors. They own people, that's what, unless they escape, like I did; but I'll tell you the truth, a lot of migrants—you know, they're Mexican-Americans like me, or black people, and a few are white, yes, but not many—they're not aware of their rights, and they're scared, and they should be. Have you seen them patrolling some of those camps? The men will ride around with guns, and the crew leaders will herd the people into the trucks to go picking. They stand them up and they look like cattle going to the market, and that's no exaggerating.

We visited the camps and the fields all through Collier County and Palm Beach County. We saw the same sites that recently shocked Senator McGovern's Select Committee on Nutrition and Human Needs: broken-down shacks, some without even windows, some nothing more than enlarged outhouses without running water or heat, a few even without electricity, all of which rent for $10, $15, even $20 a *week*. The drinking water is often contaminated, taken as it is from superficial wells located near garbage-filled swamps. Children are supposed to walk a quarter of a mile or more to unspeakably inadequate outdoor privies. There are no showers, no baths, no stoves and often no refrigerators. Entire families live in one room, sleep, if lucky, on mattresses, live on soda pop and bread and grits and fat-back and cheap candy. Yet, Collier County has no food-stamp program, no commodity food program, and no welfare program for migrants, who have been called by local officials "federal people," or "not our people." In Collier County's Immokalee, an Indian word which ironically means "my home," we saw children not only hungry and malnourished, but obviously and seriously ill, yet never seen by physicians. Born "on the road," brought up on buses and trucks, or carried from farm to farm in cars, left to themselves in the fields and, when twelve or thirteen, quietly put to work in the fields, they nevertheless have to be considered fortunate if they are still alive, since the infant mortality rate for such children in places like Collier County is estimated to be about five times that of other American children. The children are badly frightened and confused. They live unstable, chaotic lives and feel at loose ends, worthless, virtually dead.

One of us spent two years studying migrant children in Belle Glade and Pahokee, Florida, and we recently went to see some of those children, a little older now but still to be found (through a minister) in one of the camps: "Yes, we're soon to be going north again," a ten-year-old boy told us. "I'm afraid each time that we won't get back here, but we do." How did school go for him this year: "Well, I didn't get there much. We moved from place to place, and I helped with the picking a lot, and the schools, when you go to them, they don't seem to want you, and they'll say that you're only going to be there a few weeks anyway, so what's the use." What does he want to do when he gets older? "I don't know. I'd like to stay someplace, I guess, and never have to leave there for the rest of my life, that's what. I could have a job—maybe it would be where they make cars and trucks and planes. I could make plenty of money, and bring it home, and we'd all live on it, my brothers and my sister. But my mother says someone has to pick the crops, and we don't know what else there is to do, and they'll come and beat you and throw you in the canal, the crew leaders, if you cross them; and then you'd be dead in one minute. So, we'd better stay with the crops; because my mother is probably right. I hope I never fall in one of those canals. You can never get out. They're deeper than the ocean I hear. I've never seen the ocean, but I know it's not far away."

The ocean is indeed nearby—Palm Beach and all its glitter to the east, and to the west the more sedate but no less wealthy Naples, the seat of Collier County's government. One can drive the major roads of Palm Beach County or Collier County and get no idea what is happening down those dusty pathways that lead to fields and camps and "loading zones" where human beings are picked up and left off. "There's no end to it," a migrant mother said to us in Immokalee, "you just hope you'll die in between picking-time, so you're resting. I'd hate to die on the road, yes sir; my children, they'd never find their way back to Florida. I guess that's our home, yes sir. We spend more time there than in the other states; but I'll say this, they're not very good to us there, if you ask for anything."

What has she asked for? What does she need that Collier County might supply, particularly since the county's officials have publicly acknowledged that without migrant workers like her its huge farms and its dozens of well-equipped packing houses would be worthless? She is, of course, rather modest when she talks about her needs. She'd like good food for her children, particularly during those weeks when she is waiting for work. (The migrant's average annual income is $1700 a year.) She would like to be paid in full for her work. (Migrants repeatedly claim they are short-changed—given, say, five dollars at the end of a day and told that for "meals and transportation" they have been charged another five.) She would like to find decent housing and pay a reasonable amount of rent: "In Immokalee a few white men own everything. They push us into those little rooms, one for each family, and you pay $20 a week. If you go to the camps, after they deduct the rent you've got no money left, and they tell you that you owe them some, on top of it."

She is not about to fight things out with Collier County's officials. We saw a little of what frightens her—those "camp-boys" and labor contractors driving pick-up trucks fitted with gun racks that hold three or four rifles. We saw a jail in Immokalee, only recently abandoned, whose cramped and primitive quarters must rival anything that ever was or is in Siberia. On the other hand, we met up with a fine group of lawyers who are fighting hard for that woman and others like her under a program called the South Florida Migrant Legal Services, begun in April 1967 under an OEO grant. Lawyers cannot by their exertions alone bring social and economic justice to a group of people variously called in the last two or three years, not a half century ago, "the slaves we rent" or "serfs upon the land" or "America's wretched of the earth." Yet, every day migrants feel themselves victimized, cheated, deceived; and they have no past experience with lawyers, no money for them, and no belief that a law suit will lead to anything. Now, for the first time, some of those Florida migrants have found out that there are intelligent and compassionate men who know the law and are ready to represent the interests of people who haven't a cent to offer for legal fees. No social revolution has occurred in Florida, but at least a few complaints on behalf of the migrants are being made—and as a result the growers and crew-leaders and labor contractors and real estate groups that employ migrants and herd them about and rent shacks to them have become convinced that the South Florida Migrant Legal Services must be brought to an end very soon, when the OEO grant runs out. Florida's political leaders are putting strong pressure on OEO to refuse another grant, and though the agency's staff reportedly has high praise for the program, the real test will come not only when (and if) refunding takes place, but after Governor Kirk exercises his expected veto, and OEO's new chief, Donald Rumsfeld, decides either to stand firm and override the veto or allow one of the agency's best programs to be killed. It is, too, a program that aims to change things through legal action, through reliance on court orders and "due process," those quiet, slow, patient maneuvers we are daily urged to respect.

Meanwhile, Senators come and are horrified and ashamed. Tourists drive by and if they see anything, shake their heads and wonder how many miles to the next Holiday Inn. People like us quickly find ourselves out of Collier County's Immokalee and safely in Collier County's Naples—where we can eat well and take a swim, and give vent to our confusion and sadness and most galling, our frustration: how can our words do justice to the misery and heartache we have seen, and how can we describe and make unforgettable the worried, pained faces of boys and girls whose bodies are thin and covered with sores and bites and covered also with Florida's rich muckland, whose crops those children have harvested? Back in Immokalee we were offended, disgusted; later in Naples there was the tropical green water and the soft sand and a long, long pier where we could stand and discuss things with Michael Foster and Michael Kantor, two resourceful young lawyers who work for the South Florida Migrant Legal Services in Collier County and every day try to get housing codes enforced, and money paid to people who have bent and stooped from dawn to dusk, only to be denied their rightful earnings, or who have gone for weeks without work, without unemployment compensation, without relief payments.

We stood on the pier for a long time and looked at sworn affidavits that had been taken six months ago and sent up to the Justice Department, affidavits that spell out the details of peonage: "From October 17, 1968, until late in November 1968, I was only paid wages of $5.50. I went to the camp authorities to ask why I had been paid so little and they merely responded they had paid three doctors bills for me and that I was not due any money at this time. To the best of my knowledge I did not have three doctor bills while I was at Camp Happy." During her stay she "had many problems" with the camp guards. She was beaten, thrown across a room, told she might be killed. When she asked to leave, one of the camp's guards said "I could not go because I owed $25 to the company." What is more, others kept on arriving to share her fate: "On January 11, 1969, a bus with forty-two people arrived from the state of Mississippi. . . . Around half of these persons were under sixteen years of age and were not accompanied by adults. The man who brought the children to the camp was paid $15 for each person he brought." And finally, so that everybody at Camp Happy was kept happy, "persons also used to come from Fort Myers and sell narcotics at the camp. I did not know the names of these persons. They carried on their activities with the full consent of those who operated the camp."

What is to be done? The two lawyers told us they could only keep trying, keep pressing matters through the courts—though even that method has caused an uproar among Florida's political leaders. We said we could report on what we had seen and learned, even though we know that in past decades reports have been written and written—and the evident futility of all those words must haunt those who wrote them. Perhaps, we speculated, the only answer to the problem is one suggested by a tough, angry "community organizer"—an "outside agitator," no doubt about it, we met near Immokalee: "Look, you people can do your lawyering and your doctoring and your writing, but a lot of good it will do these people. They're in bondage, don't you see that? They're treated like animals—in a country that's the richest, fattest country in the world. They have no constituency, that's the problem. They don't even have the kind of constituency the blacks do in Mississippi—you know, the Northern liberals, with the voting laws they've put through, and like that. These people have nothing to fall back on but the conscience of the nation, and a lot of good that's done for them. I'll tell you, there's only one way to change things here in Florida, in Collier County. Over there in Naples there's Roger Blough of United States Steel, and there's the president of Grant's department store, and there's the president of Eli Lilly, and all the rest. They have it nice here in Florida. There's no personal income tax, and there's no tax on the corporations. I'll bet if the migrants started marching down that highway 846 to Naples, and fought their way to that Gulf Shore Boulevard there—well, I'll bet the people who live there would call in those sheriffs and county commissioners, and they'd call in the politicians who do what they're told to do, and say to all of them: boys, give them a bigger slice, because we don't want any more trouble here. You hear that! And then the migrants would be a little better off and you guys, you'd praise yourselves and all your attitudes and say like you always do: democracy, it's wonderful!"

We are in no danger of the kind of middle-class self-congratulations he scornfully described—the kind that follows a successful uprising of the poor. For there's no danger the migrants will be causing anyone much trouble. They will roam the land, follow the sun and the crops, harvest our food, and go on getting just about nothing.

16 / Equal Employment Opportunity: Public Law 88-352

The publicity directed at the clear-cut lack of equality in job opportunity due to racial discrimination in hiring led to the inclusion of an equal-employment section in the 1964 Civil Rights Act. This represented the first general commitment, in legislation, by the federal government to the concept of equal employment in both the public and private sectors. The law covers larger business firms (with 25 or more employees) and forbids not only racial, but religious, sexual, and ethnic discrimination in hiring, dismissal, referral for employment, and working conditions. The law also attempted to regulate the apprenticeship and recruitment activities of labor unions, which had an extremely bad record as far as minority-group members, especially blacks, are concerned. This represents one of the apparent paradoxes of American politics, for unions were at one time the underdogs themselves. It would seem that once a group achieves security, it denies access to newer groups.

SOURCE: *U.S. Statutes at Law* (1964), 241–268.

SECTION 701

For the purpose of this title . . .

b. The term "employer" means a person engaged in an industry affecting commerce who has twenty-five or more employees for each working day in each of twenty or more calendar weeks in the current or preceding calendar year, and any agent of such a person, but such term does not include (1) the United States, a corporation wholly owned by the Government of the United States, an Indian tribe, or a State or political subdivision thereof, (2) a bona fide private membership club (other than a labor organization) which is exempt from taxation under section 501 (c) of the Internal Revenue Code of 1954: Provided, That during the first year after the effective date prescribed in subsection (a) of section 716, persons having fewer than one hundred employees (and their agents) shall not be considered employers, and during the second year after such date, persons having fewer than seventy-five employees (and their agents) shall not be considered employers, and during the third year after such date, persons having fewer than fifty employees (and their agents) shall not be considered employers. Provided further, That it shall be the policy of the United States to insure equal employment opportunities for Federal employees without discrimination because of race, color, religion, sex or national origin and the President shall utilize his existing authority to effectuate this policy. . . .

d. The term "labor organization" means a labor organization engaged in an industry affecting commerce, and any agent of such an organization, and includes any organization of any kind, any agency, or employee representation committee, group, association, or plan so engaged in which employees participate and which exists for the purpose, in whole or in part, of dealing with employers concerning grievances, labor disputes, wages, rates of pay, hours, or other terms or conditions of employment, and any conference, general committee, joint or system board, or joint council so engaged which is subordinate to a national or international labor organization.

e. A labor organization shall be deemed to be engaged in an industry affecting commerce if (1) it maintains or operates a hiring hall or hiring office which procures employees for an employer or procures for employees opportunities to work for an employer, or (2) the number of its members (or, where it is a labor organization composed of other labor organizations or their representatives, if the aggregate number of the members of such other labor organization) is (A) one hundred or more during the first year after the effective date prescribed in subsection (a) of section 716, (B) seventy-five or more during the second year after such date or fifty or more during the third year, or (C) twenty-five or more thereafter, ...

SECTION 703

a. It shall be an unlawful employment practice for an employer—(1) to fail or refuse to hire or to discharge any individual, or otherwise to discriminate against any individual with respect to his compensation, terms, conditions, or privileges or employment, because of such individual's race, color, religion, sex, or national origin; or (2) to limit, segregate, or classify his employees in any way which would deprive or tend to deprive any individual of employment opportunities or otherwise adversely affect his status as an employee, because of such individual's race, color, religion, sex, or national origin.

b. It shall be an unlawful employment practice for an employment agency to fail or refuse to refer for employment, or otherwise to discriminate against, any individual because of his race, color, religion, sex, or national origin, or to classify or refer for employment any individual on the basis of his race, color, religion, sex, or national origin.

c. It shall be an unlawful employment practice for a labor organization—(1) to exclude or to expel from its membership, or otherwise to discriminate against, any individual because of his race, color, religion, sex, or national origin; (2) to limit, segregate, or classify its membership, or to classify or fail or refuse to refer for employment any individual, in any way which would deprive or tend to deprive any individual of employment opportunities, or would limit such employment opportunities or otherwise adversely affect his status as an employee or as an applicant for employment, because of such individual's race, color, religion, sex, or national origin; or (3) to cause or attempt to cause an employer to discriminate against an individual in violation of this section.

d. It shall be an unlawful employment practice for any employer, labor organization, or joint labor-management committee controlling apprenticeship or other training or retraining, including on-the-job training programs to discriminate against any individual because of his race, color, religion, sex, or national origin in admission to, or employment in, any program established to provide apprenticeship or other training.

e. Notwithstanding any other provision of this title, (1) it shall not be an unlawful employment practice for an employer to hire and employ employees, for an employment agency to classify, or refer for employment any individual, for labor organizations to classify its membership or to classify or refer for employment any individual, or for an employer, labor organization, or joint labor-management committee controlling apprenticeship or other training or retraining programs to admit or employ any individual in any such program, on the basis of his religion, sex, or national origin in those certain instances where religion, sex, or national origin is a bona fide occupational qualification reasonably necessary to the normal operation of that particular business or enterprise, and (2) it shall not be an unlawful employment practice for a school, college, university, or other educational institution or institutions of learning to hire and employ employees of a particular religion if such school, college, university, or other educational institution or institutions of learning is, in whole or in substantial part, owned, supported, controlled, or managed by a particular religion or by a particular religious corporation, association, or society, or if the curriculum of such school, college, university, or other educational institution or institutions of learning is directed toward the propagation of a particular religion. . . .

j. Nothing contained in this title shall be interpreted to require any employer, employment agency, labor organization, or joint labor-management committee subject to this title to grant preferential treatment to any individual or to any group because of the race, color, religion, sex, or national origin of such individual or group on account of an imbalance which may exist with respect to the total number or percentage of persons of any race, color, religion, sex, or national origin employed by any employer, referred or classified for employment by any employment agency or labor organization, admitted to membership or classified by any labor organization or admitted to, or employed in, any apprenticeship or other training program, in comparison with the total number or percentage of persons of such race, color, religion, sex, or national origin in any community, State, section, or other area, or in the available work force in any community, State, section, or other area.

SECTION 704

b. It shall be an unlawful employment practice for an employer, labor organization, or employment agency to print or publish or cause to be printed or published any notice or advertisement relating to employment by such an employer or membership in or any classification or referral for employment by such a labor organization, or relating to any classification or referral for employment by such an employment agency, indicating any preference, limitation, specification, or discrimination, based on race, color, religion, sex, or national origin, except that such a notice or advertisement may indicate a preference, limitation, specification, or discrimination based on religion, sex, or national origin when religion, sex, or national origin is a bona fide occupational qualification for employment.

SECTION 705

a. There is hereby created a Commission to be known as the Equal Employment Opportunity Commission, which shall be composed of five members, not more than three of whom shall be members of the same political party, who shall be appointed by the President by and with the advice and consent of the Senate. One of the original members shall be appointed for a term of one year, one for a term of two years, one for a term of three years, one for a term of four years, and one for a term of five years, beginning from the date of enactment of this title, but their successors shall be appointed for terms of five years each, except that any individual chosen to fill a vacancy shall be appointed only for the unexpired term of the member whom he shall succeed. The President shall designate one member to serve as Chairman of the Commission, and one member to serve as Vice Chairman. . . .

d. The Commission shall at the close of each fiscal year report to the Congress and to the President concerning the action it has taken; the names, salaries, and duties of all individuals in its employ and the moneys it has disbursed; and shall make such further reports on the cause of and means of eliminating discrimination and such recommendations for further legislation as may appear desirable. . . .

g. The Commission shall have power—(1) to cooperate with and, with their consent, utilize regional, State, local, and other agencies, both public and private, and individuals; . . . (4) upon the request of (i) any employer, whose employees or some of them, or (ii) any labor organization, whose members or some of them, refuse or threaten to refuse to cooperate in effectuating the provisions of this title, to assist in such effectuation by conciliation or such other remedial action as is provided by this title; (5) to make such technical studies as are appropriate to effectuate the purposes and policies of this title and to make the results of such studies available to the public; (6) to refer matters to the Attorney General with recommendations for intervention in a civil action brought by an aggrieved party under section 706, or for the institution of a civil action by the Attorney General under section 707, and to advise, consult, and assist the Attorney General on such matters.

h. Attorneys appointed under this section may, at the direction of the Commission, appear for and represent the Commission in any case in court. . . .

SECTION 706

a. Whenever it is charged in writing under oath by a person claiming to be aggrieved, or a written charge has been filed by a member of the Commission where he has reasonable cause to believe a violation of this title has occurred (and such charge sets forth the facts upon which it is based) that an employer, employment agency, or labor organization has engaged in an unlawful employment practice, the Commission shall furnish such employer, employment agency, or labor organization (hereinafter referred to as the "respondent") with a copy of such charge and shall make an investigation of such charge, provided that such charge shall not be made public by the Commission. If the Commission shall determine, after such investigation, that there is reasonable cause to believe that the charge is true, the Commission shall endeavor to eliminate any such alleged unlawful employment practice by informal methods of conference, conciliation, and persuasion. Nothing said or done during and as a part of such endeavors may be made public by the Commission without the written consent of the parties, or used as evidence in a subsequent proceeding. . . .

    c. In the case of any charge filed by a member of the Commission alleging an unlawful employment practice occurring in a State or political subdivision of a State, which has a State or local law prohibiting the practice alleged and establishing or authorizing a State or local authority to grant or seek relief from such practice or to institute criminal proceedings with respect thereto upon receiving notice thereof, the Commission shall, before taking any action with respect to such charge, notify the appropriate State or local officials and, upon request, afford them a reasonable time, but not less than sixty days (provided that such sixty-day period shall be extended to one hundred and twenty days during the first year after the effective day of such State or local law), unless a shorter period is requested, to act under such State or local law to remedy the practice alleged. . . .

    e. If within thirty days after a charge is filed with the Commission or within thirty days after the expiration of any period of reference under subsection (c) (except that in either case such period may be extended to not more than sixty days upon a determination by the Commission that further efforts to secure voluntary compliance are warranted), the Commission has been unable to obtain voluntary compliance with this title, the Commission shall so notify the person aggrieved and a civil action may, within thirty days thereafter, be brought against the respondent named in the charge (1) by the person claiming to be aggrieved, or (2) if such charge was filed by a member of the Commission, by any person whom the charge alleges was aggrieved by the alleged unlawful employment practice. Upon application by the complainant and in such circumstances as the court may deem just, the court may appoint an attorney for such complainant and may authorize the commencement of the action without the payments of fees, costs, or security. Upon timely application, the court may, in its discretion, permit the Attorney General to intervene in such civil action if he certifies that the case is of general public importance. Upon request, the court may, in its discretion, stay further proceedings for not more than sixty days pending the termination of State or local proceedings described in subsection (b) or the efforts of the Commission to obtain voluntary compliance.

    f. Each United States district court and each United States court of a place subject to the jurisdiction of the United States shall have jurisdiction of actions brought under this title. . . .

g. If the court finds that the respondent has intentionally engaged in or is intentionally engaging in an unlawful employment practice charged in the complaint, the court may enjoin the respondent from engaging in such unlawful employment practice, and order such affirmative action as may be appropriate, which may include reinstatement or hiring of employees, with or without back pay (payable by the employer, employment agency, or labor organization, as the case may be, responsible for the unlawful employment practice). Interim earnings or amounts earnable with reasonable diligence by the person or persons discriminated against shall operate to reduce the back pay otherwise allowable. No order of the court shall require the admission or reinstatement of an individual as a member of a union or the hiring, reinstatement, or promotion of an individual as an employee, or the payment to him of any back pay, if such individual was refused admission, suspended, or expelled or was refused employment or advancement or was suspended or discharged for any reason other than discrimination on account of race, color, religion, sex, or national origin or in violation of section 704 (a). . . .

i. In any case in which an employer, employment agency, or labor organization fails to comply with an order of a court issued in a civil action brought under subsection (e), the Commission may commence proceedings to compel compliance with such order. . . .

17 / The Mexican-American in the Southwest Labor Market

WALTER FOGEL

Employment opportunities for Mexican-Americans have been as limited as those for blacks and American Indians. Until January 1, 1965, when the *bracero,* or Mexican national farm labor, program was terminated, the majority of farm labor, a primary job market for the Mexican-American, was seasonal and very poorly paid by American standards. With the end of the *bracero* program, efforts to improve the lot of the farm worker have increased. The current activities are focused in the Great Central Valley of California, where Cesar Chavez has been leading an attempt to establish a union for farm workers (see Selection 40). The urban Mexican-American faces substantial discrimination in the labor market, as this reading selection shows. The symptoms of discrimination are the same as those associated with blacks: lower pay for the same amount of educational effort, a disproportionate number of Mexican-Americans in low-wage occupations, and lower pay in similar job classifications. As this selection shows, the con-

Source: Walter Fogel, *The Mexican-American in the Southwest Labor Market,* (Mexican-American Study Project Advance Report 10, October 1967), pp. 191–197. These materials are analyzed in broader context in Leo Grebler, Joan W. Moore, and Ralph C. Guzman, *The Mexican-American People: The Nation's Second Largest Minority* (New York: The Free Press, 1970).

ditions vary from state to state, but the general pattern remains one of unequal opportunity.

DISCRIMINATION AGAINST MEXICAN AMERICANS

Although the precise effects of labor market discrimination against Mexican-Americans were not measured in this study, the existence of discrimination was shown in several ways:

Perhaps the clearest evidence was presented in Chapter I [not reprinted here], where the incomes of Mexican-Americans and Anglos who had completed the same number of school years were compared—for the most part, incomes of Mexican-Americans were 60 to 80 percent of those of Anglos. We were not able to take account of the quality of education, and it may be that because of differing inputs to the schooling of the two groups, Mexican-Americans have less education than Anglos at each school grade level. But it does not seem possible that the quality factor could account for major portions of the income disparity which exists at each grade level.

Discrimination was also shown by the disproportionate representation of Mexican-Americans in low-wage occupations and jobs. It is true that lack of schooling is the major contributor to the inferior occupational patterns of Mexican-American employment, but our findings indicate that discrimination also contributes to these patterns. Within 6 or 7 major occupational categories, Mexican-Americans hold inferior jobs to those on which Anglos are employed. Within most major occupational categories, there is a negative association between earnings provided by the various job classifications and Mexican-American representation in them. Mexican-American employment is negatively related to size of firm and to the product market concentration of manufacturing industries. It appears to be adversely affected by strong craft unionism and is clearly very low in jobs involving supervision and persuasion of others. While the currently fashionable emphasis on formal schooling in job selection, applied to the inferior schooling of Mexican-Americans, may be instrumental in bringing about some of these adverse relationships, this emphasis itself is discriminatory when schooling is not related to job performance, which we believe to be largely the case in the manual occupations.

Finally, we believe discrimination was shown by the low earnings of Mexican-Americans compared to those of Anglos, within job classifications. Once again, it can be argued that the lower job qualifications of Mexican-Americans bring about their low earnings, but there is much less truth to this argument when it is applied to the job earnings of this minority than when it is applied to their occupational employment patterns. There is little reason for maintaining that, within job classifications, Mexican-Americans have less schooling than Anglos; from data for nonwhites we can infer that Mexican-Americans have as much schooling as Anglos within many job classifications. Furthermore, among workers in many manual job classifications, variation in experience and skill would seem to be more important to earnings than the small differences in schooling which are likely to exist. We have no knowledge of the relative job experience and skill of Mexican-Americans and Anglos. It is our belief that Mexican-Americans have low job earnings, because to a considerable extent, discrimination forces many of them to accept jobs in small, marginal firms.

DIFFERENCES AMONG THE STATES

There is a good deal of variation among the states of the Southwest in the labor market positions of urban Mexican-Americans. California and Texas are at opposite ends of the scales, with the other three states in between.

The positions of Mexican-Americans in Colorado and New Mexico are strongly influenced by economic declines or changes which have occurred in locations where they have long resided—declining industrial and farm employment in southern Colorado and declining farm employment in New Mexico. Many Mexican-Americans in these states have migrated to cities from rural areas. Employment growth in these cities has not provided enough middle- and high-wage jobs; thus, many Mexican-Americans are employed in low-wage jobs or are partially or totally unemployed. Colorado has been able to absorb the rural-to-urban migration better than New Mexico, either because it has been less in Colorado or because the growth of nonfarm jobs, which could be filled by Mexican-Americans, has been greater there. Another factor contributing to the low position of Mexican-Americans in New Mexico is a kind of insularity associated with much Mexican-American employment in white-collar occupations. Much of this employment appears to depend on the Mexican-American community rather than on the general community. As a consequence, earnings in white-collar occupations are quite low, so that the strong representation of Mexican-Americans in these occupations, in New Mexico, does not help their incomes as much as one would expect.

The similarity between the problems of Mexican-Americans in Colorado and New Mexico and those of residents of other states having depressed areas is obvious. The solution to these problems is equally obvious, though difficult to apply—movement out of the declining areas. Programs which would encourage this movement and facilitate adjustment to new jobs and locations should be encouraged.

The poor experience of Mexican-Americans in Texas is primarily a result of a large supply of unskilled labor (as a result of immigration and natural increases in population) concentrated in South Texas, where employment opportunities have not grown rapidly enough to provide good jobs and incomes for many persons of this ethnic population. The problem in Texas has been made more difficult by rapid increases in agricultural productivity, which have sent many workers from rural to urban labor markets. The problem has also been made more difficult by the existence of large numbers of Negroes in many of the large urban centers of Texas. Escape from South Texas to industrial jobs elsewhere in the state would proceed much more rapidly if there were not already such a large supply of low-skilled labor, most of it Negro, in the urban centers. Of course, Negroes trying to escape from poverty in rural Texas face the same problem. In addition to these ecological factors, there is evidence that Mexican-Americans face greater discrimination in Texas than in California or in other parts of the Southwest. This was shown by the fact that standardization for education reduced the California-Texas difference in Mexican-American relative income by less than half. It is also shown by the low relative earnings of Mexican-Americans in Texas in job classifications (intrastate regional influences on their earnings notwithstanding). The prospects for improvement in Texas are not very bright. The existence of many commuters and potential immigrants to South Texas will prevent very rapid upgrading of occupations and incomes, even if an unprecedented rate of economic growth in the area could be achieved.

In California, on the other hand, Mexican-Americans benefited substantially from the very rapid job growth which occurred during World War II. The gains established during those years are being carried forward now by a somewhat better educated generation, whose qualifications enable them to obtain many middle-income jobs. Of course, the industrial growth in California attracted many of the better-educated Mexican-Americans to the state from Texas and other parts of the Southwest. In addition, the high wage level in California has been of some help even to the *relative* earnings and incomes of Mexican-Americans. This high wage level is accompanied by an occupational earnings structure in which manual workers are better paid compared to nonmanual persons than is the case in other states of the Southwest. There is also evidence that job discrimination against Mexican-Americans is least pervasive in California; but even in California Mexican-Americans are disadvantaged. And California remains the promised land for many Americans—for those of Mexican heritage it is seen as holding forth the glowing promise of equality. Where realities do not measure up to the promise, bitterness gradually fills the gap, and so, ironically, it is in California where the pressure and confrontations are most likely to come and where, consequently, Mexican-Americans and Anglos are likely to do most in improving the terms on which the former will participate in the economic life of the region.

PROGRESS OVER TIME

Mexican-Americans made discernible gains in occupational upgrading and income between 1950 and 1960; however, the time period is too short and the data too imperfect to justify any estimates as to when they might "catch up." Their gains were greater than those made by Negroes and most other nonwhite groups. But it is also clear that Mexican-American gains during the 1950s were not as great as those which have been found for Negroes in the 1940s and, presumably, took place during that decade for Mexican-Americans as well. Thus, without social and economic changes comparable in magnitude to those of the war years, "catching up" is likely to be a slow process.

Occupational upgrading appears to have occurred a little more rapidly than increases in income. This may bring about greater income gains in the future, since incomes are more strongly related to experience in the nonmanual sector, where the upgrading is occurring, than in manual occupations.

Although the data which were available for examining long-term change were limited, they disclosed a marked upgrading of Mexican-American occupational position in the Southwest between 1930 and 1960. There were, however, large differences among the states in this regard. Much of the upgrading occurred as a result of shifts in the regional composition of the Mexican-American population—from Texas and the rest of the Southwest to California. Within California, itself, there were sharp gains in the occupational position of this group. Most of the Mexican-American gains in this 30-year period occurred during the war years, as a result of the huge increases in employment which took place in a very short time span. These increases put great pressure on labor supply and brought down many barriers of qualification and discrimination which had previously impeded Mexican-American progress. Gains in Texas were fairly small, even in the war years, not only because growth in industrial employment was less than in California, but also because, in Texas, there were large numbers of Anglo workers who, being underemployed in agriculture when the war began, moved into new industrial jobs ahead of Mexican-Americans.

The movement of the Mexican-American population from Texas and other states of the region to California contributed to the gains made by this group during the 1950s, as well as over the longer period. There are, of course, limits on the ability of California to absorb immigrants into employment. Whether these limitations will become more or less severe in the future is not known with certainty, though a decline in military expenditures by the federal government would definitely increase their severity.

SOME JUDGMENTS ABOUT THE FUTURE

Mexican-Americans will continue to make progress in the future, but the rate at which gains will be made is the important question. We believe that the pace of progress for this ethnic minority will be slow; there will not be any dramatic closure of the economic gap existing between Mexican-Americans and Anglos. This assessment is suggested by the relevant facts which are available. The gains made between 1950 and 1960, the only period for which we have much information, were rather small. The gains made between generations (nativity classes) of Mexican-Americans are also small, at least those occurring after the second generation. Indeed, the very small advances made by third and successive generations over the position of second-generation Mexican-Americans is most disturbing when we consider the future progress of this minority.

Our assessment that the rate at which Mexican-Americans will make economic progress will be slow is not altered by examination of the several influences most likely to affect that rate. One of these is the pace of immigration from Mexico. In this regard, U.S. citizens who are deeply interested in the advancement of human welfare face a real dilemma. Even though immigrants from Mexico generally hold poor jobs and receive low wages, their economic livelihood in this country is superior to the one which they have left behind, far superior in many cases.[1] For this reason unrestricted immigration from Mexico seems humane, but the large number of immigrants in the Mexican-American population do compete in job markets (and other markets, such as housing) with the native-born Mexican-American population, and, in so doing, lower the economic livelihood of the latter. The immigrants also affect the image which Anglos have of this minority group as a whole, the image which forms the basis for many hiring and promotion decisions. Gross generalizations affecting employment decisions can and should be deplored, but they will continue to be made. Immigrant additions to the Mexican-American population lower the average schooling, job skills, and language facility of this minority, and thereby help to perpetuate the Anglo generalization that Mexican-Americans are unskilled workers. At the present time a policy of numerical limitation on immigration from Mexico is under congressional study, perhaps partly as a result of the large numbers of Mexicans who have come into the United States in the last ten years or so.[2] If immigration from Mexico is restricted to a number much below the 45,000 annual average which

[1] Leo Grebler, *Mexican Immigration to the United States: The Record and Its Implications* (Mexican-American Study Project, Advance Report 2, UCLA, 1965), pp. 79–83.

[2] Grebler, pp. 95–100.

prevailed in the first half of the 1960s,[3] the rate of economic progress of the Mexican-American minority will increase, not greatly, but at least perceptibly. A program to raise sharply the rate of economic advancement for this minority would call for a complete prohibition on immigration from Mexico. But it is hardly imaginable that the U.S. citizenry could become so narrowly obsessed with its own social and economic problems that it would completely shut the doors of the country to the many disadvantaged residents of Mexico.

Future gains of the Mexican-American population also depend upon how fast the group raises its educational attainment and other job qualifications. In this respect Mexican-Americans have a very long way to go to catch up with the majority population. Signs of progress are appearing— the educational gap is much less for young Mexican-Americans than for older ones—but there is not yet enough evidence to extrapolate the future. Continuing structural shifts in the labor force, plus the ever increasing educational attainment of the majority population, accentuate the necessity for educational gains for Mexican-Americans. The most rapidly growing jobs usually employ only people who have at least a high-school education; the best paid of these jobs require more. Future generations of Mexican-Americans who enter the labor force must bring with them *much* higher levels of educational attainment than those possessed by past generations if significant economic gains are to be made. Little can be expected from the manual sector, for the number of manual jobs is growing slowly, at best; and even to compete against others for the manual jobs which do become vacant, Mexican-Americans will, in most cases, need a high-school diploma (assuming that selection for manual jobs continues to emphasize schooling). Mexican-Americans are indeed on a treadmill in their attempt to make educational progress. In twenty years they may be able to raise their average schooling to almost the level of high-school graduation, but by then the Anglo level may be only a year or two away from college graduation.[4] A more intelligent assessment by our society of the relationship of formal schooling to job performance would help Mexican-Americans, but it is unlikely to take place in the absence of severe labor shortages.

It must also be kept in mind that the economic benefits of schooling are greatest in the latter half of working lives—at ages above 45 for most people.[5] Thus, the economic gains of Mexican-Americans will lag behind whatever improvements in educational attainment they are able to make.

[3] Grebler, p. 8, table 1.

[4] This is a rough inference from data in U.S. Office of Education, Projection of Educational Statistics to 1974–75 (Washington, 1965).

[5] See Amartya K. Sen, "Education, Labor, and Learning by Doing," *Journal of Human Resources* (Fall 1966), pp. 3–21.

Finally, future economic gains of Mexican-Americans depend upon reductions in labor market discrimination. Very likely, there will be reductions in the pervasiveness of discrimination, stemming from recent antidiscrimination legislation and from increased recognition of and concern with minority-group problems on the part of employers, especially large ones, and union leaders.

18 / Urban Indian Employment in Minneapolis

ARTHUR HARKINS
RICHARD WOODS

To a limited extent, the problems faced by American Indians in finding employment are similar to those of Mexican-Americans. Indians also have lived predominantly in rural areas and have neither the training nor education to compete in the urban labor market of modern America. In addition, they frequently lack the basic English language skills to be able to apply for jobs. The major difference between the groups is that Indians have a place to return to if they fail—the reservation. This, however, may be more of a liability than an asset, because the opportunity to retreat may discourage greater effort to succeed. The federal government has attempted to assist Indians in obtaining better jobs through such programs as the adult vocational training program and through a series of grants under the war on poverty. Financial support for these efforts has not been very great, with only $12 million allocated in 1964, $15 million in 1965, and $25 million in 1968 for the vocational training program. In addition to this limited support for job training programs, the Indian faces the prob-

Source: Arthur Harkins and Richard Woods, *Attitudes of Minneapolis Agency Personnel toward Urban Indians* (Minneapolis: Training Center for Community Programs in coordination with the Office of Community Programs, Center for Urban and Regional Affairs, University of Minnesota, December 1968), pp. 2–5, 35, 37–38.

lem of prejudice. He is still stereotyped by many public and private employers as the drunken, lazy, illiterate of the nineteenth century, as the following reading indicates.

[The following are findings from a study of problem areas of Indian Americans in the urban setting by the League of Women Voters of Minneapolis in collaboration with the Training Center for Community Programs, University of Minnesota.]

EMPLOYMENT PROBLEMS OF INDIANS

1. Many Indians migrate to Minneapolis in response to the attraction of job opportunities, yet "many Indians looking for work in a competitive urban society are unprepared for it."

2. Indians new to the city may arrive with few clothes and little money. They may move in with already overcrowded friends or relatives. Such conditions make it difficult for Indians to maintain the sort of appearance necessary for finding employment.

3. Indians may be uneasy about working with non-Indians and about the prerequisites of work—"application blanks, interviews, referrals, and questions that seem too personal or irrelevant. Standardized tests are standardized for a majority, alien society."

4. Employment assistance provided by the Bureau of Indian Affairs is available by application through the Bureau's reservation offices. However, the Indian who comes to the city on his own is not eligible for help from the BIA, since BIA programs are "viewed as a part of the Bureau's responsibility as trustee of Indian lands." This is doubtless confusing to many Indians. "An Indian in a reservation area receiving services from the BIA believes that he has received these services because he is Indian, and not because of the trust status of his land. He comes to expect that he will not be eligible for assistance in the manner prescribed for non-Indians. When he comes to the city, then, he does not look for help in the channels set up to serve all citizens."

5. "City and county agencies in the metropolitan area report that Indians tend not to use their services, or that they are easily discouraged and tend not to return."

6. Indians without marketable skills or with employment problems may be eligible for Human Resources Development services of the Minnesota State Employment Service designed to improve employability. Indians seem to prefer dealing with Indian employees of the MSES. The MSES has employment specialists outstationed at the Citizens Community Centers, and it also utilizes neighborhood workers to reach the unemployed, including Indians.

7. The American Indian Employment and Guidance Center, established in 1962, was formed in the belief that special Indian problems necessitated a special Indian agency. Plagued by sporadic funding, the Center has had an intermittent history culminating in its funding by the BIA as the nation's first government-financed employment office for urban Indians. It was closed after BIA funds were discontinued at the end of fiscal 1968.

8. "It appears that Indians who come to the Indian Employment Center are persons who feel that they need an agency *for Indians*. If they are not willing or able to use the community's services, a service they *will* use may have to be provided."

9. Few Indians are government employees, perhaps due to difficulties in passing civil service examinations. Since 1962 only three formal and informal complaints have been filed by Indians with the Minneapolis Fair Employment Practices Commission.

10. A few Indians are managing to work their way around Civil Service problems through the New Careers Program.

11. The Minneapolis Rehabilitation Center's "Plans for Progress" Project is one which serves clients referred by the Youth Opportunity Center for rehabilitation of job attitudes and training for stable employment. In spring 1968 twelve of the eighteen youths in the project were Indian.

12. It appears that many Indian women seek domestic work. Placements of this sort occur regularly at the State Employment Service and at Unity Settlement House.

13. It appears that few Indians become involved with such organizations as the Career Clinic for Mature Women, TCOIC, and the Public Schools' Work Opportunity Center.

14. "The Equal Employment Opportunity Commission of the federal government reported last fall that there were 785 American Indians employed in the five-county metropolitan area. Of these, 148 held white-collar jobs and 637 (81 percent) held blue-collar jobs. The survey covered all employers having 100 or more employees, or having five or more employees and a federal government contract in excess of $50,000. According to a newspaper report, this survey covered 292,000 out of a total of 303,000 persons employed in the area."

15. "For that portion of the Indian population accepting the standards, customs and traditions of 'white America,' employment presents no real problems. However, other Indians seem to have rejected some of these values of 'getting ahead' and acquiring material wealth as having little meaning to them."

16. At various times, a center for Indian newcomers or an all-Indian workshop have been suggested as a bridge between reservation life and the city.

17. "New approaches will have to be developed for the employment of Indian citizens. Involved in such approaches must be the recognition of cultural factors, unfamiliarity and distrust of established institutions and testing techniques, and confusion caused by the proliferation of agencies that want to be of help."

ATTITUDES OF EMPLOYMENT AND OTHER AGENCY PERSONNEL TOWARD INDIANS

Personnel in six types of Minneapolis agencies were asked for their impressions of Indian adults and youth living in the Twin Cities. Their ratings were obtained by using a "semantic differential" questionnaire employing twenty-six paired adjectives. A scoring system indicated the strength and direction of responses for each pair of adjectives. The types of agencies surveyed and the number of respondents who mailed a useable questionnaire are as follows:

Agency Type	Number of Respondents
Employment	43
Health	32
Miscellaneous	88
(Park, Library, United Fund)	
Education	133
Welfare	170
Law and Corrections	230
	696

. . . These responses indicate that the agency person's view of the young Indian in the Twin Cities was predominately positive. Only respondents from health agencies made less than a favorable judgment on balance, and that judgment was neutral. Descriptive adjectives attached to Twin Cities Indian youth by respondents from *all six* agency categories were: untrustworthy, brave, unreliable, sad, honest, knowledgeable, interested, ambitious, and unwise. Consensus about descriptive adjectives for *five of the six* agency groups studied centered around the terms insincere, friendly, intelligent, cruel, active, undependable, polite and peace-loving. There was consensus among *four of the six* agency groups about the appropriateness of the terms neat, modern, and religious. *Three of the six* agency groups described young Indians as quiet and likeable.

Second, the prevailing agency view of the Indian adult in the Twin Cities tended to be negative, although one agency (welfare) produced a neutral rating, and two others (education and miscellaneous) were only slightly negative. Descriptive adjectives deemed appropriate for Twin Cities adult Indians by respondents from *all six* agency categories were: ignorant, hard-working, cruel, sincere, peace-loving, dependable, and quiet. Agreement about descriptive terms for *five of the six agency* groups studied included stupid, unsociable, rational, unlikeable, dishonest, polite, unreliable, and bored. There was consensus among *four of the six* agency groups about the appropriateness of the terms irreligious, traditionalistic, sad, active, cowardly, untrustworthy, and courteous. *Three of the six* agency groups described adult Indians as friendly and ambitious.

From these data, it can be seen that with law and corrections personnel, employment personnel rated Indian adults lowest when compared with the other four agency categories. The effects of these views upon the Indian person seeking employment are, of course, not ascertainable from these data, but it is apparent that Minneapolis employment personnel are not particularly enthusiastic about the Indian adults with whom they come into contact. It is probable that these attitudes do negatively affect the style and impact of job counselling and other forms of professional-client interaction.

chapter five

LAW ENFORCEMENT

(

19 / *Screws* v. *United States*

Screws v. *U.S.* represents in very stark terms the tremendously serious problem of the role of the police in building healthy racial understanding. The case illustrates that in the South the police have failed objectively to enforce the law and have allowed their racial attitudes to interfere with their work. It also draws attention to the broader problem of police violation if the constitutional rights of a person accused of a crime, in this case a black who was arrested by Sheriff Screws for allegedly stealing a tire and ultimately beaten to death. Screws was not accused of murder because it would have been impossible to get a conviction for that crime in his home state of Georgia; instead, he was accused of depriving the deceased of his rights under the Constitution. As a result of cases such as *Screws* v. *U.S.*, the Supreme Court has become increasingly cognizant not only of the blatant mistreatment of blacks, but of the more subtle mistreatment of all people. (Two results of the Courts awareness are the right to counsel for a defendant and the right of a voter to have his vote counted as equal to all others.)

Mr. Justice Douglas announced the judgment of the Court and delivered the following opinion, in which the Chief Justice, Mr. Justice Black and Mr. Justice Reed concur.

SOURCE: *Screws* v. *U.S.,* 325 U.S. 91, Sup. Ct. 1031, 89 L.Ed. 1495 (1945).

This case involves a shocking and revolting episode in law enforcement. Petitioner Screws was sheriff of Baker County, Georgia. He enlisted the assistance of petitioner Jones, a policeman, and petitioner Kelley, a special deputy, in arresting Robert Hall, a citizen of the United States and of Georgia. The arrest was made late at night at Hall's home on a warrant charging Hall with theft of a tire. Hall, a young negro about thirty years of age, was handcuffed and taken by car to the court house. As Hall alighted from the car at the court-house square, the three petitioners began beating him with their fists and with a solid-bar blackjack about eight inches long and weighing two pounds. They claimed Hall had reached for a gun and had used insulting language as he alighted from the car. But after Hall, still handcuffed, had been knocked to the ground they continued to beat him from fifteen to thirty minutes until he was unconscious. Hall was then dragged feet first through the court-house yard into the jail and thrown upon the floor dying. An ambulance was called and Hall was removed to a hospital where he died within the hour and without regaining consciousness. There was evidence that Screws held a grudge against Hall and had threatened to "get" him.

An indictment was returned against petitioners—one count charging a violation of §20 of the Criminal Code, 18 U.S.C. §52 and another charging a conspiracy to violate §20 contrary to §37 of the Criminal Code, 18 U.S.C. §88. Sec. 20 provides:

"Whoever, under color of any law, statute, ordinance, regulation, or custom, willfully subjects, or causes to be subjected, any inhabitant of any State, Territory, or District to the deprivation of any rights, privileges, or immunities secured or protected by the Constitution and laws of the United States, or to different punishments, pains, or penalties, on account of such inhabitant being an alien, or by reason of his color, or race, than are prescribed for the punishment of citizens, shall be fined not more than $1000, or imprisoned not more than one year, or both." The indictment charged that petitioners, acting under color of the laws of Georgia, "willfully" caused Hall to be deprived of "rights, privileges, or immunities secured or protected" to him by the Fourteenth Amendment—the right not to be deprived of life without due process of law; the right to be tried, upon the charge on which he was arrested, by due process of law and if found guilty to be punished in accordance with the laws of Georgia; . . . A like charge was made in the conspiracy count.

The case was tried to a jury. The court charged the jury that due process of law gave one charged with a crime the right to be tried by a jury and sentenced by a court. On the question of intent it charged that

". . . if these defendants, without its being necessary to make the arrest effectual or necessary to their own personal protection, beat this man, assaulted him or killed him while he was under arrest, then they would be acting illegally under color of law, as stated by this statute, and would be depriving the prisoner of certain constitutional rights guaranteed to him by the Constitution of the United States and consented to by the State of Georgia."

The jury returned a verdict of guilty and a fine and imprisonment on each count was imposed. The Circuit Court of Appeals affirmed the judgment of conviction, one judge dissenting. 140 F.2d 662. The case is here on a petition for a writ of certiorari which we granted because of the importance in the administration of the criminal laws of the questions presented. . . .

It is said, however, that petitioners did not act "under color of any law" within the meaning of §20 of the Criminal Code. We disagree. We are of the view that petitioners acted under "color" of law in making the arrest of Robert Hall and in assaulting him. They were officers of the law who made the arrest. By their own admissions they assaulted Hall in order to protect themselves and to keep their prisoner from escaping. It was their duty under Georgia law to make the arrest effective. Hence, their conduct comes within the statute. . . .

We agree that when this statute is applied to the action of state officials, it should be construed so as to respect the proper balance between the States and the federal government in law enforcement. Violation of local law does not necessarily mean that federal rights have been invaded. The fact that a prisoner is assaulted, injured, or even murdered by state officials does not necessarily mean that he is deprived of any right protected or secured by the Constitution or laws of the United States. Cf. *Logan* v. *United States,* 144 U.S. 263, dealing with assaults by federal officials. The Fourteenth Amendment did not alter the basic relations between the States and the national government. *United States* v. *Harris,* 106 U.S. 629; *In re Kemmler,* 136 U.S. 436, 448. Our national government is one of delegated powers alone. Under our federal system the administration of criminal justice rests with the States except as Congress, acting within the scope of those delegated powers, has created offenses against the United States. *Jerome* v. *United States,* 318 U.S. 101, 105. . . . It is only state action of a "particular character" that is prohibited by the Fourteenth Amendment and against which the Amendment authorizes Congress to afford relief. *Civil Rights Cases,* 109 U.S. 3, 11, 13. Thus Congress in §20 of the Criminal Code did not undertake to make all torts of state officials federal crimes. It brought within §20 only specified acts done "under color" of law and then only those acts which deprived a person of some right secured by the Constitution of laws of the United States.

This section was before us in *United States* v. *Classic,* 313 U.S. 299, 326, where we said: "Misuse of power, possessed by virtue of state law and made possible only because the wrongdoer is clothed with the authority of state law, is action taken 'under color of' state law." In that case state election officials were charged with failure to count the votes as cast, alteration of the ballots, and false certification of the number of votes cast for the respective candidates. 313 U.S. pp. 308–309. We stated that those acts of the defendants "were committed in the course of their performance of duties under the Louisiana statute requiring them to count the ballots, to record the result of the count, and to certify the result of the election." Id., pp. 325–326. In the present case, as we have said, the defendants were officers of the law who had made an arrest and who by their own admissions made the assault in order to protect themselves and to keep the prisoner from escaping, i.e., to make the arrest effective. That was a duty they had under Georgia law. *United States* v. *Classic* is, therefore, indistinguishable from this case so far as "under color of" state law is concerned. . . .

It is said that we should abandon the holding of the *Classic* case. It is suggested that the present problem was not clearly in focus in that case and that its holding was ill-advised. A reading of the opinion makes plain that the question was squarely involved and squarely met. It followed the rule announced in *Ex parte Virginia,* 100 U.S. 339, 346, that a state judge who in violation of state law discriminated against negroes in the selection of juries violated the Act of March 1, 1875, 18 Stat. 336. It is true that that statute did not contain the words under "color" of law. But the Court in deciding what was state action within the meaning of the Fourteenth Amendment held that it was immaterial that the state officer exceeded the limits of his authority. ". . . as he acts in the name and for the State, and is clothed with the State's power, his act is that of the State. This must be so, or the constitutional prohibition has no meaning. Then the State has clothed one of its agents with power to annul or to evade it." 100 U.S. at p. 347. And see *Virginia* v. *Rives,* 100 U.S. 313, 321. The *Classic* case recognized, without dissent, that the contrary view would defeat the great purpose which §20 was designed to serve. Reference is made to statements of Senator Trumbull in his discussion of §2 of the Civil Rights Act of 1866, 14 Stat. 27, and to statements of Senator Sherman concerning the 1870 Act as supporting the conclusion that "under color of any law" was designed to include only action taken by officials pursuant to state law. But those statements in their context are inconclusive on the precise problem involved in the *Classic* case and in the present case. We are not dealing here with a case where an officer not authorized to act nevertheless takes action. Here the state officers were authorized to make an arrest and to take such steps as were necessary to make the arrest effective. They acted without authority only in the sense that they used excessive force in making the arrest effective. It is clear that under "color" of law means under "pretense" of law. Thus acts of officers in the ambit of their personal pursuits are plainly excluded. Acts of officers who undertake to perform their official duties are included whether they hew to the line of their authority or overstep it. If, as suggested, the statute was designed to embrace only action which the State in fact authorized, the words "under color of any law" were hardly apt words to express the idea. . . .

But beyond that is the problem of stare decisis. The construction given §20 in the *Classic* case formulated a rule of law which has become the basis of federal enforcement in this important field. The rule adopted in that case was formulated after mature consideration. It should be good for more than one day only. We do not have here a situation comparable to *Mahnich* v. *Southern S.S. Co.,* 321 U.S. 96, where we overruled a decision demonstrated to be a sport in the law and inconsistent with what preceded and what followed. The *Classic* case was not the product of hasty action or inadvertence. It was not out of line with the cases which preceded. It was designed to fashion the governing rule of law in this important field. We are not dealing with constitutional interpretations which throughout the history of the Court have wisely remained flexible and subject to frequent reexamination. The meaning which the *Classic* case gave to the phrase "under color of any law" involved only a construction of the statute. Hence if it state a rule undesirable in its consequences, Congress can change it. We add only to the instability and uncertainty of the law if we revise the meaning of §20 to meet the exigencies of each case coming before us.

20 / Justice for Blacks

U.S. COMMISSION ON CIVIL RIGHTS

> Some people have objected that times have changed since the
> *Screws* decision in 1945. Actual evidence points to the con-
> trary. The period since the 1945 decision reveals more, not
> less, police malpractice. Similar evidence is available not only
> from other court decisions but from recent confrontations be-
> tween blacks and the community. The use of dogs, electric
> prods, high-pressure water hoses, and horses by the police in
> Birmingham, Selma, and other southern cities exposed to na-
> tional view the blatant disregard for the rights of blacks. Po-
> lice chiefs such as "Bull" Connor became associated with the
> use of the law to prevent blacks from exercising their civil
> rights. This excerpt from the report of the Civil Rights Com-
> mission represents the first attempt to document systemati-
> cally the extent of police malpractice. The result is a picture
> of verbal and physical abuse, disregard for individual rights,
> and police behavior that violates the constitutional require-
> ments of due process and equal protection under the law.

There is much to be proud of in the American system of criminal justice.
For it is administered largely without regard to the race, creed, or color of

SOURCE: U.S. Commission on Civil Rights, *Report,* Book 5, "Justice" (Washington, D.C.: U.S. Government Printing Office, 1961) pp. 105–109.

the persons involved. Most officials at all levels attempt to perform their duties within the bounds of constitutionality and fairness. Most policemen never resort to brutality, thus providing constant proof that effective law enforcement is possible without brutality. And the great majority of American policemen have an excellent record of successfully discouraging mob violence against minority group members. This record shows that policemen who make it clear that they will not tolerate vigilante violence can prevent that violence.

Unfortunately, this is not the whole story. The Commission is concerned about the number of unconstitutional and criminal acts committed by agents of American justice who are sworn to uphold the law and to apply it impartially. Perhaps the most flagrant of these acts is the illegal use of violence. Indeed, a comprehensive review of available evidence indicates that police brutality is still a serious and continuing problem.

When policemen take the law into their own hands, assuming the roles of judge, jury, and, sometimes, executioner, they do so for a variety of reasons. Some officers take it upon themselves to enforce segregation or the Negro's subordinate status. Brutality of this nature occurs most often in those places where racial segregation has the force of tradition behind it. Other types of unlawful official violence are unrelated to race or region. In Florida's Raiford Prison, recently, guards took the occasion of minor rules infractions to subject prisoners of both races to inhuman treatment. Perhaps the most frequent setting for brutality is found in the initial contact between an officer and a suspect. The fact that an officer approaches a private citizen and seeks to question him, to search him, or to arrest him, creates a tense situation in which violence may erupt at any moment. The use of brutality to coerce confessions appears to be diminishing but has not disappeared.

Complete statistics on the subject of police brutality are not available, but the Commission's comprehensive survey of records at the Department of Justice suggests that although whites are not immune, Negroes feel the brunt of official brutality, proportionately, more than any other group in American society.

The Commission has been concerned with another serious (although far less widespread) dereliction of duty by American police officers—condonation of or connivance in private violence. Although this practice appears to be on the wane, it has not been totally abandoned. The most recent victims were the "Freedom Riders" in Alabama. There are American citizens in the Deep South today who live in fear, partly because they do not know if local policemen will help them or the mob when violence strikes.

On the other hand, it is encouraging for the Commission to report that lynching, another form of mob violence which frequently involved police assistance, may be extinct. Yet, the threat lives on in the memory of many Negroes.

While the discriminatory exclusion of Negroes and other minority groups from juries has diminished during the past century, this badge of inequality persists in the judicial systems of many southern counties.

By and large, frustration and defeat face the victim of these unconstitutional practices who seeks redress—for he rarely is able to obtain immediate or effective relief. A victim of these unconstitutional practices may bring action in a State court to recover money damages from the brutal policeman. The record indicates that the prospects for a verdict for the complainant in such suits are greater than in other forms of court action either at the Federal or State level. However, most victims do not commence legal action against brutal policemen, and one of the severe drawbacks of such litigation is that even if a plaintiff overcomes the difficulties of trial and is awarded a money judgment, most municipalities are not liable for their officers' misconduct, and the policemen themselves rarely have funds to satisfy a substantial money judgment.

The victim of brutality may also request a local prosecutor to bring criminal action in a State court against the policemen. For policemen, like ordinary citizens, are subject to criminal penalties ranging from jail or fines for simple assault and battery up to the death penalty for first degree murder. Such prosecutions may have a deterrent effect on police misbehavior, but they are rare.

In addition to these State and local avenues of redress there are the Federal Civil Rights Acts, providing both civil and criminal remedies. But suits in Federal courts under these Acts are few and usually unsuccessful. The civil statutes offer the advantage of allowing the victim himself to commence action for money damages against officers who have violated his constitutional right. In a recent 2-year period, however, only 42 Federal civil suits were filed based on police brutality allegations, and none of them were successful. In a recent 2½-year period the Department of Justice authorized criminal prosecutions in 52 police brutality matters. During the same period, six prosecutions were successful. It is probable that during these periods thousands of acts of brutality were committed in this country.

There are certain inherent difficulties in suits which seek redress for acts of violence. The victim is often ignorant of remedies for police misconduct and loath, because of lethargy or fear, to report violations to responsible authorities. Even where suit is brought, there are obstacles to successful prosecution. There are frequently no witnesses and little concrete evidence to corroborate the complainant's story; the police officer usually makes a more believable witness than the complainant; and the jury is often hostile to a civil rights suit in Federal court against a local policeman. The Commission believes, however, that the Department of Justice by taking the initiative in seeking out information and, in appropriate cases, by instituting prosecutions might make the Federal Civil Rights Acts more effective instruments—despite these inherent difficulties.

Victims of civil rights violations sometimes assume that Federal officers are closely linked with local policemen. They may, therefore, be reluctant to report unlawful violence or to sign complaints. They fear that complaints either will be useless or will result in retaliation by the local policemen. It is, of course, essential that the FBI have the cooperation of thousands of local policemen to carry out its investigative mission under a long list of Federal criminal statutes not related to civil rights. Investigations of police brutality complaints may, therefore, place FBI agents in an exceedingly delicate position.

The Department of Justice policy of deference to State authorities is another problem in Civil Rights Acts prosecutions. When State authorities take steps to prosecute local law officers for acts of brutality, the Civil Rights Division of the Department suspends both investigation and prosecution. While this practice may satisfy the States, where State action proves ineffective, Federal investigation and prosecution has sometimes been made impractical by the passage of time.

When such a case does get into court, U.S. attorneys represent the Federal Government. Some U.S. attorneys have displayed unfamiliarity with the complex case law that has developed around the Federal Civil Rights Acts. Indeed, a few attorneys have displayed open hostility to Civil Rights Acts prosecutions.

There may also be other difficulties in obtaining an indictment. Grand juries in some places refuse to return indictments under the Civil Rights Acts even in the most heinous of cases; in a recent 2½-year period grand juries refused to indict in at least 16 of the 43 police brutality cases the Department of Justice filed in court. But the grand jury is not a necessary step. The Federal Government prosecutes brutal officers under section 242 of the United States Criminal Code, and since that statute defines only a misdemeanor, action may be taken by way of information (a sworn statement setting out the specific charges against the defendant) as well as by grand jury indictment. Prosecution was initiated by information in one case, brought in the early 1940s. It was successful.

Other difficulties in the prosecution of Federal criminal suits under the Civil Rights Acts arise from the 16-year-old Supreme Court decision in *Screws* v. *United States.* It was there held that to sustain a prosecution under section 242 the Government had to prove that the officers had the "specific intent" to violate the constitutional rights of the victim. If the of-

ficers merely had the general criminal intent to hurt him, the Supreme
Court explained, this would not be sufficient for a conviction under the
Federal statute. This requirement is onerous. It accounts for some of the
hesitancy of the Department of Justice to authorize prosecutions, and of
juries to render guilty verdicts. Remedial action by Congress is necessary
to make Federal criminal prosecutions effective deterrents to unlawful police violence.

The most important remedies for improper police practices, however,
lie in preventive measures on the local level. There is concrete evidence
that when a police commander indicates that he will not tolerate brutality
or other illegal practices, these practices cease. Atlanta and Chicago,
among other cities, provide examples of how positive and enlightened
leadership in the police department can reduce the incidence of unlawful
police violence. By the same token, the available evidence indicates that
some policemen have interpreted permissive leadership as a license for
brutality. Leadership may also have an impact on private violence with
police connivance, as dramatically illustrated by recent events in Alabama
and conversely, by the less dramatic but positive work of community leaders in Atlanta and, subsequent to the 1957 disturbances, in Little Rock.

Proper recruit selection standards may also reduce police misconduct.
Such standards are nonexistent in some departments; others are attempting
improvement of psychological tests to weed out those recruits prone to
violence. Training programs in human relations and in scientific police
techniques are also important factors in the prevention of violent invasions
of rights by policemen.

In 1880 the Supreme Court declared for the first time that the discriminatory exclusion of otherwise qualified citizens from jury panels was
a violation of the equal protection clause of the 14th amendment. In the
ensuing years the Supreme Court has reiterated that ruling time and time
again. It is also a Federal crime for any official to disqualify a citizen for
jury service because of his race, color, or previous condition of servitude.
One of the Civil Rights Acts (section 243) passed in 1875 makes such action punishable by a fine of $5000. But in some counties the practice of
jury exclusion is an enduring institution, and the initiative for challenging
this patently unconstitutional practice has been left by default to private
citizens. Apparently, the Department of Justice has brought only one successful section 243 prosecution, and this was in the late 1870s. The jury
exclusion issue is raised most often by Negro defendants convicted by all-
white juries. Recently, however, a colored citizen of McCracken County,
Kentucky, sought an injunction under one of the Civil Rights Acts to prevent jury officials from excluding Negroes. This action apparently has resulted in the elimination of unconstitutional jury exclusion in that county.

There can be no reasonable dissent to the proposition that all Americans, regardless of race, creed, color, or national origin, are entitled to equal justice under law. Police brutality, connivance in private violence, and exclusion of minorities from jury service violate ideals of fair play fundamental to a free society. All three are contrary to our Constitution and our heritage.

21 / The Algiers Motel Incident

JOHN HERSEY

> The tensions between the police and the urban minority com-
> munity, whether black or Mexican-American, have been the
> fuel for several of the major conflagrations of the 1960s. An ar-
> rest triggered the Watts riots; and in such cities as Newark
> and Cleveland, police-black tensions have either magnified or
> extended the conflict. In the case of Watts, statements by
> Chief of Police William Parker referring to the blacks as mon-
> keys worked to alienate the blacks further. In addition, in
> Watts and elsewhere, excessive use of force pushed neutral
> minority group members into support for the rioters, aggravat-
> ing the crisis.
>   In the Detroit riot of 1967 a group of policemen beat and
> murdered three Negro youths at the Algiers Motel on the out-
> skirts of the riot area. The incident, analyzed by John Hersey
> in this selection, contains almost all of the ingredients of po-
> lice-minority (and broader majority-minority) tension: police-
> men taking law into their own hands; racist thinking by men
> who did not believe they were racist; interracial sex; ambigu-
> ous justice in the court; and the devastation in the lives of
> both black and white in the wake of violence.

Source: From *The Algiers Motel Incident,* by John Hersey. Copyright © 1968
by John Hersey. Reprinted by permission of Alfred A. Knopf, Inc., pp. 248–249,
251–252, 271–272, 281–282.

"Before we went into the hall, we heard some other shots which sounded like to our right or the back of the building. . . ." One line of speculation followed by the investigators associates these shots with the death of Fred Temple in room A-3; the timing of this death is not agreed upon by various witnesses. "We went into the hall. There was a few people out in the hall going back and forth in the rooms and coming out. They were dressed in light-blue shirts, dark-blue pants, and were wearing helmets"—uniform, during the uprising, of the Detroit police.

"At this time," Fonger wrote in his report, "a Detroit Officer came out of the room followed by another unloading a nickel covered pistol, and saying, 'That one tried for my gun.' It is not clear to this officer if these men were City Policemen, or private policemen, as they were not wearing a badge or other identifying items." It had, however, been clear to Fonger, in the darkness at the back door, that Detroit policemen preceded him into the building.

"There were two officers that came out," Fonger testified, "and one of them had a nickel-plated revolver and he was taking the shells out of the gun and he said, 'That one tried for my gun,' . . . or, 'That one had a gun.' We then went into the room and there was a Negro male lying against the bed with numerous holes in him—or I should say—I'll have to clarify that also. He was bleeding from the front in numerous spots. His eyes were open."

"It appeared to this officer," Fonger wrote, "that this subject was still alive, as it appeared as he was breathing. . . .

"This officer then went back into the hall and observed two officers dressed as those described above, drag a Negro male with black pants and a black piece of material over his hair out of a room, and put him against a wall of the hall. Another Negro male, with only his under shorts, was then dragged out and also placed against the wall. . . . A remark was made that they should pray."

"We checked the room which would be to the front," Fonger testified, "to the west, which would be probably the southwest corner. . . . We checked this room for snipers. We checked the closet, we checked the bathroom. We came out of the room." . . .

How had Ronald August, Robert Paille, David Senak, and the other Detroit police officers at the Algiers during the incident been trained to behave in these circumstances?

The *Riot Control Plan* of the Detroit Police Department, in a chapter entitled "Guide Lines for the Individual Officer," gives these instructions:

"Maximum effectiveness will result if the officers at the scene are able to gain and hold the respect of the rioting element. This respect will be attained by a thoroughly professional approach to the problem. . . .

"Conduct: Courteous but firm. Policemen must maintain a completely neutral attitude at the scene of a disorder and completely avoid fraternization with either element. He should strenuously avoid the use of insulting terms and names. Expressions which may be used casually without thought of offending are nevertheless offensive to members of minority groups and invariably antagonize the person or group to whom they are addressed. . . .

"Listen to and take command from your superior officers. . . .

" 'Hand-to-hand' fighting or individual combat must be avoided as far as possible. . . .

"Never at any time should a single officer attempt to handle one rioter. The idea of individual heroic police action is not only unnecessary, it may be positively damaging and foolhardy. . . .

"Don't be prejudicial or guilty of unnecessary or rough handling of persons involved. Use only that force which is necessary to maintain order, effect the arrest, and protect oneself from bodily harm.

"The officer assigned to crowd control must always act in such a manner as to insure impartial enforcement of the law, and afford to all citizens the rights guaranteed to them by the Constitution and the legislative statutes." . . .

"One of the officers," Lee told me, "he said, 'We're going to get rid of all you pimps and whores.' They asked the girls did they want to die first or watch us die."

"Questioned them up against the wall," Early's notes said, "& ripped all K's clothes off & half of Juli's. Policeman said, 'Hey, you broads, do you want to die first or see the others & then go?' "

"One of the policemen," Roderick said to me, "told the girls to take off their clothes. Senak pulled them out to the center of the room. Tore one of them's dress off—hooked it with the thing on the end of his gun—and made the other one pull her dress off. He said, 'Why you got to fuck them? What's wrong with us, you nigger lovers?' "

Sortor testified in court that both girls had their dresses torn. "I seen one, had her clothes—uh—off. . . . I seen the officers pull them off. . . . The policemen . . . and some Army mens. . . . All of them pulled, pulled her clothes off her." The girl, Sortor testified, wound up naked except "just her panties."

"The officers," the police synopsis on Sortor said, "had pulled their clothes off and all they had on were their panties."

WATCHERS' FEAST

The girls were returned to the wall. "The girls' dresses were torn from behind," Dismukes told me. "The dress had fallen off one and was lying around her feet. The other was holding hers up in front."

A handful of airborne troops, "men in green uniforms," Juli testified, "came in as a group after they had ripped our clothes off." "The soldiers came in," Karen told Early, "and everyone stood around as if they were waiting for something."

The police synopsis of the statement of Wayne Henson, who had entered with Thomas and never advanced beyond the front doorway, said "Henson observed . . . 4–5 airborne police watching."

"When they'd stripped the girls down," Sortor said to me, "they told me and Lee and them to look at them. Said, 'Ain't you ashamed?' "

The men in uniform who were not hitting people at the wall, Sortor testified, were "just standing back. Just standing there laughing, you know, all like that." . . .

EXODUS

Warrant Officer Thomas was not alone in his impulse to flee after the murder of Auburey Pollard in the game that he, Thomas, had so blithely joined. The hallway was virtually clear of uniformed men in a very short time. Convenient firing was heard not far away; all but a handful ran to do their duty.

"And then some more shooting started down the block there," Greene told Eggleton. "All of them rushed out of the Manor house there and ran down the block. Two policemen were left there."

"And then I heard some more shooting from outside," Michael, who was still lying on the floor in A-4 at the time of which he was speaking, testified. "And then some of the officers and all of them went outside because I heard—let's see, the soldier told me, he say, 'That's another one of your friends out there shooting at us.' "

"I remember," Sortor testified, "that I heard officers say they were shooting down the street, and some of them ran out—ran out of there, and that's when the officer—when they left, this officer went into this room and got Michael and them up, and they told us we could leave."

SOLICITUDE

Despite the sudden fear he said he had felt, Warrant Officer Thomas did not, after all, leave. He was soon to be found in room A-4 again, with Patrolman August, the naked girl, and the half-naked girl. "These two," Karen (the one who had lost all her clothes but her panties) told Early, "were very nice."

"They then took K and J into a room (A-4)," Early's notes said. " 'What was the trouble?' They said they didn't know and they didn't ask them any more. These two were very nice. Thought Juli should go to the hospital. . . . The cop asked them if they had any robes. J & K said, 'No.' Told them to get out and get a robe."

According to the Thomas synopsis, "Warrant Officer Thomas was then asked to escort the girls to the Algiers Motel next door; as he was leaving he was joined by private watchman Dismukes and Pfc. Henson."

"I believe," Thomas testified, "it was Officer Senak that asked me to escort the women back to the motel room, their own motel room. . . . Myself, Henson, and Mr. Dismukes escorted these women back. . . . Henson, myself, and Mr. Dismukes went to the girls' room, and when they opened the door there was a colored fellow laying on the bed, and Mr. Dismukes approached him and shook the bed and woke him up. He was sleeping. And I held him at, you know, in custody more or less until Mr. Dismukes went in and checked the girl's cut on her head because she was bleeding so severely that, to see if she needed medical attention right away. I asked Mr. Dismukes to do this. And he went over and said, 'Well, it look like it will take a couple of stitches.' " (Juli had seven stitches; she also testified she suffered a slight concussion and developed a black eye.) "So I warned the girls, I told them to stay in the room until after five-thirty, until after the curfew lifted . . . and then came out because they are liable to get in trouble if they come out of the motel. I was satisfied that the girls did not need medical attention right away because she had almost stopped bleeding."

22 / Report on Investigation of Oxnard Police Department

THOMAS LYNCH

The problems of police conflict with the minority community are not limited to their relations with blacks. Mexican-Americans have asserted that they too have been the victims of verbal and physical abuse. As early as the testimony of the California Civil Rights Advisory Board to the U.S. Civil Rights Commission, members of the Mexican-American community have complained about police brutality. The response to the 1963 hearings by Los Angeles Mayor Sam Yorty and Chief of Police William Parker was to condemn the hearings as communist inspired; the presence of Bishop James Pike as commission chairman was used to justify their argument. Since those hearings, additional complaints have come out of the *barrio,* or Mexican-American ghetto. The present selection, compiled by the attorney general of California, is a series of complaints by Mexican-Americans in a community just outside of the Los Angeles area. The reader should consider at what point legitimate interrogative police methods have become police brutality, and whether the police should establish different standards of procedure for different ethnic communities.

SOURCE: Thomas Lynch, Report on Investigation of Oxnard Police Department, February 21, 1969, pp. 1, 2, 7–8, 12–13. Unpublished.

On August 21, 1968, Special Agent Richard J. Mercurio arrived in Oxnard and began the investigation. The allegations which were made included police brutality, illegal arrest, illegal search, and illegal entry. The
investigator experienced a great deal of difficulty in ascertaining what actually took place in many of the reported incidents. This was due to the
fact that many of the complaining witnesses had been under the influence
of alcoholic beverages or narcotics at the time in question. In one instance
it was due in part to a lack of clarity in a police report.

It should also be noted that in many cases there was a direct conflict
between the story told by the police and that related by the complainants.
When this occurred it was often difficult or impossible to reach any firm
conclusion as to the propriety of the police behavior. In these cases, no
finding could be made.

There were nineteen separate instances of alleged police brutality,
and one instance of alleged harassment by the police which supposedly
had been continuing for a number of years. It is significant that the complaining party or parties were under the influence of alcohol or narcotics
in twelve cases, and some degree of interference with the police, ranging
from physical assault on the officer to the giving of false information, was
present in fourteen of these cases. There were only two cases which contained no allegation of interference with an officer, or of being under the
influence of alcohol or drugs.

These facts must be considered along with the principle of law that a
police officer is legally entitled to use such force as is necessary to overcome resistance and to make an arrest. The question in these cases is not
whether the officers of the Oxnard Police Department were authorized to
use force (because clearly they were) but whether the force which they did
use was excessive.

An analysis of the facts in these twenty cases, as can be determined
from the statements of the witnesses, alleged victims, and police officers,
leads to the following results. In no case was it clear that excessive force
had been used by the police. In one case (#10) the force used may have
been excessive, but the alleged victim had given varying stories as to what
took place. In addition, the version of the incident as related by one of the
officers involved was somewhat inconsistent with the earlier written police
report, which itself suffered from a lack of clarity and detail. In view of
these facts, it is impossible to reach a conclusion concerning Case #10.

Since there was no evidence that the Oxnard Police Department had
been involved in acts of actual brutality, the investigation, and this report,
also examined instances of lesser forms of police misconduct. This includes allegations of illegal entry, search, etc. It must be recognized that in
certain situations the police have the right to forcibly enter a home, even
without announcing their presence; they sometimes have the right to arrest a

person without a warrant; and they are often able to make a legal search without a warrant. The person to be arrested had *no right to resist* that arrest, whether or not it is a lawful arrest. Some of the people who counsel and advise the complaining parties should be aware of these principles of criminal law. It appears that a number of these incidents were reported because the citizens involved were unaware that the actions of the police were lawful.

In essence, the situation in Oxnard reflects a lack of understanding on both sides. The complaining citizens do not always understand why the police take the actions that they do. Thus, even legitimate and necessary police behavior may be misunderstood and resented. The police, in turn, have apparently failed to realize that a certain degree of public hostility is based on this lack of understanding. Many irate citizens might be harboring a good-faith but mistaken belief that their constitutional rights are being violated. A brief explanation to these people might preclude a later complaint and investigation, and might also indicate to the citizen that the officer is aware of this hostility, and would like to eliminate it. While it might be technically true that a police officer need not explain his behavior to a citizen, rigid adherence to such a practice would indicate a disturbing lack of concern for the people with whom he deals.

Several of the reported cases included allegations of rudeness, or racial or ethnic slurs, by the police officers. These charges were extremely difficult to substantiate and were generally denied by the officers. While such conduct, if it occurred, may not technically be a violation of the law, it would constitute gross misconduct and would be most detrimental to proper police-public relations.

Finally, a police department should have a standard procedure for dealing with citizen complaints against police officers. This should include appropriate follow-up, so the burden is *not* on the citizen to determine the outcome of his complaint. Apparently no such system exists in Oxnard.

The following section of this report describes each of the twenty instances of alleged misconduct in greater detail. While the facts, as presented here, are very brief, they were gathered from a voluminous file prepared by the investigator. They are stated briefly as a matter of convenience. . . .

CASE # 10

Nature of Complaint Unnecessary use of force, failure to warn of rights, failure to identify self as police officer.

Principal Complainant Mr. Arnold ESTRELLA.

Facts Detectives Hurley and Bowen of the Oxnard Police Department stopped four men who were walking along the street. One of them appeared to be unable to walk by himself. The officers recognized the four as known narcotic users, and as stated in the police report, "They were highly intoxicated." The officers spoke briefly to the four men and were preparing to leave when Mr. Estrella arrived. He was antagonistic and profane, and challenged Detective Hurley to fight him.

The other four subjects left the area, but Mr. Estrella was placed under arrest for disturbing the peace and for being drunk. Mr. Estrella resisted arrest, and was forcibly subdued by Detective Hurley. At this time the other four men returned to the scene, and they were also arrested, three of them for interfering with an officer and one for being drunk.

Upon arriving at the jail, Mr. Estrella was taken into the narcotics office for individual questioning as to his use of narcotics. While in the office a fight of some kind took place involving Mr. Estrella and Detective Hurley. Mr. Estrella was then returned to the jail for booking. It was later ascertained that he had suffered a broken nose.

Conclusions Mr. Estrella claimed at one time that he had been attacked in the police station office by both Detective Hurley and Detective Bowen. He later claimed that Detective Hurley alone was responsible for his broken nose. In addition, Mr. Estrella has failed to cooperate with investigators from the Ventura County District Attorney's Office as they attempted to discover whether or not the allegations made against Detective Hurley were true. Mr. Estrella also gave evasive answers to the investigator from this office while he was looking into this situation.

All of this tends to make the charges made by Mr. Estrella highly suspect. However, there are certain factors which tend, also, to support his allegations. The police report states that while Mr. Estrella and Detective Hurley were in the narcotics office, Mr. Estrella "poked both fingers in Detective's Hurley (sic) eyes and as the detective backed off blinded, he was struck a glancing blow on the chest and throat." The report then states that Mr. Estrella "was again quickly restrained by the best known method under the circumstances. . . ." This report was not dated but was probably made out on the day of the arrest, May 1, 1968. When the Attorney General's investigator spoke to Detective Hurley on August 27, 1968, his story was somewhat different. Detective Hurley stated that he had been sitting on a desk, and when poked in the eyes by Mr. Estrella he was knocked backward on the desk and his foot come up, striking Mr. Estrella in the face. If he had, in fact, been sitting on the desk, why did the prior police report state that he had "backed off blinded" after being struck? Also a police report which states that a subject was restrained "by the best known method under the circumstances . . ." raises more questions than it answers.

The police report was "signed" by the typed names of the four officers who were involved, Hurley, Bowen, Thayer, and Skeeters, in that order. It is therefore possible that someone other than Detective Hurley made out the report.

In summary, while it is apparent that force was used on the person of Mr. Estrella while he was in the narcotics office, it cannot be said whether or not that force was justified. If Mr. Estrella did, in fact, poke his fingers into Detective Hurley's eyes, then it would be necessary to restrain him by force; but if this was done, the amount of force used *and its justification* should be clearly stated in the police report.

The claim of Mr. Estrella that the officers did not identify themselves is not valid since he later admitted that he knew them well. His claim that they did not warn him of his rights is answered by the fact that they are not compelled to do so. . . . [1]

CASE #17

Nature of Complaint Unnecessary use of force, failure to identify self as officer.

Principal Complainant Mr. John J. RODRIGUEZ.

Facts Mr. Rodriguez and a friend, Mr. Larry Richey, were in an Oxnard bar when Oxnard Detectives Bowen and Moore, in company with two other officers, entered the bar. This occurred in the early morning hours of January 11, 1968.

Mr. Rodriguez and Mr. Richey then left the bar. Detective Bowen had reason to believe that Mr. Rodriguez was selling narcotics, and could have been in possession of narcotics at that time. Detectives Bowen and Moore approached Mr. Rodriguez and his friend as they were about to get into a car. Mr. Rodriguez submitted to a search by Detective Bowen. When the officers asked Mr. Richey for some identification, he became profane. As Detective Bowen approached him, he raised his arms as if to fight, at which time Detective Moore grabbed him from the rear and restrained him by applying a choke-hold. Upon being told that the detectives, who were in plain clothes, were police officers, Mr. Richey satisfactorily identified himself.

When Detective Bowen returned to Mr. Rodriguez, he heard the latter make a threat against another person who was with the officers. Detective Bowen, who had heard threats against both himself and his family from Mr. Rodriguez then forcefully warned Mr. Rodriguez not to make such threats in the future. To emphasize his point he tapped Mr. Rodriguez on the chest with his finger.

The officers then left and no further action was taken.

[1] Recent legislation and court decisions now make it compulsory that police advise a person arrested for a crime of his or her rights.—Ed.

Conclusions Detectives Bowen and Moore had not properly identified themselves as officers prior to taking police action. Both officers received reprimands for having violated this departmental rule.

The force used against Mr. Richey could be justified, as it appeared to the officers that he was preparing to fight them. Even if they had not properly identified themselves, it would be reasonable to assume that Mr. Richey was nonetheless aware of their position. He had just watched them search Mr. Rodriguez.

The force used against Mr. Rodriguez would not appear excessive from the version of the incident as related by the police. The version as related by Mr. Rodriguez is subject to some question as he changed some facets of the story during a subsequent narration.

If further investigation of this incident is desired, then perhaps polygraph examinations would assist in reaching the truth.

23 / Justice for Indians
U.S. COMMISSION ON CIVIL RIGHTS

Because of the peculiar legal status of the Indian his law-enforcement problems are far more complex than those of either blacks or Mexican-Americans. The Indian is a member of what has been described as a "distinct," independent, political community (*Worcester* v. *Georgia,* 6 Peters 515 [1852]). It was not until 1924 that all Indians were granted United States citizenship by an act of Congress. The effect of this on the legal status of the Indian was to extend certain legal benefits to him, but to leave him in an extremely ambiguous legal position: He is still subject to the jurisdiction of Indian, state, and federal courts. In a great majority of cases he is still under the jurisdiction of tribal courts, and to the extent that constitutional protections are critical to justice, often without justice. There is no effective mechanism for transfer of appeal of a tribal court decision to a federal or state court; so if a right guaranteed by the Constitution is abridged, there is no provision for redress. In those cases where the federal or state government has jurisdictional control, the problems Indians face are the same as those of the blacks or the Mexican-Americans —police malpractice and differential court decisions.

Source, U.S. Commission on Civil Rights, *Report,* Book 5, "Justice" (Washington, D.C.: U.S. Government Printing Office, 1961), pp. 155–160.

Limited as was the Commission's study of American Indians, it disclosed sufficient evidence of unequal treatment under law to warrant action in certain areas and more searching investigation in others. It showed, for example, that some Indians are segregated in schools, and that in some instances needy Indians are denied welfare benefits in programs administered and financed by State and local government. Repeated complaints of unfair treatment by police and courts, and complaints of inadequate law enforcement on reservations in States to which the Federal Government has relinquished jurisdiction, indicate serious problems exist in the administration of justice. While no definitive investigation was made in the areas of housing and employment, such information as was received revealed that in both areas Indians run into barriers similar to those confronting the American Negro. Ironically, the study disclosed also that Choctaw Indians use waiting rooms designated "Whites Only" in Mississippi bus stations, while some towns in the Southwest still are marked by signs reading: "No Indians or Dogs Allowed." The significance of this incidental information lies in what it suggests: There is nothing exclusive about insults to human dignity.

In substance then, the civil rights problems of Indians are for the most part the same as those confronting other minorities. Yet Indians have some unique problems. Their cultures and history; their close, changing and at times turbulent relationship to the Federal Government; their battle to preserve reservation land—set them apart from others. Unlike other minorities, tribal Indians are members of semisovereign nations enjoying treaty rights with the Federal Government. They are also, however, citizens entitled to the rights and privileges of citizenship. Similarly, they are entitled to equal protection of the laws. Particularly with respect to land, tribal Indians bear a dependent relationship to the Federal Government often described, though erroneously, as that of "ward" to guardian.

The manifestations of their unique status are varied. Indians, for example, are in some respects beyond the reach of Federal and State law, including the Constitution itself. Tribal governments are not subject to the limitations imposed on governmental authority by the Bill of Rights and the 14th amendment. Indian land is, for the most part, held in trust by the Federal Government; it is tax exempt, and the Government's consent is required before it can be sold. Some Indians go to Federal, some to State, and some to mission schools. They may be subject to three kinds of law and legal procedure. They have, it appears, a strong tendency to preserve their own identities and ways of life, a tendency which is most concretely expressed in the Indian tie to reservations.

Some States resent the fact that while on a reservation, Indians are beyond the reach of State law; this resentment is occasionally expressed in attempts at "retaliation." For example, when in 1959 the Supreme Court held that Arizona had no jurisdiction over a transaction that occurred on the Navajo reservation, even though it was between a white man and an Indian, the State sought to remove all polling places from the reservation. Arizona's Attorney General issued an opinion declaring that Indians could not cast their ballots on reservations because they were not amenable to State laws. As a practical matter the removal of polling places would have disfranchised all but a few reservation Indians, for the size of the reservation would have compelled most Indians to travel great distances to cast their ballots. Though legislation was introduced to implement the Attorney General's opinion, it did not pass. The incident illustrates the Indian's ambivalent legal status, and the frustrations to which it gives rise.

Nor is it the only one. As has been noted, Indians are citizens of the United States and, as such, one would expect them to enjoy the significant protections from government encroachment contained in the Bill of Rights. They do with respect to Federal and State action, but not with respect to tribal action. Thus tribal governments can (as indeed one has) prevent tribal members on an Indian reservation from freely pursuing the religion of their choice.

Despite the recent problem in Arizona and a similar one still unresolved in New Mexico, the Indian's right to vote appears to be more secure than his other rights. Yet Indians have not gone to the polls in great numbers. A variety of explanations is offered. The high illiteracy rate among Indians (estimated to be at 50 percent) restricts registration in States that require literacy tests. Another, and more important factor, appears to be that tribal Indians are more concerned with tribal government than with white man's government. A third has to do with their close relationship to the Federal Bureau of Indian Affairs.

As to education, States with Indian populations have accepted a fair proportion of tribal children from reservations as students in public schools on a nondiscriminatory basis, although not always without special inducement by the Federal Government. As of 1960 about 60 percent of the 125,000 Indians of school age were in State schools; 27 percent were in Federal schools and 9 percent in mission schools. In some States, however, Indians are accepted in public schools only on a segregated basis. The Bureau of Indian Affairs has reported difficulty in securing admission of Indian children to public schools on a nondiscriminatory basis in Louisiana, Mississippi, and North Carolina. However, some Choctaw children in Mississippi and some Cherokee children in North Carolina do go to public schools with white children.

Apart from matters of civil rights, Indian education suffers from other limitations. Some reservations are so big and so thinly populated that it is not practical to provide schools accessible to all Indian children. Moreover, there is still some tribal resistance to compulsory education, largely because of past Federal policies under which Indian children were sent to boarding schools, forbidden to speak their native tongues and otherwise encouraged to sever tribal and cultural ties. (In some cases, families were never reunited.) A third factor is the poverty of many Indians and the reluctance to surrender wage earners to the classroom. Another is the lack of a tradition of formal education.

Complaints by Indians of discrimination in employment are similar to those of Negroes. A preliminary survey indicates some State employment offices accept and process discriminatory job orders. There are also charges that the Bureau of Indian Affairs frequently ignores its announced policy of preferential employment for Indians. Some schools, it is said, urged by parents not to permit "squaws" to teach white children, have resisted hiring qualified Indian teachers. As to private employment, many Indians express resentment over the reluctance of some employers to hire them for suitable jobs.

Indian complaints of unequal treatment in the administration of justice include charges that law and order are not adequately maintained on reservations in States to which jurisdiction has been ceded, and that there is outright ill-treatment by police and courts in towns adjacent to Indian reservations.

A final area of unequal treatment is that of public welfare—a matter of vital concern for Indians because of their general poverty. In this preliminary study there were no complaints of discrimination in the administration of public assistance programs operated by States with Federal funds. Complaints were received, however, of unequal treatment in the administration of programs financed from State and local revenue. Investigation disclosed that some States with large Indian populations do not extend their general assistance programs to Indians living on reservations. Indians, it is argued, are the special responsibility of the Federal Government. And since the legal power of a State does not ordinarily extend to Indians living on reservations—for example, Indian lands are exempt from State taxes—some States insist that their legal duty to provide care for reservation Indians is limited. Another argument is that while some individual Indians may be destitute, the tribes to which they belong are well off and should take care of their needs.

Thus the denial of equal protection of the laws to Indians appears to be severe and widespread. Some of the denials (those concerning welfare, the administration of justice and, in the recent past, voting) stem at least in part from the unique legal and political status of Indians. Others stem from the fact that, as a minority, Indians are subject to the same kinds of discrimination inflicted on other minorities. Whatever their source, the denials deserve full-fledged investigation.

Over and above matters of civil rights, we still face the problem of redeeming the past by preparing for the future, of providing Indians with the tools by which they may become economically, socially, and democratically secure. As this is done, some, if not many, of the civil rights denials will in all probability diminish. It is toward both ends then—protecting Indian rights and promoting Indian economic health—that the Federal Government should strive.

FINDINGS

General Comments

Much of what concerns the Indian is outside the specific scope of this Commission's jurisdiction—for example, his desire to retain "home rule," his worry over the loss of tribal lands, his fear that the Federal Government will abruptly end its "trusteeship," his need for economic development. Most of these were covered by the recent report to the Secretary of the Interior by the Task Force on Indian Affairs. For the present, it appears that the policy of terminating Federal supervision and special services to Indians held in abeyance in recent years, has been abandoned. The Interior Department indicates it will adopt a "new trail" for Indians stressing economic development.

Within the area of the Commission's jurisdiction, there is evidence of some serious Indian civil rights problems. But in view of the tentative nature of its study, the Commission does not offer recommendations particularly directed to such matters. However, several recommendations made elsewhere in this report would serve Indians as well as others. The following findings suggest several areas warranting further study and possibly action by appropriate Federal agencies.

1. Despite recent attempts to make it difficult for Indians on two reservations to vote, by and large Indians are free to register and cast their ballots. However, a high illiteracy rate among older Indians, and a preoccupation with tribal affairs apparently keep Indian registration figures well below the national average.

2. While the bulk of Indian children have been accepted in white public schools (although not without Federal inducement), some States have denied Indians admission to State schools because of race. With appropriate authorization by the President or Congress, the Department of Justice or the Department of the Interior might take legal action to end this discrimination against Indian children.

3. Although Indians are afforded welfare benefits much the same as other Americans in programs administered by States with Federal aid, reservation Indians in some areas have been openly denied general public assistance in localities administering programs financed out of local and State revenue. The extent to which this occurs is a matter for further study. Where it does occur, the Department of Justice or the Department of the Interior could, with appropriate authorization by the President or Congress, take legal action to end such discrimination.

4. Some State and local governments reportedly use administrative discretion as a device to prevent both reservation and nonreservation Indians from receiving welfare benefits for which they are qualified. Further study would be required to verify these reports, and to determine the extent of the practice.

5. In some cases, reservation Indians have not been provided with adequate law enforcement by the States to which the Federal Government has ceded civil and criminal jurisdiction. Further study would be needed to determine the exact extent of this problem. The problem could be dealt with in part by requiring a firm State commitment that all governmental services will be provided as a prerequisite of any future withdrawal of Federal responsibility.

6. Reservation and nonreservation Indians are treated unfairly by police and courts in many localities, particularly those adjoining large reservations. Indian neighborhoods are sometimes not given adequate police protection by local authorities. Further study would be required to determine the extent of this problem.

7. Reservation housing is generally bad. With respect to nonreservation housing, Indians face the same kinds of discrimination confronting other minorities.

8. Employment opportunities for Indians appear to be as restricted as they are for Negroes. Some State employment offices reportedly accept discriminatory job orders and some State agencies are reluctant to hire qualified Indians.

9. Unlike Negroes, Indians do not seem to be denied access to transportation and terminal facilities. (The Choctaw Indians of Mississippi, for example, use white waiting rooms.) Discrimination against Indians does exist, though on a limited basis, in many rural communities with respect to other public accommodations such as taverns, hotels, and restaurants.

10. Many American Indians are members of semisovereign tribes. They are also citizens of the United States entitled to the rights and privileges of citizenship. Indian tribal governments are not at present subject to the limitations imposed on State and Federal Governments by the Bill of Rights and the 14th amendment. Tribal governments are thus free to inhibit and have in fact in some instances inhibited the free exercise of religion by tribal members.

chapter six

VOTING AND POLITICAL PARTICIPATION

24 / *Smith* v. *Allwright*

Access to the polls has been another goal that minority
groups have fought hard to realize, and as in other areas, blacks
have led the fight. For almost 100 years after the passage of
the Fifteenth Amendment, which prohibited discrimination in
voting based on race, color, or previous condition of servitude,
the southern white devised a series of techniques to keep the
Negro from exercising his franchise. Among the better-known
methods were (1) the grandfather clause, which set arbitrary
registration requirements and then exempted those whose
grandfathers had been eligible to vote in 1960; (2) literary tests,
which were subject to the arbitrary authority of the local registrar of voting; (3) poll taxes, which were used to prevent
blacks from voting or to control how they would vote;
(4) violence and intimidation, which were particularly used by
such groups as the Ku Klux Klan; and (5) the white primary,
which kept blacks from voting in the most important election
in the one-party South. In 1944, the United States Supreme
Court concluded that the primary, as an integral part of the
total election process, had to be open to all men regardless of
race, and a major block to the vote was removed.

SOURCE: *Smith* v. *Allwright,* 321 U.S. 649 (1944).

Mr. Justice Reed delivered the opinion of the Court.

This writ of certiorari brings here for review a claim for damages in the sum of $5000 on the part of petitioner, a Negro citizen of the 48th precinct of Harris County, Texas, for the refusal of respondents, election and associate election judges respectively of that precinct, to give petitioner a ballot or to permit him to cast a ballot in the primary election of July 27, 1940, for the nomination of Democratic candidates for the United States Senate and House of Representatives, and Governor and other state officers. The refusal is alleged to have been solely because of the race and color of the proposed voter.

The actions of respondents are said to violate §§ 31 and 43 of Title 8 of the United States Code in that petitioner was deprived of rights secured by §§ 2 and 4 of Article I and the Fourteenth, Fifteenth and Seventeenth Amendments to the United States Constitution. The suit was filed in the District Court of the United States for the Southern District of Texas, which had jurisdiction under Judicial Code § 24, subsection 14.

The District Court denied the relief sought and the Circuit Court of Appeals quite properly affirmed its action on the authority of *Grovey* v. *Townsend*. We granted the petition for certiorari to resolve a claimed inconsistency between the decision in the *Grovey* case and that of *United States* v. *Classic*.

The State of Texas by its Constitution and statutes provides that every person, if certain other requirements are met which are not here in issue, qualified by residence in the district or county "shall be deemed a qualified elector." Primary elections for United States Senators, Congressmen and state officers are provided for by Chapters Twelve and Thirteen of the statutes. Under these chapters, the Democratic party was required to hold the primary which was the occasion of the alleged wrong to petitioner. These nominations are to be made by the qualified voters of the party.

The Democratic party of Texas is held by the Supreme Court of that State to be a "voluntary association," protected by § 27 of the Bill of Rights, Art. I, Constitution of Texas, from interference by the State except that:

"In the interest of fair methods and a fair expression by their members of their preferences in the selection of their nominees, the State may regulate such elections by proper laws."

That court stated further:

"Since the right to organize and maintain a political party is one guaranteed by the Bill of Rights of this State, it necessarily follows that every privilege essential or reasonably appropriate to the exercise of that right is likewise guaranteed—including, of course, the privilege of determining the policies of the party and its membership. Without the privilege of determining the policy of a political association and its membership, the right to organize such an association would be a mere mockery. We think these rights—that is, the right to determine the membership of a political party and to determine its policies, of necessity are to be exercised by the state convention of such party, and cannot, under any circumstances, be conferred upon a state or governmental agency."

The Democratic party on May 24, 1932, in a state convention adopted the following resolution, which has not since been "amended, abrogated, annulled or avoided":

"Be it resolved that all white citizens of the State of Texas who are qualified to vote under the Constitution and laws of the State shall be eligible to membership in the Democratic party and, as such, entitled to participate in its deliberations."

It was by virtue of this resolution that the respondents refused to permit the petitioner to vote.

Texas is free to conduct her elections and limit her electorate as she may deem wise, save only as her action may be affected by the prohibitions of the United States Constitution or in conflict with powers delegated to and exercised by the National Government. The Fourteenth Amendment forbids a State from making or enforcing any law which abridges the privileges or immunities of citizens of the United States, and the Fifteenth Amendment specifically interdicts any denial or abridgement by a State of the right of citizens to vote on account of color. Respondents appeared in the District Court and the Circuit Court of Appeals and defended on the ground that the Democratic party of Texas is a voluntary organization with members banded together for the purpose of selecting individuals of the group representing the common political beliefs as candidates in the general election. As such a voluntary organization, it was claimed, the Democratic party is free to select its own membership and limit to whites participation in the party primary. Such action, the answer asserted, does not violate the Fourteenth, Fifteenth or Seventeenth Amendment as officers of government cannot be chosen at primaries and the Amendments are applicable only to general elections where governmental officers are actually elected. Primaries, it is said, are political party affairs, handled by party, not governmental, officers. No appearance for respondents is made in this Court. Arguments presented here by the Attorney General of Texas and the Chairman of the State Democratic Executive Committee of Texas, as amici curiae, urged substantially the same grounds as those advanced by the respondents.

The right of a Negro to vote in the Texas primary has been considered heretofore by this Court. The first case was *Nixon* v. *Herndon*. At that time, 1924, the Texas statute, Art. 3093a, afterwards numbered Art. 3107 declared "in no event shall a Negro be eligible to participate in a

Democratic Party primary election in the State of Texas." Nixon was refused the right to vote in a Democratic primary and brought a suit for damages against the election officers under R.S. §§ 1979 and 2004, the present §§ 43 and 31 of Title 8, U.S.C., respectively. It was urged to this Court that the denial of the franchise to Nixon violated his Constitutional rights under the Fourteenth and Fifteenth Amendments. Without consideration of the Fifteenth, this Court held that the action of Texas in denying the ballot to Negroes by statute was in violation of the equal protection clause of the Fourteenth Amendment and reversed the dismissal of the suit.

The legislature of Texas reenacted the article but gave the State Executive Committee of a party the power to prescribe the qualifications of its members for voting or other participation. This article remains in the statutes. The State Executive Committee of the Democratic party adopted a resolution that white Democrats and none other might participate in the primaries of that party. Nixon was refused again the privilege of voting in a primary and again brought suit for damages by virtue of § 31, Title 8, U.S.C. This Court again reversed the dismissal of the suit for the reason that the Committee action was deemed to be state action and invalid as discriminatory under the Fourteenth Amendment. The test was said to be whether the Committee operated as representative of the State in the discharge of the State's authority. *Nixon* v. *Condon.* The question of the inherent power of a political party in Texas "without restraint by any law to determine its own membership" was left open.

In *Grovey* v. *Townsend,* this Court had before it another suit for damages for the refusal in a primary of a county clerk, a Texas officer with only public functions to perform, to furnish petitioner, a Negro, an absentee ballot. The refusal was solely on the ground of race. This case differed from *Nixon* v. *Condon* in that a state convention of the Democratic party had passed the resolution of May 24, 1932, hereinbefore quoted. It was decided that the determination by the state convention of the membership of the Democratic party made a significant change from a determination by the Executive Committee. The former was party action, voluntary in character. The latter, as had been held in the *Condon* case, was action by authority of the State. The managers of the primary election were therefore declared not to be state officials in such sense that their action was state action. A state convention of a party was said not to be an organ of the State. This Court went on to announce that to deny a vote in a primary was a mere refusal of party membership with which "the State need have no concern," while for a State to deny a vote in a general election on the ground of race or color violated the Constitution. Consequently, there was found no ground for holding that the county clerk's refusal of a ballot because of racial ineligibility for party membership denied the petitioner any right under the Fourteenth or Fifteenth Amendment.

Since *Grovey* v. *Townsend* and prior to the present suit, no case from Texas involving primary elections has been before this Court. We did decide, however, *United States* v. *Classic*. We there held that § 4 of Article I of the Constitution authorized Congress to regulate primary as well as general elections "where the primary is by law made an integral part of the election machinery." Consequently, in the *Classic* case, we upheld the applicability to frauds in a Louisiana primary of §§ 19 and 20 of the Criminal Code. Thereby corrupt acts of election officers were subjected to Congressional sanctions because that body had power to protect rights of federal suffrage secured by the Constitution in primary as in general elections. This decision depended, too, on the determination that under the Louisiana statutes the primary was a part of the procedure for choice of federal officials. By this decision the doubt as to whether or not such primaries were a part of "elections" subject to federal control, which had remained unanswered since *Newberry* v. *United States* was erased. The *Nixon Cases* were decided under the equal protection clause of the Fourteenth Amendment without a determination of the status of the primary as a part of the electoral process. The exclusion of Negroes from the primaries by action of the State was held invalid under that Amendment. The fusing by the *Classic* case of the primary and general elections into a single instrumentality for choice of officers has a definite bearing on the permissibility under the Constitution of excluding Negroes from primaries. This is not to say that the *Classic* case cuts directly into the rationale of *Grovey* v. *Townsend*. This latter case was not mentioned in the opinion. *Classic* bears upon *Grovey* v. *Townsend* not because exclusion of Negroes from primaries is any more or less state action by reason of the unitary character of the electoral process but because the recognition of the place of the primary in the electoral scheme makes clear that state delegation to a party of the power to fix the qualifications of primary elections is delegation of a state function that may make the party's action the action of the State. When *Grovey* v. *Townsend* was written, the Court looked upon the denial of a vote in a primary as a mere refusal by a party of party membership. As the Louisiana statutes for holding primaries are similar to those of Texas, our ruling in *Classic* as to the unitary character of the electoral process calls for a reexamination as to whether or not the exclusion of Negroes from a Texas party primary was state action.

The statutes of Texas relating to primaries and the resolution of the Democratic party of Texas extending the privileges of membership to white citizens only are the same in substance and effect today as they were when *Grovey* v. *Townsend* was decided by a unanimous Court. The question as to whether the exclusionary action of the party was the action of the State persists as the determinative factor. In again entering upon consideration of the inference to be drawn as to state action from a substantially similar factual situation, it should be noted that *Grovey* v. *Townsend* upheld exclusion of Negroes from primaries through the denial of party membership by a party convention. A few years before, this Court refused approval of exclusion by the State Executive Committee of the party. A different result was reached on the theory that the Committee action was state authorized and the Convention action was unfettered by statutory control. Such a variation in the result from so slight a change in form influences us to consider anew the legal validity of the distinction which has resulted in barring Negroes from participating in the nominations of candidates of the Democratic party in Texas. Other precedents of this Court forbid the abridgement of the right to vote.

It may now be taken as a postulate that the right to vote in such a primary for the nomination of candidates without discrimination by the State, like the right to vote in a general election, is a right secured by the Constitution. By the terms of the Fifteenth Amendment that right may not be abridged by any State on account of race. Under our Constitution the great privilege of the ballot may not be denied a man by the State because of his color.

We are thus brought to an examination of the qualifications for Democratic primary electors in Texas, to determine whether state action or private action has excluded Negroes from participation. Despite Texas' decision that the exclusion is produced by private or party action, federal courts must for themselves appraise the facts leading to that conclusion. It is only by the performance of this obligation that a final and uniform interpretation can be given to the Constitution, the "supreme Law of the Land." Texas requires electors in a primary to pay a poll tax. Every person who does so pay and who has the qualifications of age and residence is an acceptable voter for the primary. As appears above in the summary of the statutory provisions set out in note 6, Texas requires by the law the election of the county officers of a party. These compose the county executive committee. The county chairmen so selected are members of the district executive committee and choose the chairman for the district. Precinct primary election officers are named by the county executive committee. Statutes provide for the election by the voters of precinct delegates to the county convention of a party and the selection of delegates to the district and state conventions by the county convention. The state convention selects the state executive committee. No convention may place in platform or resolution any demand for specific legislation without endorsement of such legislation by the voters in a primary. Texas thus directs the selection of all party officers.

Primary elections are conducted by the party under state statutory authority. The county executive committee selects precinct election officials and the county, district or state executive committees, respectively, canvass the returns. These party committees or the state convention certify the party's candidates to the appropriate officers for inclusion on the official ballot for the general election. No name which has not been so certified may appear upon the ballot for the general election as a candidate of a political party. No other name may be printed on the ballot which has not been placed in nomination by qualified voters who must take oath that they did not participate in a primary for the selection of a candidate for the office for which the nomination is made.

The state courts are given exclusive original jurisdiction of contested elections and of mandamus proceedings to compel party officers to perform their statutory duties.

We think that this statutory system for the selection of party nominees for inclusion on the general election ballot makes the party which is required to follow these legislative directions an agency of the State in so far as it determines the participants in a primary election. The party takes its character as a state agency from the duties imposed upon it by state statutes; the duties do not become matters of private law because they are performed by a political party. The plan of the Texas primary follows substantially that of Louisiana, with the exception that in Louisiana the State pays the cost of the primary while Texas assesses the cost against candidates. In numerous instances, the Texas statutes fix or limit the fees to be charged. Whether paid directly by the State or through state requirements, it is state action which compels. When primaries become a part of the machinery for choosing officials, state and national, as they have here, the same tests to determine the character of discrimination or abridgement should be applied to the primary as are applied to the general election. If the State requires a certain electoral procedure, prescribes a general election ballot made up of party nominees so chosen and limits the choice of the electorate in general elections for state offices, practically speaking, to those whose names appear on such a ballot, it endorses, adopts and enforces the discrimination against Negroes, practiced by a party entrusted by Texas law with the determination of the qualifications of participants in the primary. This is state action within the meaning of the Fifteenth Amendment.

The United States is a constitutional democracy. Its organic law grants to all citizens a right to participate in the choice of elected officials without restriction by any State because of race. This grant to the people of the opportunity for choice is not to be nullified by a State through casting its electoral process in a form which permits a private organization to practice racial discrimination in the election. Constitutional rights would be of little value if they could be thus indirectly denied.

The privilege of membership in a party may be, as this Court said in *Grovey* v. *Townsend* no concern of a State. But when, as here, that privilege is also the essential qualification for voting in a primary to select nominees for a general election, the State makes the action of the party the action of the State. In reaching this conclusion we are not unmindful of the desirability of continuity of decision in constitutional questions. However, when convinced of former error, this Court has never felt constrained to follow precedent. In constitutional questions where correction depends upon amendment and not upon legislative action this Court throughout its history has freely exercised its power to reexamine the basis of its constitutional decisions. This has long been accepted practice, and this practice has continued to this day. This is particularly true when the decision believed erroneous is the application of a constitutional principle rather than an interpretation of the Constitution to extract the principle itself. Here we are applying, contrary to the recent decision in *Grovey* v. *Townsend*, the well-established principle of the Fifteenth Amendment, forbidding the abridgement by a State of a citizen's right to vote. *Grovey* v. *Townsend* is overruled.

Judgment reversed.

25 / Political Participation by Blacks

U.S. COMMISSION ON CIVIL RIGHTS

With the elimination of the white primary in 1944—a technique
for keeping blacks from the polls—many assumed that there
would be a "new day" of massive black registration and voting, which would in turn cause massive change in the social,
economic, and political institutions of the South. In fact, such
was not the case. Other legal barriers were erected in the
form of the literacy test and the poll tax. The former was suspended as a restriction of the Voting Rights Act of 1965, the
latter was eliminated by the Twenty-fourth Amendment to the
Constitution. Beyond these legal restraints, other techniques
used to keep blacks from voting or to ensure that they voted
the "right way"—that is, for the white elite—were threats of
violence to persons and property or of job loss. Thus there
was very little increase in black registration in the South, and
very few black candidates were elected to public office. The
present selection describes how these processes have worked
to exclude blacks from the voting process.

Source: U.S. Commission on Civil Rights, *Report,* "Political Participation: A
Study of the Participation by Negroes in the Electorial and Political Process in
Southern States since the Passing of the Voting Rights Act of 1965" (Washington,
D.C.: U.S. Government Printing Office, 1968), pp. 21–23, 25–26, 30–31, 34–35,
38–45, 48–49, 55, 58.

DILUTING THE NEGRO VOTE

Many new devices involve the dilution of the significantly expanded Negro vote through such measures as conversion from elections by district to elections at-large, laws permitting the legislature to consolidate predominantly Negro counties with predominantly white counties, and reapportionment and redistricting statutes.

Switching to At-Large Elections

Where Negroes are heavily concentrated in particular election districts their votes can be diluted effectively by converting to at-large elections, in which their votes are outweighed by white votes in adjoining districts. This technique has been used in Mississippi and Alabama.

Mississippi   Mississippi was strongly affected by the Voting Rights Act of 1965. Before the Act only about 7 percent (28,500) of Mississippi's Negro voting-age population was registered to vote. On the other hand, about 70 percent of the white voting-age population was registered. From the passage of the Act until the cut-off registration date for the statewide primary on June 7, 1966, Federal examiners listed 33,231 Negroes in 23 Mississippi counties to which they had been assigned. The State's total Negro registration was estimated at 132,000 that same month.

At least 30 bills relating to elections or the political process were introduced in the 1966 regular and special sessions of the Mississippi Legislature, many apparently in reaction to the increased Negro vote in many parts of the State. The legislature passed 12 bills and resolutions which substantially altered the State's election laws. . . .

Until May 1966, each Mississippi county was divided into five supervisors districts, and one member of the board of supervisors—the governing authority of the county—was elected by the voters of each district. In May, a new law granted a local option to the county boards of supervisors to provide for at-large election of members of the board. The new statute permits any board of supervisors to adopt an order under which each supervisor would be elected by all the voters in the county.

It has been contended that this enactment was racially motivated and has the effect of permitting county supervisors to dilute the Negro vote to prevent the election of Negroes to county governing bodies. Almost all sponsors of the bill in the State House of Representatives, either were from counties with potential Negro majorities or counties in which at least one supervisors district had a potential Negro majority. For example, in Oktibbeha County—home of one of the sponsors of the new act—District Five contains about 1500 more voting-age Negroes than voting-age whites. . . .

Consolidating Counties

Another device which can have the effect of diluting the Negro vote is the consolidation of counties having Negro voting majorities with counties having white voting majorities.

Less than a week after the June 1966 primary election, the Mississippi Senate and House of Representatives, respectively, passed a resolution submitting to the voters a constitutional amendment to permit the legislature by a two-thirds vote to consolidate adjoining counties. Formerly, counties could be consolidated only if a majority of voters in the affected counties voted for consolidation. The amendment was approved by the electorate of the State in a statewide referendum on November 8, 1966.

The legislative history of the amendment suggests that the legislature was motivated by racial consideration in approving the resolution. The measure passed the House in March, but was tabled in the Senate in May. In the June 7 primary the Negro candidate for U.S. Senator sponsored by the Mississippi Freedom Democratic Party—an independent Negro political organization—won majorities in two counties, including Claiborne County. The next day, Senator P. M. Watkins of Claiborne County revived the county consolidation proposal. Opponents of the resolution contended that it was designed to permit consolidation of counties heavily populated by Negroes with predominantly white counties. "All they're trying to do is avoid a few Negro votes," charged Senator E. K. Collins of predominantly white Jones County. Collins also argued that the bill was being revived in the Senate "just because a few Niggers voted down there [in Claiborne County]." Senator Ben Hilbun of predominantly white Oktibbeha County, who also opposed the measure, commented during the Senate debate: "We get so concerned because some Negroes are voting in a few counties, we are going to disrupt our entire institutions of government."

A proponent of the amendment, Senator Bill Corr from predominantly Negro Panola County, told the Senate that he had abandoned his former opposition to the bill because "a lot of things have happened" in the meantime. He referred to the primary victory of Lucius D. Amerson, Negro candidate for sheriff in Macon County, Alabama, and to the results of Mississippi's congressional primaries the day before. . . .

Reapportionment and Redistricting Measures

City dwellers and suburbanites long have had their votes diluted by legislative malapportionment and maldistricting. The apportionment and districting process also are potent weapons for dilution of Negro votes. In the South, there is evidence that these processes are being used in some areas for this purpose. . . .

Mississippi The new Mississippi election laws enacted in 1966 included several reapportionment and redistricting statutes which had the effect of diluting Negro voting strength.

In October 1965, before the 1966 regular session of the Mississippi Legislature, the Mississippi Freedom Democratic Party and several Negro plaintiffs filed a complaint in Federal district court attacking the boundaries of the State's congressional districts and the apportionment of the seats in both houses of the State Legislature on grounds of racial discrimination and gross disparity of population between districts. Before a three-judge Federal district court was convened to hear the case, the legislature enacted a bill redrawing the boundaries of the five congressional districts. The plaintiffs then amended their complaint to challenge the validity of the new legislation on the ground that it was racially motivated, that the redistricting did not follow the boundaries of the economic, geological, and geographic regions of the State, and that the effect of the plan was to deprive Mississippi Negroes of the opportunity for congressional representation by at least one Negro Congressman. The complaint alleged that Mississippi Negroes were entitled to be represented by a Negro Congressman since they constituted 43 percent of the State's population. . . .

A special session of the [Mississippi] legislature, convened in November 1966, passed a bill reapportioning the seats in both houses, and the bill was approved by the Governor on the December 1 deadline. In several instances, the legislature combined counties in which Negroes constituted a majority of the population and a majority of the registered voters in legislative districts with counties having white population and voting majorities. For example, majority Negro Claiborne County was joined in a senatorial district with majority white Hinds County. Jefferson County, with a 70 percent Negro population and a Negro voting majority, was combined with Lincoln County, which has a population 69 percent white. In both cases the resulting district had a majority white population.

The three-judge district court reconvened to consider objections to this new legislation but, consistent with its earlier position that no factors other than population disparity were to be considered, examined only the population characteristics of the new districts. It held the new legislation unconstitutional because of "glaring variations" in population figures among both House and Senate districts, and redrew the district lines itself. Under the court's plan, only six senatorial districts and only two House districts varied more than 10 percent from the population norm. Although the court stressed that it was disregarding racial considerations entirely, the effect of the court's reapportionment was to undo several districts which had combined predominantly Negro with predominantly white counties. On appeal the Supreme Court affirmed the district court's decision in a memorandum opinion without receiving briefs or hearing oral argument.

Full-Slate Voting

During the field work for this report, Negro political and civil rights leaders complained about other State legislation apparently not designed to dilute the Negro vote but allegedly having that effect. One frequently mentioned provision was the full-slate voting requirement. Under this requirement, where there is more than one post to be filled in a particular category, such as school board member, failure to vote for a number of candidates equal to the number of positions to be filled voids the ballot insofar as it applies to the offices in question. Full-slate voting creates special problems for Negro voters, who may be forced to vote for white candidates if their votes for a Negro candidate are to be counted, thus diluting the effect of their vote for the Negro candidate.

A Negro candidate in South Carolina, where such a requirement is in force, complained that unless Negroes run in numbers sufficient to occupy all the posts in a given category, the Negro vote for Negro candidates inevitably will be diluted by votes which Negro voters themselves are required to cast. For example, there are 10 at-large Richland County seats in the State house of representatives. According to the complaint, most Negroes in the community oppose contests by Negroes for all the county seats in the State legislature, fearing that such a display of aggressiveness would generate antagonism in the white community. If two or three Negro candidates seek the office, however, Negroes are forced by the statute to vote for seven or eight white candidates as well or their votes will be voided. The Negro votes for the white candidates are added to the votes cast for the white candidates by white voters, thus diluting the vote for the Negro candidates.

Persons attending a meeting of Negro political and civil rights leaders in Rocky Mount, North Carolina, made a similar complaint about the operation of the North Carolina statute.

Zelma Wyche, a Negro candidate for city alderman in Tallulah, Louisiana, complained that as a result of that State's full-slate voting requirement many inexperienced Negro voters were disqualified in the April 1966 Democratic municipal primary election. Three city aldermen were to be nominated in the primary election. To cast a valid ballot, a voter had to vote for three candidates. Wyche, the only Negro candidate, alleged that many Negroes pulled the lever of the voting machine only once to vote for him. Many Negroes were voting for the first time and, in Wyche's view, received inadequate instructions from the election officials. The disqualifications, he believes, contributed to his defeat.

PREVENTING NEGROES FROM BECOMING CANDIDATES OR OBTAINING OFFICE

Since the passage of the Voting Rights Act of 1965, measures also have been adopted to prevent Negroes from becoming candidates or obtaining office. These measures include abolishing elected offices, extending the terms of incumbent white officials, substituting appointment for election, increasing filing fees, and otherwise stiffening the requirements for getting on the ballot. In addition, Negroes elected to county office in Mississippi have encountered difficulty in securing the bonds which under state law they must obtain before assuming office. Abortive efforts also have been made to challenge the right of victorious Negro candidates to take their seats.

Abolishing the Office

When Walter Singletary, a prominent Negro farmer in Baker County, Georgia, filed to run for justice of the peace in the predominantly Negro Hoggard Mill district, the post was abolished by the county commissioners.

During the second week of February 1966, Singletary, now deceased, went to the office of the county ordinary and qualified to run for the justice of the peace position vacated by the death of the incumbent. According to the county attorney, Singletary's candidacy created the occasion for the county commissioners to re-evaluate the functions of justices of the peace in Baker County.

The minutes of the county commissioners indicate that on February 22, 1966, a special call meeting was held "at the instance and request of several citizens of the county who expressed their interest in the consolidation of several militia districts in the county into one countywide district." The minutes record that the question was discussed thoroughly and that " [i]t was generally observed that hardly any of the outlying districts actually performed any duties at all." A three-man commission was appointed to consolidate all the militia districts into one countywide district and the next day at another special call meeting the report of the commission was accepted and the change accomplished.

According to the county attorney the effect of this action was to abolish only the vacant post for which the Negro candidate had filed, since Georgia law prohibits abolition of an office during the term of the incumbent. The action of the county commissioners will not take effect in the other militia districts until the terms of the present justices of the peace expire in 1968. Although the county attorney, in a staff interview, maintained that the move was a reform measure because the county justices of the peace had been doing little business, it was the belief of a Democratic Party official and Negro residents of the county that the change was made to prevent the election of a Negro as justice of the peace.

Extending the Term of Incumbent White Officials

In Bullock County, Alabama, the county commissioners are elected to staggered terms. Primary elections to nominate candidates for two county commission seats were scheduled to be held on May 3, 1966. In July 1965, shortly before enactment of the Voting Rights Act of 1965, legislators representing Bullock County, where the Negro voting-age population is almost twice as large as the white voting-age population, introduced local legislation to extend for two years the terms of office of the Bullock County commissioners. The bill was passed by both houses and approved by the governor on August 20, 1965, two weeks after passage of the Voting Rights Act. The effect of the new law was to cancel the previously scheduled primary election. . . .

Substituting Appointment for Election

For many years county superintendents of education in Mississippi were elected at the same time and in the same manner as other county officers. A statute passed after the June 1966 primary election established a mechanism generally applicable throughout the State by which the office may be made appointive. The act itself made the office appointive in certain counties.

Under the new act the voters of a county may require the county board of supervisors to hold an election on the question of whether the school superintendent must be appointed by presenting a petition containing the names of 20 percent of the qualified electors of the county. The act, however, *requires* that the superintendent be appointed by the county board of education in Madison, Holmes, Humphreys, Noxubee, Jefferson, Claiborne, Lincoln, Coahoma, Copiah and Hancock counties. . . .

Another Mississippi statute enacted in 1966 provided that where territory is added to a municipal separate school district, the school trustee representing the supplemental area shall be elected. An exception was made for Grenada County, where Negroes constitute close to a majority of the population. The statute provides in effect that the school trustee representing the area outside the municipality of Grenada must be appointed by the county board of supervisors rather than elected by residents of the area.

Increasing Filing Fees

In at least one Alabama county, filing fees have been raised apparently to preclude Negroes from running for office.

Under the rules of the Alabama Democratic Party, filing fees for most candidates seeking county office are set by the county Democratic Executive Committee. In February 1966—six months after Lowndes County had been designated for a Federal examiner—the Lowndes County Democratic Executive Committee raised the filing fee for candidates in the Democratic primary tenfold. For example, the filing fee for the office of sheriff was raised from $50 to $500 and for members of the board of education from $10 to $100. . . .

Adding Requirements for Getting on the Ballot

In Mississippi, State statutes have added to the requirements for qualifying as a candidate for the apparent purpose of preventing Negroes from running for office.

For example, a statute passed by the Mississippi Legislature directly after the June 1966 Democratic primary stiffened the requirements for qualifying as an independent candidate in the general election. The new law increased the number of signatures of registered voters required on the nominating petition; required each elector "personally" to sign the petition and include his polling place and county; required independent candidates to file their petitions before or on the day of party primary elections, and disqualified any person voting in a primary election from running as an independent candidate in the general election. As of November 1967, 19 independent Negro candidates reportedly had been disqualified under this statute, most under the provision disqualifying a person who votes in a primary from running as an independent in the general election. . . .

Withholding Information

In some areas of the South during 1966, public and party officials reportedly failed or refused to provide prospective Negro candidates with pertinent information about elective office.

Dallas County, Alabama Organizers of the Dallas County Independent Free Voters Organization—an independent Negro political organization—reported difficulty in obtaining the necessary information to run independent Negro candidates for county and State offices in the November 1966 general election. . . .

Taliaferro County, Georgia In Taliaferro County, Georgia, four of six Negroes who sought to qualify in 1966 as candidates for membership on the county Democratic Executive Committee failed, according to their accounts, because the committee called a convention to nominate candidates for committeeman without adequate notice, and because party officials discriminatorily withheld necessary information, made false statements with respect to required procedure, and refused to permit them to qualify before the deadline. . .

Withholding Certification of Nominating Petition

Another tactic reportedly employed in some areas of Mississippi to forestall Negro candidacy or harass prospective Negro candidates has been to withhold or delay the required certification of the nominating petition.

The Mississippi statute, passed after the June 1966 primary election which increased the number of signatures required on the nominating petitions of independent candidates, also added a requirement that there be attached to each nominating petition a certificate from the registrar of each county in which the candidate is running showing the number of signatures of qualified electors appearing on the petition. . . .

Imposing Barriers to the Assumption of Office

For many of the Negroes who successfully ran for office in the November 1967 election in Mississippi, winning a majority of the votes was not the last hurdle to overcome before assuming office. In Mississippi, Negroes elected to office had difficulty in obtaining bonds. Mississippi law requires most county officials to post a bond to cover any losses they might cause. If these officials do not post bond in time for their swearing-in ceremonies their positions can be declared vacant and new elections held. Although all finally were successful, the oath-taking for some came only after a long struggle to find companies willing to write the required bonds. Their final success in obtaining bonds was attributed to the efforts of lawyers and civil rights groups in the North and South in putting pressure on the bonding companies and to "the glare of publicity."

26 / Victory at the Polls for Blacks
EDITORS, *COMMONWEAL*
RICHARD G. HATCHER

One of the last techniques to be thwarted in the South for preventing blacks from full political participation was the literacy test. With the passage of the Voting Rights Act in 1965, these tests were suspended, and the prospects for greater political power for blacks seemed bright. Some of these hopes have been realized; the election of Charles Evers, a black, as mayor of Fayette, Mississippi, is one example of this increased power. For the northern black the problems of political power were different. He was not denied access to the polls, but he did not have much influence. As a result of housing segregation and economic discrimination, the blacks have been concentrated in small areas, and their votes were neutralized except in national presidential elections. Until 1966, when Carl Stokes was elected mayor of Cleveland and Richard Hatcher was elected mayor of Gary, Indiana, few blacks were successful in being elected to positions that required any support from white voters. The Stokes and Hatcher victories seemed to signal a breakthrough, but the victory of Sam Yorty over

SOURCE: "Mayor Stokes' West Side Story," *Commonweal*, November 28, 1969, pp. 270–271; reprinted by permission of Commonweal Publishing Co., Inc.; Richard G. Hatcher, "The Black Role in Urban Politics," *Current History*, November 1969, pp. 287–289, 306–307.

Thomas Bradley in the Los Angeles mayoralty election of 1969
indicated that white voters had not totally accepted black candidates.

MAYOR STOKES' WEST SIDE STORY

—Editors, *Commonweal*

Cleveland's charismatic black Mayor picked up his most surprising vote
gains in the November 4 elections in two predominantly white West Side
wards. The sociological composition of the area is such that some might
consider it a bailiwick of Richard Milhous Nixon's "forgotten people." In
Ward 7, Carl Stokes received 35.2 percent of the vote as against 28.5 percent in 1967; in Ward 8 he received 32 percent to '67s 22.8 percent.
Stokes' 1967 vote in the two wards was 2411; his plurality in the entire
city, 3753. The increases were achieved in a heavily European ethnic section of the city against Republican Ralph Perk, the son of Czechoslovak
immigrants.

Experts had said all along that the battle would be won or lost on the
white West Side. A drop in registration of 10,000 East Side Negro voters
had made the West Side performance all the more critical. (The Mayor's
actual vote in some all-black wards dropped by more than 7000.) The
"near" West Side, or Wards 7 and 8, just over the bridge from downtown
Cleveland, is still the kind of melting pot New York City was in the early
1900s. The population is a mix of Southern Appalachians fleeing the poverty of West Virginia and Kentucky, first and second-generation Europeans (Czechs, Slovenians, Hungarians, Russians, Ukrainians, Poles. Greeks,
Germans and Italians), Anglo-Saxon Protestants and Irish Catholics,
Puerto Ricans and relocated American Indians. Only a possible 5 percent
are Negroes.

For the most part the people are poor because underemployed or on
welfare, or are slightly better-off blue-collar steel, automotive and other
factory workers who live in houses with small, neat yards; the kind of people who for American journalists have become a symbol of white backlash.

The near West Side has its share of problems: Saturday night shoot-
ings at bars, glue-sniffing and beer-drinking by minors, racial and national
tensions among gangs of kids. Though the near West Side has its gentle
people too, some people on the far (and more affluent) West Side consider
it pretty rough territory. White liberals living in Cleveland's integrated East
Side suburbs have suspected it to be a hotbed of bigotry.

Why did such a potentially hostile area (frequently hostile in practice)
up Carl Stokes' margin so dramatically? Cleveland newspaper reporters

have arbitrarily attributed the Mayor's success in Wards 7 and 8 to "a large influx of Puerto Rican voters" and to "the Democratic party's decision to expose Stokes to large numbers of West Side voters during the last weeks of the campaign."

Sorry, wrong on both counts. The Puerto Rican population is fairly stable, and has not experienced any tremendous upsurge in the two years since 1967; even now the total count of registered Puerto Rican voters in 7 and 8 is only 788. Though the Puerto Ricans were solidly behind Carl Stokes, worked hard for his election, and gave him probably his most jubilant campaign reception on the West Side, they comprise only 7.6 percent of the near West Side voting population.

On the second count, "exposure to West Side voters," the Mayor owes the Democratic party less than he thinks. (Most West Side Democratic councilmen avoided being seen with him during the campaign.) Weeks, and even months before Election Day, large numbers of near-West Side voters had made up their minds to vote for Carl Stokes.

In mid-October, not long after Robert Kelly's bitter law-and-order primary campaign had stirred up the old hates and the "nigger" talk, Stokes canvassers warily picked up their telephones to find out the lay of the land. What they discovered was substantial support for the Mayor, some purely on the basis of party loyalty ("My husband wouldn't care if a man was blue, green or purple, so long as he was a Democrat"), but just as much based on performance. "He's for the underdog," an elderly Italian voter said with a heavy accent. "This town had been dead for 20 years until he took over," said another voter. "He's a good man, whether he's white or black," commented a lady with a West Virginia accent. "And I surely appreciate those new lights down the street."

A resident of a Polish, Russian and Ukrainian precinct observed that services were beginning to improve in the neighborhood, and that Mayor Stokes "is always the perfect gentleman." (Little old ladies love to watch the Mayor on television. "He's smooth as wax," one said. "I noticed Mr. Perk's collar was rumpled last week when I saw him.")

A neighborhood organizer, asked why a group of Southern Appalachians, who had been angry with the Mayor in the spring, now intended to vote for him: "It's simple. They know he's halfway responsive to their needs. They want to be sure they have the same guy to fight this time. Let's face it. Stokes has made poor people's claims legitimate. He's legitimized community control."

It should be pointed out, however, that the racists were still there, passing out hate literature, and that a couple of West Side windows with Stokes signs were shattered by bullets and rocks.

An important factor in "The West Side Story," as the *Cleveland Press* called Stokes' win, was the tight and bouncy campaign run in Wards

7 and 8 by Bill Hale, young Texas-raised director of the West Side Community House. "We didn't have any money, but we had the manpower," Hale says. The votes were there, and Hale was determined to get them. The regular Democratic party offered no help, but a grass roots corps of dedicated neighborhood workers had sprung up; swarms of college students from Oberlin, Antioch, Wooster College and Ohio State descended on the office on Election Day to help get voters to the polls. "Perk simply didn't have the manpower or the personal contacts over here in 7 and 8," Hale maintains. . . .

THE BLACK ROLE IN URBAN POLITICS

—Richard G. Hatcher

Black political contributions in the United States can be real and tangible only when black communities have evidence from the nation's polling places of the importance of their participation. Blacks must have lasting and visible leverage. When entire communities finally accept black leadership as they do Irish leadership, or Italian leadership, as an established fact, and do not regard it as a passing poignancy—a latter day Reconstruction phenomenon of temporary dimensions—then relevancy will come. When there is an end to attempts to beat black hands off the lever of political power or to slide the fulcrum from under the lever, then the larger questions of the meaning of black power can be asked intelligently and answered meaningfully.

Black political power today is most visible and most meaningful in urban America. Yet in the cities where black power is important, the realization of black political hope is threatened today by a two-pronged attack. By cutting away territory where black people have gained some measure of reasonable influence, or by adding territory around the black center, the opponents of change seek to weaken whatever momentum black political action can generate.

The politics of abandonment is at work in urban America in some quarters; the politics of envelopment is manifest in others. The difference is most often the difference between Metro Government—an enlargement of the metropolis—on the one hand, and moves toward disannexation—neighborhood independence from cities—on the other. It is a difference in the shape of shadows.

In Gary, Indiana, for example, there are those in a large, virtually wholly white section of the city, Glen Park, who would like to disannex from the city proper. The intensity of their desire to leave Gary and incorporate separately is unfurling now, and remains to be formally tested. Those who support disannexation seem to believe that by changing the name of their community, by becoming known as something other than Gary, they will escape the turbulence and the challenges of the times. The price of disannexation for Glen Park would be high in a number of ways, and there are many motives for this aggressive pursuit of urban fractionalization. Yet its supporters seem to press for disaffiliation from the city despite all practical considerations.

The specter raised by the Gary disannexation movement is a specter of national significance. Glen Park holds about 36,000 of Gary's more than 180,000 citizens. The area is separated from the rest of the city by a highway, a river, and perhaps some several generations of social thought. The latter will better be known when the disannexation drive either folds up under its own weight or proceeds aggressively with wide support.

Regardless of its support in Glen Park, the questions posed by disannexation remain real. If Glen Park can disannex, can United States Steel, the vast industrial complex at the north edge of the city, also cut loose—taking its 40 percent of the city's tax base with it?

If Glen Park can disannex, can an industrial park in a medium sized community in Massachusetts explore the economic potential in such a step? Can it set up new political sovereignty, financially independent of the community that provides its manpower—the community that supports that manpower with services from schools to water?

If Glen Park can disannex, what are the possibilities in major cities like Chicago, Los Angeles or Detroit when they first elect a black mayor? Will these cities, brittle with anxiety, shatter into separate units, each with cutting edges turned toward the others?

The thrust of the Glen Park disannexation effort puts pressure on Los Angeles, Boston and innumerable cities between. It is a blunt and costly response to black realization, an embryonic American version of apartheid.

To Glen Parkers, disannexation will cost money. Under present law, they are not able to incorporate and, as an unincorporated area, they would have to rely on county services. Since Glen Park could not disannex from some other government units, such as the School City, additional complications would arise. The cost of setting up a government (if and when incorporation became a fact) would be great, and without the advantage of United States Steel's contribution to tax revenues, taxes would certainly rise.

All this and more has been detailed at length to Glen Parkers, yet some of them continue to attempt to obscure the real issues and the actual costs of disannexation. They claim that Gary's city services are not up to par, and that this is a major consideration of the politics of abandonment. On the other hand, many disinterested citizens maintain that city services have never been at such a high level of efficiency. In any event, the "services" argument is weak in the face of the historic facts of Gary. Interestingly, there were no organized attempts to build a disannexation drive in years past when Gary was governed by mayors who went to jail for sundry misdeeds.

In a recent national magazine interview, the leading exponent of Glen Park disannexation was quoted at length on his perception of the city he serves. The major revelatory impact of his remarks had nothing to do with garbage collection—his remarks reveal a white supremacist view of history and a distrust of the mode and manner of black people.

There can be little doubt what disannexation is all about in Gary. It is, at the core, white reaction to black ascendency. Gary suffers from the social schizophrenia of our times, with the 10 major metropolises of the nation headed inexorably toward black majorities.

Metro Government

There is another contemporary non-solution to urban problems that is achieving new currency and a more respectable momentum. This second tine of the sharp-pointed fork of unresponsiveness to city needs is one aspect or another of the modern phenomenon known as Metro Government, or Uni-Gov or whatever euphemistic label is logically popular. In the urban areas that are moving in this direction, it is not the chipping away of the urban mass that appeals, but the drawing of ever larger concentric circles of governmental structure that just as effectively enervates the strength of the inner city. Need is not abandoned with this technique. It is smothered.

Like a doctor's prescription scrawled in Latin, the processes of traditional Establishment rule have long been kept from the uninitiated black and poor and powerless communities. Every American city of any size supports a black ghetto teeming with the disadvantaged, the alienated, the suppressed. These ghettos are growing in anger and political and social sophistication. They are closing in on once hidden power, the power that will give them an equal voice and equal opportunity. Today they are learning how the political game is played. At the same time, the Establishment is trying to change the rules.

No one has a right to be dismayed if the ghetto does not swing enthusiastically behind the area government concept. Good intentions notwithstanding, to the ghetto Metro Government means more of the same tired struggle. To the ghetto, with its accelerating awareness, Metro Government is one more flanking maneuver—another way, however subtle, to offer oblique reaction to needs that require honest response.

Enlightened leaders make a persuasive case for Metro Government. They talk sensibly of the proliferation of tax districts without contiguous boundaries, from Mosquito Abatement districts to school districts. They deplore, with reason, the confusion these many overlapping authorities can cause.

Enlightened leaders speak of political and social problems that do not end at traditional political lines; they speak of the need for coordination and overall planning in the megalopolises. They are, of course, right. They even decry the usually toothless attempts of Metropolitan Area Planning Commissions to fill the bill for the larger community, and they are right again.

To the ghetto, it still looks as if whitey is trying to mute black voices by diluting the vote of these new huddled masses. And the ghetto, too, is right. Whatever the motives for Metro Government, at the theory's end, the practical effect is to undermine black power.

Indeed, if the choice is between deferrring the black dream—already deferred beyond all human understanding—or of deferring the eminent logic of Metro Government, the choice is clear. Metro Government must wait.

Nonetheless, the apologists for area-wide government make too much sense to be lightly dismissed. They have too much logic on their side. They are doing more than saying "no" to black America. In most cases, the "no" is merely a byproduct of a sincerely held conviction that many of our problems must be dealt with on an area-wide basis if they are to be dealt with at all.

Rapid metropolitan growth has been no respecter of political boundaries, and communities today spill across city lines in a stretching, reaching urban sprawl of constantly remagnified proportions. In such a situation, inter-governmental communication is an absolute necessity. The awesome problems of air and water pollution cannot be attacked tellingly when they are attacked by isolated units. Such battles, to be won, must become area-wide battles rather than isolated skirmishes.

In addition, the tax calls on citizens are topping out; they approach levels beyond which further taxes cannot be tolerated. Simultaneously, citizen demands increase. If the social flow is ever to be reversed, if the poverty cycle is to be broken, these requirements must be met now. Ten years from now may be too late. Economies, then, must be effected, and area cooperation is one route to new economy.

Cooperation in areas such as interdepartmental police communication would be of great value. The list of needs requiring cooperation multiplies with the complexities of our burgeoning population in a mathematical progression of unmet problems. The solutions so far offered to these clear requirements for mutual assaults on mutual enemies are largely variations on, or degrees of, Metro Government. In some instances, they are bureaucratic preambles to Metro Government.

Unfortunately, if such solutions are incautiously handled, the black community—a body that is just beginning to flex its political muscles—will see its main chance disappearing even as it recognizes that chance. If the answers sap sovereignty from emerging black political power, what answers to their own destiny will be left to blacks? The alternatives to viable political participation for blacks are bleak indeed. With the removal of traditionally accepted avenues of progress, new avenues will be carved out of society by a righteous, justified and impatient black minority. Then the social acceleration of black action, and white suppression in reaction, will set in with a vengeance that can only vitiate the promise of democracy.

The dialogues around such solutions as Uni-Government, two-tiered governments, cooperative buying, suburban/city trade-offs, complete consolidation and, finally, abdication of responsibility to another, larger governing unit—these dialogues are too often exercises in futility. A vital element is most often left out of such discussions.

Whither black America in these experimental machinations?

The importance of black participation in politics, black leadership in the democratic processes, and the contribution blacks can make to urban solutions all become academic if black hopes are cut off at the political pass by tactical devices. This is true whether the denial to blacks is calculated—as in disannexation—or accidental, even incidental, as in Metro Government.

The problems raised by Metro Government partisans are real and should be met. The problems created by Metro Government plans in regard to black power are also real, and must be anticipated. The dilemma offered by these two considerations may be more apparent than real.

Some of the answer may lie in our political parties, either those that exist now, or those that are destined to flourish if the two major parties do not strike postures of more courage and constancy than they have found so far.

The traditional coalitions that have provided the glue for Democrats and Republicans alike are moribund. The opportunism inherent in attempts to build a "party for everyone" is failing. Paucity of principle needs to be supplanted by coalitions of conscience: when and if that happens, black communities can move closer to political parity.

But there can be no waiting for that distant day. The isolated salients established by black political awareness must be protected now. At the same time, the call for intergovernmental cooperation must be heeded, lest the problems it would confront grow so monumental as to defy solution. Black leaders must join efforts to answer those difficulties now, if only for the preservation of the minor black gains made so far. If they do not join in seeking honest answers while protecting emerging black power, supra-governments will be formed around them to answer those problems—and will inevitably diffuse and dilute the little black equity that does prevail. With or without black contributions, intergovernmental cooperative ventures will be developed. They must not be developed in a closet populated by white planners who have only rarely been sensitive to black destiny.

27 / Politics and Policies of the Mexican-American Community

RALPH GUZMAN

For the Mexican-American, the problems of voting and political power are somewhat different from those of either the black or the Indian. On the one hand, he has not been the victim of systematic exclusion from the polls; on the other hand, he has been denied access through threats or the actual use of a literacy test because of his failure to read and/or write English. Because much of the work available to the Mexican-American is farm labor, he has been kept from the polls by residency requirements that his migratory occupation precludes. Today, the problem is more one of apathy than disenfranchisement, a continuing lack of education, cultural biases against women participating in politics, gerrymandering to neutralize the impact of any effort at bloc voting, and, as the present selection indicates, splintering of groups in the community. There are at least five active organizations: MAPA (Mexican-American Political Association), LULAC (League of United Latin American Citizens), CSO (Community Service Organization), American GI Forum, and PASSO (Political Asso-

Source: Ralph Guzman, "Politics and Policies of the Mexican-American Community," from *California Politics and Policies*, edited by Eugene P. Dvorin and Arthur J. Misner, 1966, Addison-Wesley, Reading, Mass., pp. 357, 372–373, and 381–383.

ciation of Spanish Speaking Organizations). They are region-
ally based, competitive within themselves, and as a result, far
less effective than their counterparts in the black community.

In California, two political campaigns, both organized in East Los Angeles, reveal how campaign strategy was adjusted in order to achieve limited
ethnic goals. The campaign of Edward R. Roybal, when he first ran for
Councilman in the Ninth District of the City of Los Angeles, is one example. A second is Leopoldo Sanchez' campaign for Municipal Court Judge
in the East Los Angeles Judicial District. Both candidates were resisted by
Anglo politicians. And both men wore the ethnic label. Yet each resolved
the conflict of ethnic goals and Anglo power in different ways.

Roybal's effort was set in Boyle Heights, an east side community
where there was much interaction between Anglo and Mexican and also a
substantial amount of conflict. On the other hand, the Sanchez judicial
campaign was launched in Belvedere, where there was little Mexican-An-
glo interaction but a great deal of conflict. Another important difference is
time. The Roybal campaign was initiated shortly after World War II, when
Mexican social issues, sometimes provoked by the Los Angeles police,
were immediate and urgent. By contrast, the Sanchez campaign took place
in the late 1950s after great political momentum had been gathered and
when police brutality, discrimination in housing, unequal educational opportunities, and other social problems seemed less urgent. However, it is
in the area of ethnic goals that the greatest disparity between Roybal and
Sanchez is seen. Roybal, recruited by a group of Mexican businessmen as
an ethnic candidate to replace an aging Anglo in City Hall, dispensed with
pure ethnic politics early in his campaign. Sanchez, on the other hand,
maintained an ethnic platform in which he stressed that the majority of the
people who came before the east side judiciary were Mexican, and that a
Mexican from the local area could best administer the law for Mexicans.

While Roybal's district was heavily Mexican, the Mexicans were
widely interspersed with other minority groups. Consequently, victory for
Roybal depended on the successful blending of minority voting blocs (i.e.,
Mexican, Jewish, Negro, Oriental) along with pockets of Anglo votes. The
Roybal strategy, to which no Mexican Democratic Party campaign organizer contributed personally, deemphasized the image of a "Mexican" poli-
tician.

Sanchez' East Los Angeles Judicial District included a heavily Mexican section (around Belvedere and Maravilla), several neighborhoods
where Mexicans were interspersed with Jews, and a heavy concentration of
Anglos in the Montebello area. In terms of voting blocs, Sanchez faced a
more difficult path to victory than Roybal.

Ethnic goals in the Sanchez campaign, while clear from the beginning, were placed in sharp relief by opposition from Governor Brown. And, unlike Roybal who had the invaluable services of a professional Anglo organizer, Sanchez counted on a few friends, mostly from the American G.I. Forum, a Mexican civic action group. Reconciliation of ethnic goals with Anglo political power came early in the Roybal campaign because the issues were specific, e.g., discrimination in housing, in employment, and before the law. For Sanchez, the issues were vague, e.g., the need for Mexican representation and the need for justice. Sanchez noted that "bread and butter issues are not at stake in a judicial campaign" [1] In the Roybal effort the issues concerned a candidate for a legislative post.

Today, several years later, both men remain important ethnic symbols. However, neither seems exclusively concerned with the ethnic goals that appeared sharp and urgent at the outset of their campaigns. Both seek effective involvement of Mexicans in the American political system.

ETHNIC GOALS AND ETHNIC ORGANIZATION

Civic organizations have been vehicles for the accomplishment of minority goals. However, American society has changed, and so have the goals of the minorities. The result is that new models of the vehicles of social change have emerged.

The following typologies of Mexican organizations is useful to the understanding of the creation of Mexican organizations and of the shifting patterns of ethnic goals: (1) assimilation into American society, and (2) participation in the American political system. Seven selected organizations illustrate this pattern of changing group goals. These organizations, arranged chronologically in terms of the period in history when they were created, are as follows:

1. The Mexican Liberal Party (MLP), organized September 28, 1906
2. The Order of Sons of America, founded circa 1920
3. The League of United Latin-American Citizens (LULAC), established in 1927
4. Community Service Organization (CSO), chartered in 1947
5. American G.I. Forum, organized in 1948
6. Mexican-American Political Association (MAPA), founded in 1959
7. Political Association of Spanish Speaking Organizations (PASSO), founded in 1960.

Concern for social assimilation as expressed in the constitution of the organization, recruitment pamphlets, house organs, news releases, and

[1] Interview with Leopoldo Sanchez, East Los Angeles Municipal Court Judge.

public statements by elected officials are used to classify organizations in terms of high, medium, or low intent to become socially assimilated. Some groups, for example, express organizational goals of complete integration into American society, with small concern for retention of things Mexican or a Mexican way of life. At the other extreme, some organizations emphasize retention of things Mexican or a Mexican way of life and only small concern for integration into American society (Table 1). . . .

Table 1   Suggested Typologies of Mexican-American Organizations

Social Intent (Assimilation)

		High	Medium	Low
Political Intent (Participation)	High		Mexican-American Political Association (MAPA), 1959 Political Association of Spanish-Speaking Organizations (PASSO), 1960	
	Medium	League of United Latin-American Cit-izens (LULAC), 1927 The Order of Sons of America, 1920	Community Service Organization (CSO), 1947 American G.I. Forum, 1948	
	Low			Mexican Liberal Party (MLP), 1906

In addition to general social goals, all organizations seem to have a high, medium, or low intent to become politically partisan. Some groups, for example, are highly active politically. On the other hand, some organizations are studiously nonpolitical. . . . Ultimately, the Political Association of Spanish-Speaking Organizations (PASSO) became the name of the new national organization. In California, however, both MAPA and the CSO refused to subsume their activities beneath the PASSO label.

Today, PASSO maintains a high level of political participation, mainly in the State of Texas. Like MAPA in California, PASSO concentrates on direct political action. Recently, in 1963, PASSO, joined by the Teamsters' Union and other organizations, helped to elect a completely Mexican slate of city officials in Crystal City, Texas. The Crystal City victory appeared to be a high-water mark of political activity for PASSO.

Like MAPA, the Texas-based PASSO does not seem to have much

concern for social assimilation. PASSO, again like MAPA, reflects explicitly partisan political goals, in spite of the apparent ambiguity that its organizational label proclaims. A woman orator at a PASSO rally said:

> Los Mexicans han estado en el back seat for muchos años. (The Mexicans have been in the back seat for many years.) Let's get in the front seat and go. We, the Mexicans, deserve a few paved streets and a little self-dignity, and we're going to get it.[2]

PORTENTS OF CHANGE

It has been said that the majority group determines the behavior of the minority. This relationship is evident in the politics of the Southwest. The California context is different from that of Texas. In California, Mexicans were able to organize the Mexican American Political Association, an unquestionable Mexican organization with untarnished ethnic goals. On the other hand, a clear ethnic identity in Texas was possible only briefly, when the Mexican-Americans for Political Action was formed. In California, prejudice against Mexicans is considerably less than it is in Texas and in other parts of the Southwest. It is easier (and safer) to say "Mexican" in California than it is in other states. In Texas, for example, "Mexican" has unmistakable pejorative implications derived from a heritage of conflict.

Politics

The political effectiveness of MAPA and PASSO is much debated by Mexicans and non-Mexicans alike. Among Mexicans it seems generally agreed that both MAPA and PASSO perform an essential gadfly function that has on occasion caused the donkey to bray and the elephant to trumpet. However, a significant section is concerned lest the image of a stoical, uncompromising Mexican supplant that of the docile bracero. One non-Mexican, a defeated officeholder in Mathis, Texas, said:

> I don't know what it is they want. These people on the other side have got so bitter. I asked one of the Mexican leaders, "What are you people up to? What have we done?" All he could say was, "We want to get on top." [3]

Voting

Mexican leaders at a 1965 meeting in Los Angeles said, "The Mexican vote, once a monolithic Democratic vote, has shrunk and so has our political effectiveness." [4] The voting strength of the Mexican in California has,

[2] Carl D. Howard, "A Tale of Two Texas Cities," The National Observer, Vol. 4, No. 15 (April 12, 1965), p. 13.

[3] Howard, p. 13.

[4] Meeting of Mexican-American Leaders, New Federal Building, September, 1965.

indeed, dropped. Massive voter registration drives, once common in East Los Angeles, have been replaced by occasional specialized and narrowly focused efforts in selected Spanish-surname precincts. Out of a 1960 potential voting population of more than 600,000 Spanish-surname people in California, less than 20 percent were registered voters, and fewer yet were brought to the polls. In Los Angeles County a potential Spanish-surname vote of 256,000 was never activated. An estimate of comparative voting strength between Negro and Mexican voters (U.S. citizens only), based on 1960 Census data, suggests a potential Negro vote on the State level of 454,000 and a Mexican vote of 633,000. In Los Angeles County, the population of U.S. citizens in both groups is more nearly equal. Negro voters are computed at 243,400 and Mexicans (Spanish surnames) at 256,800. The combined potential of these two enormous minority groups has long been a prominent point in majority group conversation. . . .

Race Relations

Substantial support has been given to the Mexican people by other minority groups and by members of the Anglo majority. That Jewish organizational know-how and Jewish funds have helped the Mexican people of California is slightly known. Less known is the political and financial aid that was rendered by the Negro community.

In California, there have been two examples of Negro cooperation and assistance to the Mexican community. One involved a group of Mexican and Negro citizens from El Centro, California who, in 1955, jointly filed a class suit in a Federal district court in an effort to end school segregation in California. The case, called *Romero* v. *Weakley,* was sponsored by the Alianza Hispano-Americana and the National Association for the Advancement of Colored People (NAACP). Several other organizations, among them the American Civil Liberties Union, the American Jewish Committee, and the Greater Los Angeles CIO Council, filed an *Amicus Curiae* (Friend of the Court) brief supporting the Mexican and Negro plaintiffs. A news release from the Alianza Hispano Americana announced:

> This [case] marks the first time in U.S. history that the Negro and Mexican communities have joined hands, as American citizens, to fight for a common social problem.[5]

Three years later, in 1958, a Negro woman lawyer, representing a coalition of Mexican and Negro politicians, nominated Henry P. Lopez, a Mexican Attorney, for the office of Secretary of State at a convention in Fresno, California. That same year the Democratic Minority Conference, a predominantly Negro association, organized and financed an intensive

[5] News release from the Alianza Hispano Americana of September 2, 1965.

voter registration drive among Mexican and Negro voters that netted 25,000 new voter registrations within a three-month period.

Comparable cooperation between these two massive minorities no longer prevails. Mexicans and Negroes have long shared similar economic and social distress in the large urban centers of the Southwest. And yet today, meaningful dialogue between responsible Mexican and Negro leaders is not heard. However, with the increasing pressure of the Negro Civil Rights movement, it seems likely that Mexicans will eventually seek renewed contact with the Negro people.

28 / Voting on Indian Reservations

**HOUSE COMMITTEE ON INTERIOR
AND INSULAR AFFAIRS**

Of the three minority groups, Indians enjoy probably the least
use of their legal right to participate in the political process.
The Indian's record of voting is the lowest, and there are far
fewer elected or appointed officials of Indian origin than of
black or of Mexican-American origin. There is one congressman of Indian background and fifteen legislators at the state
level. The two political parties show no leadership from the
group. There is only one major national organization representing Indians—the National Congress of Indians—while
there are several speaking for the other two groups. The
causes of these conditions appear to lie with the confused
legal status of the Indian, his delayed entry into full citizenship status (in Maine he did not gain the right to vote until
1953, and in Arizona and New Mexico, with large Indian
populations, not until 1948), lack of trust in the white man's
word (the result of many years of treaties being broken by
the federal and state government), lack of experience with
the democratic process, inaccessibility of polling places, and

SOURCE: House Committee on Interior and Insular Affairs, *Present Relations of Federal Government to the American Indian*. 85th Congress, 2d Session, House Commission Print #38 (Washington, D.C.: U.S. Government Printing Office, 1959), pp. 161–162, 164–165, 172–173, 175–179.

199

the related procedural barriers described in this reading selection. The result of these factors is that a very low percentage of the Indians eligible to vote exercise their franchise. (In Minneapolis, Minnesota, a very recent survey showed that 44 percent had never voted in a public election.) The lack of societal concern over the political rights of the Indian is demonstrated by the scarcity of material on the subject. The most recent substantial work was done in 1958, over twelve years ago.

ABERDEEN AREA OFFICE, SOUTH DAKOTA

Cheyenne River Indian Agency, South Dakota

This agency indicated that there were polling places at all towns on the reservation and at the following places in addition: Bridger, Cherry Creek, Moreau, Promise, Laplant, and Agency Districts. The number of nonvoting Indians was explained by (*a*) apparent indifference, (*b*) transportation difficulties, and (*c*) unusual expense entailed in traveling to the polls.

Crow Creek Reservation, South Dakota

There are six polling places on the Crow Creek Reservation, namely: Pershing No. 5, Buffalo County; Wilson No. 6, Buffalo County; Victory No. 7, Buffalo County; Paradise Valley, Hughes County; Joe Creek, Hughes County; and Stephan Store, Hyde County. The number of nonvoting Indians is explained in 72 percent of the cases as due to apparent indifference, in 16 percent of the cases as due to transportation difficulties, in 6 percent of the cases as due to ill health, in 3 percent as due to illiteracy, and in 3 percent as due to inability to speak English.

Fort Berthold Reservation, North Dakota

The number of nonvoting Indians is explained to the extent that apparent indifference accounts for approximately 10 percent, inability to speak English about 1 percent, and ill health about 1 percent. . . .

ANADARKO AREA OFFICE, OKLAHOMA

Kiowa Area Field Office, Oklahoma

Kiowa, Comanche, and Apache Tribes, Oklahoma It is believed that apparent indifference is the largest factor controlling the number of nonvoting Indians. Elections are conducted with standing votes in the tribe. In tribal council proceedings, the standing vote or the show of hands are generally used. On some occasions, secret balloting has been ordered.

Wichita, Caddo, and Delaware Tribes, Oklahoma Local politicians have made efforts in the past to encourage voting by explaining the privileges and obligations and attempting to assist them in registering. Lack of registration may account for some nonvoting.

Fort Sill Apache Tribe, Oklahoma Apparent indifference is the explanation as to why the number of nonvoting Indians is high in this group. Fort Sill Apache are unorganized and transact very little business as a tribal organization.

Cheyenne-Arapaho Area Field Office, Oklahoma

Cheyenne and Arapaho Tribes, Oklahoma These Indians vote in the same polling places as non-Indians. Apparent indifference would cover approximately 75 percent of the nonvoting. A large percentage of this number do not register, or do not know how to go about qualifying themselves to vote. There are some who have been informed as to how they can register but are afraid to and are not interested enough to go and register. . . .

Kickapoo Tribe of Kansas No reason for nonvoting is indicated. The secret ballot is used in tribal elections but standing vote or show of hands is used in council proceedings.

Potawatomi Tribe of Kansas No reason for nonvoting is indicated. . . .

Osage Agency, Okla.

Osage Tribe of Oklahoma The secret ballot is used in the election of tribal officials and on important issues involving the welfare of the tribe. The tribal council uses both secret ballot and show of hands, depending on the issue involved.

GALLUP AREA OFFICE, NEW MEXICO

Consolidated Ute Agency, Colorado

Southern Ute Tribe, Colorado, New Mexico Polling places are located in the following towns within the reservation area: Ignacio, Bayfield, Allison, and Oxford. Apparent indifference seems to be the explanation for the low population of Indian voters. There is a legal cloud existing regarding the right of Indians to vote and a State attorney general's opinion is necessary to remove this cloud. There has been apparently little encouragement to the Indians to register to vote. Secret ballot is used in tribal elections and occasionally in council meetings.

Ute Mountain Tribe, Colorado   A polling place exists at Towaoc for the Utes living near Blanding, Utah, on allotments. The nearest polling place is in Blanding. Illiteracy and inability to speak English have contributed to nonvoting. The polling place was first set up on the reservation within the last year and many have registered for the first time. Show of hands has been the procedure in general council meetings rather than secret ballot primarily because of illiteracy of members.

Mescalero Apache Tribe, New Mexico   A polling place is set up at Bent, N. Mex., which is 5 miles from the reservation line. Indians who have reached the age of 21 since 1949 have not made any effort to register at the county seat, which is 35 miles from the reservation. No apparent indifference is indicated but the matter of registering has not been explained to those reaching eligible age. The secret ballot is used in tribal elections and the polling place for these elections is usually a community hall. Poll boxes are set up within a closed voting booth and pencils and ballots are furnished. In the tribal council pieces of paper are distributed to each member and the latter indicates his choice on the paper and folds it. Voting by show of hands is used sometimes in general meetings.

BILLINGS AREA OFFICE, MONTANA

Blackfeet Agency, Montana

There are 13 polling places on the reservation and 6 polling places located just off the reservation, and in no case more than 2 miles off the reservation boundary. The polling places on the reservation are as follows: Seville, Browning, Glacier Park, Blackfoot, Browning (2), Browning (3), McKelveys, Babb, Family, DeMartins, Starr, Browning (4), and Heart Butte. All of the foregoing are in Glacier County except Heart Butte, which is in Pondera County. About 70 percent of the Indians are registered to vote and probably indifference accounts for the remainder not registering. Secret ballot is used for all tribal and council elections.

Crow Indians, Montana

Polling places are set up on the reservation as follows: St. Xavier Public School, Pryor Public School, recreation hall at Crow Agency, public school and American Legion hall at Lodge Grass, and Wyola Public School and Kirkemo Ranch at Two Leggin. Apparent indifference appears to be the chief obstacle to voting, followed by illiteracy and inability to speak English, ill health and transportation difficulties. Both secret ballot and voice and show-of-hands procedures are used in council meetings. The secret ballot is used on most votes on important issues.

Flathead Agency, Montana

There are 27 polling places where Indians vote in Lake County, Sanders County has 8 voting precincts where Indians vote, and Missoula County 1 precinct. The non-Indian population outnumbers the Indian population about 10 to 1 within the reservation boundary. It has been difficult for the Indians of this reservation to quickly evaluate their privileges to vote. This is particularly true of the fullbloods. The secret ballot is used in tribal elections but not in tribal council proceedings, except where open votes will injure the best interests of the tribe. In council meetings voting is accomplished by show of hands as a general practice.

Fort Belknap, Montana

Polling places exist at the agency, Hays, Lodge Pole, Harlem, and Dodson. The last two are just off the reservation. Apparently the candidates for office have not reached the Indians to the extent that they will take an interest in voting. Although tribal elections are by secret ballot, the normal tribal business is conducted by show-of-hands method as a matter of expediency.

Rocky Boy, Montana

There is a polling place on the reservation in the tribal council room of the Rocky Boy Subagency office. Most of the nonvoting is due to apparent indifference but to a minor degree to illiteracy and inability to speak English. The secret ballot is used in tribal elections but the tribal business committee uses show of hands.

Fort Peck, Montana

Polling places are established by precincts in all towns on the reservation. Rural precincts vote at schoolhouses. Apparent indifference is the only important factor in nonvoting. . . .

Navajo, New Mexico, Arizona, Utah Polling places on the Navajo Reservation are located as follows: (1) In New Mexico: Ramah, Hospah, Crownpoint, Thoreau, Rehoboth, Fort Wingate, Whitewater, Mentmore, Gamerco, Tohatchi, Shiprock, Bloomfield; (2) in Arizona: Puerco, Lupton, Ganado, St. Michaels, Fort Defiance, Salina, Chinle, Lukachukai, Rough Rock, Denehotso, Sweetwater, Kayenta, Keams Canyon, Teesto, Tuba City. In New Mexico only Tohatchi and Shiprock are on the reservation while in Arizona only Puerco is off. Illiteracy is a major obstacle to voting in State and national elections, particularly in Arizona. Inability to speak English is also important. Transportation difficulties play a considerable part as it is difficult for many families to reach polling places on election day, especially in inclement weather. The secret ballot is used in tribal elections, which is a paper ballot containing pictures of the various candidates for office and is marked with a pencil in the proper square under the candidate representing the voter's choice. Manner of voting in the tribal council is not indicated. . . .

PORTLAND AREA OFFICE, OREGON

Colville Reservation, Washington

Polling places are located at Nespelem, Keller, Inchelium, and East Omak. The reason for nonvoting would be apparent indifference, particularly among the younger generation. The secret ballot is used in tribal elections and council proceedings.

Spokane, Washington

A polling place is located at St. Augustine School at Wellpinit. Apparent indifference would explain nonvoting. The secret ballot is used in tribal elections and council proceedings.

Klamath, Oregon

Polling places are set up at Beatty, Sprague River, and Chiloquin. Apparent indifference explains the percentage of nonvoters. The secret ballot is used in tribal elections and standing-vote procedures in tribal council proceedings.

Northern Idaho Indian Agency, Idaho and Washington

This includes four reservations on which polling places are set up, both on and off each reservation. Apparent indifference is the main reason for not voting. Voice and show of hands are the general procedures for both the general and tribal council proceedings. The report for this agency did not include detailed information for Nez Perce, Coeur d'Alene, Kalispel, and Kootenai Reservations.

Umatilla, Oregon

Polling places are as follows: Tillicum Grange, about three-quarters mile from the agency office, and Gibbon, Oregon, about 15 miles from the agency office. There is a lack of interest in local government on the part of the Indians. Candidates for offices in primary and general elections this year have apparently displayed little interest in the Indian vote. In tribal elections the secret ballot is used, but in the general council only seldom.

Warm Springs, Oregon

There is a polling place located at Warm Springs, Oregon. Indians of the Simnasho district in the northern part of the reservation must go 15 miles to Wapinitia, Oregon, to vote. The local Indians are more or less indifferent to State and National political issues and elections. However, the younger Indians are showing considerable interest in voting. The secret ballot is used at all local elections.

Chehalis, Washington

No information was secured regarding polling places. The secret ballot is used in elections and controversial issues. . . .

Yakima Agency, Washington

Yakima Reservation, Washington   Polling places are on or adjacent to the reservation. A small percentage do not vote because they fear they will have to pay taxes. The secret ballot is not used in the tribal elections nor the tribal council proceedings. They vote by raised hands or standing as this is the traditional method. The secret ballot has been explained but met with violent opposition.

Fort Hall, Idaho   Public schools on and adjacent to the reservation are used as polling places, e.g., at Fort Hall, Bannock Creek, on the reservation; and at Tyhee off the reservation. The Legion Hall in Blackfoot is a polling place for a few Indians residing on the reservation. The secret ballot is used in tribal elections.

SACRAMENTO AREA OFFICE, CALIFORNIA

Polling places are actually set up on reservations in only a few instances. Among the reasons for nonvoting, apparent indifference is of chief importance. In general, a secret ballot is used in conducting tribal elections. On most reservations, tribal or group proceedings involving other than election of officers are conducted by show of hands or standing vote.

NONAREA OFFICE INDIANS

Cherokee Indian Agency, North Carolina and South Carolina

Cherokee Reservation, North Carolina   Polling places are set up in each of the six townships of the reservation for tribal elections. For county, State, and National elections, the polling places are off the reservation and members of the band must travel from 3 to 20 miles, depending on the location of their homes, in order to vote. Nonvoting is explained as primarily due to transportation difficulties. In order to get to the polls the Indians must hire taxis, or ride with neighbors or other persons who own cars; it is an unusual expense to travel to the polls therefore. Since 1947, there has been a gradual increase in the number of Indians taking advantage of the voting privileges in county, State, and National elections. There are less than 150 persons of voting age estimated as illiterate. The most recent survey showed that there were only 54 persons of adult age who could not speak English. There are also a number of disqualifications for voting by reasons of health in terms of those bedfast at home, hospitalized at time of election, and abnormal mentally. The secret ballot is used in tribal elections and is very satisfactory. In tribal council proceedings, it is rarely used and the more common method is by voice, show of hands, or by standing, as directed by the chairman. There are 18 Indians on the reservation not members of the tribe. Absentee voting is not permitted in tribal elections and residence in respective townships for 90 days prior to voting is required in tribal elections.

Catawba Reservation, South Carolina   There are no polling places on the Catawba Reservation for county, State, or National elections. Those who vote must go to the nearby precinct in Leslie, traveling from 1 to 5 miles, depending on the location of their homes. To vote in tribal elections a member must attend the general council meeting at the public schoolhouse on the reservation. Apparent indifference and the fact that 65 percent of the families have 1 white spouse would be the main reason for nonvoting. The secret ballot is used for tribal elections but the show-of-hands method has also been used occasionally. For council proceedings the most common methods are: show-of-hands, standing, or voice vote. There are two Indians married to Catawbas living on the reservation who are not members of the tribe. There are also 67 non-Indians married to Indians living on the reservation and 13 Indians married to non-Indians living on the edge of or in the immediate vicinity of the reservation. Absentee voting is not permitted in tribal elections.

chapter seven

ATTITUDES AND SELF-IMAGE

29 / Black Rage

WILLIAM H. GRIER
PRICE M. COBBS

At the core of change in the political, economic, and social needs of minority groups is the problem of a positive self-image. Minority groups have been told by the majority society that for either racial, cultural, or language reasons they are different and therefore inferior. As a result, minority group members begin life with a lack of confidence in their basic human abilities. For many of them, particularly boys, this is further complicated by the absence of a strong male adult after whom to model themselves. In the United States, where sexual roles are so important, blacks have been particularly hurt by the heritage of the slavery system and white attitudes toward them. Slave families were systematically destroyed by the selling of husbands and wives to different owners. Despite the emancipation of the slaves the black family structure has remained weak as a result of economic problems. Many black men have been unable to find jobs that pay enough to support a family, so they have to live at home supported by the wife or leave so their families can obtain welfare payments. In either case, sons lack the strong male image.

SOURCE: From *Black Rage,* pp. 206–213, by William H. Grier and Price M. Cobbs. © 1968 by William H. Grier and Price M. Cobbs. Basic Books, Inc., Publishers, New York.

207

The facts, however obfuscated, are simple. Since the demise of slavery black people have been expendable in a cruel and impatient land. The damage done to black people has been beyond reckoning. Only now are we beginning to sense the bridle placed on black children by a nation which does not want them to grow into mature human beings.

The most idealistic social reformer of our time, Martin Luther King, was not slain by one man; his murder grew out of that large body of violent bigotry America has always nurtured—that body of thinking which screams for the blood of the radical, or the conservative, or the villain, or the saint. To the extent that he stood in the way of bigotry, his life was in jeopardy, his saintly persuasion notwithstanding. To the extent that he was black and was calling America to account, his days were numbered by the nation he sought to save.

Men and women, even children, have been slain for no other earthly reason than their blackness. Property and goods have been stolen and the victims then harried and punished for their poverty. But such viciousness can at least be measured or counted.

Black men, however, have been so hurt in their manhood that they are now unsure and uneasy as they teach their sons to be men. Women have been so humiliated and used that they may regard womanhood as a curse and flee from it. Such pain, so deep, and such real jeopardy, that the fundamental protective function of the family has been denied. These injuries we have no way to measure.

Black men have stood so long in such peculiar jeopardy in America that a *black norm* has developed—a suspiciousness of one's environment which is necessary for survival. Black people, to a degree that approaches paranoia, must be ever alert to danger from their white fellow citizens. It is a cultural phenomenon peculiar to black Americans. And it is a posture so close to paranoid thinking that the mental disorder into which black people most frequently fall is paranoid psychosis.

Can we say that white men have driven black men mad?

> An educated black woman had worked in an integrated setting for fifteen years. Compliant and deferential, she had earned promotions and pay increases by hard work and excellence. At no time had she been involved in black activism and her only participation in the movement had been a yearly contribution to the NAACP.
>
> During a lull in the racial turmoil she sought psychiatric treatment. She explained that she had lately become alarmed at waves of rage that swept over her as she talked to white people or at times even as she looked at them. In view of her past history of compliance and passivity, she felt that something was wrong with her. If her controls slipped she might embarrass herself or lose her job.

A black man, a professional, had been a "nice guy" all his life. He was a hard-working non-militant who avoided discussions of race with his white colleagues. He smiled if their comments were harsh and remained unresponsive to racist statements. Lately he has experienced almost uncontrollable anger toward his white co-workers, and although he still manages to keep his feelings to himself, he confides that blacks and whites have been lying to each other. There is hatred and violence between them and he feels trapped. He too fears for himself if his controls should slip.

If these educated recipients of the white man's bounty find it hard to control their rage, what of their less fortunate kinsman who has less to protect, less to lose, and more scars to show for his journey in this land?

The tone of the preceding chapters has been mournful, painful, desolate, as we have described the psychological consequences of white oppression of blacks. The centuries of senseless cruelty and the permeation of the black man's character with the conviction of his own hatefulness and inferiority tell a sorry tale.

This dismal tone has been deliberate. It has been an attempt to evoke a certain quality of depression and hopelessness in the reader and to stir these feelings. These are the most common feelings tasted by black people in America.

The horror carries the endorsement of centuries and the entire life-span of a nation. It is a way of life which reaches back to the beginning of recorded time. And all the bestiality, wherever it occurs and however long it has been happening, is narrowed, focused, and refined to shine into a black child's eyes when first he views his world. All that has ever happened to black men and women he sees in the victims closest to him, his parents.

A life is an eternity and throughout all that eternity a black child has breathed the foul air of cruelty. He has grown up to find that his spirit was crushed before he knew there was need of it. His ambitions, even in their forming, showed him to have set his hand against his own. This is the desolation of black life in America.

Depression and grief are hatred turned on the self. It is instructive to pursue the relevance of this truth to the condition of black Americans.

Black people have shown a genius for surviving under the most deadly circumstances. They have survived because of their close attention to reality. A black dreamer would have a short life in Mississippi. They are of necessity bound to reality, chained to the facts of the times; historically the penalty for misjudging a situation involving white men has been death. The preoccupation with religion has been a willing adoption of fantasy to prod an otherwise reluctant mind to face another day.

We will even play tricks on ourselves if it helps us stay alive.

The psychological devices used to survive are reminiscent of the years of slavery, and it is no coincidence. The same devices are used because black men face the same danger now as then.

The grief and depression caused by the condition of black men in America is an unpopular reality to the sufferers. They would rather see themselves in a more heroic posture and chide a disconsolate brother. They would like to point to their achievements (which in fact have been staggering); they would rather point to virtue (which has been shown in magnificent form by some blacks); they would point to bravery, fidelity, prudence, brilliance, creativity, all of which dark men have shown in abundance. But the overriding experience of the black American has been grief and sorrow and no man can change that fact.

His grief has been realistic and appropriate. What people have so earned a period of mourning?

We want to emphasize yet again the depth of the grief for slain sons and ravished daughters, how deep and lingering it is.

If the depth of this sorrow is felt, we can then consider what can be made of this emotion.

As grief lifts and the sufferer moves toward health, the hatred he had turned on himself is redirected toward his tormentors, and the fury of his attack on the one who caused him pain is in direct proportion to the depth of his grief. When the mourner lashes out in anger, it is a relief to those who love him, for they know he has now returned to health.

Observe that the amount of rage the oppressed turns on his tormentor is a direct function of the depth of his grief, and consider the intensity of black men's grief.

Slip for a moment into the soul of a black girl whose womanhood is blighted, not because she is ugly, but because she is black and by definition all blacks are ugly.

Become for a moment a black citizen of Birmingham, Alabama, and try to understand his grief and dismay when innocent children are slain while they worship, for no other reason than that they are black.

Imagine how an impoverished mother feels as she watches the light of creativity snuffed out in her children by schools which dull the mind and environs which rot the soul.

For a moment make yourself the black father whose son went innocently to war and there was slain—for whom, for what?

For a moment be any black person, anywhere, and you will feel the waves of hopelessness that engulfed black men and women when Martin Luther King was murdered. All black people understood the tide of anarchy that followed his death.

It is the transformation of *this* quantum of grief into aggression of which we now speak. As a sapling bent low stores energy for a violent backswing, blacks bent double by oppression have stored energy which will be released in the form of rage—black rage, apocalyptic and final.

White Americans have developed a high skill in the art of misunderstanding black people. It must have seemed to slaveholders that slavery would last through all eternity, for surely their misunderstanding of black bondsmen suggested it. If the slaves were eventually to be released from bondage, what could be the purpose of creating the fiction of their subhumanity?

It must have seemed to white men during the period 1865 to 1945 that black men would always be a passive, compliant lot. If not, why would they have stoked the flames of hatred with such deliberately barbarous treatment?

White Americans today deal with "racial incidents" from summer to summer as if such minor turbulence will always remain minor and one need only keep the blacks busy till fall to have made it through another troubled season.

Today it is the young men who are fighting the battles, and, for now, their elders, though they have given their approval, have not joined in. The time seems near, however, for the full range of the black masses to put down the broom and buckle on the sword. And it grows nearer day by day. Now we see skirmishes, sputtering erratically, evidence if you will that the young men are in a warlike mood. But evidence as well that the elders are watching closely and may soon join the battle.

Even these minor flurries have alarmed the country and have resulted in a spate of generally senseless programs designed to give *temporary summer jobs!!* More interesting in its long-range prospects has been the apparent eagerness to draft black men for military service. If in fact this is a deliberate design to place black men in uniform in order to get them off the street, it may be the most curious "instant cure" for a serious disease this nation has yet attempted. Young black men are learning the most modern techniques for killing—techniques which may be used against *any* enemy.

But it is all speculation. The issue finally rests with the black masses. When the servile men and women stand up, we had all better duck.

We should ask what is likely to galvanize the masses into aggression against the whites.

• Will it be some grotesque atrocity against black people which at last causes one-tenth of the nation to rise up in indignation and crush the monstrosity?

• Will it be the example of black people outside the United States who have gained dignity through their own liberation movement?

• Will it be by the heroic action of a small group of blacks which by its wisdom and courage commands action in a way that cannot be denied?

• Or will it be by blacks, finally and in an unpredictable way, simply getting fed up with the bumbling stupid racism of this country? Fired not so much by any one incident as by the gradual accretion of stupidity into fixtures of national policy.

All are possible, or any one, or something yet unthought. It seems certain only that on the course the nation now is headed it will happen.

One might consider the possibility that, if the national direction remains unchanged, such a conflagration simply might *not* come about. Might not black people remain where they are, as they did for a hundred years during slavery?

Such seems truly inconceivable. Not because blacks are so naturally warlike or rebellious, but because they are filled with such grief, such sorrow, such bitterness, and such hatred. It seems now delicately poised, not yet risen to the flash point, but rising rapidly nonetheless. No matter what repressive measures are invoked against the blacks, they will never swallow their rage and go back to blind hopelessness.

If existing oppressions and humiliating disenfranchisements are to be lifted, they will have to be lifted most speedily, or catastrophe will follow.

For there are no more psychological tricks blacks can play upon themselves to make it possible to exist in dreadful circumstances. No more lies can they tell themselves. No more dreams to fix on. No more opiates to dull the pain. No more patience. No more thought. No more reason. Only a welling tide risen out of all those terrible years of grief, now a tidal wave of fury and rage, and all black, black as night.

30 / Life Styles in the Black Ghetto

WILLIAM McCORD
JOHN HOWARD
BERNARD FRIEDBERG
EDWIN HARWOOD

The results of the destruction of a positive self-image for a minority group member are varied but almost always negative.
He generally attempts to compensate for his inability to relate
to others on an equal basis by creating some artificial social
structure. For example, in the urban ghetto the gang has been
created to provide a social group within which the minority
group male is able to find ego reinforcement. As research in
Watts just after the riot of 1965 indicated, the members of
these teen-age gangs all were big men "within the group." No
one challenged the position of another; all demonstrated a
thin veneer of bravado over an empty core of self-deprecation.
This, of course, is not the only response to the white ideology.
For some, withdrawal functions as a "safe" way to avoid confrontation with an unpleasant environment. For others, a shell
of protection via religion or through education is created, with
the hope that it will ward off antagonism.

SOURCE: Reprinted from *Life Styles in the Black Ghetto* by William McCord,
John Howard, Bernard Friedberg, Edwin Harwood, pp. 106, 138–139, 166–167,
169–170, 184, 187, 189, 199, 201, 202–203, 217–219, 237, 256–257. By permission
of W.W. Norton & Company, Inc. Copyright © 1969 by W. W. Norton & Company,
Inc.

Stoicism, of course, has many colloquial meanings: apathy, indifference to pleasure and pain, the ability to repress feelings, endurance, insensibility.[1] Using the word in all its varied shadings, we believe that four rather distinct types of stoics exist in the Negro population.

• *The Religious Stoic,* who, like Mrs. Madison, says he finds the strength to endure life by belonging to a conventionally oriented church.

• *The Cultist Stoic,* who, like some members of the Black Muslims, strives to maintain his dignity by membership in a deviant, ascetic religious group.

• *The Cool Stoic,* who apparently does not care for religion but tries to maintain a "cool" front (an apparent indifference to pain) and pursues some kind of illegitimate but nonviolent "hustle" (racket).

• *The Passive Stoic,* who says he finds little consolation either in religion, a cult, or in a "hippie" life but simply accepts the humiliations of being a Negro in a white society, without overtly rebelling.

Despite their differences, these four types of people share certain characteristics: a relative indifference toward politics or participation in the civil rights movement; a belief that certain feelings must be repressed or controlled; and a conviction that their destiny is largely controlled either by "higher forces" or, at least, by circumstances beyond their control. . . .

"I was just born black, poor, and uneducated," a Harlem drug addict told Kenneth Clark, "and you only need three strikes all over the world to be out. . . . I have nothing to live for but this shot of dope." [2] This man, aged twenty-six, had given up all hope for a "normal" life, a regular job, or a decent marriage with a woman who did not "turn tricks." "Your environment, I read somewhere, is just a mirror of yourself," he said. "So what can I do? . . . I don't think I could be rehabilitated, you know, not now, in this society." [3] He counted himself as enlisted for life in the ranks of defeated men: those who have fled the harsh realities of life to seek solace in dreams, hallucinations, or the total extinction of feeling.

Surely escapism or complete withdrawal are attractive alternatives for those who must endure the humiliations and brutalities of the ghetto. It is not surprising, therefore, that a relatively high proportion of American Negroes find an outlet for their miseries in drugs, alcohol, or psychotic delusions.

---

[1] After much debate, we settled on the term stoic as an admittedly vague label for a large group. Other terms—the "uninvolved," the "resigned," the "passive"—could also be applied. Obviously, we are not using the term stoic in its literal, classical sense.

[2] Quoted in Kenneth Clark, *Dark Ghetto* (New York: Harper & Row, 1965), p. 95.

[3] Clark, *Dark Ghetto,* pp. 96–97.

While national statistics seldom reveal a true picture of the situation, almost all studies indicate an uncommon tendency for urban Negroes to seek release in ways disapproved by our society:

• Urban Negro alcoholism rates are two to four times higher than white rates.[4]
• Urban Negroes account for approximately 60 per cent of identified drug addicts.[5]
• The incidence of Negro psychoses, particularly schizophrenia, exceeds white rates by about 200 per cent.[6]

Whatever the many differences in causation, these three life styles have several characteristics in common. They all represent ways of withdrawing from reality; they are—at least in the eyes of an outside observer—self-destructive; and they are, in one fashion or another, an admission of defeat, a confession that one no longer wishes to confront every-day life. One would expect, then, that American Negroes would also choose the ultimate escape of suicide more frequently than American whites. The opposite is true; Negroes commit suicide about half as often as whites.[7] . . .

Frank Wright,[8] Negro, aged fifty, has been running all of his life to outdistance himself. "I am always competing—not to be better than other people, but just to be the best in whatever I do." Raised on an impoverished Iowa farm and later a hand in Pittsburgh's steel mills, Wright is now one of the nation's most distinguished lawyers.

His grandmother served as a washerwoman for a wealthy Chicago white family. She passed on this family's values of "success," leading one of her daughters to attend "normal school" and enter a teaching career. She in turn raised a son who went from honor to honor. At great financial sacrifice, she and her husband put her son through high school. Frank Wright finished as salutatorian. He still felt apologetic, in a 1967 interview, for not having been valedictorian and explained his "failure" as due to an illness during high school.

[4] Muriel W. Sterne, "Drinking Patterns and Alcoholism Among American Negroes," October 1966 Social Science Institute "Occasional Paper" No. 7, Washington University, St. Louis. In Houston, although the statistics are far from accurate since police do not record all offenses, the Negro incidence of arrests for drunkenness exceeds the white rate by 50 per cent. Los Angeles and the Bay Area approximate the national rate. Conceivably, since more Houstonians have arrived from rural areas, this difference may reflect a true rural-urban differential.

[5] John A. Clausen, "Drug Addiction" in *Contemporary Social Problems,* R. K. Merton and R. A. Nisbet, eds. (New York: Harcourt, Brace & World, 1961).

[6] For a perceptive discussion of the problem, see Ann Hallman Pettigrew, "Negro American Health" in *A Profile of the Negro American* by Thomas F. Pettigrew (Princeton, N.J.: D. Van Nostrand, 1964).

[7] Pettigrew, "Negro American Health."

[8] Fictitious name.

At college Wright served as class president for four years and was also student-body president, a track star, an orchestra leader, and editor of the school paper. He graduated six months ahead of his class with honors in a double major of mathematics and sociology. He published poetry, composed operettas, and learned fluent German.

Wright served as a pilot in World War II, and after the war he became a regional general manager for an insurance firm and simultaneously attended an Ivy League law school. After graduation he became one of the youngest law deans in the country. He was subsequently dean of several other law schools and then, at forty-five, decided to enter private law practice. . . .

What motivates Frank Wright? Why should he have escaped the poverty, the sense of futility, the defeated attitude that affects so many Negroes?

During the interview Wright tried frankly to analyze his character. "I remember," he said, "a Negro spiritual which told of keeping your head high, of being proud despite what others think of you. Probably I just wanted social acceptance by whites."

Beyond this need, Wright observed, "I wanted to get even with the oppressor. I wanted to prove myself to be not only as good but better than the whites. I, like most middle-class Negroes, want to show our kids that you can make it, even if the whites try to keep you down." . . .

The factors that pushed Frank Wright into his high achievements seem rather clear. First, his mother strongly encouraged him to better his lot, to attain a higher status than her or his father. She indoctrinated him with the "Protestant ethic" in its purest form. Second, his father and, particularly, his elder brother supported this drive with both moral encouragement and material support. Third, the family consciously shielded him from the most debilitating aspects of living in a ghetto and being a Negro.

Surrounded by foreign ethnic groups in Pittsburgh, Wright seldom thought of himself as a "Negro." One day, when he was twelve, he read of the lynching of a Negro doctor who had tried to help a wounded white woman. "Suddenly I knew there was a difference," he said. "I became a Negro." After reading of the incident, he went to see a Polish boy, who was his best friend. They had a habit of hitting each other in the solar plexus, supposedly to enhance the tone of their stomach muscles. Engulfed with anger, Wright hit the other boy with all his strength.

"I will never forget it," he recalls. "I had hurt my best friend, simply because I suddenly realized that I was a 'Negro' and he was white. I shall always feel guilty."

Another time, a white doctor refused to treat Wright's sister after she had been involved in an auto accident. Again, Wright said, "It was impressed on me that I was a Negro. I wanted to kill that doctor. Even today, I would still kill him."

Wright had learned what it means to be a Negro in America. Yet his mother kept preaching "Christian love" to him and he controlled or repressed his anger toward whites. Today Wright avoids involvement in the civil rights movement, although he maintains a token membership in the NAACP. . . .

Most of the exploiters in the slums are *not* Negroes, and certainly not all of the businessmen or professionals who work in the ghetto treat their clients unfairly. Yet there is a small group of the "black bourgeoisie" who bilk their fellow Negroes. As E. Franklin Frazier noted years ago:

> With the emergence of the new black bourgeoisie, the standards of consumption which the 'sporting' and criminal elements are able to maintain have become the measure of success among the black middle class. The standards which they set are emulated by Negroes in the professional classes—doctors, dentists, and lawyers, and even teachers as far as they are able to do so.[9]

Most significantly, Frazier went on to observe that "in order to secure the money necessary to maintain these standards, Negro professional men engage in the same 'rackets' as the successful Negroes in the underworld." [10]

The exploitation of one's own social group is a common phenomenon throughout the world. It was practiced by Benedict Arnold, by a few Jews in the concentration camps, by Cabinet ministers in Ghana, to mention only a few. Consequently, as with all the life styles we discuss, one should not draw the conclusion that this is a uniquely *Negro* way of adapting to a difficult situation. If people have traditionally been closed off from the usual avenues to "success," it is hardly surprising that a minority will turn to illegitimate (or semilegitimate) ways of earning a living. . . .

In their specific opinions about civil rights, the exploiters did not differ greatly from the general Negro population. Approximately equal proportions of the exploiters and the random sample believed that the pace of integration was moving too slowly (38 per cent vs. 44 per cent) and about the same proportion believed that integration was coming at "about the right speed" (48 per cent vs. 51 per cent). Equal proportions of both groups (82 per cent) had apparently never participated in civil rights demonstrations, protests, or picketing.

The exploiters, however, deviated from the general population in their beliefs about which groups would be most effective in aiding the Negro cause. Most of the exploiters put their faith in the efficacy of the NAACP, while they generally had little respect for either the churches' influence or that of "militant" groups (*e.g.*, PUSH, SNCC, and CORE). . . .

. . . [V]iolent Negroes ("rebels without a cause") also most often

[9] E. Franklin Frazier, *Black Bourgeoisie* (New York: The Free Press—paperback, 1957), p. 128.

[10] Frazier, *Black Bourgeoisie,* p. 128.

choose white people with power as their most admired figures. Perhaps the exploiters and the violent criminals have one element in common: an overweening desire for power and a consequent admiration for those who possess it. . . . The contemporary Negro exploiter tends to accept the status quo and, for economic reasons, prefers society in its present form. While he claims to favor more speed in civil rights and at least gives lip service to religion, he in fact thrives on a segregated system. Compelled by circumstances or his own character, such a person truly leads a double life. . . . What produces the "rebel without a cause" in the urban ghetto? Why does the subculture of crime flourish there? Why has the ghetto crime rate increased since the early 1920s and shows every sign of increasing still further? A brief look at the theories about ghetto crime can help answer these questions.

THE SUBCULTURE OF CRIME

American society has sentenced most of today's urban Negro to live in neighborhoods that are breeding grounds for crime. These are the "ports of entry"—transitional, dilapidated, economically deprived areas—that have always been the way stations for generations of newly arrived immigrants to American cities until they are able to move to better quarters. In an interesting study, Pauline Young demonstrated that if immigrants moved into a high-delinquency area the incidence of crime among them was 5 per cent during their first five years of residence, 46 per cent after another five years, and 83 per cent after another twenty years.[11] . . .

Yet although most urban Negroes are exposed to all of the cultural conditions that promote violence, only a minority become "rebels without a cause." Admittedly, these broad social factors contribute strongly to the high rate of violent ghetto crime, but one must probe into the nature of the family to find out why one young Negro becomes a rebel while another chooses a different life-style. . . .

Despite the severe limitations imposed by the small number of men examined, the results of the Cambridge-Somerville study made it clear that the backgrounds and personalities of the deviants—before they became deviant—differed substantially; that distinct differences appeared between the violent rebels and both the noncriminals and "property" criminals; and that the differences applied to both Negro and white offenders.

1. The potential murderers came from homes devoid of love. Their parents hated each other and their children. From early childhood onward, there-

---

[11] Pauline V. Young, "Urbanization as a Factor in Juvenile Delinquency," *Publications of the American Sociological Society,* Vol. 24, 1930, pp. 162–166.

fore, the violent rebels intimately experienced a world full of conflict and hatred.

2. Their mothers either neglected them or tried to dominate every aspect of their lives. Consequently, in their early lives, these men had not experienced a feminine environment in which they were treated warmly yet allowed some identity of their own.

3. Their fathers, if present in the home at all, were generally highly aggressive men who quite often had criminal records themselves. They taught the child, at least implicitly, that one could express violent tendencies without inhibitions and they offered the child a model of violence.

4. Typically, the parents disciplined the potential violent criminals in an extraordinarily erratic manner: sometimes they overlooked a transgression entirely while at other times they brutally punished the boy for the same action. . . .

Following the publication of E. Franklin Frazier's *Black Bourgeoisie* it became fashionable to condemn the Negro middle class for, among other things, its lack of leadership in the struggle against segregation and discrimination. Such accusations notwithstanding, however, insofar as there has been sustained active opposition to American racism it has come from the black bourgeoisie. This can be accounted for not in terms of any special virtue of this group, but probably in terms of status inconsistency.

Historically, members of the middle class took the lead in mounting the first protests against the crippling confines of caste at the turn of the century, and fifty years later middle-class Negro college students initiated the sit-ins which in turn gave impetus to the massive assault on racism of the early and middle 1960s. If these middle-class reformers—from W. E. B. DuBois to the students of the early '60s—did not turn to radicalism and condemn the basic political and social system in the United States in toto, it was because so many of them had enjoyed a certain degree of educational and occupational mobility, which convinced them that the system was not inherently defective but needed reform rather than complete transformation.

POST-SELMA REFORMERS

Following the passage of civil rights legislation in 1964 and 1965 many people, black and white, had the feeling that the corner had been turned as regards Negro rights. The Watts riot of August 1965, however, graphically demonstrated that the game was not even close to being over. The massive march in Selma, Alabama, and the 1965 voting rights act were only turning points. After Selma the focus shifted from the largely nonviolent, relatively integrated demonstrations and confrontations in the South to the ghettos of the North and West.

The post-Selma struggle has been much more complex than the pre-Selma struggle—the issues are more involved, the identity of major actors less clear. It is the purpose of this section of the chapter to analyze the post-Selma phase of the movement, which in many ways is more important than the pre-Selma phase. The early movement dealt with narrowly defined racial issues such as discrimination at lunch counters. The later movement has tended to focus on class deprivation and has called for remedies relevant not only for blacks, but for all class have-nots—Puerto Rican, Mexican-American, American Indian, and white.

In very broad terms, three groups have emerged in the post-Selma movement—the ghetto rioter, black students, and the politically mobilized poor. Riots and rioters are dealt with in other sections of this book. Let us deal here with the other two groups. Both have been militant but as of the spring of 1968 neither has turned to violence except for sporadic student rebellions. . . . There are many kinds of black revolutionaries. The alarmed white, listening to voices from the ghetto, hears only bits of the various revolutionary cantos. To the white they seem to be a single chorus of hate. His ear is not attuned to the differences of style and tempo from one revolutionary to the next, and to the clashing and discordant notes that separate them.

Let us attempt to identify the varying revolutionary orientations by discussing their proponents. The revolutionaries share with other blacks a growing belief in the importance of black pride, an interest in re-examining African history, and in reaffirming the importance of the Negro's contribution to American culture. Unlike other blacks, however, they are more likely to repudiate nonviolence and to seek black control of institutions in the ghetto, and some even demand actual geographical separation of the races. The major themes shift from one revolutionary to the next. . . .

In the nature of things black revolutionaries are not easy to study. Often access is closed to white social scientists and there are not that many black social scientists around. Certain things do emerge, however, from the literature on revolutionary organizations in the ghetto. They seem to appeal most strongly to the most dispossessed of the ghetto's young men. The typical Muslim and the typical Panther are alike in being young, unskilled, in trouble with the law, and out of school. These are individuals who are failures even by the standards of the ghetto, and even the modest legitimate aspirations most ghetto residents have are closed to them.

These rootless young men are precisely the people least likely to be seen by polltakers. They are not residentially stable and if caught at home by a polltaker would probably think he was a bill collector or a policeman and refuse to be questioned. It follows, then, that their opinions are probably underrepresented in the various surveys of what people in the ghetto think. Ghetto support for revolutionary organizations is probably a little broader than survey research efforts would have us believe.

The amount of influence the revolutionaries have is probably related to the type of atmosphere in which they attempt to exercise influence. In general their influence is limited, but in a riot situation, for example, where the usual norms are suspended, they may be able to sway individuals who ordinarily would not find their message appealing.

Participation in the affairs of revolutionary organizations probably allows these alienated and dispossessed young men to assume a male role. As Patrick Moynihan has pointed out, discrimination and segregation deny many black men the opportunity to meet the conventional expectations of the man's role. He cannot achieve occupationally if his education has been stunted. He cannot support his family if his income is low. The kinds of handicaps Moynihan discusses seem to apply most directly to the typical rank-and-file recruit to the Muslims and Panthers, which provide opportunities to fulfill at least some of the dimensions of the male role. They are paramilitary in structure and their use of uniforms, titles, and arms undoubtedly gratifies a certain sense of manliness for individuals denied more conventional forms of achievement. This is not to say that the Panthers' resort to arms for purposes of self-defense might not be a realistic adaptation to the particular situation they face (it probably is), but only to indicate that there are psychodynamic dimensions to their behavior that are also relevant.

It has been suggested at several points in this chapter that the larger society makes the revolutionary. Like the mad scientists in horror movies, society then becomes fearful of its own creation. The white community's response to the revolutionaries seems to be a mixture of fear, hatred, and paranoia. A more useful response would be to attempt to develop creative opportunities to channel the revolutionaries' drives. If the revolutionaries are damaged individuals due to no fault of their own, those responsible might at least accept the challenge and inconvenience of developing the kinds of programs that would open up possibilities for life without deprivation or despair.

31 / The Changing Image of the Black

ELDRIDGE CLEAVER

> The issue of psychological need is intimately intertwined with
> cultural identity. This is most dramatically seen in the debate
> currently raging on many college (and public school) cam-
> puses over ethnic study programs. Many militant black and
> Mexican-American leaders are calling for segregated pro-
> grams with the explicit goal of building a greater sense of
> identity in and pride for the minority child's ethnic or racial
> heritage. The phrase "Black is beautiful" is another manifesta-
> tion of the recognition that a positive identification with a sub-
> culture is necessary for successful participation in a pluralistic
> society such as the United States. For a black, the develop-
> ment of this identification is particularly difficult because (1)
> he has been trained to believe that black is bad or ugly, (2) his
> cultural development has been within this nation rather than in
> a "pure"—less pluralistic—setting such as the Mexican-Amer-
> ican or Indian cultures, and (3) his music, art, and literature
> are set in the American context.

After reading a couple of James Baldwin's books, I began experiencing
that continuous delight one feels upon discovering a fascinating, brilliant

SOURCE: From *Soul on Ice* by Eldridge Cleaver, pp. 97, 99–101, 105–106,
110–111. Copyright © 1968 by Eldridge Cleaver. Used with permission of McGraw-
Hill Book Company.

talent on the scene, a talent capable of penetrating so profoundly into one's own little world that one knows oneself to have been unalterably changed and *liberated,* liberated from the frustrating grasp of whatever devils happen to possess one. Being a Negro, I have found this to be a rare and infrequent experience, for few of my black brothers and sisters here in America have achieved the power, which James Baldwin calls his revenge, which outlasts kingdoms: the power of doing whatever cats like Baldwin do when combining the alphabet with the volatile elements of his soul. (And, like it or not, a black man, unless he has become irretrievably "white-minded," responds with an additional dimension of his being to the articulated experience of another black—in spite of the universality of human experience.) . . .

There is in James Baldwin's work the most grueling, agonizing, total hatred of the blacks, particularly of himself, and the most shameful, fanatical, fawning, sycophantic love of the whites that one can find in the writings of any black American writer of note in our time. This is an appalling contradiction and the implications of it are vast.

A rereading of *Nobody Knows My Name* cannot help but convince the most avid of Baldwin's admirers of the hatred for blacks permeating his writings. In the essay "Princes and Powers," Baldwin's antipathy toward the black race is shockingly clear. The essay is Baldwin's interpretation of the Conference of Black Writers and Artists which met in Paris in September 1956. The portrait of Baldwin that comes through his words is that of a mind in unrelenting opposition to the efforts of solemn, dedicated black men who have undertaken the enormous task of rejuvenating and reclaiming the shattered psyches and culture of the black people, a people scattered over the continents of the world and the islands of the seas, where they exist in the mud of the floor of the foul dungeon into which the world has been transformed by the whites.

In his report of the conference, Baldwin, the reluctant black, dragging his feet at every step, could only ridicule the vision and efforts of these great men and heap scorn upon them, reserving his compliments—all of them left-handed—for the speakers at the conference who were themselves rejected and booed by the other conferees because of their reactionary, sycophantic views. Baldwin felt called upon to pop his cap pistol in a duel with Aimé Césaire, the big gun from Martinique. Indirectly, Baldwin was defending his first love—the white man. But the revulsion which Baldwin felt for the blacks at this conference, who were glorying in their blackness, seeking and showing their pride in Negritude and the African Personality, drives him to self-revealing sortie after sortie, so obvious in "Princes and Powers." Each successive sortie, however, becomes more expensive than the last one, because to score each time he has to go a little farther out on the limb, and it takes him a little longer each time to hustle back to the cover and camouflage of the perfumed smoke screen of his prose. Now and then we catch a glimpse of his little jive ass—his big eyes peering back over his shoulder in the mischievous retreat of a child sneak-thief from a cookie jar.

In the autobiographical notes of *Notes of a Native Son,* Baldwin is frank to confess that, in growing into his version of manhood in Harlem, he discovered that, since his African heritage had been wiped out and was not accessible to him, he would appropriate the white man's heritage and make it his own. This terrible reality, central to the psychic stance of all American Negroes, revealed to Baldwin that he hated and feared white people. Then he says: "This did not mean that I loved black people; on the contrary, I despised them, possibly because they failed to produce Rembrandt." The psychic distance between love and hate could be the mechanical difference between a smile and a sneer, or it could be the journey of a nervous impulse from the depths of one's brain to the tip of one's toe. But this impulse in its path through North American nerves may, if it is honest, find the passage disputed: may find the leap from the fiber of hate to that of love too taxing on its meager store of energy—and so the long trip back may never be completed, may end in a reconnaissance, a compromise, and then a lie.

Self-hatred takes many forms; sometimes it can be detected by no one, not by the keenest observer, not by the self-hater himself, not by his most intimate friends. Ethnic self-hate is even more difficult to detect. But in American Negroes, this ethnic self-hatred often takes the bizarre form of a racial death-wish, with many and elusive manifestations. Ironically, it provides much of the impetus behind the motivations of integration. And the attempt to suppress or deny such drives in one's psyche leads many American Negroes to become ostentatious separationists, Black Muslims, and back-to-Africa advocates. It is no wonder that Elijah Muhammad could conceive of the process of controlling evolution whereby the white race was brought into being. According to Elijah, about 6300 years ago all the people of the earth were Original Blacks. Secluded on the island of Patmos, a mad black scientist by the name of Yacub set up the machinery for grafting whites out of blacks through the operation of a birth-control system. The population on this island of Patmos was 59,999 and whenever a couple on this island wanted to get married they were only allowed to do so if there was a difference in their color, so that by mating black with those in the population of a brownish color and brown with brown—but never black with black—all traces of the black were eventually eliminated; the process was repeated until all the brown was eliminated, leaving only men of the red race; the red was bleached out, leaving only yellow; then the yellow was bleached out, and only white was left. Thus Yacub, who was long since dead, because this whole process took hundreds of years, had finally succeeded in creating the white devil with the blue eyes of death. . . .

I am not interested in denying anything to Baldwin. I, like the entire nation, owe a great debt to him. But throughout the range of his work, from *Go Tell It on the Mountain,* through *Notes of a Native Son, Nobody Knows My Name, Another Country,* to *The Fire Next Time,* all of which I treasure, there is a decisive quirk in Baldwin's vision which corresponds to his relationship to black people and to masculinity. It was this same quirk, in my opinion, that compelled Baldwin to slander Rufus Scott in *Another Country,* venerate André Gide, repudiate *The White Negro,* and drive the blade of Brutus into the corpse of Richard Wright. As Baldwin has said in *Nobody Knows My Name,* "I think that I know something about the American masculinity which most men of my generation do not know because they have not been menaced by it in the way I have been." O.K., Sugar, but isn't it true that Rufus Scott, the weak, craven-hearted ghost of *Another Country,* bears the same relation to Bigger Thomas of *Native Son,* the black rebel of the ghetto and a man, as you yourself bore to the fallen giant, Richard Wright, a rebel and a man? . . .

I, for one, do not think homosexuality is the latest advance over heterosexuality on the scale of human evolution. Homosexuality is a sickness, just as are baby rape or wanting to become the head of General Motors.

A grave danger faces this nation, of which we are as yet unaware. And it is precisely this danger which Baldwin's work conceals; indeed, leads us away from. We are engaged in the deepest, the most fundamental revolution and reconstruction which men have ever been called upon to make in their lives, and which they absolutely cannot escape or avoid except at the peril of the very continued existence of human life on this planet. The time of the sham is over, and the cheek of the suffering saint must no longer be turned twice to the brute. The titillation of the guilt complexes of bored white liberals leads to doom. The grotesque hideousness of what is happening to us is reflected in this remark by Murray Kempton, quoted in *The Realist:* "When I was a boy Stepin Fetchit was the only Negro actor who worked regularly in the movies. . . . The fashion changes, but I sometimes think that Malcolm X and, to a degree even James Baldwin, are *our* Stepin Fetchits."

Yes, the fashion does change. "Will the machinegunners please step forward," said LeRoi Jones in a poem. "The machine gun on the corner," wrote Richard Wright, "is the symbol of the twentieth century." The embryonic spirit of kamikaze, real and alive, grows each day in the black man's heart and there are dreams of Nat Turner's legacy. The ghost of John Brown is creeping through suburbia. And I wonder if James Chaney said, as Andrew Goodman and Michael Schwerner stood helplessly watching, as the grizzly dogs crushed his bones with savage blows of chains—did poor James say, after Rufus Scott—*"You took the best, so why not take the rest?"* Or did he turn to his white brothers, seeing their plight, and say, after Baldwin, "That's your problem, baby!"

32 / The Mexican-Americans of South Texas

WILLIAM MADSEN

The Mexican-American is experiencing a renaissance similar
to that of the American Indian. He is more fortunate than the
black because he has a cultural heritage to regain. He is also
more fortunate than the Indian because his culture is tied to a
single language tradition, whereas the Indian has many different languages. The Mexican-American's tradition, however, is
a blend of Spanish and Indian cultures, although in the last
several years, both in Mexico and the United States, there has
been an effort to redirect attention toward the Indian or native
components of the Mexican-American and Mexican culture.
Mexican-Americans in the Southwest have followed the same
pattern as blacks, rather than that of Indians—that is, they
have pressured the existing educational system to provide
their youth with exposure to the cultural heritage of their
group rather than to create separate schools. Mexican-Americans differ from the other two groups to the extent that the
language which carries much of their cultural heritage already
is generally spoken in the home, so they are not faced with
having to reeducate their children in such a rudimentary skill.
Rather, they desire bilingual education to permit the

SOURCE: Reprinted from Chapter Two of *The Mexican-Americans of South
Texas* by William Madsen. Copyright © 1964. Reprinted by permission of Holt, Rinehart and Winston, Inc.

Mexican-American child to compete in school on an equal basis with the white Anglo child.

SPATIAL AND SOCIAL SEPARATENESS

The historical past is not forgotten despite the growing tolerance and friendliness in the valley. Incidents such as the Bloody Hour reinforce the barrier between Anglos and Latins created by differences in appearance, language, custom, and class. This division is both social and spatial.

The larger towns in Hidalgo County still maintain the planned geographical separation of Latin and Anglo populations initiated by the land development companies in the early part of the twentieth century. Today, each town and city is neatly divided into an Anglo and a Latin community. The dividing line is usually a railroad or a highway. Until the end of World War II, this boundary commonly served as effectively as an electrified fence to socially separate the two ethnic groups. Mexican-American entry to the Anglo side was restricted to employment situations or shopping expeditions. A Latin crossing the line at night was subject to police questioning or taunts and violence at the hands of Anglo teen-agers. Similarly, the Latin side of town was regarded as unsafe at night for Anglos, especially women. However, groups of Anglo males made occasional slumming trips to the Latin cantinas in search of beer and excitement.

The geographical division of the community is marked by speech differences. English is the predominant language on the Anglo side of town while Spanish prevails on the Latin side. The Spanish dialect of this region is commonly called Tex-Mex because it includes many hispanicized English words. Each side of town has distinctive labels. The Spanish-speaking population refers to the Latin community as *el pueblo mexicano* (the Mexican town), *Mexiquito* (Little Mexico), or *nuestro lado* (our side). They designate the Anglo section as *el pueblo americano*. The Anglos also refer to "our side" and "their side" and speak of the Latin community as being "over there." They generally designate the Latin side as "Meskin town."

The two sides of the tracks reflect the class differences between most Anglos and most Latins. Most Anglo homes are well-constructed and well-equipped with luxuries such as TV sets, washing machines, and air conditioning. They are situated in shady, well-kept yards. On the Latin side of town, homes are smaller and obviously of cheaper frame construction. Some are drab shacks with peeling paint, bare yards, and rundown outhouses. Others display fresh coats of paint in the lively pastel colors so loved in Mexico. Even the poorer homes maintain an appearance of brightness by decorating the yards with arrays of gaily-colored flowers neatly arranged in earthen pots or painted tin cans.

There is a noticeable difference in the pace, atmosphere, and noises characteristic of each side of town. The Anglo commercial area buzzes with the traffic din and the hustle of busy shoppers. The determined look of an Anglo housewife may be seen on the faces of women out to buy particular items of clothing in the near panic of a department store sale. People hurry along the streets with an appearance of definite purpose. Even coffee breaks are marked by the concentrated effort of purposeful conversation.

The Latin shopping areas lack the plush department stores of the Anglo side of town. Small stores sell produce, Mexican magazines, cotton clothing, or sundries. There may be a tiny hole in the wall specializing in medicinal herbs. The shoppers are more relaxed and there is more casual visiting. Pleasantries are exchanged between buyer and seller. From the cantinas come the strains of the gay-sad music of Mexico played on juke boxes. Traffic noises are less pronounced on the streets, many of which are dusty and unpaved. The Latin side is poorer but it seems gayer than the Anglo side. There are more children and dogs and more laughter on the Latin side.

Since 1946, the apartness of the two sides of town has been decreasing. Today, almost any Anglo neighborhood may have some Latin residents. In the evenings, Spanish-speaking families may be seen strolling to the movies in the Anglo downtown section. During the day, increasing numbers of Anglos go to Mexican town to eat enchiladas and tacos and drink beer. In one town, a Mexican-American judge settles complaints brought by Anglos and Latins.

CULTURAL IMAGES

Despite the growing tolerance and intermingling between the two ethnic groups, each is still keenly aware of the differences that divide them. Feelings of resentment stem from a mutual lack of understanding and stances of superiority. Each group finds the other lacking in propriety of behavior and each feels superior in some respects. These attitudes are manifest in the labels by which each group distinguishes the other. Each group has polite terms for the other to be used in face-to-face contact and in press releases. These respectful terms include: Anglo, Anglo-American, Latin, and Latin-American. Anglos refer to themselves as Americans and use the term Mexican or Meskin for both the Mexican national and the Mexican-American. Depending on the particular usage, the term Mexican may be merely descriptive or derogatory. A decreasing minority of Anglos still use the face-slapping term "greaser" for the Latin citizen. Derogatory terms used by Latins to designate Anglos include: gringo, *bolillo,* and *gabacho.* Among themselves, Latins may refer to a respected Anglo as an

Americano. Mexican-Americans [1] call themselves *tejanos* and sometimes speak of the Anglos as *extranjeros* (foreigners). Latins use the words *mexicanos* and *chicanos* for both Mexican-Americans and Mexican nationals.

Anglos reserve the racial term "white" for their exclusive use in the valley. This tendency is deeply resented by the Latins who see themselves lumped together with the Negroes as colored. The only similarity the average Latin sees between himself and the Negro is that they both belong to minority groups. Neither Latins nor Anglos have much direct contact with Negroes—who constitute less than one percent of the population of Hidalgo County. Until quite recently, the Negroes attended their own segregated schools. The Negro district in one urban center is often called "Niggertown" by both Anglos and Latins. Most Mexican-Americans say that they feel no hostility toward the Negroes but one Latin added, "Of course, I wouldn't want my daughter to marry a Negro." Negroes are almost never entertained in Latin homes.

There can be no doubt that the Anglo has a higher regard for the Latin than for the Negro. As an uneducated Anglo put it, "The Meskin's not a white man but he's a hell of a lot whiter than a nigger." Anglos regard the Latin field hand as superior to the Negro although they sometimes complain about the unreliability of the Latin. Many Anglos claim that the Latin is basically lax and unreliable but does a good day's work once he starts. An Anglo farmer pointed toward a group of Mexican-American crop pickers in a carrot field and commented, "They're all right if they have their own boss supervising them. Basically, they're lazy." This particular crew had been working at stoop labor for hours without a break. Another Anglo regarded Latins as the best of all farm laborers, "Man for man, a Mexican can out-plant, out-weed, and out-pick anyone on the face of the earth." Most Latins would agree with him. They think the Negro is too clumsy and the Anglo too weak to do a good day's work in the fields.

Anglos express different opinions on the Latin contribution to the development of Hidalgo County. Some say the area would still be a desert if it had remained Mexican. Another point of view was expressed by an Anglo rancher, "We've got to give them a lot of credit. They conquered the Indians and had ranches going here while much of our West was still wild." Perhaps the most common Anglo sentiment was voiced by a rancher, "If it were not for those hard working Meskins, this place wouldn't be on the map. It is very true about the Anglo know-how, but without those Meskin hands no one could have built up the prosperity we have in this part of the nation."

Although the Anglos fully recognize the economic importance of unskilled Latin labor, they tend to regard the Mexican-American as child-

[1] Mexican-American and Latin are interchangeable terms.

like, emotional, ignorant, and in need of paternalistic guidance. The American zeal for bettering people leads to the popular conclusion that the Latin should be educated and remade in an Anglo mold. At the same time, employers do not want to educate the Latin to the point of losing their labor force. The Anglo white-collar worker sees the educational upgrading of the Mexican-American as a threat to his job with the increasing employment of Latins in office and mercantile work at lower salaries.

The Mexican-American resents the economic dominance of the Anglo and his associated air of superiority. The Latin also objects to Anglo intolerance of Mexican-American ways and the pressures put on minority groups to conform to the American way. A Latin high school teacher summed up this attitude:

> The Anglo-American sees himself as the most important being that ever lived in our universe. To him the rest of humanity is somewhat backward. He believes his ways are better, his standard of living is better, and his ethical code is better although it is of minor importance. In fact, he believes that his whole way of life is the best in the world. He is appalled to find people on the face of the earth who are unable or unwilling to admit that the American way of life is the only way.

Many Latins believe that Anglos lack true religion and ethics and are concerned only with self-advancement. When one Mexican-American expressed the opinion that Anglos were not religious, another protested by saying, "Look at the number of people in their churches every Sunday." The first man replied, "But have you looked at the altar? No crucifix. Only a bank book." As the conversation continued, a third man said, "The Anglo will do anything to get ahead, no matter who gets hurt. Of course, it's usually one of us who is hurt." A similar view came from the teacher quoted above, "Personal gain and achievement are the main Anglo goals in life and the ethics used to attain these goals will be worked out along the way." A Latin crop picker phrased the same sentiment in more transcendental terms, "The Anglo does what his greed tells him. The Chicano does what God tells him." He added somewhat hopefully, "I think that Anglos will be discriminated against in heaven."

The Latin feels that blind dependence on science and the ceaseless push for advancement have fettered the Anglo's integrity and intellectual ability. The Latin male sees himself meeting life's problems with intelligence and logic, which he finds lacking in the Anglo. An educated Latin pointed up the contrast in these words, "The Mexican-American has no disdain for thinking, no mistrust of it. He wants to arrive at his own convictions, do his own thinking. The Anglo-American will fit into almost any organization in most any way if he can only get ahead. He is often so overworked that even if he had faith in thinking, he would have little time for it. He accepts many facts although he does not understand them."

DECREASING DISCRIMINATION

Despite such unflattering images, the overt relationship between Latin and Anglo shows signs of improvement. Latins are well aware of the fact that discrimination is becoming increasingly rare. All can remember the days of segregated schools, direct insult, and unequal rights before the law. The Mexican-American sees the current change as a result of his efforts rather than a product of increasing Anglo democracy. "When we stand together for our rights, we will get what we should," is a common sentiment. The Anglo knows that when Latins do stand together they will control 75 percent of the votes. This realization makes Anglos more considerate of Latins.

Latins are listened to when they stand up to the Anglo now. Francisco advised a younger Latin to stand up and hold still in order to get the respect of the Anglo:

> We never used to do this. Instead we would take our hats in our hands and look at the gringo's feet. It was bad in those days before the war. The Mexicans suffered very much. They discriminated against us more than now. So, when the law came to make me go to war, I told them that before I was not good because I was Mexican. I was not treated as a citizen. Why was I good enough now to go to war? I told them I would go on not being good, just a Mexican. I said I wouldn't go to war. They went away and left me. Later I was a soldier and a good one. But I went to war because I wanted to. No Tejano runs from a fight. I went because I wanted to, not because anyone told me to. It pays to be a man.

As opportunities open for economic advancement and social acceptance of the Mexican-American, he still resists complete conformity to Anglo patterns. This resistance puzzles, and at times, angers the Anglo-Americans. Nevertheless, many Mexican-Americans are unwilling to abandon their cultural heritage from south of the border. The Latin pride in heritage was espoused by a college student:

> We're not like the Negroes. They want to be white men because they have no history to be proud of. My ancestors came from one of the most civilized nations in the world. I'm not going to forget what they taught me. I'm proud of being an American but I won't become a gringo. Now they're offering us equality. That's fine. I want to be equal before the law and have a chance to make

money if I choose. But the Anglos are denying me the right to be myself. They want me to be like them. I want the chance to be a Mexican-American and to be proud of that Mexican bit. The Anglos offer us equality but whatever happened to freedom?

I asked the same Latin gentleman why the Magic Valley seemed so friendly when so much emotional hostility boiled beneath the surface. "I think," he replied, "that the Anglos smile at us because they need to be liked. We smile back because we're polite."

33 / Indian Arts

U.S. INDIAN ARTS AND CRAFTS BOARD

The use of the term "Indian renaissance" to describe the increasing interest in cultural identity among American Indians indicates the difference between Indians and blacks. Renaissance means rebirth, and for the Indian the task has been to reintroduce the youth to their own special heritage. This effort has coincided with the recent revitalization of a romantic spirit in the country as a whole and the resulting growth of interest in native or folk culture. For the first time in many years "Indianness" is attractive to the youth, both Indian and white. The nonmaterialistic, community-oriented values of the tribe are similar to the values reached by many of the critics of contemporary America. This combination of forces is producing a growing movement of Indian cultural regeneration in all forms —the arts, dance, and music are all receiving greater support than they have in many years, especially from college-attending Indians.

The basic goal of the traditional American educational system has been to prepare all individuals to function effectively in an average middle class

Source: U.S. Indian Arts and Crafts Board, Native American Crafts, *Institute of American Indian Arts,* No. 1 (Washington, D.C.: U.S. Government Printing Office, 1968), pp. 5–6, 8, 10, 12.

society. But, ideal as this goal may be, the processes of mass education do not always lend themselves to singular problems and since this country is comprised of varied groups requiring singular attention, some failures are inevitable. Over a period of time, these have occurred in sufficient number and with sufficient force to cause general concern and give rise to questioning from many quarters as to the soundness of the principles involved. Efforts are now being made on a wide front to reconsider the goals and the methods and to search out new educational approaches that will better solve the problems of special groups. This is a particularly urgent cause in the case of education for the North American Indian. The task of setting up and administering educational programs for the American Indian has been fraught with seemingly insurmountable problems and inbuilt frustrations for both the Indian population of the country and the Federal Government. The circumstances need to be examined briefly in order to understand past failures and present needs.

The American Indian has never truly subscribed to the Common American Middle Class Dream, largely because of the fundamental differences existing between his lifegoals and those of society at large. The Indian value system always has been centered on the idea that man should seek to blend his existence into the comparatively passive rhythms of nature, as opposed to the dominant society's quest for control of nature through scientific manipulation of its elements. This schism, alone, has been a formidable barrier to the establishment of a constructive interrelationship between the protagonists.

Another factor with important bearing on the Indian's negative reaction to some of the general goals set forth *for* him has been his original indigenous relationship to the *land* of America, his position and attitudes in this respect being dramatically different from those of the immigrant groups by whom he was eventually surrounded. Psychologically, the American Indian generally has remained aloof from the melting pot concept upon which this country was structured.

The language barrier must be placed high on the list of circumstances which have worked to the detriment of both the Indian and the Government. The grammar and semantics of Indian languages differ so widely from English that they impede communication and are a major deterrent to successful education for the Indian child who, on entering school, has to contend with the requirements of a curriculum based in English which, to him, is a strange and uncomfortable foreign language. The child has difficulty learning under these conditions, not because he is unintelligent but, rather, because the educational offering has not been structured to his special needs.

The heterogeneous makeup of the Indian population has been the source of many frustrations for Indian and Anglo, alike. According to the

U.S. Bureau of the Census the Indian population in 1960 numbered 552,000 and according to the Bureau of Indian Affairs this number sorts itself into 263 separate Indian tribes, bands, villages, pueblos and groups in states other than Alaska, plus 300 Native Alaskan communities. The job of creating and administering programs of health, education and welfare for such diverse groups as these, with language barriers and culturally unique concepts of life, can hardly be viewed as an easy one. And, unfortunately, some early efforts of the Government to bridge the many gaps proceeded erroneously, based on the premise that the Indian, if given the opportunity, would relinquish his "Indianness" sooner or later and fit himself into the overall plan of American life. History points sadly to the flaws in this assumption.

For the past century the Indian has clung tenaciously to his way of life and has managed to quietly reject any event that seemed to threaten it. Overtures made in his behalf which do not fit *his* sense of need were frequently received with submerged hostility, often manifested by the kind of deadly passivity that kills any cooperative program far more effectively than open warfare. This kind of a situation amounts to an impasse; with the Indians on one hand being labeled: unresponsive; and the Government on the other hand being labeled: inept; and with neither side achieving constructive goals.

Social and technological changes, and the rapidity with which they have occurred, have made the old Indian way of life increasingly less viable. The Indian finds himself pressured on many fronts, particularly economically, to fall in line and cope with the changes, but in most cases and for obvious reasons he is ill equipped to do so. The following statistics quoted from President Lyndon B. Johnson's Address To Congress, March 6, 1968, shed some light on present conditions:

> —Fifty percent of Indian families have cash incomes below $2000 a year; 75 percent have incomes below $3000.
> —Nearly 60 percent have less than an eighth grade education.

The President states the problem concisely in the following paragraph:

> The American Indian, once proud and free, is torn now between white and tribal values; between the politics and language of the white man and his own historic culture. His problems, sharpened by years of defeat and exploitation, neglect and inadequate effort, will take many years to overcome.

This official awareness is encouraging and one can feel hope in the fact that many plans are being initiated to overcome the problems. Experimental kindergarten workshops are now being conducted where the pupil's Native language is used as a preliminary to the introduction of English;

new opportunities in adult education have been provided in many areas; stepped-up programs in vocational training and bringing industry to the reservations are two of the Government's major efforts toward alleviating the unemployment problem; and the Indian population, for its part, has an awakened attitude toward matters of self-determination.

Also, the Federal Government has recognized, with some alarm, the possible dissipation of American Indian art forms as a National resource. In response to the advice of the Indian Arts and Crafts Board, the Bureau of Indian Affairs is working on new programs concerned with Native culture in Alaska as well as in the rest of the United States.

In establishing the Institute of American Indian Arts six years ago, the Bureau recognized the special needs of Indian youth and provided an institution which was set up to make special curriculum provisions geared to their particular needs, in an attempt to turn the potential disadvantage of the cultural transition to advantage and to stimulate extensions of American Indian expressions in the arts.

The underlying philosophy of the program is that unique cultural tradition can be honored and can be used creatively as the springboard to a meaningful contemporary life.

The Institute holds that cultural differences are a rich wellspring from which may be drawn new creative forces relevant to contemporary conditions and environments. We believe that, ultimately, by learning to link the best in Indian culture to contemporary life, the young Indian will be able to solve his own problems and enrich the world scene in the process.

We do not believe that it is possible for anyone to live realistically while shut in by *outmoded* tradition. We do believe that each generation must evolve its own art forms to reflect its own times and conditions, rather than turn to the hopeless prospect of mere remanipulation of the past. The Indian artist who draws on his own tradition to evolve new art forms learns to stand on his own feet, artistically, avoiding stultifying cliches applied to Indian art by purists who, sometimes unwittingly, resent any evolution of forms, techniques, and technology in Indian art.

In general, the Institute plans its programs around the special needs of the individual, as best these can be determined. It attempts continuously to expand its understanding of student problems as they emanate from Indian cultural origins. The goal of the programs is to develop educational methods which will assist young Indian people to enter contemporary society with pride, poise, and confidence.

The school offers an accredited high school program with emphasis on the arts, and a post-high vocational arts program as preparation for college and technical schools and employment in arts-related vocations. The age range of the student body is from 15 to 22.

Most of these young people have suffered from cultural conflict and economic deprivation. They are beset with misunderstandings regarding race, color and religion; and are lost in a labyrinth, in search of identity; they are stung by memories of discrimination. Among them are the revolutionists, the nonconformists, and the unacademically-minded who find no satisfaction in the common goals set for them in the typical school program. They typify that percentage of creative individuals to be found in all cultural groups who seek new ways of self-expression and who are bent on searching out very personal and creative approaches to problem solving. Holding standards which are at odds with the majority, they reject and are rejected by the typical school program.

Without the opportunity to attend a school catering to their particular drives, such students are most likely to join ranks with the growing number of dropouts who represent one of today's major problems in education. Such misfits, when measured in terms of their ultimate contributions to humanity, very often stand in indictment of a system which categorically has excluded them.

In contemplation of his immediate position, the Indian youth may easily view himself as a sorely disadvantaged, second-rate citizen—and act accordingly. He may tend to equate his problems with the simple fact of being Indian and may, consciously or subconsciously, reject *himself* and engage in acts of self-denigration such as drinking to excess, flaunting the law, fighting publicly, and other antisocial behavior; or, he may go to the other extreme and take refuge in "Indianism," seeking to live in an atmosphere of complete chauvinism and false pride, in which case he may withdraw in a state of indifference and lethargy; or, he may be astride a fence, torn in both directions, in a state of complete frustration.

At the same time, the Indian youth shares in the general concerns of the typical American teen-ager; he wears mod clothes, does the latest dances, engages in TV hero worship, and is generally cognizant of the significant youth movements of search and protest. In short, he has all the problems common to the youth of this era and, in addition, the difficult problem of making a satisfactory psychological reconciliation between the mores of two cultures.

In all cases, the Institute's primary goal is to give the student a basis for genuine pride and self-acceptance. At the outset and at a very personal level, he is made aware of the fact that we know, in general, what his problems are, and that we are on hand to discuss them with him and look into what can be done to help in his particular circumstances; he is made aware of the fact that we respect him both as an individual and as an Indian, and that we cherish his cultural traditions. The school operates in a general aura of honor and appreciation for the Indian parent and the world he represents.

All students at the Institute are oriented in the history and aesthetics of Indian accomplishments in the arts. They view exhibitions of the choicest collections of fine Indian art pieces, listen to lectures with slides and films covering the archaeology and ethnology of Indian cultures, and take field trips into the present-day cultural areas of the Southwest groups. They are encouraged to identify with their total heritage, harkening back to the classic periods of South and Central American cultures—heydays of artistic prowess in the New World. And they are exposed to the arts of the world, to give them a basis for evaluating and appreciating the artistic merits of the contributions made by their ancestors. Each student is led to investigate the legends, dances, materials, and activities pertaining to the history of his own particular tribe.

Through this process, he gradually increases his awareness of himself as a member of a race tremendously rich in cultural accomplishments and gains a feeling of self-worth.

In a curriculum unusually rich in art courses . . . a student, who may have become dulled to the excitement of personal accomplishment as a result of unsatisfactory experiences with academic subjects in his early years, can be revitalized through the experience of creative action. He may have an undiscovered aptitude for music, dancing, or drama; a natural sense of color and design, a sensitivity for three-dimensional form, or a way with words. All students at the Institute elect studio art courses. Sooner or later, with a great deal of sensitive cooperation on the part of the faculty, a field is found in which a student can "discover" himself. His first successful fabric design, ceramic bowl, piece of sculpture, or performance on stage may be his very first experience with the joy of personal accomplishment. His reaction is one of justifiable pride, and sometimes a shade of disbelief, at having produced something of worth, and he equates it with his own personal worth. For him, this is a great personal discovery. It is, also, a most potent form of motivation toward personal growth.

To date, our approach is happily justified in a look at the progress of young Indian students at the Institute. Art critics of stature are excited by the work. The quality of design and workmanship, equal in its own way to the finest traditional approaches, is easily discernible in the work being produced in sculpture, painting, and the various crafts. New sources of richness and beauty are reflected in poetry and prose. Early developments in drama and music are gratifying.

As impressive as these results are in terms of artistic accomplishments, the real value of the program lies in the general personal growth of the student and in his discovery of newly found strength and its carry over into his academic efforts and social behavior.

A continuous effort is made in the Academic Department to find more effective ways to correct the academic deficiencies all too common to

Indian students who come from the disadvantaged backgrounds previously explained. Special attention is given to students who have language handicaps. New approaches are sought continuously for expanding intellectual growth based upon ways compatible with the cultural mores of the student's background.

In the dormitories, living conditions are planned especially to broaden the student's exposure to the behavioral expectations of a contemporary society. Here, he learns the social amenities necessary to democratic living in the world at large as well as within his own cultural group.

As a result of these procedures, most students seem to gain self-affirmation. They emerge strengthened, proud, and confident, exercising newly found powers of self-direction. Figures for the past three years (1966, 1967 and 1968) reveal that 86.2% of the students in the graduating classes (12th, 13th and 14th years) have continued their educational pursuits beyond the high school level. A breakdown of this figure shows that 23.2% go into college or college-level arts schools, while 63% return to the Institute or enroll in formal vocational training programs. Significantly, students in the 14th year, who have been with us two additional years beyond the 12th year, matured sufficiently to show a college entrance figure of 42.2%. Of the total student body, 11.9% left the Institute prior to the end of a school year and did not transfer to any other educational program.

Since we must deal with the fact that no group ever will be 100% college oriented for various legitimate reasons, the Institute is currently planning a practically based terminal program for the talented but non-college directed art student who presently has no place to go for completion of his vocational art training at a professional level.

In summary, the Institute of American Indian Arts is embarked on an exploratory program, with many steps yet to be taken. We are aware that cultural change is always difficult, and even traumatic when it involves alteration of one's own traditional foundation in favor of new values—especially when the latter emanate from an alien source. But, we must assume that change is inevitable. Therefore, the need is to find ways to encompass it healthily, taking care to avoid the *destruction* of ethnic traditions.

The entry to the Institute's campus theater announces an evening of Native American drama and dance, one of several programs produced during the year by the students. An additional and larger facility comprising a 2000 seat outdoor amphitheater, now under construction at the Institute, will serve as a national center for the development of Native American drama.

During the school year Institute students plan and stage events that reflect historic Native American culture. Here, Herbert Stevens (Apache / Arizona) is assisted with preparations for a special weekend of tribal dancing and traditional cooking.

Buildings on the campus of the Institute, a remodeled facility of an earlier Bureau of Indian Affairs school, located in Santa Fe, New Mexico, feature Spanish-American Colonial adobe-style architecture. The contemporary design of proposed new structures for the campus . . . reflects the Institute's interest and needs for experimentation and diversity in its educational program for Native American youth.

Thus far in our job, we have found that by stressing cultural roots as a basis for creative expression and by offering a wide range of media in which to work, Indian students can be inspired to new personal strengths in dimensions heretofore unrealized. As a result of the Institute's heritage-centered approach, a gratifying number of its students do discover who they are and what it is they have to say to the world; and they develop the self-respect and confidence to express themselves accordingly. They are helped to function constructively, in tune with the demands of their contemporary environment but without having to sacrifice their cultural being on the altar of either withdrawal or assimilation.

This method of dealing with Indian minority problems seems to hold promise of being an effective educational approach for dealing with the needs of other minority groups in the United States and throughout the world, wherever similar problems prevail.

It cannot be overemphasized that the program at the Institute could not succeed without the presence of a sensitive, creative, alert faculty who are attuned to the youth of today and are immediately empathetic; who appreciate and use wisely the great storehouse of positive ethnic forces that can be turned to the advantage of our Indian students.

II methods of change

chapter eight

THE MINORITY ESTABLISHMENT: APPEAL TO TRADITIONAL STRUCTURES

34 / The Souls of Black Folk

W. E. B. DUBOIS

The first major organizing effort by the black community in the twentieth century produced the National Association for the Advancement of Colored People (NAACP). The impetus for the organization came from W. E. B. DuBois, one of the most controversial black leaders in American history. DuBois very strongly opposed Booker T. Washington's proposals for black and white separation, and acceptance of black inferiority. He wrote one of the greatest studies of black Americans, *The Souls of Black Folk,* in response, and began to organize opposition to Washington. The first meeting of DuBois and others sympathetic with his position produced the Niagara Movement and the famous Protest Platform. The result, as far as an organization, was the NAACP. It is important to keep in mind that the group considered itself a protest group, but chose the description "colored people" and used the most conservative branch of government, the courts, to attempt to rectify the inequities it felt existed. Within a few years the NAACP achieved substantial legal success with the victory in the case of *Buchanan* v. *Worley* (1917).

SOURCE: From W. E. B. DuBois, *The Souls of Black Folk* (Chicago: A. C. McClurg and Company, 1903), pp. 41–42, 50–55, 58–59.

245

Easily the most striking thing in the history of the American Negro since 1876 is the ascendancy of Mr. Booker T. Washington. It began at the time when war memories and ideals were rapidly passing; a day of astonishing commercial development was dawning; a sense of doubt and hesitation overtook the freedmen's sons—then it was that his leading began. Mr. Washington came, with a simple definite program, . . . His program of industrial education, conciliation of the South, and submission and silence as to civil and political rights, was not wholly original; the Free Negroes from 1830 up to war-time [1860] had striven to build industrial schools, and the American Missionary Association had from the first taught various trades; and Price [a Free Negro leader] and others had sought a way of honorable alliance with the best of the Southerners. But Mr. Washington first indissolubly linked these things; he put enthusiasm, unlimited energy, and perfect faith into this program, and changed it from a by-path into a veritable Way of Life. And the tale of the methods by which he did this is a fascinating study of human life. . . .

Mr. Washington represents in Negro thought the old attitude of adjustment and submission; . . . This is an age of unusual economic development, . . . an age when the more advanced races are coming in closer contact with the less developed races, and the race-feeling is therefore intensified; and Mr. Washington's programme practically accepts the alleged inferiority of the Negro races. Again, in our own land, the reaction from the sentiment of war time has given impetus to race-prejudice against Negroes, and Mr. Washington withdraws many of the high demands of Negroes as men and American citizens. . . .

. . . Mr. Washington distinctly asks that black people give up, at least for the present, three things—

- First, political power,
- Second, insistence on civil rights,
- Third, higher education of Negro youth.

and concentrate all their energies on industrial education, the accumulation of wealth, and the conciliation of the South. This policy has been courageously and insistently advocated for over fifteen years [about 1885–1900], and has been triumphant for perhaps ten years. As a result of this tender of the palm-branch, what has been the return? In these years there have occurred:

1. The disfranchisement of the Negro.
2. The legal creation of a distinct status of civil inferiority for the Negro.
3. The steady withdrawal of aid from institutions for the higher training of the Negro.

These movements are not, to be sure, direct results of Mr. Washington's teachings; but his propaganda has, without a shadow of doubt, helped their speedier accomplishment. The question then comes: Is it possible, and probable, that nine millions of men can make effective progress in economic lines if they are deprived of political rights, made a servile caste, and allowed only the most meagre chance for developing their exceptional men? If history and reason give any distinct answer to these questions, it is an emphatic *No.* And Mr. Washington thus faces the triple paradox of his career:

1. He is striving nobly to make Negro artisans business men and property-owners; but it is utterly impossible, under modern competitive methods, for workingmen and property-owners to defend their rights and exist without the right of suffrage.
2. He insists on thrift and self-respect, but at the same time counsels a silent submission to civic inferiority such as is bound to sap the manhood of any race in the long run.
3. He advocates common-school and industrial training, and depreciates institutions of higher learning; but neither the Negro common-schools, nor Tuskegee itself, could remain open a day were it not for teachers trained in Negro colleges, or trained by their graduates.

This triple paradox in Mr. Washington's position is the object of criticism by two classes of colored Americans. One class is spiritually descended from Toussaint the Savior, through Gabriel, Vesey, and Turner, and they represent the attitude of revolt and revenge, . . .

The other class of Negroes who cannot agree with Mr. Washington has hitherto said little aloud. They deprecate the sight of scattered counsels, of internal disagreement; and especially they dislike making their just criticism of a useful and earnest man an excuse for a general discharge of venom from small-minded opponents. Nevertheless, the questions involved are so fundamental and serious that it is difficult to see how men like the Grimkes, Kelly Miller, J. W. E. Bowen [the opponents of Washington], and other representatives of this group, can much longer be silent. Such men feel in conscience bound to ask of this nation three things:

1. The right to vote
2. Civic equality
3. The education of youth according to ability

. . . They do not expect that the free right to vote, to enjoy civic rights, and to be educated, will come in a moment; they do not expect to see the bias and prejudices of years disappear at the blast of a trumpet; but they are absolutely certain that the way for a people to gain their reasonable rights is not by voluntarily throwing them away and insisting that they do not want them; that the way for a people to gain respect is not by continually belittling and ridiculing themselves; that, on the contrary, Negroes must insist continually, in season and out of season, that voting is necessary to modern manhood, that color discrimination is barbarism, and that black boys need education as well as white boys.

The black men of America have a duty to perform, a duty stern and delicate—a forward movement to oppose a part of the work of their greatest leader. So far as Mr. Washington preaches Thrift, Patience, and Industrial Training for the masses, we must hold up his hands and strive with him, rejoicing in his honors and glorying in the strength of this Joshua called of God and of man to lead the headless host. But so far as Mr. Washington apologizes for injustice, North or South, does not rightly value the privilege and duty of voting, belittles the emasculating effects of caste distinctions, and opposes the higher training and ambition of our brighter minds—so far as he, the South, or the Nation, does this—we must unceasingly and firmly oppose them. By every civilized and peaceful method we must strive for the rights which the world accords to men, clinging unwaveringly to those great words . . . : "We hold these truths to be self-evident: That all men are created equal; that they are endowed by their Creator with certain unalienable rights; that among these are life, liberty, and the pursuit of happiness." . . .

WHY THE NAACP IS NEEDED

The first exclamation of any one hearing of this new movement will naturally be: "Another!" Why, we may legitimately be asked, should men attempt another organization after the failures of the past? We answer soberly but earnestly, "For that very reason." Failure to organize Negro-Americans for specific objects in the past makes it all the more imperative that we should keep trying until we succeed. . . .

WHAT THE NIAGARA MOVEMENT PROPOSES TO DO

What now are the principles upon which the membership of the Niagara Movement are agreed? As set forth briefly in the constitution, they are as follows:

    a. Freedom of speech and criticism
    b. An unfettered and unsubsidized press
    c. Manhood suffrage
    d. The abolition of all caste distinctions based simply on race and color
    e. The recognition of the principle of human brotherhood as a practical present creed

f. The recognition of the highest and best training as the monopoly of no class or race

g. A belief in the dignity of labor

h. United effort to realize these ideals under wise and courageous leadership

All these things we believe are of great and instant importance; there has been a determined effort in this country to stop the free expression of opinion among black men; money has been and is being distributed in considerable sums to influence the attitude of certain Negro papers; the principles of democratic government *are* losing ground, and caste distinctions are growing in all directions. Human brotherhood is spoken of today with a smile and a sneer; effort is being made to curtail the educational opportunities of the colored children; and while much is said about money-making, not enough is said about efficient, self-sacrificing toil of head and hand. Are not all these things worth striving for? *The Niagara Movement* proposes to gain these ends. All this is very well, answers the objector, but the ideals are impossible of realization. We can never gain our freedom in this land. To which we reply: We certainly cannot unless we try. If we expect to gain our rights by nerveless acquiescence in wrong, then we expect to do what no other nation ever did. What must we do then? We must complain. Yes, plain, blunt complaint, ceaseless agitation, unfailing exposure of dishonesty and wrong—this is the ancient, unerring way to liberty, and we must follow it. I know the ears of the American people have become very sensitive to Negro complaints of late and profess to dislike whining. Let that worry none. No nation on earth ever complained and whined so much as this nation has, and we propose to follow the example. Next we propose to work. These are the things that we as black men must try to do.

- To press the matter of stopping the curtailment of our political rights
- To urge Negroes to vote intelligently and effectively
- To push the matter of civil rights
- To organize business co-operation
- To build school houses and increase the interest in education
- To open up new avenues of employment and strengthen our hold on the old
- To distribute tracts and information in regard to the laws of health
- To bring Negroes and labor unions into mutual understanding
- To study Negro history . . .
- To attack crime among us by all civilized agencies. In fact to do all in our power by word or deed to increase the efficiency of our race, the enjoyment of its manhood, rights and . . . duties. . . .

This is a large program. It cannot be realized in a short time. But something can be done and we are going to do something.

35 / The Legal Attack to Secure Civil Rights

THURGOOD MARSHALL

> The NAACP continued to be the most "successful" black civil
> rights organization so long as the main agency for redress of
> black grievances was the Supreme Court of the United States.
> From the victories in housing and in voting cases during World
> War I, through the famous school desegregation decision in
> 1954, the NAACP compiled the most outstanding record of any
> group that brought cases before the Court. The man who in-
> creasingly came to symbolize this incredible success in the
> law was Thurgood Marshall. He argued the appeal in the
> *Brown* case and in other major cases in the 1940s and 1950s.
> Subsequently he became the Solicitor General of the United
> States, the first black to hold such a high legal post in the fed-
> eral government. In 1967 he became the first black to become
> a member of the body before which he had achieved such
> success fighting for his people, the United States Supreme
> Court.

The struggle for full citizenship rights can be speeded by enforcement of
existing statutory provisions protecting our civil rights. The attack on dis-

SOURCE: Thurgood Marshall, "The Legal Attack to Secure Civil Rights," an address delivered July 13, 1944, at the NAACP Wartime Conference. Reprinted with
permission of the author.

crimination by use of legal machinery has only scratched the surface. An understanding of the existing statutes protecting our civil rights is necessary if we are to work toward enforcement of these statutes.

The titles "civil rights" and "civil liberties" have grown to include large numbers of subjects, some of which are properly included under these titles and others which should not be included. One legal treatise has defined the subject of civil rights as follows: "In its broadest sense, the term civil rights includes those rights which are the outgrowth of civilization, the existence and exercise of which necessarily follow from the rights that repose in the subjects of a country exercising self-government."

The Fourteenth and Fifteenth Amendments to the Constitution are prohibitions against action by the states and state officers violating civil rights. In addition to these provisions of the United States Constitution and a few others, there are several statutes of the United States which also attempt to protect the rights of individual citizens against private persons as well as public officers. Whether these provisions are included under the title of "civil rights" or "civil liberties" or any other subject is more or less unimportant as long as we bear in mind the provisions themselves.

All of the statutes, both federal and state, which protect the individual rights of Americans are important to Negroes as well as other citizens. Many of these provisions, however, are of peculiar significance to Negroes because of the fact that in many instances these statutes are the only protection to which Negroes can look for redress. It should also be pointed out that many officials of both state and federal governments are reluctant to protect the rights of Negroes. It is often difficult to enforce our rights when they are perfectly clear. It is practically impossible to secure enforcement of any of our rights if there is any doubt whatsoever as to whether or not a particular statute applies to the particular state of facts.

As to law enforcement itself, the rule as to most American citizens is that if there is any way possible to prosecute individuals who have willfully interfered with the rights of other individuals such prosecution is attempted. However, when the complaining party is a Negro, the rule is usually to look for any possible grounds for *not* prosecuting. It is therefore imperative that Negroes be thoroughly familiar with the rights guaranteed them by law in order that they may be in a position to insist that all of their fundamental rights as American citizens be protected. . . .

During the present administration of Attorney General Francis Biddle there have been several instances of prosecution of members of lynch mobs for the first time in the history of the United States Department of Justice. There have also been numerous successful prosecutions of persons guilty of peonage and slavery. However, other cases involving the question of the beating and killing of Negro soldiers by local police officers, the case involving the action of Sheriff Tip Hunter of Brownsville, Tennessee, who killed at least one Negro citizen and forced several others to leave town, the several cases of refusal to permit qualified Negroes to vote, as well as other cases, have received the attention of the Department of Justice only to the extent of "investigating." Our civil rights as guaranteed by the federal statutes will never become a reality until the U.S. Department of Justice decides that it represents the entire United States and is not required to fear offending any section of the country which believes that it has the God-given right to be above the laws of the United States and the United States Supreme Court.

One interesting example of the apparent failure to enforce the criminal statutes is that although the statute making it a crime to exclude persons from jury service because of race or color was declared unconstitutional by the U.S. Supreme Court in 1879, and is still on the statute books, there have been no prosecutions by the Department of Justice in recent years for the obvious violations of these statutes. The Department of Justice has most certainly on several occasions been put on notice as to these violations by the many cases carried to the Supreme Court by the NAACP and in which cases the Supreme Court has reversed the convictions on the ground that Negroes were systematically excluded from jury service. One whole-hearted prosecution of a judge or other official for excluding Negroes from jury service because of their race would do more to make this particular law a reality than dozens of other cases merely reversing the conviction of individual defendants. . . .

But back to the voting case. The affidavits must be presented to the United States Attorney with a demand that he investigate and place the evidence before the Federal Grand Jury. At the same time copies of the affidavits and statements in the case should be sent to the National Office. We will see that they get to the Attorney General in Washington. I wish that I could guarantee you that the Attorney General would put pressure on local United States Attorneys who seem reluctant to prosecute. At least we can assure you that we will give the Attorney General no rest unless he gets behind these reluctant United States Attorneys throughout the south.

There is no reason why a hundred clear cases of this sort should not be placed before the United States Attorneys and the Attorney General every year until the election officials discover that it is both wiser and safer to follow the United States laws than to violate them. It is up to us to see that these officials of the Department of Justice are called upon to act again and again wherever there are violations of the civil rights statutes. Unfortunately, there are plenty of such cases. It is equally unfortunate that there are not enough individuals and groups presenting these cases and demanding action.

The most important of the civil rights provisions is the one which provides that "every person who, under color of any statute, ordinance, regulation, custom or usage of any state or territory subjects or causes to be subjected any citizen of the United States or person within the jurisdiction thereof to the deprivation of any rights, privileges or immunities secured by the Constitution and laws shall be liable to the party injured in an action at law, suit in equity or other proper proceeding for redress." Under this statute any officer of a state, county or municipality who while acting in an official capacity, denies to any citizen or person within the state any of the rights guaranteed by the Constitution or laws is subject to a civil action. This statute has been used to equalize teachers' salaries and to obtain bus transportation for Negro school children. It can be used to attack *every* form of discrimination against Negroes by public school systems.

The statute has also been used to enjoin municipalities from refusing to permit Negroes to take certain civil service examinations and to attack segregation ordinances of municipalities. It can likewise be used to attack all types of discrimination against Negroes by municipalities as well as by states themselves.

This statute, along with other of the civil rights statutes, can be used to enforce the right to register and vote throughout the country. The threats of many of the bigots in the south to disregard the ruling of the Supreme Court of the United States in the recent Texas Primary decision has not intimidated a single person. The United States Supreme Court remains the highest court in this land. Election officials in states affected by this decision will either let Negroes vote in the Democratic Primaries, or they will be subjected to both criminal and civil prosecution under the civil rights statutes. In every state in the deep south Negroes have this year attempted to vote in the primary elections. Affidavits concerning the refusal to permit them to vote in Alabama, Florida and Georgia have already been sent to the United States Department of Justice. We will insist that these election officials be prosecuted and will also file civil suits against the guilty officials.

It can be seen from these examples that we have just begun to scratch the surface in the fight for full enforcement of these statutes. The NAACP can move no faster than the individuals who have been discriminated against. We only take up cases where we are requested to do so by persons who have been discriminated against.

Another crucial problem is the ever-present problem of segregation. Whereas the principle has been established by cases handled by the NAACP that neither states nor municipalities can pass ordinances segregating residences by race, the growing problem today is the problem of segregation by means of restrictive covenants, whereby private owners band together to prevent Negro occupancy of particular neighborhoods. Although this problem is particularly acute in Chicago, it is at the same time growing in intensity throughout the country. It has the full support of the real estate boards in the several cities, as well as most of the banks and other leading agencies. The legal attack on this problem has met with spotty success. In several instances restrictive covenants have been declared invalid because the neighborhood has changed, or for other reasons. Other cases have been lost. However, the NAACP is in the process of preparing a detailed memorandum and will establish procedure which will lead to an all-out legal attack on restrictive covenants. Whether or not this attack will be successful cannot be determined at this time.

The National Housing Agency and the Federal Public Housing Authority have established a policy of segregation in federal public housing projects. A test case has been filed in Detroit, Mich., and is still pending in the local federal courts. The Detroit situation is the same as in other sections of the country. Despite the fact that the Housing Authority and other agencies insist that they will maintain separate but equal facilities, it never develops that the separate facilities are equal in all respects. In Detroit separate projects were built and it developed that by the first of this year every single white family in the area eligible for public housing had been accommodated and there were still some 800 "white" units vacant with "no takers." At the same time there were some 45,000 Negroes inadequately housed and with no units open to them. This is the inevitable result of "separate but equal" treatment. . . .

It should also be pointed out that many of our friends of other races are not as loud and vociferous as the enemies of our race. In northern and mid-western cities it repeatedly happens that a prejudiced southerner on entering a hotel or restaurant, seeing Negroes present makes an immediate and loud protest to the manager. It is very seldom that any of our friends go to the managers of places where Negroes are excluded and complain to them of this fact. Quite a job can be done if our friends of other races will only realize the importance of this problem and get up from their comfortable chairs and actually go to work on the problem.

Thus it seems clear that although it is necessary and vital to all of us that we continue our program for additional legislation to guarantee and enforce certain of our rights, at the same time we must continue with ever-increasing vigor to enforce those few statutes, both federal and state, which are now on the statute books. We must not be delayed by people who say "the time is not ripe," nor should we proceed with caution for fear of destroying the "status quo." Persons who deny to us our civil rights should be brought to justice now. Many people believe the time is always "ripe" to discriminate against Negroes. All right then—the time is always "ripe" to bring them to justice. The responsibility for the enforcement of these statutes rests with every American citizen regardless of race or color. However, the real job has to be done by the Negro population with whatever friends of the other races are willing to join in.

36 / We Must Use Every Tool

ROY WILKINS

In many of the minority group organizations the impact of the younger, more militant leaders on their older, more traditional counterparts can be seen very dramatically in the types of statements made recently by Roy Wilkins, national director of the NAACP. The legalistic orientation has given way to proposals for action against more central power holders, public and private. The language is more emotional and less cautious, and the appeal to the black community is for action of a far more militant character, and to the white community for greater support for corrective policies before more destruction occurs. These statements reflect the dilemma of older leaders such as Wilkins. The grievances of the minority, especially in urban ghettoes, are clearly valid, and the younger leaders play upon these real grievances and upon the failure of the older leaders to achieve action. Wilkins and others have appealed to the white community to help before their credibility is destroyed and the more militant, younger leaders take over, thus further undercutting the moderates and forcing them to take a

SOURCE: Roy Wilkins, "Excerpt from Remarks of Roy Wilkins of New York City, Executive Secretary of the National Association for the Advancement of Colored People, at the Annual Dinner of the Southern Regional Council, Atlanta, Georgia, January 29, 1964," printed as "Freedom Tactics for 18,000,000" in the Southern Regional Council's organ, *New South,* 18, 2 (February 1964), 3–7. Reprinted with permission of Roy Wilkins.

> more militant stance to keep any influence. Unfortunately, the
> white community has responded by inaction.

We cannot have meaningful change in human relations, especially if these involve the revision of laws and the uprooting of tradition, without confrontation, tension and occasional strife. Thoughtful students of the national scene have marked the frank talk and direct negotiations of the Sixties as a most significant gain in the assault upon citizenship inequities based upon race.

In no quarter has the value of supplementary direct action and individual involvement been acknowledged more readily and with more warmth than among those who had employed other approaches and had found these, in and of themselves, agonizingly slow in producing the results desired.

But a program of conciliation alone (such as the early Interracial Commissions) or of court action alone (such as the 1917 decision against municipally-established ghettos) or of legislation alone (such as certain of the state and municipal civil rights laws) did not meet our varied needs and situations.

Events in both the North and the South would seem to suggest that today we need to study the efficacy of the exclusive direct action approach. Such a study should recognize the very obvious fact that circumstances may differ even when they appear similar. For example, is any different procedure indicated in a city at a time when desegregation is under way than at the time when the segregation front was solid?

If the problem in a public school system is the junior high school feeder system, is a city-wide, all-level pupil boycott the effective tactic to achieve the end desired? If a neighborhood selective buying campaign can win the employment of supermarket checkout cashiers, can the same tactic win jobs for unemployed laborers as electricians or sheet metal workers?

Negro doctors last year staged a dramatically informative and persuasive picketing of the American Medical Association. They do not expect, however, that a picket line will solve the intricate, tradition-and-income-and-prestige encrusted problem of hospital staff appointments, among other problems.

It may be that the time has now arrived when the civil rights forces need to go to a quarterback clinic. The goal of a football team is to make points enough to win the game. If points cannot be made with touchdowns, field goals can be called upon. If the line of the opposition is unyielding, end runs or forward passes are tried. No quarterback worth his salt keeps pounding away with line bucks that yield at best a yard or, worse still, a yardage loss.

The enterprise that engages us is not one against a single restaurant in Atlanta, Ga., or a single school board in Malverne, N.Y., or an employment policy in St. Louis, Mo., or police action in Plaquemine, La., or a single hotel in Salt Lake City, Utah. We are engaged in a comprehensive campaign for the civil rights of 18 million citizens scattered in 50 states, living under varied economic, social and political conditions and functioning with a variety of education and technical knowledge, training and skill.

The 18 millions are a minority in 186 millions of citizens. Thus even elementary reasoning would seem to indicate that allies among the majority must be won and held if the minority's efforts are not to end in frustration and failure.

Craven tactics do not win allies; instead, they pile up contempt. Unending patience, ultra-conservatism and continuous conciliation win nothing except an occasional crumb or bone and the deeper entrenchment of the status quo.

But uni-racial assaults, brave and dedicated though they may be, which are rooted in one tactic and in no critical appraisal of pertinent factors in a particular encounter, could not only fail in their immediate objective, but could set back the whole civil rights army across the entire action front.

Is it too old-fashioned to suggest that we may need more flexibility in our campaign? Where our opponents have been most inflexible, they have been most vulnerable and we have won undisputed psychological victories, even though practical advances may have been delayed. When the Trojans . . . [made] a frontal assault ineffective . . . [the Greeks] used a wooden horse. Hannibal surprised the Romans by bringing elephants the back way across the Alps. David spurned the traditional sword against Goliath and used a slingshot. The Germans added Stuka dive bombers and V-2 rockets in World War II and the Japanese went them one better with their suicidal pilots.

A bulldozer can excavate for a foundation but a block and tackle is required to get a piano into the ninth floor.

Let us not become so inflexible in thought and method that we too, become vulnerable. In some places outside the South some of our tactics are causing questions to be raised about our campaign among, not our expected opponents, but among some of our own people and our potential allies.

Here in the South some procedures are undermining those persons in strategic positions who have supported us. These procedures are also reviving hard-core opponents who had been repudiated and all but forgotten in the struggle. And, most seriously, some tactics have won support for the segregationists from that reservoir of public opinion that might well have been won—or neutralized—by us.

The plain lesson is that we must use every method, every technique, every tool available. We need to devise new tools. Our attack must be across the board and must be leveled at all forms and degrees of second class citizenship. Where one weapon is sufficient, let it be employed. Where a combination is required, let it be used. Where variations in timing and methods will be effective, by all means let us employ these. But let none of us, in the North or in the South, "activists" or not, fall into the trap, at this crucial stage, of attempting to solve all problems everywhere by a single method.

If Negro citizens today need to re-examine their position, white people are under no less obligation to review theirs. Despite the bitter-enders, the question of the day is not whether racial inequality and its principal tool, segregation, shall survive. The question is only on the means and the pace of eliminating it. Die-hard opposition will but delay matters; it cannot win. . . .

. . . American Negro citizens are a unit in insisting that the Constitution of the United States guarantees protection of their citizenship rights against the abridgements and denials of any racist doctrine or practice, in Atlanta or in Spokane.

In 1964 they expect to move at an accelerated pace toward the practical realization of that goal. Peaceful, mutually respectful and brisk progress can result if the white majority will acknowledge the realities of the day and not persist in using turn-of-the-century blinders.

37 / League of United Latin
American Citizens

RUTH S. LAMB

In the Mexican-American community a large number of groups of a traditional orientation have existed for many years. The first such organization, the Mexican Liberal party, was organized in 1906, predating the NAACP. It was not until much later, however, that any concerted effort was made to organize a substantial number of Mexican-Americans. In the 1920s the Order of the Sons of America was started, but it too had little lasting effect. Another group, LULAC (League of United Latin American Citizens), emerged in the late 1920s and still exists. It is similar to the Sons of America in placing a very high emphasis on assimilation into the American society. After World War II, several more politically sophisticated groups developed, the first two being CSO (Community Service Organization), in 1948 and American GI Forum, in 1947. In the late 1950s MAPA (Mexican-American Political Association), CMAA (Council for Mexican-American Affairs), and PASSO (Political Association of Spanish Speaking Organizations) emerged. The more moderate of the three have been CSO and GI Forum, although they did not begin as such. This selection describes the aims and purposes of LULAC as set forth in their 1929

Source: From Ruth S. Lamb, *Mexican-Americans: Sons of the Southwest,* Ocelot Press, Claremont, California, 1970, pp. 115–118.

convention and recent objectives discussed at the 1969 convention.

The ideal of unity continued to be sought and in 1929 three distinct groups made an effort to achieve this. These included the League of Latin American Citizens, and the others that had seceded from the Order Sons of America, one of which was the San Antonio Council and the other was Council No. 4 of Corpus Christi. A convention set for February 17, 1929, made it possible to organize the League of United Latin American Citizens. They agreed that membership would be confined to American citizens of Latin extraction. They also recognized all local councils in the convention as members of the new organization. They arranged for the calling of a convention to meet in Corpus Christi the following May 18th and 19th to adopt a permanent constitution. The Constitution as adopted by the second convention consists of nine articles. The first article establishes the name of the organization as "The League of United Latin American Citizens." Article II presents the aims and purposes of the organization which are of interest and may be quoted in full as follows:

The Aims and Purposes of This Organization Shall Be:
- To develop within the members of our race the best, purest and most perfect type of a true and loyal citizen of the United States of America.
- To eradicate from our body politic all intents and tendencies to establish discriminations among our fellow citizens on account of race, religion, or social position as being contrary to the true spirit of Democracy, our Constitution and Laws.
- To use all the legal means at our command to the end that all citizens in our country may enjoy equal rights, the equal protection of the laws of the land and equal opportunities and privileges.
- The acquisition of the English language, which is the official language of our country, being necessary for the enjoyment of our rights and privileges, we declare it to be the official language of this organization, and we pledge ourselves to learn and speak and teach same to our children.
- To define with absolute and unmistakable clearness our unquestionable loyalty to the ideals, principles, and citizenship of the United States of America.
- To assume complete responsibility for the education of our children as to their rights and duties and the language and customs of this country; the latter, in so far as they may be good customs.
- We solemnly declare once for all to maintain a sincere and respectful reverence for our racial origin of which we are proud.
- Secretly and openly, by all lawful means at our command, we shall assist in the education and guidance of Latin Americans and we shall protect and defend their lives and interest whenever necessary.

• We shall destroy any attempt to create racial prejudices against our people, and any infamous stigma which may be cast upon them, and we shall demand for them the respect and prerogatives which the Constitution grants to us all.

• Each of us considers himself with equal responsibilities in our organization, to which we voluntarily swear subordination and obedience.

• We shall create a fund for our mutual protection, for the defense of those of us who may be unjustly persecuted and for the education and culture of our people.

• This organization is not a political club, but as citizens we shall participate in all local, state, and national political contests. However, in doing so we shall ever bear in mind the general welfare of our people, and we disregard and abjure once for all any personal obligation which is not in harmony with these principles.

• With our vote and influence we shall endeavor to place in public office men who show by their deeds, respect and consideration for our people.

• We shall select as our leaders those among us who demonstrate, by their integrity and culture, that they are capable of guiding and directing us properly.

• We shall maintain publicity means for the diffusion of these principles and for the expansion and consolidation of this organization.

• We shall pay our poll tax as well as that of members of our families in order that we may enjoy our rights fully.

• We shall diffuse our ideals by means of the press, lectures, and pamphlets.

• We shall oppose any radical and violent demonstration which may tend to create conflicts and disturb the peace and tranquility of our country.

• We shall have mutual respect for our religious views and we shall never refer to them in our institutions.

• We shall encourage the creation of educational institutions for Latin Americans and we shall lend our support to those already in existence.

• We shall endeavor to secure equal representation for our people on juries and in the administration of governmental affairs.

• We shall denounce every act of peonage and mistreatment as well as the employment of our minor children of scholastic age.

• We shall resist and attack energetically all machinations tending to prevent our social and political unification.

• We shall oppose any tendency to separate our children in the schools of this country.

• We shall maintain statistics which will guide our people with respect to working and living conditions and agricultural and commercial activities in the various parts of our country.

The League of United Latin American Citizens has debated the main problems of the Latin Americans for four decades. It started and had its major successes in Texas, though since then several chapters have appeared in California in Los Angeles County. The issues have usually been clear and well stated though remedies were not always available.

In June of 1969 Robert Ornelas of the 100,000-member League of United Latin American Citizens called on the Nixon Administration to "make a forward thrust right now." Speaking at a press conference at LULAC's national convention in a Long Beach hotel, Ornelas charged that the Nixon Administration made a serious tactical error by appointing Governor Nelson Rockefeller rather than a person of Latin American descent to conduct a fact-finding mission to Latin America.

However, Ornelas went on to say that President Nixon had appointed two qualified Mexican Americans to important governmental positions: Hilary Sandoval as administrator of the Small Business Administration and Tony Rodríguez as chairman of the United States section of the United States–Mexico Joint Border Commission.

He also praised Mr. Nixon's continuation of the Inter-Agency Committee on Mexican-American Affairs which coordinates efforts of all government agencies dealing with Mexican-American matters. But he called upon the Administration to take the following steps to provide better working conditions and homes, more governmental appointments and more jobs for Mexican-Americans:

• Take a positive stand on the rights of California grape workers to organize and be included among the unions whose rights are guaranteed under the National Labor Relations Act.

• Urge stronger controls which will guarantee running water, showers, and other facilities in migrant workers' homes while establishing a program which will provide decent low-income housing for Mexican-Americans everywhere.

• Appoint qualified Mexican-Americans as assistants to Cabinet members, administrative assistants to the President, and to civil service at all levels.

• Back increased appropriations for the bilingual education act which provides that young school children be taught in two languages to make their transition to English a gradual one.

38 / NCAI and the March on Washington

EDITORS, *NCAI SENTINEL*

One of the oldest Indian organizations is the National Congress of American Indians (NCAI), founded in 1944. A coalition of tribal groups, the NCAI focuses a considerable amount of its efforts on presentations before the United States Congress and other federal agencies. In addition, it attempts to publicize efforts by Indians to develop businesses through conferences held in conjunction with such agencies as the Office of Economic Opportunity and the Department of Commerce. The organization is thus implicitly committed to the American political and economic "system." As a result, it took a somewhat negative position toward the Poor People's March on Washington of 1968 and was criticized by some of the younger and more militant Indians. The group then felt obligated to "clarify" its attitudes toward the march and, in addition, criticized the younger Indians for having become involved only recently in activities to improve the lives of their people, while the NCAI had been active since World War II. This conflict over the march and similar issues also occurred between traditional minority organizations (black and Mexican-American) and the younger and more militant groups.

Source: From *NCAI Sentinel,* quarterly publication of the National Congress of American Indians, 1346 Connecticut Ave., N.W., Washington, D.C. 20036. Summer 1968, pp. 7–11.

In early May, hundreds of members of the Poor People's March, sponsored by the Southern Christian Leadership Conference, came from all parts of the country to Washington, D.C., erected a tent village called "Resurrection City" near the Lincoln Memorial, and through the rain-drenched weeks that followed started their campaign to focus the attention of the country and especially the Congress on the plight of the nation's poor.

To clarify NCAI's position on the march—especially in view of the publicity being received by some of the Indian participants—the Washington office issued the following statement on May 3:

> The National Congress of American Indians, representing some 105 major American Indian Tribes and Alaska Native Villages, wishes to take this opportunity to clarify its position on the Poor People's March presently arriving in the Nation's Capital. We feel that it is incumbent on us to do so because of the inescapable significance the March has in reflecting the discontent which exists within American society—a discontent understood and felt, in a very real sense, by the American Indian community.
>
> An official endorsement of the Poor People's March in the form of a NCAI policy statement would constitute a commitment of support which NCAI cannot make at this time. When NCAI decides upon and addresses itself to a policy position as an official commitment, it strives to confine these occasions to cases where the commitment reflects a near unanimous conviction on the part of its membership.
>
> In view of the common bond of concern and experience that links the American Indian community with other sectors of the disadvantaged population, the membership of NCAI is near unanimous in its belief that present political, economic and social conditions precipitated the March and that its ultimate goals and aims are legitimate. Where there is not unanimity in the NCAI membership is in the conviction that the March as it is presently conceived —with particular respect to the intended and prolonged camp-in in Washington—holds no particular optimistic prospects for producing satisfactory results relevant to the wants of its participants before their thresholds of frustration have been exceeded.
>
> The Poor People are supposed to stay encamped in Washington until Congress responds with a legislative program satisfactory to the interests of the marchers. However, there is no defined criteria as to what a satisfactory program would be, hence, what achieved goals will terminate the March. Even if Congress knew exactly what legislative measures the marchers deem necessary, and if actual violence does erupt out of the March it is quite possible that the only result will be a Congress even less receptive to the demands of the marchers. Already, Congress is becoming less than sympathetic to these demands.

Now we Indians are not necessarily against the use of violence as a means of defending group interests against encroachments by the mainstream society. In the last one hundred and fifty years, we feel that we have compiled an extensive record of experience and experiments in this approach. However, the results of most of this experience have been sufficiently disenchanting so as to necessitate weighing the alternatives of violence with carefully measured considerations. Violence would be used if—and only if—it holds some promise of producing certain desired results, which it seldom ever does.

In this case, already the press is observing that some of the Marchers want to return home and are doing so. This suggests that as time wears on only the most militant, irresponsible, and dedicated will remain, concentrating the intensity of the mood at the camp-in. As time goes on, the Marchers will become bored and unoccupied, crowded and uncomfortable—conditions certain to amplify their sense of frustration. When this set of circumstances takes place in a city already in a restless and dire mood, the situation looks extremely volatile.

In conclusion, as we of NCAI see it, the success of the Poor People's Campaign will depend largely on the success of the Southern Christian Leadership Conference to juggle with iron discipline the politically awesome threat of potential violence against the rigid restraint of that violence. We offer the SCLC every encouragement in doing this. If SCLC is successful, it will be a monumental victory deserving complete endorsement of their right to leadership in social issues. It will also provide the country, white and black, red and yellow, with a model of what is truly possible in American life.

However, in this not-so-best-of-all-possible worlds, complete success seems doubtful. And it is this doubt which restrains much of the membership of NCAI from giving its unqualified endorsement to the Campaign.

On June 10, Senator Paul Fannin of Arizona, in his remarks which appeared in *The Congressional Record,* stated that,

Much has been made of the inclusion of American Indians in the poor march in Washington. Actually the plight of the American Indian is by and large one of the foremost examples of what can happen when a segment of the population becomes substantially dependent upon the Government for its sustenance. I think those who are demanding to be dandled in the lap of Government should take a good look at the guarantees the U.S. Government has offered to the American Indians and how the Government has not lived up to those agreements. They will see that Government has neither the will nor the ability to take care of individual wants and needs.

What I wish to point out is that the Indians have some very real grievances. They are in the nature of broken treaties and misadministration of programs designed to assist the Indians. I know something about this problem, since there are more Indians in my State of Arizona than in any other. Presently I serve on the Subcommittee on Indian Education of the Committee on Labor and Public Welfare, and we are very much aware of these problems and are seeking satisfactory solutions to them. The late beloved Senator from New York, Mr. Kennedy, was chairman of that subcommittee, and I know that he shared a deep concern for these difficulties.

It should be noted that the National Congress of American Indians, one of the most outstanding organizations interested in the affairs of Indians, has voiced its opposition to the Poor March in Washington and has courageously pointed out that without definite realistic and achievable goals there can be little hope of success. The NCAI has wisely called for a restatement of the long-range collective goals of the Indians, presented in an orderly and proper way to the various branches of Government.

Mr. President, it is high time that we took more notice of, and thereby encouraged, those who recognize the proper and effective way of presenting petitions to Congress. We cannot have progress unless we have order. If we are to "selectively disobey" those laws which we do not like, then we should put a plainer label on our action and call it by its proper name of "anarchy" or "nihilism."

Mr. President, I commend the action of the NCAI in its plans to be responsible and reasonable in presenting the case for the Indians to the Congress and ask that a statement issued by the NCAI on June 8, and a list of the supporters of that statement be printed in the RECORD."

There being no objection, the statement and list were ordered to be printed in the RECORD, as follows (from the National Congress of American Indians, June 3, 1968):

THE NATIONAL CONGRESS OF AMERICAN INDIANS CALLS EXECUTIVE COMMITTEE MEETING

President Wendell Chino of the National Congress of American Indians has called an emergency session of the NCAI Executive Committee June 6–8, 1968, at the Albuquerque Indian School, Albuquerque, New Mexico, to formulate position papers on various social and economic issues now being aired by the Indian participants in the Poor People's Campaign in Washington, D.C.

According to John Belindo, Executive Director of NCAI, the real issues of unemployment, education, housing, and hunting and fishing rights now being raised in Washington are being clouded by the emotional appeals and accusations of some of the individual marchers. To offset the arguments being posed by this group, the

NCAI wishes to present its ideas and recommendations—in the form of a long-term program of economic development—to various Departments of the Government.

Because of the size and diversity of its membership—some 105 major American Indian Tribes and Alaska Native Villages—the NCAI feels that it represents the collective interests of the Indian Community more so than any other organization and must, therefore, pursue policies which are oriented to answer the wants of the majority on occasions where such wants may be at cross purposes with the desires of individual segments.

In a statement on the Poor People's Campaign issued May 31, the NCAI refused to give official endorsement of the March because of the lack of any unanimous conviction among its membership that the March as it is presently conceived can produce satisfactory results before the thresholds of frustration of its participants have been exceeded.

Recent events in the nation's capital have brought home to us the great gap between performance and publicity. Indian demonstrators have gained a certain amount of headlines with their venture into the Supreme Court and it seems that certain of them feel that "nothing" has ever been done for the Indians until they came on the scene.

In a hearing a few weeks back, some of the more militant angrily asked the NCAI, "Where were you when we needed you?" as if they had been the only ones ever to have done anything to get Indians a fair shake.

Also, some churches and organizations who cannot tell the difference between racism and nationalism have dedicated themselves to attacking the "establishment" and word has reached us that NCAI is classified as the "establishment."

So we challenge the Johnny Come-Lately group with the same question they recently asked us: "Where were you when we needed you?" It is fairly easy to get out in the streets and raise hell. In fact, it does not take any sense at all. But to work steadily day after day on programs and unspectacular legislative problems is another thing altogether. That takes dedication and faith in Indian people that somehow, someday, Indians will unite and become the force that they should.

So we ask: Where were you when:

• NCAI secured legislation for restoration of ceded and unentered land to the Crow, Coeur d'Alene, Fort Peck, Hoopa Valley, and Spokane reservations?
• NCAI promoted the enactment of legislation that made it unlawful for anyone to destroy, deface, or remove certain boundary markers on Indian reservations?
• NCAI promoted the enactment of legislation that made it unlawful for trespassers to hunt, fish or trap on Indian reservations?

• NCAI impeded attempts to offset payments for social programs in Indian Claims judgments?

• NCAI promoted the enactment to establish the Indian Claims Commission in 1946 and supported the acts of 1956 and 1961 that extended the life of the Commission to grant continuing adjudication of claims.

• NCAI assisted in resolving Indian Voting Rights in Arizona, New Mexico and Utah?

• NCAI sponsored a Washington conference on "termination" in 1954 and blocked termination-without-consent legislation.

• NCAI launched a major study of economic resources on Indian reservations for the benefit of Indian Tribes in 1965 and 1966.

• NCAI defeated a bad heirship bill.

• NCAI fought to keep an Indian desk in OEO.

• NCAI uncovered the Omnibus Bill that "didn't exist."

• NCAI fought Calvert's Whiskey Ad.

• NCAI helped postpone construction of Stampede Dam to assist Pyramid Lake.

• NCAI pushed the passage of the Erwin Amendments for Civil Rights for Indians.

• NCAI helped the Tlingit and Haidas get their claims bill through.

• NCAI opposed the Colville Termination.

• Above all, where were all the heroes who are now in the streets when the extension of the Indian Claims Commission was being discussed?

• And where are all the churches and street people when the current demonstrations are over? They will return to the normal humdrum existence and do very little but the NCAI will still be in Washington trying to get good legislation through, supporting appropriations for programs, working in a variety of fields to see that Indians are not trampled under foot by government agencies.

So we are not impressed with claims that we were not around when we were needed. Too many tribes know differently. And when the publicity has died we will still be working to ensure that Indians are heard in our nation's capital.

We are not denying that much is left to be done. We wish more tribes could realize that through unity and willingness to work hard together much can be done. But it is absurd to pretend that nothing has been done until a few people went to demonstrate in the streets of Washington.

Where were the heroes when the going was tough?

chapter nine
EARLY MILITANCY: NEGOTIATION AND DEMONSTRATIONS

39 / To Be Equal
WHITNEY YOUNG

The Urban League, organized in 1911, represents one of the oldest of the organizations working for the improvement of the life of blacks. It has focused rather extensively on the problem of employment, although the ties between this aspect of a person's life and housing, education, and political power are not overlooked. The League has emphasized negotiation and bargaining as techniques for obtaining better jobs for blacks, rather than following the tactics of the union movement or even of Mexican-Americans such as Cesar Chavez. It would thus be identified as a moderate-to-conservative group in the general spectrum of organizations speaking for a minority. The current director, Whitney Young, demonstrates the validity of this characterization of the general group, for he is one of the few more established leaders who has not modified his position in response to the militancy of the newer leaders and is a supporter of the Nixon administration. In the proposals he makes in this selection he uses a model of federal aid for blacks that is very much a product of the premilitant period.

SOURCE: From *To Be Equal* by Whitney M. Young, Jr., pp. 27–33. Copyright © 1964 by Whitney M. Young, Jr. Used with permission of McGraw-Hill Book Company.

The American Negro has been out of the mainstream for more than three centuries and a special effort must be made to bring him into the central action of our society. The effects of more than three centuries of oppression cannot be obliterated by doing business as usual. In today's complex, technological society, a sound mind, a strong back, and a will to succeed are no longer sufficient to break the bonds of deprivation as was the case with minority groups in the past.

A comparable effort must also be made for millions of other Americans of minority groups—the Mexican-Americans, Puerto Ricans, and others—so that these millions will also benefit. I am confining my remarks to Negroes, because I am more expert on the problems of my own people, and because their plight is worse than that of any other minority (except perhaps for our seven hundred thousand Indians). However, I ought to make it clear that I do not believe in extraordinary measures to help more Negroes progress and become self-supporting simply because they are Negro. I believe we must receive assistance until we can make use of equal opportunities now opening to us because we are Americans, and no Americans ought to be deprived or disenfranchised economically, politically, or socially.

Thus our call for an immediate, dramatic, and tangible domestic Marshall Plan is aimed at closing the intolerable economic, social, and educational gap that separates the vast majority of us Negro citizens from other Americans. Unless this is done, the results of the current heroic efforts in the civil rights movement will be only an illusion, and the struggle will continue, with perhaps tragic consequences.

In our plea for such a domestic Marshall Plan, we are asking for *special effort,* not for special privileges. Our program is designed to reverse economic and social deterioration of urban families and communities and to help develop the tools and understanding that will prevent such deterioration in the future. Here is the proposed *special effort* program:

1. Our basic definition of equal opportunity must include recognition of the need for special effort to overcome serious disabilities resulting from historic handicaps. When you find a man in the wilderness dying from malnutrition you don't just bring him to civilization and turn him loose with a pat on the back saying, "We've saved you, now you're on your own; lots of luck!" He is on the point of starvation. He requires special attention, careful diet and rest, and psychological and physical aid to readjust to civilization.

The Negro has been starving, not in the wilderness, but in the midst of the world's richest nation in the period of its greatest prosperity in history. He has been sighted, but whether his true condition has been "diagnosed" accurately and will be corrected by the majority is yet to be seen.

2. America must recognize and assess at a higher value than ever before the human potential of its Negro citizens, and then our society must move positively to develop that potential.

It is no accident that the U.S. Department of Labor and economists such as Gunnar Myrdal, Eli Ginzberg and others agree that the Negro population is America's greatest undeveloped natural resource. The extraordinary contributions to America of those Negro citizens who have overcome incredible handicaps merely hint at the tremendous benefits that will be ours when Negroes can participate freely in our society.

3. The best schools and the best teachers are needed:

—to instill in Negro children and other educationally disadvantaged youth a desire for excellence;

—to motivate them to achieve and prepare them to advance up the economic ladder with full understanding of the rewards they will receive.

We do not need more examples of school boards treating ghetto schools as the Siberias of their systems, relegating to them largely the problem teachers, probational teachers, neophyte teachers on a "make or break" basis. We need insight, courage, understanding, and an educational value system which parallels that of the medical profession, where doctors and nurses who selflessly devote themselves to combatting an epidemic, for example, earn greater prestige than those who dispense pills for allergies and colds in the suburbs.

4. A conscious, planned effort must be made to bring qualified Negroes into "entrance jobs" in *all* types of employment, to upgrade them and aid them to qualify for advancement, and to place them in positions of responsibility, *including the full range* of management positions. The day is past when token integration and pilot placement of Negroes in business and industry, labor and government can be considered solutions. These devices never were acceptable nor adequate, except to white Americans.

For employers the special effort, domestic Marshall Plan approach means exercising the same creative zeal and imagination to include Negro workers at all levels that management has used throughout the years in excluding them. And incorporating Negroes into the work force will not happen automatically by taking down a sign, pasting up a poster, or autographing the President's Plans for Progress Program—a statement of fair-hiring practices. It means honest, realistic seeking out of workers, for fillable jobs, not just positions for which industry can't find whites—such as nuclear physicists, or secretaries who look like Lena Horne and can type 120 words per minute.

Special effort means not hiding behind lame excuses. Any employer who does not want to hire can find excuses. This approach suggests that if a business has never hired Negroes in its offices or plants and two equally qualified people apply, it should hire the Negro to redress the injustice previously visited upon him. Such action has double virtue: it gives Negro youth a new role model and promotes the image of a truly American company.

5. Effective, positive action must be taken to destroy the racial ghetto and to open housing opportunities of all types on the basis of need and ability to buy or rent. Too long the cancerous sore of the ghetto has festered in our urban communities, spewing forth human wreckage and the major portion of criminal offenders; draining our body politic of treasure; robbing us of the meaningful contributions of hundreds of thousands of citizens whose lives and ambitions have been thwarted and truncated.

6. Health and welfare agencies, both public and private, must bring to the ghettoized population their best services and most competent personnel. Needed are trained workers who understand the myriad ills that afflict ghetto dwellers —unstable family patterns, illegitimate births, the direct relationship between low socio-economic status and social problems—and how to rehabilitate urban Negro families.

7. Qualified Negroes should be sought and named to all public and private boards and commissions, particularly those that shape policy in the areas of employment, housing, education, and health and welfare services. These are the key areas in which the racial differential is greatest and the need for dramatic change—meaning the inclusion of Negro citizens in decision-making —is most urgent.

To achieve this, strong leadership within the Negro community must be encouraged and developed. This leadership will then be ready to step into the vanguard of the teamwork effort so imperative in resolving the smoldering problems of civil rights. The experiences of 1963 should have made clear, if it was not evident before, that the era of paternalistic handling by whites of the needs and ambitions of Negro citizens is gone. American Negroes are done with being "done *for*"; they demand the right to participate, to do for themselves and determine their own destiny.

8. Every opportunity to acquire education and technical skills must be utilized to the fullest. Every means of strengthening the social and economic fabric of the Negro community must be employed.

Negro citizens, adults as well as young people, must maintain and even accelerate the sense of urgency that now characterizes the drive for first-class citizenship.

9. It is vital that government at all levels, philanthropic foundations, labor, business, and industry reassess their financial support of, and cooperation with, established organizations committed to securing equal opportunity for Negro citizens to share in the fundamental privileges and rights of American democracy.

It is imperative that all of these major sources of support increase substantially their contributions, both financial and nonfinancial, to the preventive and remedial programs carried on by responsible Negro leadership organizations. These agencies aid Negroes to help themselves by staying in school, registering and voting, making use of adult education classes and retraining centers. For far too long the agencies that have seen the needs and attempted unspectacularly but effectively to meet them have suffered from a crippling anemia of finances, caused by the acute myopia of government, philanthropy, business, and labor.

10. Negro citizens must exert themselves energetically in constructive efforts to carry their full share of responsibilities and to participate in a meaningful way in every phase of community life. It is not enough to man the machinery of protest. Equally important today and twice as important tomorrow is participation in the responsibilities and opportunities of full citizenship in our democracy. This means Negroes moving not only onto the picket lines but also into PTA meetings, moving not only into lunch counters but also into libraries, moving into both community facilities and committee rooms, into both public accommodations and public hearings, and, finally, moving onto the commissions and boards to exercise their rights and insure their fair share.

The *special effort* program outlined above represents a mature, realistic, broad-front attack on the existing problems, a program through which significant breakthroughs of sufficient scale and extent can be accomplished. The program has a simple, practical aim: to provide the Negro citizen with the leadership, education, jobs, motivation and opportunities which will permit him to help himself. It is not a plea to exempt him from the independence and initiative demanded by our free, competitive society. Just the opposite. It is a program crafted to transform the dependent man into the independent man. It makes practical economic sense as a measure to reduce unemployment and welfare costs and to increase our productivity and national income by including Negro citizens in the benefits of our rich society. The President's economic advisers estimate that our Gross National Product could be raised 2.5 percent if the Negro worker's earnings were commensurate with the nation's average.

This program makes historical sense as a rehabilitation of the damage inflicted upon the Negro by generations of injustice and neglect. He, too, has given his blood, sweat, and tears to build our country. Yet, where the labor and initiative of other minority groups have been rewarded by assimilation into the society, the black American has been isolated and rejected.

There are profound moral and religious justifications in this domestic Marshall Plan. Our country is in sharp jeopardy as long as it has within its body politic a socially and economically deprived group of citizens, whether they are actually enslaved or denied the full benefits of equality and freedom by an insidious economic and psychological slavery. In this sense, the crash program proposed is not an effort to impose the guilt and sins of a past generation on our present white community. This is rather an appeal for all Americans, working together, to rid present-day America of its sickening disease, its moral shame.

This is what *special effort* means. It is this kind of *in*clusion, selection, and "preference" which responsible Negro leadership advocates. The nation should not be misled by sloganeers of dubious motivation who conjure up fright phantoms by waving trigger phrases such as "preferential treatment," "reverse discrimination," "indemnification," and "reparation" before unsuspecting, unthinking, and uninformed Americans.

Some ask, why single out the Negro, since there are whites who have been disadvantaged. Yet nobody complained when Helen Keller, for example, spoke out for the blind and said the people who have this handicap need new facilities, new resources, and new assistance in their particular difficulty. Further, she said, where they qualify they should be given special consideration.

With infantile paralysis Franklin D. Roosevelt made a similar effort. There are millions more Americans with cancer, heart trouble, or diabetes. But nobody bothered to ask why he singled out polio for his attention because everyone recognized the truth of the assertions and the special qualifications of Roosevelt as an advocate to speak on this matter.

My basic contention here is that Negroes are subjected to all of the hazards that other Americans face—they may be mentally retarded, have heart trouble, cancer, be lazy or brilliant or lame—but the additional fact of color complicates and aggravates every other hazard. This is why the Negro requires special attention and special effort.

The concept of special effort for Negro citizens may be difficult for the majority of white citizens to accept for three reasons: first, to accept the need for such programs means necessarily to admit that there has existed deliberate or unconscious discrimination in this country. Second, to accept the concept is to admit that the whites themselves have been beneficiaries of a preferential system—and nobody really wants to admit this. Finally, it is extremely difficult for a society that has only recently begun to adjust itself to affording equal opportunity for all its citizens to find itself suddenly called upon to offer special treatment as well.

As in the case of the GI Bill of Rights, the Marshall Plan in Europe, and the use of preventive medicine, this crash program should be seen as an investment rather than a give-away program. It constitutes an investment in human resources, and it will pay off—just as the Marshall Plan paid off in a prosperous Western Europe of strong and friendly allies; just as the GI Bill paid off in better-educated Americans, a revitalized housing industry, etc. The hundreds of millions of dollars poured into medical research through our National Institutes of Health do not disappear into the sand. They have an economic payoff in increasing longevity, improving the level of health and making possible more years of productivity by millions of our citizens. These additional productive years and reduced public payments for medical rehabilitation yield tax revenues which more than offset the federal funds committed.

Finally, and most important, it provides a meaningful and constructive alternative to continuing demonstrations, unrest, despair, tension, and outright racial conflict.

The Negro is in revolt today not to destroy the fabric of our society nor to seek an insulated compartment in it, but to enter into full partnership in that society. We have the materal and spiritual resources as a country to meet the challenge and to accomplish the urgent task ahead. All we need is the will to act and the spirit of decency and sacrifice that abounds in our land.

40 / Cesar Chavez

EDITORS, *TIME*

The methods followed by the Urban League represent the "old guard." In the black and Mexican-American communities in particular they are being replaced by many young, more militant leaders. The transition is similar to the general historical evolution of the labor movement from the early company unions through the American Federation of Labor and the more militant Congress of Industrial Organization. Dr. Martin Luther King, Jr., and his successor, Dr. Ralph Abernathy, have led the Southern Christian Leadership Conference and other civil rights groups in supporting the attempts of southern blacks to improve their economic position; they have led marches and boycotts for better jobs. In the Mexican-American community, Cesar Chavez, in particular, has moved his people to more militant efforts for the improvement of their lives. Through the UFWOC (United Farm Workers Organizing Committee), he has led a strike (*huelga*) of the grape workers in the Central Valley of California, using all of the classical union tactics, as well as marches to Sacramento, the state capitol, similar to the black marches from Birmingham to Selma. By 1971, more than 80 percent of the farms had been unionized, but much remains to be done.

SOURCE: Reprinted by permission from *Time,* The Weekly Newsmagazine, July 4, 1969, pp. 16–21; Copyright Time Inc. 1969.

Item: At a dinner party in New York's Westchester County, the dessert includes grapes. The hostess notices that her fellow suburbanites fall to with gusto; the guests from Manhattan unanimously abstain.

Item: At St. Paul's, a fashionable New Hampshire prep school, grapes are the only part of the meal invariably left untouched.

Item: In San Francisco, a Safeway official observes: "We have customers who come to the store for no other reason than to buy grapes. They'll load up their car with grapes and nothing else."

Item: In Oakland, a conscience-ridden housewife explains apologetically to her dinner companions: "I really wanted to have this dessert, and I just decided that one little bunch of grapes wouldn't make that much difference."

Item: In Honolulu, the Young Americans for Freedom organizes an "emergency grape lift" by jet from the mainland, inviting "all of those starved for the sight of a California grape to come to the airport."

Why all the excitement about this smooth, sweet and innocent fruit? The answer is that the table grape, *Vitis vinifera,* has become the symbol of the four-year-old strike of California's predominantly Mexican-American farm workers. For more than a year now table grapes have been the object of a national boycott that has won the sympathy and support of many Americans—and the ire of many others. The strike is widely known as *la causa,* which has come to represent not only a protest against working conditions among California grape pickers but the wider aspirations of the nation's Mexican-American minority as well. *La causa's* magnetic champion and the country's most prominent Mexican-American leader is Cesar Estrada Chavez, 42, a onetime grape picker who combines a mystical mien with peasant earthiness. *La causa* is Chavez's whole life; for it, he has impoverished himself and endangered his health by fasting. In soft, slow speech, he urges his people—nearly 5,000,000 of them in the U.S.—to rescue themselves from society's cellar. As he sees it, the first step is to win the battle of the grapes. . . .

Governor Ronald Reagan calls the strike and boycott "immoral" and "attempted blackmail." Senator George Murphy, like Reagan an old Hollywood union man-turned-conservative, terms the movement "dishonest." The Nixon Administration has seemed ambivalent, putting forward legislation that would ostensibly give farm workers organization rights but would also limit their use of strikes and boycotts. The Pentagon has substantially increased its grape orders for mess-hall tables, a move that Chavez and his followers countered last week by preparing a lawsuit to prevent such purchases on the ground that grapes are the subject of a labor dispute. Some auto-bumper stickers read: NIXON EATS GRAPES. The growers' answering slogan: EAT CALIFORNIA GRAPES, THE FORBIDDEN FRUIT.

Edward and Ethel Kennedy, following the late Robert Kennedy's example, have embraced Cesar Chavez as a brother. The so-called Beautiful People, from Peter, Paul and Mary to the Ford sisters, Anne Uzielli and Charlotte Niarchos, are helping to raise funds for the strikers. That support is one of the few issues that find Chicago Mayor Richard Daley, iconoclastic writer Gloria Steinem, and liberal Senators Jacob Javits and George McGovern in total agreement. Ralph Abernathy lends black help to what is becoming the Brown Power movement.

The fact that it is a movement has magnified *la huelga* far beyond its economic and geographic confines. At stake are not only the interests of 384,100 agricultural workers in California but potentially those of more than 4,000,000 in the U.S. Such workers have never won collective bargaining rights, partially because they have not been highly motivated to organize and partially because their often itinerant lives have made them difficult to weld into a group that would have the clout of an industrial union. By trying to organize the grape pickers, Chavez hopes to inspire militancy among all farm laborers. Because most of the grape pickers are Mexican Americans, he also believes that he is fighting a battle on behalf of the entire Mexican-American community, which as a group constitutes the nation's second biggest deprived minority.

UNLETTERED AND UNSHOD

Like the blacks, Mexican Americans, who are known as *Chicanos,* are a varied and diverse people. Only recently have they emerged from a stereotype: the lazy, placid peasant lost in a centuries-long siesta under a sombrero. Unlike the blacks, who were brought to the U.S. involuntarily, the *Chicanos* have flocked to the U.S. over the past 30 years, legally and illegally, in an attempt to escape the poverty of their native Mexico and find a better life. Whatever their present condition may be, many obviously find it better than their former one, as evidenced by the fact that relatives have often followed families into the U.S. The *Chicanos* do not speak in one voice but many, follow no one leader or strategy. Their level of ambition and militance varies greatly from *barrio* to *barrio* between Texas and California.

No man, however, personifies the *Chicanos'* bleak past, restless present and possible future in quite the manner of Cesar Chavez. He was the unshod, unlettered child of migrant workers. He attended dozens of schools but never got to the eighth grade. He was a street-corner tough who now claims as his models Emiliano Zapata, Gandhi, Nehru and Martin Luther King. He tells his people: "We make a solemn promise to enjoy our rightful part of the riches of this land, to throw off the yoke of being considered as agricultural implements or slaves. We are free men and we demand justice." . . .

Because of his own experience of poverty and acquaintance with prejudice, Cesar Chavez has made *la causa* more than a labor movement. He is determined to better the lot of all Mexican Americans. There is much room for improvement. There have never been Jim Crow laws against them, like those against blacks, but overt discrimination undeniably exists. *Chicanos* still find it hard to get into the barbershops and public swimming pools of south Texas. Still, though the *Chicano* is set apart by language, assimilation is often easier for him than for the Negro. For this reason, and because most of the *Chicano* population lives in relative obscurity in the *barrios* or rural areas, the Mexican-American community has been slow to develop aggressive leadership.

Now, because they have seen that organized black action gets results, the *Chicanos* have begun to stir with a new militancy. They have formed the Brown Berets, modeled on the Black Panthers, and set up a $2,200,-000 Mexican-American Legal Defense and Educational Fund, financed by the Ford Foundation. "We are about ten years behind the Negroes, and we must catch up," says Dr. Daniel Valdes, a Denver behavioral scientist. "But I think we will do it without extreme violence." Lawyer Donald Pacheco puts the plight of the Mexican American more bluntly: "We're the 'nigger' of ten years ago."

If he is a migrant farm worker, the Mexican American has a life expectancy of about 48 years *v.* 70 for the average U.S. resident. The *Chicano* birth rate is double the U.S. average—but so is the rate of infant mortality. More than one-third live below the $3000-a-year level of family income that federal statisticians define as poverty. Eighty percent of the Mexican-American population is now urban, and most live in the *barrio*.

FORBIDDEN LANGUAGE

The overwhelming majority work as unskilled or semiskilled labor in factories and packing plants, or in service jobs as maids, waitresses, yard boys and deliverymen. Particularly in Texas, Mexican Americans sometimes get less pay than others for the same work. Even the few who have some education do not escape discrimination. *Chicano* women find that jobs as public contacts at airline ticket counters are rarely open; they are welcome as switchboard operators out of the public eye. Mexican-American men who work in banks are assigned to the less fashionable branches. Promotions come slowly, responsibility hardly ever.

One major impediment to the Mexican American is his Spanish language, because it holds him back in U.S. schools. Mexican Americans average eight years of schooling, two years less than Negroes and a full four years less than whites. Often they are forced to learn English from scratch in the first grade, and the frequent result is that they become not bilingual but nearly nonlingual. In Texas, 40% of *Chicanos* are considered functionally illiterate. In Los Angeles, only an estimated 25% can speak English fluently. *Chicano* children in some rural areas are still punished for speaking Spanish in school. Only this year, *Chicano* students at Bowie High School in El Paso—in a predominantly Mexican-American section —managed to get a rule abolished that forbade the speaking of Spanish on the school grounds.

The *Chicano* is as vulnerable to mistreatment at the hands of the law as the black. Seven Mexicans were beaten by drunken policemen at a Los Angeles police station on Christmas Eve, 1952; six of the officers were eventually given jail terms. During an 18-month period ending last April, the American Civil Liberties Union received 174 complaints of police abuses from Los Angeles Mexican Americans. Two of the recent landmark Supreme Court decisions limiting police questioning of suspects involved Mexican Americans—*Escobedo* v. *Illinois* and *Miranda* v. *Arizona.* Many Mexicans still look on the Texas Rangers and U.S. border patrols with terror.

PLURALISM V. THE MELTING POT

That Chavez had dramatized the problems of Mexican Americans in the city as well as on the farm seems beyond dispute. Father Bernardo Kenny, a Sacramento priest with a sizable Mexican-American congregation, believes that even if Chavez never wins his strike he will have made a "tremendous contribution." Says Kenny: "He focused attention on the problem of the farm workers, and he made the Mexican Americans proud to be Mexican Americans. Chavez must be given credit, I think, for really starting the Mexican-American civil rights movement." Ironically, mechanization hastened by unionization may eventually diminish Chavez's farm-labor base—but it will not slow the momentum of *la causa.*

The new Mexican-American militancy has turned up a mixed *piñata* of leaders, some of them significantly more strident than Chavez. In Los Angeles, 20-year-old David Sanchez is "prime minister" of the well-disciplined Brown Berets, who help keep intramural peace in the *barrio* and are setting up a free medical clinic. Some of them also carry machetes and talk tough about the Anglo. Reies Lopez Tijerina, 45, is trying to establish a "Free City State of San Joaquin" for *Chicanos* on historic Spanish land grants in New Mexico; at the moment, while his appeal on an assault conviction is being adjudicated, he is in jail for burning a sign in the Carson National Forest. Denver's Rudolfo ("Corky") Gonzales, 40, an ex-prize-fighter, has started a "Crusade for Justice" to make the city's 85,000 Mexican Americans *la causa*-conscious.

As with the blacks, the question for those who lead the *Chicanos* is whether progress means separatism or assimilation. Cal State Professor Rafael Guzman, who helped carry out a four-year Ford Foundation study of Mexican Americans, warns that the *barrio* is potentially as explosive as the black ghetto. He argues for a new pluralism in the U.S. that means something other than forcing minorities into the established Anglo-Saxon mold; each group should be free to develop its own culture while contributing to the whole.

Yet there is no real consensus in the *barrio*. The forces for assimilation are powerful. A young Tucson militant, Salomon Baldenegro, contends: "Our values are just like any Manhattan executive's, but we have a ceiling on our social mobility." While federal programs for bilingual instruction in Mexican-American areas are still inadequate, that kind of approach—if made readily available to all who want it—leaves the choice between separatism and assimilation ultimately to the individual *Chicano* himself. He learns in his father's tongue, but he also learns in English well enough so that language is no longer a barrier; he retains his own culture, but he also knows enough of the majority's rules and ways to compete successfully if he chooses to.

Cesar Chavez has made the *Chicano's* cause well enough known to make that goal possible. While *la huelga* is in some respects a limited battle, it is also symbolic of the Mexican-American's quest for a full role in U.S. society. What happens to Chavez's farm workers will be an omen, for good or ill, of the Mexican-American's future. For the short term, Chavez's most tangible aspiration is to win the fight with the grape growers. If he can succeed in that difficult and uncertain battle, he will doubtless try to expand the movement beyond the vineyards into the entire Mexican-American community.

41 / The Fish-Ins

STAN STEINER

The techniques for changing the current distribution of jobs
are similar among the three minority groups in general. The
one major difference among them is use of direct violation of
the law by the Indians, a reference to the now-famous "Fish-
In" on the Columbia River by the Nisqually, Yakima, and other
northwestern Indian tribes of the state of Washington in 1964.
This form of direct action was intended to dramatize that new
state laws were denying the Indians access to fishing waters
they used to maintain their livelihood. The decision by the Indians to violate the law was an important political event because: (1) it was the result of cooperative effort between the
usually fragmented tribes; (2) it was led by the National Indian
Youth Council, thus indicating the emergence of the new,
younger leaders; and (3) it showed that the reticence of many
Indians to confront the organized governmental structure was
ending. The protest attracted support from tribes all over the
United States, along with such personalities as Dick Gregory
and Marlon Brando. (As a sidelight, the Supreme Court in 1969
ruled against the Indians when the case growing out of the
fish-ins reached it.)

Source: From pp. 50–54 of *The New Indians* by Stan Steiner. Copyright ©
1968 by Stan Steiner. Reprinted by permission of Barthold Fles Literary Agent and
Harper & Row, Publishers.

The Fish-Ins had begun. . . .

Hundreds of Indians stood on the banks of the river, watching the fishermen row out. The winds of Puget Sound tore at them. On the Quillayute River the Indians were uneasy. The tribe was small. It had never done anything this bold; for fishing off the reservation, without licenses, was an act of civil disobedience to the game laws, and to the State Supreme Court decisions that confined net fishing by Indians to their reservations. And the wardens were white with wrath.

The Indians were not fearful. But they were troubled. One who shared their apprehension was Mel Thom, then president of the National Indian Youth Council, which had organized the Fish-In as their first direct action.

> In the beginning the Indians just watched [Thom said]. The riverbanks were crowded. It was tense. The tone of the crowd was rather tense. You could feel the hostility build up against the game wardens. The authorities, the people with the law, were really mad at us for being there.
>
> We knew the game wardens would make arrests. They did. This was not going to be a cowboys-and-Indians story.
>
> And then a funny thing happened. The Indians began to enjoy it. They were happy to see some direct action. Then the tenseness broke. You would see kids running back and forth on the riverbanks and laughing.
>
> And some of the Indians took out their cameras and began taking pictures of the game wardens. Most times you see white people taking pictures of Indians, but this time it was Indians taking pictures of *mad* white people. That made them madder. It was our turn.
>
> You could feel there was a squaring off [Thom said] ; it was the first time in recent history that we were publicly demonstrating what we privately felt.

And before it had ended the hundreds of Indians had swelled to thousands. There were Fish-Ins on half a dozen rivers. There were dozens of arrests, war dances on the steps of the capitol rotunda, an Indian protest meeting of several thousand at the state capital. There were Treaty Treks on the streets of the cities and Canoe Treks, of sixty miles, through Puget Sound. There was a gathering of more than one thousand Indians from fifty-six tribes throughout the country who came to join their brothers.

Seminoles of Florida, Winnebagos of Nebraska, Navajos of New Mexico, Blackfeet of Montana, Potawatomis of Michigan, Iroquois of New York, Shoshone of Wyoming, Sioux of the Dakotas, Kiowas and Poncas of Oklahoma, Nez Percés and Coeur d'Alenes of Idaho. . . .

"We were ending the government's divide-and-rule system among Indians," said Mel Thom.

"It was the first full-scale intertribal *action* since the Indians defeated General Custer on the Little Big Horn," said Herbert Blatchford, then executive secretary of the Youth Council.

The Quillayute River and Puyallup River and Yakima River and Nisqually River and Columbia River and Green River became political battlefields. And there was fighting on the rivers. Women and children stood on the riverbanks and threw sticks and rocks at the state police and game wardens who came to arrest their men. The men in the boats fought back with their fists. Jails became familiar to the Indian fishermen. There were several arrested for the Fish-In on the Quillayute. Later, more were arrested on the Puyallup. Half a dozen were arrested on the Nisqually; four more on the Green. And these jailed fishermen joined the more than forty Indians arrested in the previous eighteen months.

"I think the State of Washington will fill the jails with Indians. But the Indians have no choice," said Bruce Wilkie, one of the young leaders of the Fish-Ins.

Mel Thom quietly said: "Laws or no laws, if people are downtrodden, if your treaty rights are violated, if there's police brutality, and these are things you feel and know, then, regardless of what the penalty is, any group will defy the law to correct a wrong. All I know is that when there is a problem the only thing that takes care of it is direct-action!"

On the coastal rivers and along Puget Sound up to 75 percent of the Indians earned much of their livelihood, and obtained much of their food by fishing. It was estimated that 25 percent of the income of the Yakimas and the Columbia River tribes depended on their fish catches. Without fish their families would not eat.

One of the Nisqually who was jailed, Don McCloud, said he pulled in about $20 a day fishing when "the fish were running." But much of the year his family of nine children was on relief. Let the state feed them if they jailed him, he said angrily: "They can eat what the governor told them to eat—sympathy."

The temper of the Indians was voiced by another of the Nisqually tribe, Alvin James Bridges, who had been arrested twice. He had failed to appear in court, and in response to a court order "to show cause" why he should not be jailed for contempt he blurted forth the anger his tribesmen felt:

> I went to jail last year to test the state's jurisdiction and was treated by the Supreme Court of Washington State as an animal with no rights whatsoever, e.g., "Menagerie Theory"—which in essence means that we (like the deer and bear) reserved within the treaty the rights to go to the river for a drink of water, and not to fish.
>
> New devices are dreamed up to place us in jail, further impov-

> erishing and humiliating our position. Our boats have been confiscated, supposedly for evidence. Yet they never appear in court. The State of Washington is attempting to deprive us of our fishing rights, using illegal chicanery, political-minded judges and the militant Nazi-like Game and Fisheries Departments as weapons against us.
>
> For these reasons I feel compelled to avoid the courts who are avoiding justice. . . . If I were ignorant of my rights, perhaps I would not feel so bitter toward the judges, who I know are not ignorant of my rights.

More than a dozen Yakimas were then arrested on the Columbia River. And the Yakimas took up arms.

The conservative Yakimas had refused to join the Fish-Ins. Located in the fertile bend of the Columbia and Yakima rivers, on the orchard lands of Washington's famous "fruitbowl," their huge reservation is one of the richest in the state. For years they fished from the banks of the Horse Heaven Hills across river from the Hanford Project of the Atomic Energy Commission. The Yakimas seemed unconcerned—at first. Besides, the U.S. Government, desirous of keeping the tribe amiable in view of their precarious location, had offered them $15 million in payment for the destruction of their ancient fishing sites by the construction of the Dalles Dam on the Columbia.

So the tribal leaders counseled moderation. When the jailings began, the Yakimas felt betrayed. They took up arms. Young men of the tribe put on their discarded Marine Corps and Army uniforms and shouldered their old M-1 rifles. The armed Yakimas patrolled the banks of the rivers, guarding the tribal fishermen. There were guns along the rivers for the first time since the Yakima Wars, one hundred years before. Rifles in hand the Yakimas cast their nets.

The upheaval wrought by the first tribal direct action of the ten young university Indians who had met that sultry day a few years ago surprised even them. It was they who planned, launched, organized, and guided the Fish-Ins. The response of the tribes had astounded the youth, and everyone else.

It had all begun one day in February of 1964. The tribal council of the Makahs had decided that the small and scattered tribes of Washington State could never win their fishing rights until they got together.

"As one, we can win," the Makahs said. The elders of the tribe sent word to the university boys and girls of the Youth Council to come. Let us organize the tribes everywhere in the state, they said, and do something together that the white men will not forget. The Red Muslims among the younger members were eager for direct action, any action. "Just a little

field study of some of that sociology we had learned in college," one of
them said.

Urgent messages were sent to fifty tribes to come to a council meeting. More than forty came. There, in that meeting of tribal elders and
young university Indians, the Fish-Ins were planned. It was the first time
in the history of the tribes that so many had come together for a modern
political battle.

And the youths were asked to lead it. In proper academic jargon the
university youths named the tribal direct action the "Washington State
Project." Mel Thom said of it:

> Long, too long, the State of Washington had been denying the
> Indians their treaty fishing rights and the Indians were never able
> to do much about it. Whenever the Indians got into federal court
> they won, but in the local courts they never took the federal trea-
> ties and laws into consideration. It looked hopeless. And the Bu-
> reau of Indian Affairs and the Department of Justice were very re-
> laxed; they would not protect the Indians.
>
> Someone had to do something about it. And the Youth
> Council decided to go in with the Northwest Indians and stage the
> first tribal direct action in modern history.

It was an unprecedented task. The more so because of the lethargy
and disarray that plagued the tribal spirit and structure of the scattered
and disunited thirty thousand Indians in the state. Remnants of the tribes
in the Pacific Northwest were so dissipated and divided that some were
tribal skeletons. The government had recognized twenty-six tribes in the
state, though the Indians spoke of dozens of scattered bands. A few had
some acreage, but there were others who owned nothing more than a tribal
anthill: the Puyallups' reservation had thirty-three acres of tribal-owned
land; the Nisquallys had two acres; the Snohomish had sixteen acres; the
Suquamish had forty-one, while the Muckleshoot tribes of three hundred
members shared a tribal-owned reservation of one-quarter of an acre. The
tribes were pathetic. Politically the scraggly bands of Indians, on a pittance
of land, were incapable of resisting the powers of the state. If the last ves-
tiges of their heritage, their fishing rights, were to be denied them, they
seemed too weak and powerless to do anything.

> In the beginning tribal support was a little difficult to get
> [was the laconic understatement of Mel Thom]. Being a conserva-
> tive people, as they are, the tribal leaders had never had the oppor-
> tunity to be aggressive. For long they had been dominated and run
> by the government. So action, direct action, was something they
> were not sure about. These tribes had never used direct action.

Was it "the Indian way"? What would happen to them if they protested! Would all their rights be taken away?

The Indian had been stereotyped to act in certain ways; he was not supposed to take direct action, or to picket, or to demonstrate. People were curious to see if the Indians could do these things. So were the Indians!

Could a handful of tribal Indians undo the stereotype of the communications industry and the image machinery of a society? Could these Indians who "had been stereotyped to act in a certain way" break free of their image of themselves?

"If we were going to make any headway the stereotyped image had to be done away with," Mel Thom said, "so we decided to do something dynamic and different. We decided on the Fish-Ins."

chapter ten

MILITANCY GROWS: MARCHING AND SIT-INS

42 / Black Hope, White Hope

JOHN PEKKANEN

The technique most greatly used since the late 1950s to solve
the problems identified in Part I has been the demonstration.
The first major use of the demonstration was by Dr. Martin Luther King, Jr., in Birmingham as a protest against segregated
public buses. The most noteworthy organization to use the
demonstration is CORE (Congress of Racial Equality), which
began in 1942–1943 as an outgrowth of a Quaker organization,
and was, like the NAACP, dominated by whites in its early
years. It emphasized nonviolent direct action and the sit-in,
and during the 1950s, it was the major group using direct action. It lost prominence for a time but regained it in the early
1960s under James Farmer, who has now moved to a more
militant position though he now has joined the Nixon administration. The most articulate spokesman today for demonstrations is Jesse Jackson, a Chicago clergyman. His program
combines not only the demonstration, but personal pressure
on elected officials and a form of religious charisma. Jackson
is seen as the probable heir to King's position as the major
spokesman for nonviolent demonstration, although he is a
more militant and flamboyant leader than was King.

SOURCE: From "Black Hope, White Hope," by John Pekkanen, *Life* Magazine,
November 21, 1969, © 1969 Time Inc.

On Saturday mornings, just before 10, Jesse Jackson, 28 years old, ambles onstage at Chicago's Capitol Theater for the weekly broadcast of Operation Breadbasket. Resplendent in turtleneck and bell-bottoms, he strides to the podium and the audience of 4000, mostly well-dressed black women, rises. Ben Branch's gospel band reverberates with *Hard Times,* the Breadbasket choir belts out the words, and there is rhythmic applause. Jackson gives a palms-down signal and the audience sits, and he offers a prayer, his reverence real and moving.

Then he preaches—often on the economic disparity between rich and poor and what may be required to end it. "They talk about America being a melting pot, but it is more like a vegetable soup and we've been pushed down to the bottom of the pot. We are going to come up and be recognized or turn the pot over." Sometimes he preaches on the legacy of slavery, and one senses that as he stands up there, his eyes ablaze, arms flailing, neck veins rigid, he is feeling every lash of every old whip. During these sermons Jackson sweats profusely, the only visible symptom of sickle-cell trait, a chronic blood disease that saps his stamina but which he ignores in the drama of the moment. . . . Possessing a monumental ambition, an iron will and a facile mind, he was Mr. Everything in high school and college—star athlete, student body president, top scholar. Then he became a civil rights leader, and he wants to be a star there too. He likes it up there where the applause is deafening and the adulation endless, and he wants to keep on going. All this explains much about him, including the fact that he is constantly late. He held up two graduation ceremonies at which he received honorary doctorates of divinity, and he was 40 minutes late for an appointment with the mayor of Peoria, whose support he was seeking. About to meet Chief Justice Warren at a graduation ceremony some time ago, he muttered, "A few years ago I'da popped over and said, 'Yessuh, Mr. Chief Justice, Sir.' But no more, brother. Let him come over here." I'm important now, Jackson seems always to be saying, and you're going to have to wait a little bit until I get ready to see *you.* You can see it when he orders around a coterie of aides, men older than he, who forever get his food, run his baths, pack his bags and laugh when he tells them something is funny. It is an enormous ego at work, one that perhaps grew large before he was fully ready for it, but it is getting results.

Jesse Jackson has been hailed both as the great white hope because he is successfully nonviolent and as the great black hope because he is successfully pursuing economic parity for blacks. Nothing exemplifies this success better than the A&P fight Operation Breadbasket waged in Chicago. It began in July 1968, when staff members of Breadbasket, making their periodic check of businesses in the black areas of Chicago, found that A&P was not complying with its 1967 pledge to hire 770 blacks. When negotiations between A&P and Breadbasket broke down, the alarm to boycott was sounded. The word not to buy at A&P went out to black Chicago from the pulpits of the more than 100 black churches that form Breadbasket's organizational network.

Within a few weeks all of the 40 A&P stores in black Chicago were being picketed. A group of 900 sympathetic whites from the wealthy suburbs that stretch from Evanston to Highland Park joined in the boycott and picketed, hitting an additional 60 stores in white areas. Half the A&P stores in metropolitan Chicago were under siege. "It was a process," Jackson recalls, "of squeezing a company's vitals, and a company's vitals is its profit margin."

After 14 weeks, its sales down substantially, A&P capitulated. The "convenant" it signed with Breadbasket is enormous in scope. Beside providing for the hiring of hundreds of black employes, it requires A&P stores in black neighborhoods to use black janitorial, extermination and garbage-collection services; to give prominent shelf display to black products such as Mumbo Barbecue Sauce and Joe Louis Milk; to use black contractors for construction of new stores in black areas; the use of black media to advertise; the hiring of a black public relations firm; the promise of investment in black banks; the creation of "sensitivity seminars" for A&P executives to attune them to the racial situation; and, finally, a monthly meeting between Breadbasket and A&P to assure compliance. "It was," Jackson says, "a historic document for black people." An A&P spokesman will say only that Breadbasket took too much credit for it.

The Chicago branch of Operation Breadbasket was formed in February 1966. For two years prior to that, Jackson, after graduating from North Carolina's A&T College at Greensboro, was a student at the Chicago Theological Seminary and also worked part time for the Coordinating Council of Community Organizations (CCCO), a loose-knit coalition of civil rights organizations which became the local base for Martin Luther King's Chicago Freedom Movement.

In January of 1966, when King came to Chicago, he urged the 60 ministers who were a part of CCCO to begin a local Breadbasket program. The Breadbasket idea, which had enjoyed moderate success in gaining jobs for blacks in Atlanta, was based on the concept of "selective buying," a tactic used effectively in the early '60s by the Reverend Leon Sullivan in Philadelphia. The Chicago ministers quickly put the organization together and suggested Jackson, with whom they had worked, as its director. King had observed Jackson's work in civil rights causes, was impressed with him and approved of the appointment. Jackson, tired of "Bible stories," was attracted by the idea of action rather than contemplation and left the seminary several months short of graduation.

"What I feared then, and what I still fear," he says, "is that black power would remain at the level of psychological self-esteem. That we would stop with new hair styles instead of striving onward for new life styles." With Jackson as its director, Breadbasket began functioning in Chicago and was taken under the organizational umbrella of King's Southern Christian Leadership Conference. Jackson brought his tactical skill to bear by relying heavily on the black church, still the most vital institution in the black community, as the basis of Breadbasket's structure—and Breadbasket soon got results. Dairies were boycotted that spring because, Jackson explains, "milk can't sit too long," and soft drink companies were hit in the summer, the peak season.

In August 1967, King tapped Jackson to be national director of Operation Breadbasket, an organization with branches similar to Chicago's in 15 cities. By then, Breadbasket's reputation had become so firmly established in Chicago that many ghetto businesses capitulated merely at the threat of boycott. Today, after three years in Chicago, Breadbasket has obtained more than 4000 jobs directly and an estimated 10,000 by indirect influence, and has brought black businessmen good markets for their products. "We dare any cat in the ghetto to take us on," Jackson will say. "We'll destroy him."

Nevertheless, Breadbasket has had and continues to have many internal troubles. From the beginning, the more militant black members were resentful of Jackson's key use of white people, many of whom Jackson brought with him from the seminary. Jackson sympathized with their objections but fought vigorously to keep Breadbasket integrated, and at a showdown threatened to resign if the "all-black" faction prevailed. He won.

The hunger drive, in May, was part of the second phase of the Poor People's Campaign begun in Resurrection City in 1968. While the drive failed to rouse the national conscience as Jackson hoped it would, it did succeed in influencing the Illinois legislature in Springfield to accept two of its four major demands. The first was a free-lunch program for poor schoolchildren. The second, on which Jackson had only slight effect, was to place a higher tax levy on corporations than on individuals under a new state tax law passed by the legislature.

Jackson's maneuvering during the hunger campaign left no doubt that he is far and away the most astute black political leader in the state, perhaps in the nation. Dealing with the entrenched political leadership in Springfield, he was able to shift effortlessly from the area of economics and civil rights protest to politics and self-promotion. Early in the hunger drive, the conservative speaker of the Illinois House, Representative Ralph Smith (now U.S. senator), introduced a bill to cut the state welfare budget by $1.25 million, or about $15 per person per month. Declaring the bill "open warfare against poor people," Jackson quickly arranged for 3000 people to protest at the capitol in Springfield. The day they arrived from Chicago, Jackson met privately with Governor Richard Ogilvie, who admitted Smith's bill was bad and indicated to Jackson he would see to it that it was killed. Aware of the value of a public victory for himself and the hunger drive, Jackson answered that if the bill were to be killed, *he* would help kill it, and the execution would not be in the quiet confines of the governor's office. The next day Jackson appeared to testify before the entire House on Speaker Smith's bill. Rather than testimony, he delivered a sermon that attacked the bill and decried the plight of the poor. It was a masterful show, with Jackson exerting total control over the gallery, which was packed with his followers. Man legislators resented his takeover of their chamber. One of them, a Republican known for his backlash sentiments, was so incensed he muttered obscenities and repeatedly kicked the wall until two fellow legislators quieted him.

Jackson had given his speech and captured the headlines. But almost ignored in the drama was the fact that Smith's bill, now dead, had been killed before Jackson ever entered the House that day. Earlier that morning, Smith publicly read a letter from Governor Ogilvie, a close personal friend, which said that the state could meet its welfare budget without the proposed cut. In a move unprecedented for a speaker, Smith withdrew the bill. Not surprisingly, however, Jackson was publicly hailed as the man who forced Smith to back down. The response from black people around the state was enormous; Jackson could no longer be fairly labeled as a man who fought only for the black middle class. A welfare mother marching in a Jackson-led hunger march in Peoria spoke for many: "If they cut the welfare it would have killed me and my kids. But Reverend Jackson wouldn't let them do it. . . ."

After Martin Luther King was shot, nationally syndicated columnists called for Jackson to assume the presidency of SCLC. This was impossible, for, as one high-ranking SCLC board member later explained: "If anybody but Ralph Abernathy had taken over, the organization would have been in a shambles, because on one would have followed Jesse or any of the younger ones. We always fought like hell over things, and Dr. King and Ralph were the only two with enough stature to arbitrate them." Fulfilling King's wish, Reverend Ralph Abernathy became the new leader of SCLC, but there were soon rumors of internecine intrigues, with Jackson always in the picture.

There were reasons for the rumors, the strongest being that Jackson, despite all the disclaimers and denials, really doesn't respect Abernathy's leadership (Jackson gave Abernathy this backhanded compliment: "Ralph says all the right things. So what if he doesn't say them well.") There was also a bitter fight between Jackson and the volatile Hosea Williams over the mayoralty of Resurrection City last summer. Jackson was appointed by Abernathy to the job, but Williams took it over, and the resultant clash exasperated Abernathy and strained his relations with Jackson, who was reassigned and left the camp before the summer ended.

The fact is that, since the 1965 Selma march, SCLC has not scored a major success other than Breadbasket, and this raises the question of who needs whom more. Should the two organizations go their separate ways, Jackson would be hurt little. The chances are, however, that he will stay with SCLC—his loyalty to Martin Luther King is stronger than his lack of enthusiasm for Abernathy.

With Chicago's black middle class already largely committed to him and a solid footing now in the long-ignored, hunger-driven black underclass, Jackson has created a Chicago constituency that is cohesive, responsive and self-reliant. He has broadened his scope considerably. He is virtually on a national speaking tour all the time. He is also a major catalyst in the black protest against the construction unions in Chicago. A Chicago reporter who has watched him for several years observes: "Jesse is the man right now. He's moving in many directions, creating for himself the kind of power base in the black community that Daley has in the white community: a broad appeal to all factions and recognition that he's the one to come to when you want something done."

Jackson has stature and he knows it, but there are times when he seems insensitive to its implications. He can weep openly at the sight of a malnourished child, as he did recently during a hunger tour of Rockford, and then arrive for the next tour in Peoria in a rented Cadillac limousine, courtesy of SCLC, and appear oblivious when eyebrows are raised. He is vain almost to the point of narcissism, unable to resist peeking at himself in every mirror he passes. He once ordered his car stopped in traffic and told an aide to fetch him a copy of *Time* magazine when he was told there was a story about him appearing. He has demonstrated little capacity for self-criticism, he calls criticism from others "unfair," and he labels praise as "the truth." These are troublesome but not fatal flaws, and Jackson will acknowledge that he might have shortcomings. "It ain't nothing," he'll tell you, "for God to speak through imperfect people."

43 / Why We Can't Wait

MARTIN LUTHER KING, JR.

By 1964 the selection reprinted here had been published, and Martin Luther King, Jr., had become the most important single figure in the civil rights movement in the United States. He had reached national prominence six years earlier when, as a young minister, he led the Montgomery, Alabama, bus boycott, which ultimately resulted in desegregation of the public transportation system in that city. He had become a central figure in the 1960 presidential election when he was jailed in Birmingham, Alabama, trying to focus the attention of the entire nation on the denial of voting rights to blacks in the South. Public indignation over the treatment of blacks in Selma, coupled with President Kennedy's assassination, led to the 1965 Civil Rights Act. Before he was killed by an assassin in April 1968, Dr. King had received the Nobel Peace Prize, led the famous March on Washington, D.C., in August 1963, and had also led nonviolent demonstrations to focus worldwide attention on racial discrimination in almost every walk of life and in all parts of the country. As a follower of Mahatma Gandhi, he gave his life to the nonviolent pursuit of racial brotherhood in the United States.

Source: From pp. 134–140 in *Why We Can't Wait* by Martin Luther King, Jr. Copyright © 1964 by Martin Luther King, Jr. Reprinted by permission of Harper & Row, Publishers.

Among the many vital jobs to be done, the nation must not only radically readjust its attitude toward the Negro in the compelling present, but must incorporate in its planning some compensatory consideration for the handicaps he has inherited from the past. It is impossible to create a formula for the future which does not take into account that our society has been doing something special *against* the Negro for hundreds of years. How then can he be absorbed into the mainstream of American life if we do not do something special *for* him now, in order to balance the equation and equip him to compete on a just and equal basis?

Whenever this issue of compensatory or preferential treatment for the Negro is raised, some of our friends recoil in horror. The Negro should be granted equality, they agree; but he should ask nothing more. On the surface, this appears reasonable, but it is not realistic. For it is obvious that if a man is entered at the starting line in a race three hundred years after another man, the first would have to perform some impossible feat in order to catch up with his fellow runner.

Several years ago, Prime Minister Nehru was telling me how his nation is handling the difficult problem of the untouchables, a problem not unrelated to the American Negro dilemma. The Prime Minister admitted that many Indians still harbor a prejudice against these long-oppressed people, but that it has become unpopular to exhibit this prejudice in any form. In part, this change in climate was created through the moral leadership of the late Mahatma Gandhi, who set an example for the nation by adopting an untouchable as his daughter. In part, it is the result of the Indian Constitution, which specifies that discrimination against the untouchables is a crime, punishable by imprisonment.

The Indian government spends millions of rupees annually developing housing and job opportunities in villages heavily inhabited by untouchables. Moreover, the Prime Minister said, if two applicants compete for entrance into a college or university, one of the applicants being an untouchable and the other of high caste, the school is required to accept the untouchable.

Professor Lawrence Reddick, who was with me during the interview, asked: "But isn't that discrimination?"

"Well, it may be," the Prime Minister answered. "But this is our way of atoning for the centuries of injustices we have inflicted upon these people."

America must seek its own ways of atoning for the injustices she has inflicted upon her Negro citizens. I do not suggest atonement for atonement's sake or because there is need for self-punishment. I suggest atonement as the moral and practical way to bring the Negro's standards up to a realistic level.

In facing the new American dilemma, the relevant question is not:

"What more does the Negro want?" but rather: "How can we make freedom real and substantial for our colored citizens? What just course will ensure the greatest speed and completeness? And how do we combat opposition and overcome obstacles arising from the defaults of the past?"

New ways are needed to handle the issue because we have come to a new stage in the development of our nation and of one in ten of its people. The surging power of the Negro revolt and the genuineness of good will that has come from many white Americans indicate that the time is ripe for broader thinking and action.

The Negro today is not struggling for some abstract, vague rights, but for concrete and prompt improvement in his way of life. What will it profit him to be able to send his children to an integraged school if the family income is insufficient to buy them school clothes? What will he gain by being permitted to move to an integrated neighborhood if he cannot afford to do so because he is unemployed or has a low-paying job with no future? During the lunch-counter sit-ins in Greensboro, North Carolina, a nightclub comic observed that, had the demonstrators been served, some of them could not have paid for the meal. Of what advantage is it to the Negro to establish that he can be served in integrated restaurants, or accommodated in integrated hotels, if he is bound to the kind of financial servitude which will not allow him to take a vacation or even to take his wife out to dine? Negroes must not only have the right to go into any establishment open to the public, but they must also be absorbed into our economic system in such a manner that they can afford to exercise that right.

The struggle for rights is, at bottom, a struggle for opportunities. In asking for something special, the Negro is not seeking charity. He does not want to languish on welfare rolls any more than the next man. He does not want to be given a job he cannot handle. Neither, however, does he want to be told that there is no place where he can be trained to handle it. So with equal opportunity must come the practical, realistic aid which will equip him to seize it. Giving a pair of shoes to a man who has not learned to walk is a cruel jest.

Special measures for the deprived have always been accepted in principle by the United States. The National Urban League, in an excellent statement, has underlined the fact that we find nothing strange about Marshall Plan and technical assistance to handicapped peoples around the world, and suggested that we can do no less for our own handicapped multitudes. Throughout history we have adhered to this principle. It was the principle behind land grants to farmers who fought in the Revolutionary Army. It was inherent in the establishment of child labor laws, social security, unemployment compensation, manpower retraining programs and countless other measures that the nation accepted as logical and moral.

During World War II, our fighting men were deprived of certain advantages and opportunities. To make up for this, they were given a package of veterans rights, significantly called a "Bill of Rights." The major features of this GI Bill of Rights included subsidies for trade school or college education, with living expenses provided during the period of study. Veterans were given special concessions enabling them to buy homes without cash, with lower interest rates and easier repayment terms. They could negotiate loans from banks to launch businesses, using the government as an endorser of any losses. They received special points to place them ahead in competition for civil-service jobs. They were provided with medical care and long-term financial grants if their physical condition had been impaired by their military service. In addition to these legally granted rights, a strong social climate for many years favored the preferential employment of veterans in all walks of life.

In this way, the nation was compensating the veteran for his time lost, in school or in his career or in business. Such compensatory treatment was approved by the majority of Americans. Certainly the Negro has been deprived. Few people consider the fact that, in addition to being enslaved for two centuries, the Negro was, during all those years, robbed of the wages of his toil. No amount of gold could provide an adequate compensation for the exploitation and humiliation of the Negro in America down through the centuries. Not all the wealth of this affluent society could meet the bill. Yet a price can be placed on unpaid wages. The ancient common law has always provided a remedy for the appropriation of the labor of one human being by another. This law should be made to apply for American Negroes. The payment should be in the form of a massive program by the government of special, compensatory measures which could be regarded as a settlement in accordance with the accepted practice of common law. Such measures would certainly be less expensive than any computation based on two centuries of unpaid wages and accumulated interest.

I am proposing, therefore, that, just as we granted a GI Bill of Rights to war veterans, America launch a broad-based and gigantic Bill of Rights for the Disadvantaged, our veterans of the long siege of denial.

Such a bill could adapt almost every concession given to the returning soldier without imposing an undue burden on our economy. A Bill of Rights for the Disadvantaged would immediately transform the conditions of Negro life. The most profound alteration would not reside so much in the specific grants as in the basic psychological and motivational transformation of the Negro. I would challenge skeptics to give such a bold new approach a test for the next decade. I contend that the decline in school dropouts, family breakups, crime rates, illegitimacy, swollen relief rolls and other social evils would stagger the imagination. Change in human psychology is normally a slow process, but it is safe to predict that, when a people is ready for change as the Negro has shown himself ready today, the response is bound to be rapid and constructive.

While Negroes form the vast majority of America's disadvantaged, there are millions of white poor who would also benefit from such a bill. The moral justification for special measures for Negroes is rooted in the robberies inherent in the institution of slavery. Many poor whites, however, were the derivative victims of slavery. As long as labor was cheapened by the involuntary servitude of the black man, the freedom of white labor, especially in the South, was little more than a myth. It was free only to bargain from the depressed base imposed by slavery upon the whole labor market. Nor did this derivative bondage end when formal slavery gave way to the de-facto slavery of discrimination. To this day the white poor also suffer deprivation and the humiliation of poverty if not of color. They are chained by the weight of discrimination, though its badge of degradation does not mark them. It corrupts their lives, frustrates their opportunities and withers their education. In one sense it is more evil for them, because it has confused so many by prejudice that they have supported their own oppressors.

It is a simple matter of justice that America, in dealing creatively with the task of raising the Negro from backwardness, should also be rescuing a large stratum of the forgotten white poor. A Bill of Rights for the Disadvantaged could mark the rise of a new era, in which the full resources of the society would be used to attack the tenacious poverty which so paradoxically exists in the midst of plenty.

The nation will also have to find the answer to full employment, including a more imaginative approach than has yet been conceived for neutralizing the perils of automation. Today, as the unskilled and semiskilled Negro attempts to mount the ladder of economic security, he finds himself in competition with the white working man at the very time when automation is scrapping forty thousand jobs a week. Though this is perhaps the inevitable product of social and economic upheaval, it is an intolerable situation, and Negroes will not long permit themselves to be pitted against white workers for an ever-decreasing supply of jobs. The energetic and creative expansion of work opportunities, in both the public and private sectors of our economy, is an imperative worthy of the richest nation on earth, whose abundance is an embarrassment as long as millions of poor are imprisoned and constantly self-renewed within an expanding population.

In addition to such an economic program, a social-work apparatus on a large scale is required. Whole generations have been left behind as the majority of the population advanced. These lost generations have never learned basic social skills on a functional level—the skills of reading, writing, arithmetic; of applying for jobs; of exercising the rights of citizenship, including the right to vote. Moreover, rural and urban poverty has not only stultified lives; it has created emotional disturbances, many of which find expression in antisocial acts. The most tragic victims are children, whose impoverished parents, frantically struggling day by day for food and a place to live, have been unable to create the stable home necessary for the wholesome growth of young minds.

Opportunities and the means to exploit them are, however, still inadequate to assure equality, justice and decency in our national life. There is an imperative need for legislation to outlaw our present grotesque legal mores. We find ourselves in a society where the supreme law of the land, the Constitution, is rendered inoperative in vast areas of the nation. State, municipal and county laws and practices negate constitutional mandates as blatantly as if each community were an independent medieval duchy. In the event that strong civil-rights legislation is written into the books in the session of Congress now sitting, and that a Bill of Rights for the Disadvantaged might follow, enforcement will still meet with massive resistance in many parts of the country.

44 / What Is MAPA?

VENTURA COUNTY MAPA

One of the few minority group organizations that has explicitly identified its commitment to political activity is the Mexican-American Political Association (MAPA). Although the group claims to be nonpartisan, it is more accurately bipartisan, but only to a degree. It has consistently supported Democratic party candidates, and it is considered generally by both parties as a captive of the Democratic party. Its usual sympathy for the Democrats was intensified in 1960 by the religious affiliation of John Kennedy, and little has happened in the intervening years to reduce that support. MAPA enjoys more prestige than probably any other Mexican-American organization, with the possible exception of UFWOC under Cesar Chavez. This was demonstrated by the appearance of Bert Corona, California State President of MAPA, at the 1968 Democratic Convention (the only Mexican-American representative to address either convention). In recent years, the group has been moving in much the same direction as the older, more established groups in the black community—that is, toward more militant statements and activity, in response to the younger, more aggressive organizations. At the same time, MAPA demonstrates the frustration of these older groups because it frequently does the hard negotiating, while the younger groups spend their efforts criticizing without developing specific alternatives.

SOURCE: From Ventura County MAPA, *What is MAPA?* pp. 1–3, undated.

MAPA is an organization of politically-minded Mexican-Americans who have an interest in improving our ethnic group's standing in our community. MAPA is building and enlarging a MEXICAN-AMERICAN POLITICAL POWER STRUCTURE.

WHAT IS A POWER STRUCTURE?

It is an organization that functions using the art of politics and is formed so that its beliefs, desires and voice are considered by the governing bodies in our society. A political power structure has the power to request and receive realistic answers on issues and questions affecting its membership and whoever that structure represents.

WHY DO MEXICAN-AMERICANS NEED A POLITICAL ORGANIZATION?

The plight of many Mexican-Americans can be directly attributed to the lack of a strong and vocal political voice. Although various individuals within our ethnic group have achieved degrees of high social standing, our vast majority remains inferior. As we all will agree, progress is considerably slower among our group than in any other group in the nation.

In the area of politics it is particularly very much the case. Example: In most cities of California our leadership is mostly questionable, mainly because our leaders are not really chosen by our group but rather by the "Anglo Power Structure" whose interests our so-called leaders serve. In most cases our leaders are chosen not for ability but rather by whether these persons are acceptable to the power structure. In very few cases are Mexican-American votes sufficient to elect Mexican-Americans who are vocal and who have "agitated the power structure's status quo." Among those considered agitators by the WASP community and by the "Nice" Mexican-American members of their respective communities are Congressman Edward Roybal of Los Angeles, Congressman Henry Gonzales of Texas, and such educators as Doctor Ernesto Galarza.

IS IT IMPORTANT TO HAVE A MEXICAN-AMERICAN POLITICAL ORGANIZATION?

The answer is unquestionably YES! During election time we are deluged by waves of propaganda from individuals seeking our votes. Some candidates are even so phony as to try to address us in Spanish, which they do badly, but this only demonstrates their almost complete lack of sophistication, because we as voters know that they had never taken the time to learn Spanish and after the election they continue to ignore our native language, our culture, and our people until the next election. In the case of Mexican-American candidates the evidence is more pronounced. Because we lack a large and well-funded political organization, we fail to build our own potential candidates. Consequently those ambitious individuals that desire political power "self appoint" themselves, and we are faced with the fact that 99% of our Mexican-American candidates had never in the past really taken an honest stand in behalf of us.

In most cases our Mexican-American elected officials shy away constantly from facing the community in any controversial issue and usually once elected find themselves bending over backward in not being prejudiced in behalf of Mexican-Americans.

Mexican-American candidates capitalize on the fact that they are "Chicanos" or that they run a small business or that they have an education and a profession. Some have even joined MAPA chapters throughout the state (30 days before elections), only long enough for an endorsement and then pulling out, succeeding only in splintering MAPA chapters in the process.

Mexican-Americans must have a strong political organization. We can avoid the above pitfalls that have plagued us in the past. Politics are here to stay, and in the name of good government we must become expert politicians. We will no longer continue to be used by the "Coyote" the "nice, acceptable Mexican." We will investigate, debate, and take appropriate action.

chapter eleven

BLACK, BROWN,
AND RED NATIONALISM

45 / The Black Muslims
in America

C. ERIC LINCOLN

The recent movement for black separatism has been identified
with the Black Muslims (or the Black Nation of Islam) more
than with any other organization. The Black Muslims are not
the first to press for separatism. During the 1920s and early
1930s Marcus Garvey became the first major figure to press
for separatism. The Muslims differ from Garvey in that he
wanted blacks to return to Africa, while they want land in the
United States. The Muslims are probably the largest black nationalist group in terms of followers, although no accurate
data are available. (Almost all nationalist groups claim that
they keep their membership list secret in order to protect their
members, but it also permits them to claim almost any number
of supporters.) The two most famous Muslims have been Malcolm X, who left the movement and, it appears, was killed by
Muslims, and Mohammad Ali, the heavyweight champion of the
world. The movement has been led by Elijah Muhammad
throughout its life, although its founder is supposed to be Wal-
lace D. Fard. The beliefs of the Muslims are a mixture of puri-
tanical moral beliefs (no smoking or drinking), hatred of

Source: From *The Black Muslims in America* by C. Eric Lincoln, pp. 68–69,
72, 75, 80–83, 85, 87–88, 90. Reprinted by permission of the Beacon Press, copyright © 1961 by C. Eric Lincoln.

whites, and the demand for the physical separation of the races. The Muslims call themselves "Black Men" and reject white men's names. They do not endorse violence, contrary to the assumption of many whites. One of the strongest advantages of the movement is that it emphasizes self-respect and the rebuilding of the image of the black male.

Like all other black nationalists, the Muslims do not consider themselves "Negroes." They resent and reject the word and its implications: it is no more than "a label the white man placed on us to make his discrimination more convenient." For this reason, they rarely use the word "Negro" without the qualifier "so-called."

The Muslims prefer to be called "Black Men." . . .

America's so-called Negroes, say the Muslims, have been kept in mental slavery by the white man, even while their bodies were free. They have been systematically and diabolically estranged from their heritage and from themselves. "They have been educated in ignorance," kept from any knowledge of their origin, history, true names or religion. Reduced to helplessness under the domination of the whites, they are now so lost that they even seek friendship and acceptance from their mortal enemies, rather than from their own people. They are shackled with the names of the Slavemasters; they are duped by the Slavemaster's religion; they are divided and have no language, flag or country or their own. Yet they do not even know enough to be ashamed.

The most unforgivable offense of these so-called Negroes is that they "are guilty of loving the white race and all that that race goes for . . . [for] the white race [is] their arch deceiver." . . .

The Negro's plight was forced upon him by the white man, but it persists because the Negro has been willing to remain "in a land not his own." It can only be solved by separation. So long as Negroes live among whites, they will be subject to the white man's abuse of power—economic and political. Separation will provide the only realistic opportunity for mutual respect between the races.

But the Muslims are hardly planning to abandon the country to the white man. They emphasize that the white man's home is in Europe and that justice requires a separate "Black Nation here in America," built on "some of the land our fathers and mothers paid for in 300 years of slavery . . . right here in America." Marcus Garvey wanted to found a Black Nation in Africa. Elijah Muhammad thinks America will do. . . .

The Original Man is, by declaration of Allah himself, "none other than Black Man." Black Man is the first and last: creator of the universe and the primogenitor of all other races—including the white race, for which Black Man used "a special method of birth control." White man's history is only six thousand years long, but Black Man's is coextensive with the creation of the earth. Original Man includes all non-white people, and his primogeniture is undeniable: "everywhere the white race has gone on our planet they have found the Original Man or a sign that he has been there previously." [1]

The so-called Negro in America is a blood-descendant of the Original Man. "Who is better knowing of whom we are than God Himself? He has declared that we are descendants of the Asian Black Nation and of the tribe of Shabazz," [2] which "came with the earth" when a great explosion divided the earth and the moon "sixty-six trillion years ago." The tribe of Shabazz was first to explore the planet and discover the choicest places in which to live, including the Nile Valley and the area which was to become the Holy City of Mecca in Arabia.

All so-called Negroes are Muslims, whether they know it or not. It is the task of Elijah Muhammad and his followers to teach the so-called Negroes that they are of the tribe of Shabazz and, therefore, "Original." Once they understand this, they will know themselves to be Muslims, heart and soul. Christ himself was a Muslim prophet, and several of his parables refer to the so-called Negroes, especially those of the Lost Sheep, the Prodigal Son and the Raising of Lazarus. The so-called Negroes are good people and religiously inclined by nature. In fact, "the Black Man by nature is divine." . . .

The reprehensible behavior of the so-called Negro preachers stems primarily from their desire to be acceptable to the white churches and other religious organizations. Hence the black preacher is far more zealous about adhering to what he has been told are Christian principles than is the white man. The white man does not believe in trying to perfect himself morally, but he wants the Negro to be "past-perfect." As a result, the black preacher is so busy trying to gain the white man's approval by doing what the white man himself has never done, and has no intention of doing, that he has no time to concern himself with the real issues, such as economic justice and the freedom to walk the streets as a man.

MUSLIM MORALITY

In their day-to-day living, the Black Muslims are governed by a stringent code of private and social morality. Since they do not look forward to an afterlife, this morality is not related to any doctrine of salvation. It is, quite simply, the style of living appropriate to a divine Black Man in his capacity as true ruler of the planet Earth. . . .

[1] Elijah Muhammad, *The Supreme Wisdom* (2d ed.), p. 39.
[2] *The Supreme Wisdom*, p. 33.

Certain foods, such as pork and corn bread, are forbidden to the Muslim, for "they are a slow death" to those who eat them. Many other foods common to the diet of Negroes, especially in the South, are not to be eaten, since they constitute a "slave diet" and "there are no slaves in Islam." Lamb, chicken, fish and beef are approved, but all foods must be strictly fresh. The hog is considered filthy—"a poison food, hated of Allah"—and was never intended to be eaten except by the white race.[3]

One Muslim minister explained why the eating of pork is prohibited: "The hog is dirty, brutal, quarrelsome, greedy, ugly, foul, a scavenger which thrives on filth. It is a parasite to all other animals. It will even kill and eat its own young. Do you agree? In short, the hog has all the characteristics of a white man!" Asked to explain the analogy implied in the reference to the hog eating its young, he replied, "Didn't they father a million half-blacks during slavery and sell them off like cattle—for money? Aren't they still bastardizing the race today to keep their wives in servants at subsistence wages? This is eating your own young and picking your teeth with the bones!"

Muhammad himself is vociferous in his dislike of pork and those who eat it:

> The hog is absolutely shameless. Most animals have a certain amount of shyness, but not the hog or its eater. . . . The hog eater, it is a fact, will go nude in public if allowed. His temper is easily aroused . . . and he will speak the ugliest, vilest, and most filthy language. . . .[4]

Tobacco is also forbidden, and Muslims are admonished against overeating—a habit to which the so-called Negroes are alleged to be particularly susceptible. An overweight Muslim may be penalized by a fine, which continues until he reduces. In general, one meal a day is considered sufficient, for such restraint eliminates physical and mental sluggishness and leaves more time for industry. . . .

Sexual morality is defined in ultra-puritanical terms and is said to be strictly enforced. Any philanderer is answerable to the quasi-judicial militia, the FOI. Courtship or marriage outside the group is discouraged, and unremitting pressure is put on non-Muslim spouses to join the Black Nation. Divorce is frowned upon but allowed. No Muslim woman may be alone in a room with any man except her husband; and provocative or revealing dress, including cosmetics, is absolutely forbidden. Any Muslim who participates in an interracial liaison may incur severe punishment, even expulsion, from the Movement. Clear lines are drawn to indicate the behavior and social role appropriate to each sex; and Muslim males are

[3] See *The Supreme Wisdom*, pp. 21 and 42.
[4] *The Supreme Wisdom*, p. 22.

expected to be constantly alert for any show of interest in a Muslim woman on the part of a white man, for whom sex is alleged to be a degrading obsession.

The regeneration of criminals and other fallen persons is a prime concern of the Black Muslims, and they have an enviable record of success. Muhammad claims that his Movement has done more to "clean up the so-called Negroes" than all the churches and social agencies combined. . . .

But the rank-and-file Muslim is expected to evince general character traits that can only benefit the society as a whole. Men are expected to live soberly and with dignity, to work hard, to devote themselves to their families' welfare and to deal honestly with all men. They are expected to obey all constituted authority—even the usurped and corrupt authority of the white man, until the Black Nation returns to power. Women are especially enjoined not to imitate "the silly and often immoral habits of the white woman," which can only wreck their marriages and their children. While equal in every way to their husbands, they are taught to obey them. Modesty, thrift and service are recommended as their chief concerns. . . .

The Muslim ideal is "a United Front of Black Men," who will "take the offensive and carry the fight for justice and freedom to the enemy." Through such a United Front, "the American Negroes will discover themselves, elevate their distinguished men and women . . . give outlets to their talented youth, and assume the contours of a nation" [5] Because he pursues a United Front, Muhammad's attacks against Negro leadership have been mainly retaliatory, and the necessity for such a public display of disunity is distressing to him. . . .

The Black Muslims demand absolute separation of the black and the white races. They are willing to approach this goal by stages—the economic and political links, for example, need not be severed immediately —but all personal relationships between the races must be broken *now*. Economic severance, the next major step, is already under way, and political severance will follow in good time. But only with complete racial separation will the perfect harmony of the universe be restored.

Those so-called Negroes who seek integration with the American white man are, say the Muslims, unrealistic and stupid. The white man is not suddenly going to share with his erstwhile slaves the advantages and privileges he has so long pre-empted. America became the richest and most powerful nation in the world because she harnessed, for more than three hundred years, the free labor of millions of human beings. But she does not have the decency to share her wealth and privileges with "those who worked so long for nothing, and even now receive but a pittance."

[5] *Los Angeles Herald-Dispatch,* February 6, 1958.

The so-called Negroes are still "free slaves." Millions of them are not allowed to vote, and few are permitted to hold office. None can wholly escape the implications of color. Ralph Bunche, the most distinguished American Negro on the world scene, refused a sub-Cabinet post in the federal government because he could not live and move in the nation's capital with the freedom accorded to the most illiterate white thug. Even the recognized enemies of the country, so long as they are white, come to America and immediately enjoy the privileges of freedom. To American Negroes—hundreds of thousands of whom have fought and died for their nation—these same privileges are denied. . . .

The call for a Black Front has important economic overtones, for the Muslims' economic policies are a fundamental aspect of the total Movement. Their basic premise is that the white man's economic dominance gives him the power of life and death over the blacks. "You can't whip a man when he's helping you," says Muhammad; and his oft-quoted aphorism is economically, if not socially or politically, cogent.

Economic security was stressed from the first days of the Movement. As early as 1937 it was observed that:

> The prophet taught them that they are descendants of nobles. . . .
> To show their escape from slavery and their restoration to their
> original high status, they feel obliged to live in good houses and
> wear good clothes . . . and are ashamed that they have not been
> able to purchase better commodities or rent finer homes.[6]

As we have seen, the pendulum has swung back toward the center. The Muslims still prize industriousness and a sense of responsibility, but they shy away from conspicuous consumption. They do not live in the residential section generally preferred by the Negro business and professional classes, and they do not sport the flashy automobiles usually associated with Negro revivalistic cults. On the contrary, they strongly affirm their identity with the working class. There is a strong emphasis on the equality of the ministers and the "brothers," and all tend to live pretty much alike in terms of housing—in the Black Ghetto—and visible goods.

Thrift is encouraged; and while credit purchasing is not forbidden, Muslims are reminded that "debt is slavery." These counsels have had a clearly salutary effect. Indeed, the more faithful a Muslim is to the teachings of his leaders, the better his economic condition is likely to be.

[6] Erdman D. Benyon, "The Voodoo Cult among Negro Migrants in Detroit," *The American Journal of Sociology,* 43, No. 6 (May 1938), 905–906.

46 / Malcolm X Speaks

MALCOLM X

This selection is by perhaps the most influential black author-
leader of the 1960s. Malcolm X, or Malcolm Little as he was
originally known, made a greater impact on the young black
community in the year after he broke with the Black Muslims
(1964–1965) than any other leader in this decade. Why this
should be is revealed in his writing. He rejected the traditional
techniques of the black leadership that arose after the school
desegregation decision and replaced their vocabulary of pas-
siveness, brotherhood, and acceptance of small changes with
a bravado and strength that has proved to be a welcome tonic
to the frail egos of ghetto youth. At the same time he did not
preach the virulent hatred expressed by the Muslims. In this
transition from the separatist doctrine of the Muslims to the
more ambiguous position of his Organization of Afro-American
Unity, he left blacks with the courage to stand up to the white
community, but at the same time he did not have any specific
resolution of racial differences. He realized that not all whites
were evil and left this as a final positive heritage for race relations.

Source: From *Malcolm X Speaks,* pp. 12–14, 16–17, 24, 31; copyright © 1965
by Merit Publishers and Betty Shabazz.

Just as the slavemaster of that day used Tom, the house Negro, to keep the field Negroes in check, the same old slavemaster today has Negroes who are nothing but modern Uncle Toms, twentieth-century Uncle Toms, to keep you and me in check, to keep us under control, keep us passive and peaceful and nonviolent. That's Tom making you nonviolent. It's like when you go to the dentist and the man's going to take your tooth. You're going to fight him when he starts pulling. So he squirts some stuff in your jaw called novacaine, to make you think they're not doing anything to you. So you sit there and because you've got all that novacaine in your jaw, you suffer peacefully. Blood running all down your jaw, and you don't know what's happening. Because someone has taught you to suffer peacefully.

The white man does the same thing to you in the street, when he wants to put knots on your head and take advantage of you and not have to be afraid of your fighting back. To keep you from fighting back, he gets these old religious Uncle Toms to teach you and me, just like novacaine, to suffer peacefully. Don't stop suffering, just suffer peacefully. As Rev. Cleage pointed out, they say you should let your blood flow in the streets. This is a shame. You know he's a Christian preacher. If it's a shame to him, you know what it is to me.

There is nothing in our book, the Koran, that teaches us to suffer peacefully. Our religion teaches us to be intelligent. Be peaceful, be courteous, obey the law, respect everyone; but if someone puts his hand on you, send him to the cemetery. That's a good religion. In fact, that's that old-time religion. That's the one that Ma and Pa used to talk about: an eye for an eye, and a tooth for a tooth, and a head for a head, and a life for a life. That's a good religion. And nobody defends that kind of religion being taught but a wolf, who intends to make you his meal.

This is the way it is with the white man in America. He's a wolf and you're sheep. Any time a shepherd, a pastor, teaches you and me not to run from the white man and, at the same time, teaches us not to fight the white man, he's a traitor to you and me. Don't lay down a life all by itself. No, preserve your life, it's the best thing you've got. And if you've got to give it up, let it be even-steven.

The slavemaster took Tom and dressed him well, fed him and even gave him a little education—a *little* education; gave him a long coat and a top hat and made all the other slaves look up to him. Then he used Tom to control them. The same strategy that was used in those days is used today, by the same white man. He takes a Negro, a so-called Negro, and makes him prominent, builds him up, publicizes him, makes him a celebrity. And then he becomes a spokesman for Negroes, and a Negro leader. . . .

It's just like when you've got some coffee that's too black, which means it's too strong. What do you do? You integrate it with cream, you make it weak. But if you pour too much cream in it, you won't even know you ever had coffee. It used to be hot, it becomes cool. It used to be strong, it becomes weak. It used to wake you up, now it puts you to sleep. This is what they did with the march on Washington. They joined it. They didn't integrate it, they infiltrated it. They joined it, became a part of it, took it over. And as they took it over, it lost its militancy. It ceased to be angry, it ceased to be hot, it ceased to be uncompromising. Why, it even ceased to be a march, it became a picnic, a circus. Nothing but a circus with clowns and all. You had one right here in Detroit, I saw it on television with clowns leading it, white clowns and black clowns. I know you don't like what I'm saying but I'm going to tell you anyway. Because I can prove what I'm saying. If you think I'm telling you wrong, you bring me Martin Luther King and A. Philip Randolph and James Farmer and those other three, and see if they'll deny it over a microphone.

No, it was a sellout. It was a takeover. When James Baldwin came in from Paris, they wouldn't let him talk, because they couldn't make him go by the script. Burt Lancaster read the speech that Baldwin was supposed to make; they wouldn't let Baldwin get up there, because they know Baldwin is liable to say anything. They controlled it so tight, they told those Negroes what time to hit town, how to come, where to stop, what signs to carry, what songs to sing, what speech they could make, and what speech they couldn't make; and then told them to get out of town by sundown. And every one of those Toms was out of town, by sundown. Now I know you don't like my saying this. But I can back it up. It was a circus, a performance that beat anything Hollywood could ever do, the performance of the year. Reuther and those other three devils should get an Academy Award for the best actors because they acted like they really loved Negroes and fooled a whole lot of Negroes. And the six Negro leaders should get an award too, for the best supporting cast.

Before we try and explain what is meant by the ballot or the bullet, I would like to clarify something concerning myself. I'm still a Muslim, my religion is still Islam. That's my personal belief. Just as Adam Clayton Powell is a Christian minister who heads the Abyssinian Baptist Church in New York, but at the same time takes part in the political struggles to try and bring about rights to the black people in this country; and Dr. Martin Luther King is a Christian minister down in Atlanta, Georgia, who heads another organization fighting for the civil rights of black people in this country; and Rev. Galameson, I guess you've heard of him, is another Christian minister in New York who has been deeply involved in the school boycotts to eliminate segregated education; well, I myself am a minister, not a Christian minister, but a Muslim minister; and I believe in action on all fronts by whatever means necessary.

Although I'm still a Muslim, I'm not here tonight to discuss my religion. I'm not here to try and change your religion. I'm not here to argue or discuss anything that we differ about, because it's time for us to submerge our differences and realize that it is best for us to first see that we have the same problem, a common problem, a problem that will make you catch hell whether you're a Baptist, or a Methodist, or a Muslim, or a nationalist. Whether you're educated or illiterate, whether you live on the boulevard or in the alley, you're going to catch hell just like I am. We're all in the same boat and we all are going to catch the same hell from the same man. He just happens to be a white man. All of us suffered here, in this country, political oppression at the hands of the white man, economic exploitation at the hands of the white man, and social degradation at the hands of the white man. . . .

So, where do we go from here? First, we need some friends. We need some new allies. The entire civil-rights struggle needs a new interpretation, a broader interpretation. We need to look at this civil-rights thing from another angle, from the inside as well as from the outside. To those of us whose philosophy is black nationalism, the only way you can get involved in the civil-rights struggle is to give it a new interpretation. That old interpretation excluded us. It kept us out. So, we're giving a new interpretation to the civil-rights struggle, an interpretation that will enable us to come into it, take part in it. And these handkerchief-heads who have been dilly-dallying and pussyfooting and compromising—we don't intend to let them pussyfoot and dillydally and compromise any longer.

How can you thank a man for giving you what's already yours? How then can you thank him for giving you only part of what's already yours? You haven't even made progress, if what's being given to you, you should have had already. That's not progress. And I love my brother Lomax, the way he pointed out we're right back where we were in 1954. We're not even as far up as we were in 1954. We're behind where we were in 1954. There's more segregation now than there was in 1954. There's more racial animosity, more racial hatred, more racial violence today in 1964, than there was in 1954. Where is the progress?

It's time for you and me to stop sitting in this country. Letting some cracker senators, Northern crackers and Southern crackers, sit there in Washington, D.C., and come to a conclusion in their mind that you and I are supposed to have civil rights. There's no white man going to tell me anything about my rights. Brothers and sisters, always remember, if it doesn't take senators and congressmen and presidential proclamations to give freedom to the white man, it is not necessary for legislation or proclamation or Supreme Court decisions to give freedom to the black man. . . .

Last but not least, I must say this concerning the great controversy over rifles and shotguns. The only thing that I've ever said is that in areas where the government has proven itself either unwilling or unable to defend the lives and the property of Negroes, it's time for Negroes to defend themselves. Article number two of the constitutional amendments provides you and me the right to own a rifle or a shotgun. It is constitutionally legal to own a shotgun or rifle. This doesn't mean you're going to get a rifle and form battalions and go out looking for white folks, although you'd be within your rights, I mean, you'd be justified; but that would be illegal and we don't do anything illegal. If the white man doesn't want the black man buying rifles and shotguns, then let the government do its job. That's all. And don't let the white man come to you and ask you what you think about what Malcolm says—why, you old Uncle Tom. He would never ask you if he thought you were going to say, "Amen!" No, he is making a Tom out of you.

I would like to mention just one other thing quickly, and that is the method that the white man uses, how the white man uses the "big guns," or Negro leaders, against the Negro revolution. They are not a part of the Negro revolution. They are used against the Negro revolution.

When Martin Luther King failed to desegregate Albany, Georgia, the civil-rights struggle in America reached its low point. King became bankrupt almost, as a leader. The Southern Christian Leadership Conference was in financial trouble; and it was in trouble, period, with the people when they failed to desegregate Albany, Georgia. Other Negro civil-rights leaders of so-called national stature became fallen idols. As they became fallen idols, began to lose their prestige and influence, local Negro leaders began to stir up the masses. In Cambridge, Maryland, Gloria Richardson; in Danville, Virginia, and other parts of the country, local leaders began to stir up our people at the grass-roots level. This was never done by these Negroes of national stature. They control you, but they have never incited you or excited you. They control you, they contain you, they have kept you on the plantation.

As soon as King failed in Birmingham, Negroes took to the streets. King went out to California to a big rally and raised I don't know how many thousands of dollars. He came to Detroit and had a march and raised some more thousands of dollars. And recall, right after that Roy Wilkins attacked King. He accused King and CORE [Congress of Racial Equality] of starting trouble everywhere and then making the NAACP [National Association for the Advancement of Colored People] get them out of jail and spend a lot of money; they accused King and CORE of raising all the money and not paying it back. This happened; I've got it in documented evidence in the newspaper. Roy started attacking King, and

King started attacking Roy, and Farmer started attacking both of them. And as these Negroes of national stature began to attack each other, they began to lose their control of the Negro masses.

The Negroes were out there in the streets. They were talking about how they were going to march on Washington. Right at that time Birmingham had exploded, and the Negroes in Birmingham—remember, they also exploded. They began to stab the crackers in the back and bust them up 'side their head—yes, they did. That's when Kennedy sent in the troops, down in Birmingham. After that, Kennedy got on the television and said "this is a moral issue." That's when he said he was going to put out a civil-rights bill. And when he mentioned civil-rights bill and the Southern crackers started talking about how they were going to boycott or filibuster it, then the Negroes started talking—about what? That they were going to march on Washington, march on the Senate, march on the White House, march on the Congress, and tie it up, bring it to a halt, not let the government proceed. They even said they were going out to the airport and lay down on the runway and not let any airplanes land. I'm telling you what they said. That was revolution. That was revolution. That was the black revolution. . . .

47 / La Raza:[1] Mexican-Americans in Rebellion

JOSEPH L. LOVE

A major proponent of Mexican-American nationalism and separatism is Reies Tijerina. He has attempted, through a series of actions described in this selection, to dramatize the failure of the white Anglo society to respect the rights of his people. His efforts have been focused primarily on obtaining control over a piece of land in New Mexico that he claims belongs to the Mexican-Americans, a result of the treaty of Guadalupe Hidalgo (1854), signed by the United States and Mexico to signal the end of the war between them. The Mexican-Americans claim that the treaty not only guarantees land titles in existence at the time of the treaty, but also bilingual education and their right to continue to use Spanish as a primary language. Tijerina speaks for a large group of underprivileged Mexican-Americans, and is seen by some as a modern-day Emilio Zapata. (Zapata, one of the modern folk heroes of the militant younger Mexican-Americans, led a group of poor farmers and peasants in a bloody uprising against the central government.) Tijerina's group is not only pressing for land return, but also is working to create cooperative economic

[1] The Race

SOURCE: An edited version of Joseph L. Love, "La Raza: Mexican Americans in Rebellion," *TRANS-action,* February, 1969. Copyright © February 1969, by TRANS-action Inc., New Brunswick, New Jersey.

315

strength for the Mexican-American through a group known as the Tierra Amarilla Cooperative.

In early June, 1967 a group of Spanish-speaking Americans who call themselves the *Alianza Federal de Mercedes* (Federal Alliance of Land Grants) and claim that they are the legal and rightful owners of millions of acres of land in Central and Northern New Mexico, revolted against the governments of the United States of America, the State of New Mexico, and Rio Arriba (Up River) County, formally proclaiming the Republic of Rico Chama in that area.

On June 5 an armed band of forty or more *Aliancistas* attacked the Tierra Amarilla courthouse, released 11 of their members being held prisoner, and wounded a deputy sheriff and the jailer. They held the sheriff down on the floor with a rifle butt on his neck, searched for the District Attorney (who wasn't there) and for an hour and a half controlled the village (population 500). They took several hostages (later released when the getaway car stuck in the mud).

Despite some of the melodramatic and occasionally comic opera aspects of the affair, both the members of the *Alianza* and the local and state authorities take it very seriously. This is not the first time the Aliancistas have violated federal and state law, attempting to appropriate government property (in October, 1966, for instance, their militants tried to take over Kit Carson National Forest, and to expel the rangers found there as trespassers); nor is it the only time their activities have resulted in violence. In this case the state government reacted frantically, sending in armored tanks, 300 National Guardsmen and 200 state police. They rounded up dozens of Spanish-speaking persons, including many women and children, and held them in a detention camp, surrounded with guns and soldiers, for 48 hours. The raiders got away, but in several days all of them—including their fiery leader, former Pentecostal preacher Reies López Tijerina—were captured.

It has become common to associate these actions of the Alianza with other riots or revolts by poor, dark-skinned and disaffected Americans—with Watts, Newark and Detroit. Tijerina himself helps reinforce this impression by occasionally meeting with, and using the rhetoric of, some leaders of the black urban revolt. The fact is, however, that the Alianza movement is really a unique example in the United States of a "primitive revolt" as defined by Eric Hobsbawm, a kind almost always associated with developing nations rather than advanced industrialized countries—and which includes such diverse phenomena as peasant anarchism, banditry and millenarianism (the belief that divine justice and retribution is on the side of the rebels and that the millennium is at hand). The attack on the courthouse, in fact, had more in common with the millenarian Sioux Ghost Dance cult of 1889–1890 than with Watts.

As the Aliancistas see it, they are not violating any legitimate law. The territory around Rio Arriba belongs to them. They demand the return of lands—primarily common lands—taken from *Hispano* communities, most of which were founded in the Spanish colonial era. Their authority is the famous *Recopilación de leyes de los Reinos de Indias* (*Compilation of Laws of the Kingdoms of the Indies,* generally shortened to *The Laws of the Indies*) by which the Crown of Castile governed its New World possessions. They claim that according to these laws common lands were inalienable—could not be taken away. Since most of such lands were in existence when the Treaty of Guadalupe Hidalgo was signed in 1848— and since in that treaty the United States government pledged itself to respect property rights established under Mexican rule—the Alianza insists that those land grants remain valid. The members speak primarily of common lands, rather than individual heirs, and define the towns in question as "closed corporations, with membership restricted to the descendants and heirs of the founding fathers and mothers"—that is, themselves.

The Alianza's interpretations of law and history are, of course, selective, and tend to ignore inconvenient facts and other interpretations. It claims that *The Laws of the Indies* were not abrogated when "Mexico invaded and occupied New Mexico," nor when the United States did the same in 1846. The Aliancistas are the early settlers, the legitimate heirs.

THE MAXIMUM LEADER

The Alianza and its actions cannot really be understood without knowledge of its background and its leader. First, the people from whom it draws its members and its strength—the Mexican-American minority in the US—and specifically New Mexico; second, the rapid economic changes throughout the area since World War II that have so greatly affected their lives; and last but surely not least the dynamism, determination and charisma of Reies Tijerina, without whom the movement would probably never have arisen. . . .

New Mexico is a distinctive area of Latin culture. It was the last state in the Southwest to be overwhelmed by Anglo-American civilization, and is the only one with two official languages. The Mexican-American population has been traditionally located along the Rio Grande and its tributaries, and extends into southern Colorado.

Until recent years, the Mexican Americans of New Mexico have been isolated from other members of *la raza* (the Mexican-American "race"). Texas and California have more than 80 percent of the Mexican-American population of the Southwest, yet most of these crossed over from Mexico after 1900, or descended from persons who did. But, the New Mexican *Hispanos* (the local name) have resided there for many generations, and some strains go back to the seventeenth century (Santa Fe was founded in 1609). Moreover, large numbers of English-speaking Americans only began to compete seriously for rural property in the 1880s, and appropriation continued into the 1920s. . . .

The Alianza was born in 1963, partly to combat the alienation and isolation of the Hispanos, but specifically to reclaim lands taken from the Spanish-speaking population since 1848. In colonial New Mexico (1598–1821), Spanish officials made land grants of indeterminate size to both individuals and to communities as commons, and the latter were respected through the era of Mexican rule (1821–1848). When Anglo-Americans began to enter New Mexico in significant numbers in the 1880s, they found it possible to wrest lands from the native inhabitants through the legal and financial devices of land taxes, mortgages, and litigation over disputed titles. By 1930, through legal and extralegal means, the Anglos had taken over most of the farming and ranching land in the state, and the state and federal governments appropriated much of the common lands that had previously belonged to the incorporated towns and villages. The Spanish-speaking population ultimately lost 1.7 million acres of community lands and two million acres in private holdings. The Hispanos sporadically reacted to this process by forming secret societies and vigilante groups; but at most this constituted harassment rather than effective resistance.

The Alianza now demands the return of these lands.

Yet in all probability, the Alianza would not exist but for the efforts of a single man, a leader who devotes his life to his cause, and inspires his followers to do likewise. Reies López Tijerina is a man of rare charisma who is most in his element when haranguing a large crowd. Of average height, he seems to have great physical strength as he grasps a microphone with one sinewy arm and gesticulates artfully and furiously with the other. He sometimes shouts violently as he asks rhetorical questions of his audience in Spanish—the language he uses by preference—and gets "Sí!" and "No!" bellowed back in appropriate cadences. The author witnessed a Tijerina performance last fall on the steps of the state capitol in Austin, Texas, where the Alianza leader told a group of Mexican-American Labor Day marchers he supported their demand for a state minimum wage of $1.25 an hour, but did so "with shame." Why should Mexican-Americans in Texas ask so little of the Anglos, whose government had repeatedly broken the Treaty of Guadalupe Hidalgo?

Reies Tijerina uses a demagogic style before a crowd, but he holds the tenets of his faith with unshakeable conviction: "It's something in me that must come out," Tijerina proclaims. His followers regard him with awe. He is "Caudillo" (leader) of the Alianza, but disclaims any desire to be dictator. He points out that a Supreme Council has ultimate control—though he, clearly, makes the decisions. It seems obvious that no one could step into his shoes, nor has anyone been groomed to do so. . . .

Yet there is a sinister element in the apocalypse which must precede the millennium: Anglos must be driven out. And Hispanos will be judged by whether they aided, stood aside from, or hindered the cause. Those who hindered will be treated harshly. . . .

While waiting trial on the multiple charges of the June '67 raid and appealing against the decision in the first case, Tijerina and his co-defendants were once more released on bond. On January 3, 1968, again in Tierra Amarilla, Deputy Sheriff Eulogio Salazar was kidnapped and beaten to death. Governor David Cargo, Campbell's successor, immediately revoked the bonds. Protests rapidly poured into the Governor's office from SNCC, MAPA, and other organizations, and a short time later Tijerina was out on bail again.

Since that time legal problems have necessarily absorbed most of Tijerina's energies, as he appealed the verdict of the first trial and prepared for the more serious set of charges (including kidnapping) stemming from the Tierra Amarilla affair. But the Caudillo found time to break into national headlines again in May and June when he led his followers at the Poor People's March on Washington. Alleging that the Negro leaders of the march refused to grant Mexican-Americans an adequate place in the sun, Tijerina cancelled Alianza participation in Resurrection City. Instead, he made use of his appearance in Washington to lecture State Department officials on the meaning of the Guadalupe Hidalgo Treaty—namely, the legitimacy of the Spanish land grants.

Tijerina had hoped to run for governor in the November 1968 elections, but the New Mexico Supreme Court disallowed his candidacy in October because of his conviction the previous year. Meanwhile the second (Tierra Amarilla) trial took place, during which Tijerina dramatically dismissed his lawyers and conducted his own defense. In mid-December his self-confidence was justified by his acquittal of kidnapping and two lesser counts. Other charges against him and nine other defendants had yet to come before the courts at the end of 1968. . . .

The disintegration of the traditional Hispano community seems well underway, and Tijerina articulates widely-shared feelings that his people do not want to assimilate into Anglo culture. He also rejects relief as demoralizing to its recipients, stating again and again, "We will no longer take powdered milk in exchange for justice." Recent increases in welfare assistance may actually have aggravated the situation by raising the Hispanos' hopes for greater improvement. . . .

Reaction to social disintegration can take many forms, and the Hispanic religious tradition—plus Tijerina's own background as a Pentecostal preacher—have helped channel it into millenarianism. In the 1930s a religious group called the Allelujahs, an Hispano version of the Holy Rollers, became popular, and before it faded out as many as half the people of some northern New Mexico communities had joined, taking part in religious services in which "Passages from the Revelation of St. John are favorite texts [according to a 1937 report], and lead to frenzies of religious ecstasy." The Allelujah experience has helped prepare the ground. So perhaps have the *Penitentes,* a lay brotherhood of Hispano mystics and self-flagellants that traces its origins back to the colonial era.

When the Alianza failed to obtain redress through the courts, the hope for and belief in extra-legal and supernatural means of relief—natural enough in the presence of the charismatic and fiery Tijerina—became exacerbated. When the National Forest Service recently cut back the use of grazing lands because of drought, the Hispanos were the hardest hit—and Tijerina was at hand to transform frustration into action. The frequency of millenarianism when belief in and identity with the dominant society are lost has been well documented in sociological literature. The Alianza constitutes an almost classic case.

Yet there is a "modern" dimension to the Alianza, and this is a direct outgrowth of its appearance in an industrial society with rapid transcontinental communications and ever-vigilant news media. The Alianza fits the requirements of a "primitive rebellion" or "revitalization movement," but its links with urban radical and reformist groups outside New Mexico show its potential for evolving into something more modern. Thus there are two distinct dimensions of the movement—the "primitive," rural, grassroots constituency on the tributaries of the upper Rio Grande; and the "modern," urban, nationally-connected leadership in Albuquerque. The "visible" media-oriented sector is modern, but the "invisible" millenarian sector is not.

Tijerina's primary concern is still regaining lost community lands, as his action at the Poor People's March showed. The hunger for community lands—the *ejidos*—remains the basis for the "real" movement, despite manifestos of solidarity with the Black Panthers and denunciations of the war in Vietnam.

The ignorance of government officials of the basic nature of the movement is almost monumental. They tend to explain the Alianza away by easy, modern clichés. Some find in the references to common lands the spore of modern communism.

At the November 1967 trial, the prosecuting attorney declared, "This is not a social problem we're trying. This is a criminal problem." Even some sympathetic observers have used singularly inappropriate terms. Tom Wicker of the *New York Times* and Congressman Joseph Resnick, chairman of the House Agriculture Subcommittee on Rural Development, have both referred to Rio Arriba County as a "rural Watts."

But Rio Arriba has little in common with Watts. The majority of Aliancistas, the rural grassroots, are not industrial proletarians but primitive rebels—peasants reacting and striking back in millenarian fashion against the modernization that is tearing their society apart.

48 / The Red Muslims

STAN STEINER

For the American Indians the issues of nationalism and separatism are different from that of blacks and Mexican-Americans, because the Indians have their own land. However, to call some of the barren waste areas the Indians were relegated to "their own land" is perhaps deceptive; in virtually every case the white settlers and authorities of the United States government took the best land from the tribes that had lived on it and crowded the Indians onto the least productive and desirable space. In Arizona for example, the Navaho and Hopi tribes were put on reservations of desert sand and rock. As a result, they have been unable to develop an economy except for the grazing of sheep and the production of goods for tourists. In other areas, such as the Midwest, the federal government developed what has come to be known as the "termination policy," which sets as its goal the termination of United States government supervision of reservation policy. The fruits of such terminations have been the loss of even more land by the Indians. In response, the Indians have set goals and organized policies to maintain possession of their physical lands and to rebuild an identity for the increasing number of nonres-

SOURCE: From pp. 39–40, 42–43, and 46–47, *The New Indians* by Stan Steiner. Copyright © 1968 by Stan Steiner. Reprinted by permission of Barthold Fles Literary Agent, and Harper & Row, Publishers.

ervation Indians who have left these remaining "islands" of Indianness.

It began in a too small and stuffy room on the wrong side of the railroad tracks in the highway town of Gallup, New Mexico. On that August 10, 1960, the nondescript and dusty Indian Community Center was suffocated by the unbelievably hot, burnt morning air that seemed to evaporate in one's mouth. Ten young Indians, who were to be known as the Red Muslims, sat in a circle like a modern war council.

Whistles of the wailing freight trains drowned their words. In the streets tens of thousands of tourists and Indians milled about. They had come to see the ceremonials. Hour upon hour the ten young Indians talked —a Paiute, a Mohawk, a Ute, a Ponca, a Shoshone-Bannock, a Potawatomi, a Tuscarora, two Navajos, and a Crow. These university youths had come from diverse and distant tribes. One had written, "Of course I'll go into hock to meet with you. . . . I may be forced to travel by oxcart, but I shall be there." But, once there, seated in a circle of decision, with their angers and determinations, they were uncertain. This was not the Cathedral of St. Francis or the University of Chicago. Now their destiny was their own to decide.

"If we organize are we really trying to help our people, or are we going to seek status for ourselves?" asked Clyde Warrior.

The Mohawk girl Shirley Witt was troubled by this too: "Is there any way by which this organization can guard against political climbing? Can we prevent its being used as a lever to gain high position?"

The university Indians talked of their desire to "find a place for themselves, *as a group,* within the Indian world. Some of the members stated that, though their training in school would not be of direct help to the Indian people, nonetheless they felt a very strong need to serve those at home. Several members added their voices to this.

"Most of all," the minutes of that meeting concluded, "the group felt that it was vital to retain the beauty of the Indian heritage."

Little by little the image of the new Indians emerged. A Winnebago girl, Mary Natani, said that they "must identify themselves as Indian and still adjust to another culture. But not leave behind what is really Indian." The new Indians would be "hybrids." Blatchford said, and would create a synthesis of the two cultures in their Indianness.

On that day the idea of a new tribalism—red nationalism—began to take form. (One girl, at the meeting, admitted that she had never been to a "regular powwow.") The form was, however, still uncertain; the leaders were yet unchosen; and the organization was nonexistent.

It was the Paiute Mel Thom who proposed the organizational principles of the new Youth Council. He thought that "political climbing" was a concept of the white man that was inherent in the structure and goals of his society. It was not tribal nor Indian. Let us organize "in the Indian way" on the "high principles derived from the values and beliefs of our ancestors," he said. " [And let us] consider rules based on Indian thinking as being sufficient."

Thom later elaborated on these beliefs: "The movement grew in the Indian way. We had decided what we needed was a movement. Not an organization, but a movement. Organizations rearrange history. Movements make history. That's what we decided to do. That's what we did.

"Long ago the Indians knew how to use direct action. You might say that was the traditional way that Indians got things done," Thom went on. "We were concerned with direct action: Indians moving out and doing something. The younger Indians got together in the Youth Council because they didn't feel that the older leadership was aggressive enough. And we felt that Indian affairs were so bad that it was time to raise some hell.

"But it had to be done in the Indian way," he added. . . .

> In the country today we are undergoing some kind of revolution. The young people in the whole country are not satisfied. Being an Indian and being young means you are twice as dissatisfied. You can hold a people down just so long. Then, pretty soon, they are going to kick back. And that's what's happening with some of the Indian tribes. It has already happened with the young Indians.

Young Thom, as the leader of the Youth Council, and as tribal chairman, combines within himself the new and old tribalism. He was one of its political architects.

> The Indians are the only tribal people, really tribal people, in this country, who don't have the same system, the same values as urban America, Thom said. And even though what exists in the Indian world is inconsistent with urban America, we've got to recognize this different way of life. If we continue to look at the Indian as a 'problem' that can be worked out by making him look like any other American, well, it wouldn't work.
>
> The Indian way, or what you might call Indian culture, is the way the Indian people live today. The government and the people of this country seem to feel that the Indian heritage, or Indian culture, is the way we look, or dance, or sing. But Indian culture is the way people live today.
>
> And there is a way! The young, educated Indian people know this way, this tribal way, and they like it.

Generations ago, in the last gasp of the "Indian revivalists," it was the Paiute prophet Wovoka whose religious visions of the rebirth of the old tribalism inspired the Ghost Dances. In the fading years of the nineteenth century his prophecy swept the defeated reservations like a prairie fire. Wovoka was a tribal ancestor of young Thom's on the Walker River Reservation. The old prophet's grave, where he was buried under his Christian name of Jack Wilson, lay not too far from the office of the new tribal chairman.

In his belief in a new tribalism, Mel Thom is heir to tradition. The Paiutes of Walker River were one of the last tribes to lay down their arms. It was not until 1911 that the final "battle" of the old Indian Wars had been fought on the alkali flats of the Nevada desert. It was known in history books as the "Paiute Outbreak," but the tribe itself called it "The Massacre of the Black Desert."

"My father knew two children who were caught by the U.S. Army in that massacre. They died. They died of heartbreak," Thom said. Like the tribal memory of Wovoka, these inheritances were in young Mel Thom's thoughts and in his bones.

He even spoke of modern "Indian Wars." His voice had that defiant, unflinching, but calm tone of a modern warrior: "Let us take a look around our great country and see what the red man of today is fighting," Thom said. "There is definitely a battle going on, no question about that. This is not a fictitious 'nothing fight' like that on TV and in the movies. This is a different kind of war—a cold war, one might say. Fortunately, for someone, this is not a hot war; otherwise the Indians might not have so many friends and experts.

> The opposition to Indians is a monstrosity which cannot be beaten by any single action, unless we as Indian people could literally rise up, in unison, and take what is ours by force. We see, however, that our Indian is small, confused, and regretfully does not include all our Indian people. We know the odds are against us, but we also realize that we are fighting for the lives of future Indian generations.
>
> The weakest link in the Indian's defense is his lack of understanding of this modern-type war. Indians have not been able to use political action, propaganda, and power as well as their opponents. Enemy forces have successfully scattered the Indian people and got them divided against themselves. The enemy has made notable gains; they deployed their forces well. But there is increased activity over on the Indian side. There is disagreement, laughing, singing, outbursts of anger, and occasionally some planning. Given some time, it looks like an effort can be put forth. If we can hold

our ranks together, our chances of gaining in our modern campaign are good. There is growing hope.

We are convinced, more than ever, that this is a real war. . . . No people in this world ever has been exterminated without putting up a last resistance [Thom said]. The Indians are gathering. . . .

The young Chickasaw Kenneth Kale wrote:

We know all about
Our redskinned counterpart
Of Martin, Gregory, and Stokely
Rolled into one—
Like an angry "Red Muslim"
With work to be done. . . .

I've often wondered why it is said
That the Indian Spirit is broken and dead
When in their midst like a grizzly bear
Is the sleeping redskinned giant
Now on the prowl. . . .

The voice of the new Indian was heard in the land. What he had to say was a choral chant of tribal resurgence that was articulated in the themes and words of modern man. Yet what he had to say was old.

In the beginning there had been an educational explosion. Now the young Indians were lighting the fuse of a political explosion. "We in the National Indian Youth Council were looking for a target area. We were looking for a target area for direct action," Mel Thom said.

On the wild rivers of the State of Washington the new Indians found their target.

chapter twelve
BLACK, BROWN, AND RED POWER

49 / Black Power

STOKELY CARMICHAEL
CHARLES V. HAMILTON

In September 1966 the slogan "Black Power" was coined by
Stokely Carmichael, the then-head of the Student Nonviolent
Coordinating Committee. It caused more negative reaction
than any other phrase in the history of civil rights. For most of
those who opposed its use, the slogan was interpreted to mean
that blacks would use violence to force whites to change their
behavior. As a result, the slogan was associated with the riots
of 1965 and of other racial riots since then. For others, the
phrase had far less explosive implications and was seen simply as a recognition that if the black community was to develop as an equal participant in the political process, it would
have to look not to white sympathizers for support, but to its
own economic, political, and human resources. This implied a
rejection of the concept of integration as it has been proposed
in the 1950s and 1960s and a move back toward at least the
temporary maintenance of segregated communities. It also implied that white supporters were less important in the ghettoes,
and so they were often urged to do less in the ghettoes but to
work harder at changing the attitudes of other whites. Carmichael and Hamilton present these themes in this selection.

SOURCE: From *Black Power,* pp. 44, 52–53, by Stokely Carmichael and
Charles V. Hamilton. Copyright © 1967 by Stokely Carmichael and Charles V.
Hamilton. Reprinted by permission of Random House, Inc.

The adoption of the concept of Black Power is one of the most legitimate and healthy developments in American politics and race relations in our time. The concept of Black Power speaks to all the needs mentioned in this chapter. It is a call for black people in this country to unite, to recognize their heritage, to build a sense of community. It is a call for black people to begin to define their own goals, to lead their own organizations and to support those organizations. It is a call to reject the racist institutions and values of this society.

The concept of Black Power rests on a fundamental premise: *Before a group can enter the open society, it must first close ranks.* By this we mean that group solidarity is necessary before a group can operate effectively from a bargaining position of strength in a pluralistic society. Traditionally, each new ethnic group in this society has found the route to social and political viability through the organization of its own institutions with which to represent its needs within the larger society. . . .

> . . . America has asked its Negro citizens to fight for opportunity as *individuals,* whereas at certain points in our history what we have needed most has been opportunity for the *whole group,* not just for selected and approved Negroes.
> . . . We must not apologize for the existence of this form of group power, for we have been oppressed as a group and not as individuals. We will not find our way out of that oppression until both we and America accept the need for Negro Americans, as well as for Jews, Italians, Poles, and white Anglo-Saxon Protestants, among others, to have and to wield group power.[1]

A key phrase in our buffer-zone days was non-violence. For years it has been thought that black people would not literally fight for their lives. Why this has been so is not entirely clear; neither the larger society nor black people are noted for passivity. The notion apparently stems from the years of marches and demonstrations and sit-ins where black people did not strike back and the violence always came from white mobs. There are many who still sincerely believe in that approach. From our viewpoint, rampaging white mobs and white night-riders must be made to understand that their days of free head-whipping are over. Black people should and must fight back. Nothing more quickly repels someone bent on destroying you than the unequivocal message: "O.K., fool, make your move, and run the same risk I run—of dying."

When the concept of Black Power is set forth, many people immediately conjure up notions of violence. The country's reaction to the Deacons for Defense and Justice, which originated in Louisiana, is instructive. Here is a group which realized that the "law" and law enforcement agencies

[1] National Council of Churches statement, *The New York Times,* July 31, 1968.—Ed.

would not protect people, so they had to do it themselves. If a nation fails to protect its citizens, then that nation cannot condemn those who take up the task themselves. The Deacons and all other blacks who resort to self-defense represent a simple answer to a simple question: what man would not defend his family and home from attack?

But this frightened some white people, because they knew that black people would now fight back. They knew that this was precisely what *they* would have long since done if *they* were subjected to the injustices and oppression heaped on blacks. Those of us who advocate Black Power are quite clear in our own minds that a "non-violent" approach to civil rights is an approach black people cannot afford and a luxury white people do not deserve. It is crystal clear to us—and it must become so with the white society—*that there can be no social order without social justice*. White people must be made to understand that they must stop messing with black people, or the blacks *will* fight back!

Next, we must deal with the term "integration." According to its advocates, social justice will be accomplished by "integrating the Negro into the mainstream institutions of the society from which he has been traditionally excluded." This concept is based on the assumption that there is nothing of value in the black community and that little of value could be created among black people. The thing to do is siphon off the "acceptable" black people into the surrounding middle-class white community.

The goals of integrationists are middle-class goals, articulated primarily by a small group of Negroes with middle-class aspirations or status. Their kind of integration has meant that a few blacks "make it," leaving the black community, sapping it of leadership potential and know-how.

It is a commentary on the fundamentally racist nature of this society that the concept of group strength for black people must be articulated—not to mention defended. No other group would submit to being led by others. Italians do not run the Anti-Defamation League of B'nai B'rith. Irish do not chair Christopher Columbus Societies. Yet when black people call for black-run and all-black organizations, they are immediately classed in a category with the Ku Klux Klan. This is interesting and ironic, but by no means surprising: the society does not expect black people to be able to take care of their business, and there are many who prefer it precisely that way.

In the end, we cannot and shall not offer any guarantees that Black Power, if achieved, would be non-racist. No one can predict human behavior. Social change always has unanticipated consequences. If black racism is what the larger society fears, we cannot help them. We can only state what we hope will be the result, given the fact that the present situation is unacceptable and that we have no real alternative but to work for Black Power. The final truth is that the white society is not entitled to reassurances, even if it were possible to offer them. . . .

50 / Another Defector from the Gringo World

RAMON RUIZ

The call for group power has come from the youth in the Mexican-American community as it has in the other two minority
communities. A variety of organizations have sprung up, none
of which presently enjoys national prominence comparable to
the Black Panthers. In California, the largest is the Brown Berets, who have modeled themselves to an extent on the Panthers. Other groups exist in California, especially on college
campuses. In New Mexico, a group known as Lodlanos has
been organized. In Chicago, the group is known as LADO
(Latin American Defense Organization) and is made up of
more Puerto Ricans than Mexican-Americans. In Texas, one of
the groups is known as MANO (Mexican-American Nationalist
Organization). The groups share a number of characteristics:
They single out the police as the particular agency in society
to criticize (see Selection 22); they reject any assimilation into
the white Anglo society; and they preach solidarity between
the members of "La Raza" (The Race). Finally, they all imply
in their public statements that the use of force and violence is
a form of power they consider acceptable as a solution to
their problems.

SOURCE: From Ramon Ruiz, "Another Defector from the Gringo World," *The New Republic*, July 27, 1968, p. 11. Reprinted by permission of *The New Republic*, ©1968, Harrison-Blaine of New Jersey, Inc.

Amidst the frustrations that accompanied the faulty organization and flabby leadership of the Poor People's Campaign in Washington, one hope burned brightly, auguring a new day for a minority long silent in the American Southwest. The minority is the Mexican-American and the spokesmen for that awakening are Rodolfo "Corky" González and his band of Denver militants who had lodged themselves in the basement of the Hawthorne School in the nation's capital. González rejects not merely the commonly held belief that poverty is the inevitable lot of his people, but the standards by which Mexican-Americans formerly measured success. A former prizefighter with a national ranking, the father of eight children, and once a businessman, González heads the first organization of Mexican-Americans in Denver that strives to achieve through militant means the social and economic betterment of 75,000 people who have furnished much of the physical labor to develop Colorado but have shared almost none of the rewards of progress.

González and his group ask for more than just the opportunity to share in the American success story. All Mexican-American leaders demand better jobs and schooling for their followers. The uniqueness of González lies in his intellectual and cultural vision of the future for Mexican-Americans. Until this man and his band appeared in Denver, what nearly all Mexican-Americans wanted was the opportunity to join their Anglo neighbors—to assimilate and be assimilated; to learn English, to adopt "American" manners. Their leaders advocated cutting all ties with the culture of their immigrant parents—of Mexican stock and almost always of semi-literate or illiterate peasant background. They explicitly condemned any interest in the country of their parents or grandparents— Mexico.

González and the new leadership break abruptly with this opinion. To them, the hero and example is Emiliano Zapata, the Mexican agrarian leader whose deeds form much of the mythology of the Mexican Revolution of 1910. Benito Juárez is another. Both Juárez and Zapata were of Indian background. The new creed among Mexican-Americans upholds not just the need to feel pride in Mexico, but specifically in the *Indian* heritage. "The Spaniards," says González, "came to Mexico to exploit, not to build."

Many members of ethnic minorities have traveled similar paths. Yet the new Mexican-Americans, much like militant black nationalists, want to use their heritage in a very different manner. They seek to preserve it, and to develop and strengthen it within themselves, in order not only to build an identity and to gain a measure of self-respect, but also to protect their community from the dangers of assimilation. Militant Mexican-Americans fight to keep their communities intact. As one of them put it, "we don't want to live in the world of the gringo, where people live in identical homes, mow their lawns at the same time, and compete with each other from dawn to dusk." The "barrio" provides another life, more sedate, stronger spiritually. To destroy it in behalf of assimilation and success in the gringo manner would be idiotic.

The story of Ernesto Vigil, a 20-year-old native of Denver and the first Mexican-American to refuse induction into the armed forces, illustrates the new approach. Vigil, an associate editor of *El Gallo,* the newspaper of Denver Mexican-Americans, spent last year at Goddard College in Vermont. He dropped out because, as he explains, life away from his barrio alienated him from his people, and from everything that made his life meaningful. He cannot conceive of life in an Anglo-Saxon community. Thus, he gave up his scholarship and returned home. When Vigil argued his point he had the sympathetic understanding of every member of the contingent at the Hawthorne School. All of them take immense pride in Vigil's refusal to fight against "brown brothers in Vietnam."

Vigil's stand on Vietnam brings out another facet of the changing attitudes. In the past, Mexican-Americans served with distinction in World War II and the Korean War, while their spokesmen publicly expressed support of American foreign policy—even when in conflict with the best interests of Spanish speaking Latin-Americans. No Mexican-Americans protested the invasion of Guatemala in 1954 by CIA-sponsored forces, or the Bay of Pigs fiasco. The Dominican tragedy passed virtually unnoticed by them.

González claims the cause of the Cuban Revolution as his; the slogan *venceremos* is as much his as Castro's, for the young leader looks with sympathy upon the Cuban's efforts to rebuild the island's society. With the cry, *Viva la Raza,* the new Mexican-Americans demand that public schools in the Southwest teach Mexican history and folklore and hire Mexican-American teachers to teach Mexican-Americans. In Denver, González and his supporters will frighten the white community accustomed to dealing with a docile people. But to the restless young generation of Mexican-Americans the Denver "revolutionaries" carry the light of hope.

51 / Paleface Power: The Problems of Reservation Indians

YALE REPORTS

For the Indian, the concept of Red Power is slightly different from that of Black Power or Brown Power. It identifies the same roots of power—economic and political resources—but it sees the reservation as an historical separation of the Indian nations from the white society as the source of building this power. The goal of Red Power is the maintenance of a separate Indian culture, a goal similar to the goals of the blacks and Mexican-Americans; however, because of the physical separation between the Indians and the white man, this goal is potentially easier to achieve. The barriers to the successful achievement of Red Power are similar again to those of the blacks and Mexican-Americans. First, government policy is based on the theory that its ultimate goal is the assimilation of all groups into the American process, and so separateness is discouraged. Second, because most businesses discourage the use of any language but English, of dress other than a conventional type, or of behavior outside a narrow pattern, holding a job requires the loss of cultural differences. Finally, until recently, the groups themselves have accepted the idea that they were destined, in fact, to be assimilated.

SOURCE: From "Paleface Power: The Problems of Reservation Indians," *Yale Reports,* 509 (March 30, 1969), pp. 1–8.

Since white power came to America, palefaces have pushed American Indians further and further into geographical enclaves called reservations.

Those Indians who live *off* these reservations have all the rights and responsibilities of any American citizen. However, reservation Indians have many services such as education and relocation provided to them by the Bureau of Indian Affairs, part of the Federal Government. Many of these services are derived from promises made during the treaty days of the last century.

At the same time, many reservation Indians have records falling far below those of most Americans. For Indians, the average age of death is 45; the average reservation child stays in his government school only five or six years, and the average reservation family earns only $1500 a year.

If the resources of Federal Government are at the disposal of the reservation, how has this happened? William Byler, executive director of the Association on American Indian Affairs, Dr. Carl Mindell, assistant professor of psychiatry and former director of a community mental health program on the Pine Ridge Indian Reservation, and Sam Deloria, a student at Yale Law School and member of the Standing Rock Sioux tribe, explore the reasons.

DR. MINDELL: I think the influence of the policies of government has really been very far-reaching in terms of the way that people on the reservation feel about themselves. It would not be unfair to think of the government agencies, vis à vis the tribal people, as functioning as colonial administrators, that is, coming in with set ideas about how things ought to be done and having the policy of getting the Indian people into the mainstream of American life as if what Indian people have and have had was worthless.

This is especially reflected in the policies in the schools. For example, if you ask the teachers and the administrators what they mean by the policy of getting the Indian into the mainstream of American life, it is very difficult to come up with a positive meaning. Invariably, the meaning is to deemphasize anything Indian, so that even today we find teachers who will become very angry at Indian children for speaking in their own language as if it is a terrible thing to do. One of the things we found in our community mental health program on the reservation was that Indian students felt the problems on the reservation were their own internal problems (they were no good, Indians are lazy, they are loafers, they are heavy drinkers) rather than seeing that the problems have to do with the difficulties in finding jobs, difficulty in finding high-status jobs, and the very fact that Indian people have little or no say over their own destiny on the reservation.

MR. DELORIA: One of the things that struck me is the kind of 1984 quality of reservation life. The government controls so much which is not noticeable to a visitor to the reservation. The services that an Indian person gets generally come from this monolithic agency. He knows, for instance, that when he misbehaves in school, it is not like a regular community where the school is a separate agency and has its problems getting along with the other public agencies in the community. It is all one big happy family. The school teacher can talk to the welfare worker, who can talk to the relocation man, who can talk to the superintendent, and the land-management man. Pretty soon you find that whole family has got the entire system down on it.

Because of the shift from an oral tradition to a people who seem to worship pieces of paper, there is a great fear of documents. The bogeyman that they use in schools, "This will go down on your record and follow you through life," is true on the reservation. They know it is true. They know it is down on your record. Not only will that follow you through school, but the same record then goes down the street so that when you apply for relocation to get job training of some sort, they look at that and say, "Ha, ha, we see you spoke Indian at recess in second grade. Now, that's not the attitude we like to encourage around here."

DR. MINDELL: Certainly the idea that the service-providing individual is the servant of the people is not existent. With the structure of the Bureau of Indian Affairs and the Indian Health Service which is part of Health, Education, and Welfare set up so that the people in charge are responsible to area office people and from there to Washington headquarters, it makes it theoretically possible for agency people to be entirely responsive and responsible to their own agencies rather than the people they are serving. The issue of power and powerlessness is extremely important on the reservation.

MR. DELORIA: This is becoming quite an issue in welfare rights organizations around the country. But it is even more so on the reservation for at least two reasons.

One is that there is much more propaganda and much more pressure towards acculturation. These people who are supposed to be serving have a mandate to go in and make substantial changes in a person's culture and his values.

The second is that the sense of powerlessness is terrifically reinforced by the symbolic tribal councils which exist but have no power over the services that are provided. It is a mock government, almost mocking the people. You get to have elections, but do not ever make the mistake of thinking that this is going to have any effect over the services that are in the community. . . .

MR. DELORIA: I think the change we are seeing is the early beginnings of a real change. These problems are beginning to be currency, vocabulary, part of the things that people discuss.

MR. BYLER: They need to be implemented.

MR. DELORIA: They need to be implemented. Society, Congress, everybody, has to develop a new way of looking at these things, a new way of understanding.

For instance, if you give money to the tribal government, that is fine. But if you also set such guidelines and attach such strings to that money that all you are doing is having brown people be punitive and push other people around rather than white people who are on Civil Service, you have not really changed things. So it remains to be seen how much a change this is. All you have really done is say you do not have to be on Civil Service, you can work for the tribe, but we still want you to do the same thing, rather than recruit Indians on Civil Service in the Bureau to do these things.

MR. BYLER: Yes, but the tribe is politically responsive to the people.

MR. DELORIA: Right.

MR. BYLER: The bureaucracy is not politically responsive.

DR. MINDELL: If the bureaucracy will leave the tribal elections alone.

MR. BYLER: Yes, that is the key point.

DR. MINDELL: What is currently happening on the reservations is that these policies people are talking about at high levels in Washington get considerably toned down when they get to the reservation bureaucracy. What we see now is the fad of talking about involvement. Everyone on the reservation talks about involvement with the Indian people which is, for the most part, talk. The people who are providing services feel no need to really be involved and to see the Indian person as a needed participant in the provision of services. It is talk, it is theory, but it is not really believed in.

MR. DELORIA: Sometimes when I am pessimistic, I think if there is a new awareness of the Indian desire to be left alone and to be individuals, the effect is simply that it is going to move society's masochism to another level. . . . This society loves to punish itself about how terrible it is to Indians. Now it will be a little more sophisticated and say, "Look, we are invading their privacy too. Oh, my, we are terrible." But it will not really change. I think in a lot of ways this may be about all it amounts to.

There are enough problems there so that a lot of things have to be worked out, a lot of attitudes have to change. This may be the beginning of an important change. Then again, the bureaucracy is almost as resilient as the spirit of the Indian people and both can bounce back and assert themselves pretty well . . .

MR. DELORIA: The kinds of decisions that are made are difficult to attack if you are within the value system of this society because they are so easily justified on that very basis. Everyone agrees that if you have 12 people living in a one-room log cabin there are going to be certain problems. So it is very easy for a social worker to justify taking all the kids away. Then, obviously, it is much more comfortable.

MR. BYLER: Clearly there are problems, not just in house design, but problems such as the high rate of problem drinking on the reservations. On some reservations the incidence of alcoholism (whatever that means) is as high as 70 per cent. Can we assume, therefore, that 70 per cent of those parents are unfit? Yet state laws, and I think of the State of North Dakota, indicate that it is enough to show that the parents are habitual drinkers to separate the child from the family. You do not have to look into what actually goes on in the home, whether the child is happy or not.

It is also state law that a child can be separated from his parents if he is habitually dependent upon the state for support. In this particular tribe, 90 per cent of the people are on welfare. Under the state law, 90 percent of the children could be taken away.

Immoral conduct is another state standard by which to judge the suitability of a home. Clearly, in questions of morality, I think there are cultural and personal factors that should not be judged by the state when it determines whether or not to break up a family.

MR. DELORIA: By those same criteria, you could probably depopulate most of the Eastern Seaboard if you really wanted to be meticulous about it. Many suburban communities would be childless.

DR. MINDELL: Another reason underlying the high rates of foster children on reservations is that the welfare agencies themselves are understaffed and child-welfare services in some reservations are nonexistent altogether. There are not enough people there and those who are there are generally very poorly trained. It becomes much easier for the agency to remove the child from the family rather than to try to keep the family together when meeting with a problem.

MR. BYLER: I think this is a central point. Despite all the services that there are on reservations, there is a notable lack of preventive and rehabilitation services to families in trouble.

Separating the child from the family destroys the incentive for the family to continue as a unit in many ways. We find that rather than diminishing the problems of the parents, you tend to aggravate the problem of the parents by taking the child away.

MR. DELORIA: When breaking up a family becomes the easiest administrative decision, I think a lot of human values are sacrificed.

I think when people are willing to break up a family for the sake of education or for the sake of their judgments about suitable homes, they have made decisions that reach farther than they realize.

There is the terrible story in John Collier's book about the Navajo family that ran off and hid in the hills because their youngest child was supposed to go to school and they were trying to keep her out of school. When they investigated they discovered that those people had ten other children, all of whom were taken away at the age of six or seven, all of whom never returned, and died of various diseases in institutions. Naturally, the family is not too anxious to send their last one away. But some children are raised in boarding schools, and of course, there is going to be no family integrity after that. . . .[1]

MR. BYLER: What some of these services can mean can be illustrated by the boarding school at Busby on the Northern Cheyenne Reservation.

Two years ago during a two-month period ten per cent of the teenage population at that school attempted suicide. The response was swift when publicity was given to this and mental health professionals were made available to the school. The attempted suicide rate dropped to nothing for the remainder of the term.

MR. DELORIA: I thought you were going to say they passed a regulation against attempted suicide.

The Bureau of Indian Affairs has been in operation for well over a hundred years and has been involved in education most of that time. They did not always run it themselves. I think it was about a year ago that they hired their first psychologist in the education branch.

DR. MINDELL: The issue of children needing care after they finish their eight hours in the classroom is rarely approached. There are many young children, five, six, and seven years old, in boarding schools where the ratio of caring adults to child is anywhere from one person to 30 on up to one to 250.

MR. BYLER: I would like to move to another area where the system works against the Indian. A system of credit that is inspired by greed provides a good illustration of the kind of web that the Indian is caught in.

We have heard a lot about hunger in the United States in the last several months. It has been discovered. Indian people have known there has been hunger on the reservation since there has been a white man. The Federal Government attempts to meet the problem of hunger on the reservation by providing commodities and providing welfare checks to those who do not have jobs. (And on most reservations there are not jobs for the majority of the population.)

Indian people trade generally at a local white store that caters almost exclusively to Indians. On the reservations the stores are crammed with food. The problem is for the Indian to utilize what little cash he has to buy that food.

---

[1] See Selection 8 for more information on Indians in boarding schools.—Ed.

DR. MINDELL: If I can just interject one statement. Although the stores may have plenty of food, in general prices are different from prices in surrounding areas off reservation. They are much higher.

MR. BYLER: Yes, I would say 25 to 50 per cent higher on an average. The Federal Government bases its welfare check on the assumption that prices are normal. Prices are not normal on the reservations, so that that child or family is eating 25 to 50 per cent less food because the prices are pegged that high.

The system works to keep the Indian trading at that store through credit, and this is how it works. Very often the postmaster of the community who receives the welfare checks will also operate the trading post. When the welfare check comes in, he requires that the Indian sign it over. He takes the check to liquidate the debt. Then the person, if he wants to eat for the rest of the month, has to go to him for credit again. So there is very little way out for the Indian. The Federal Government makes this all the more difficult because when you apply for welfare you have to wait one month to get your check. Therefore, for one month you have to be on credit. And that first month stretches out into years.

One thing that would be helpful in trying to resolve some of this would be for the Federal Government to make a check available on application. This would then enable an Indian to trade at stores immediately at lower prices and perhaps keep him out of the whole vicious credit cycle.

The powers of the state are often brought in against the Indian when he has a debt owing to the store. It is typical for a trader to require an Indian to sign a blank check as a record of the debt. The Indian will explain he has no bank account. The storekeeper will say that he knows that, this is just for bookkeeping purposes. Yet, should the Indian fail to make payment from his welfare check, or if he is employed, from his employment check, the merchant will deposit the check in the bank. The check will bounce and the police powers of the state are then called down upon the Indian and he is threatened with jail. There are Indians today in jail for failure to make that payment.

MR. DELORIA: Not even should he fail to make payment on the principal. He may pay it off and may pay a reasonable interest, only pay 100 per cent or 200 per cent interest. If the storekeeper does not like him, that may not be enough. We have all found interest rates getting up into 1000 per cent. So that it really is unlimited power.

The credit system has lasted a lot longer than it should partly because of the same cultural gap that exists on the reservation. People who are in a position to do something about the credit system find that they are more comfortable talking to the storekeepers than they are to the people in the community. They are willing to overlook these little flaws in the storekeeper's operation. In fact, they may consider him to be a community leader because they can talk to him, so they are reluctant to do anything to change the system. In fact, this storekeeper may have a lot to say on whether a person gets on welfare or stays on. He has tremendous power in the community, and the community again is powerless.

Generally a lot of the problems we have been talking about go back to an assumption on the part of society with respect to Indian people, but also with respect to poor people, black people, Spanish-American people, that the society has a right and a responsibility to act in their best interest by making them over in the image of some mythical ideal man. People have to have autonomy, they have to have considerable say over what happens to them. The services that are provided to them have to be voluntary. They can not be a condition on his welfare check. An Indian can not be forced to promise that if he leaves the reservation for job training he will never come back. This is something they try to do.

DR. MINDELL: We have been talking in terms of the larger community changing its policy so that the Indian community has more power and autonomy. The question comes up of the Indian people taking power. Are they banding together, lobbying to increase the power available to them?

I think of the stresses that are hindering this, one important stress is the fear of termination of services. The general idea is that if the tribe gets to look too good, the government then will terminate needed services to them as they have done in the past to some tribes.

MR. BYLER: The problem of acculturation, that is, attempts by the society to acculturate the Indians, ignores the strengths of the Indian communities, the genius of the Indian people. If society is successful in this effort it will have robbed itself of a great opportunity to continue to learn from Indian people what we have been learning since the Europeans landed on this shore.

MR. DELORIA: It is a larger version of the decision of the social worker that we were talking about before. Because there are problems in an Indian community which the social worker sees, that the Bureau of Indian Affairs sees, that society sees, in order to remedy those problems you do not break up the community, thereby breaking up the integrity of the people and their sense of identity.

chapter thirteen

IS VIOLENCE THE ANSWER?

52 / The Riot Area—Before and After

WILLIAM McCORD
JOHN HOWARD
BERNARD FRIEDBERG
EDWIN HARWOOD

In August 1965, the worst conflict between the black community and the total society occurred in Watts, or Watts-Willowbrook, a section of south-central Los Angeles. The conflict began after the arrest of a young black male for drunkenness. The result was the destruction of more than forty lives and the loss of many millions of dollars in property. The famous Watts riot or revolt (depending on one's perspective) came as almost a total surprise to the leadership of the city and to the traditional black leadership as well.

Los Angeles seemed to be a good place for blacks to live, but in fact this was illusionary. The unemployment rate in the ghetto was several times higher than that of the white population; housing conditions were typically substandard; there was a long history of tension between the police and ghetto residents; educational opportunities were inferior; hospital facilities did not exist; and businesses serving the ghetto residents charged the usual usurious rates. The explosion that rocked

SOURCE: Reprinted from *Life Styles in the Black Ghetto* by William McCord, John Howard, Bernard Friedberg, Edwin Harwood, pp. 58–62, 64–67. By permission of W. W. Norton & Company, Inc. Copyright © 1969 by W. W. Norton & Company, Inc.

Los Angeles in August 1965 was the first of several in northern cities, including Detroit, Newark, and Cleveland. Unfortunately, it has resulted in few improvements in the lives of the people of Watts.

Again, in May 1964, Assistant Attorney General Howard H. Jewel explicitly warned that demonstrations in Los Angeles could well be joined by the entire Negro community. Jewel wrote:

> In Los Angeles if demonstrators are joined by the Negro community at large the policing will no longer be done by the Los Angeles Police Department, but by the State Militia. If violence erupts millions in property damage may ensue, untold lives may be lost and California will have received an unsurpassed injury to her reputation.[1]

Mayor Sam Yorty, Chief of Police William Parker, and Governor Edmund Brown ignored these repeated predictions. When the riots broke out in 1965, Yorty flew to San Francisco, apparently believing that police could handle the situation. And Governor Brown expressed both his shock and his naïveté when, after viewing the effects of the Watts riot, he commented, "Here in California, we have a wonderful working relationship between whites and Negroes. We got along fine until this happened. . . ."

Later almost all responsible officials recognized that they had failed to understand the scope of the problem. "We just did not communicate with the right people," said Mrs. Ethel Bryan, a Negro executive assistant to Mayor Yorty. "We only talked to middle-class 'leaders' when, really, Watts had no leaders at all." Similarly, in 1967, a police inspector admitted the same problem: "Soon, I hope, we will have a conference between officers and the true leaders down there . . . but we will all check our guns outside."

For anyone who talked with the people of Watts during the tragic days of August 1965 the true feelings of the Negro community soon became apparent. However inchoately expressed, the rioters again and again said that they had rebelled for three reasons: to protest against "police brutality," to get all the material goods that "whitey" had, and to demonstrate their manhood and dignity. To understand this reasoning is a first step in comprehending why Watts exploded.

[1] Letter from Howard H. Jewel to Attorney General Stanley Mosk, May 25, 1964.

"POLICE BRUTALITY"

"Never again," said Marquette Frye, whose arrest triggered the riot, "never again in this neighborhood will any young man, like my brother and me, stand by and take abuse from an officer." [2] Rightly or wrongly, almost every Negro who participated in the riot echoed this sentiment. "Police brutality is like when they arrest you where it can't be seen and whip you," a twenty-two-year-old Negro explained to reporters Jerry Cohen and William Murphy. "They grab you when you walk down the street. They pull you over and beat on you. That ain't right. Man, I was born in California—in Long Beach. But I'm a Negro, so I been arrested." [3]

I [4] found no evidence of the kind of true brutality I saw in Mississippi where, at first hand, I witnessed police terrorism,[5] but my evaluation must be tempered by two qualifications.

First, the Los Angeles police admittedly participated in sweeps of "duck ponds"—areas of high criminality—before the riots of 1965. During these raids, police randomly selected people on the street, interrogated them, and checked, for example, to see if they had failed to pay a traffic penalty. These "field investigations" were conducted regularly in Watts but never in the rich suburbs of Los Angeles. At the minimum, therefore, the Los Angeles police submitted the people of Watts to a continuing surveillance which most Negro citizens considered an insult to their dignity.

Second, during the riot itself, individual policemen may well have acted in a brutal fashion. There is conflicting testimony on this issue, so no final conclusion may be drawn. In the midst of flames and snipers, however, it is certain that some officers reacted with a fear and hatred that normally they would have controlled.

The story of Laurence Jacques, which was contradicted by the testimony of the police officers involved, typifies what many Negroes—with or without valid reason—believed happened during the riots.[6]

Jaques witnessed the shooting of one looter and the arrest of another. He, too, was then arrested, although he claimed he had done nothing, and was forced to lie on the ground with another Negro. Jacques said later that one policeman had asked another, "How many did you kill?"

The second man, supposedly answered, "I killed two niggers. Why don't you kill those two lying on the ground?"

[2] Jerry Cohen and William Murphy, *Burn, Baby, Burn* (New York: E. P. Dutton, 1966), p. 47.

[3] Cohen and Murphy, p. 204.

[4] The "I" in this case is William McCord.

[5] William McCord, *Mississippi: The Long Hot Summer* (New York: W. W. Norton, 1965).

[6] Cohen and Murphy, p. 179.

According to Jacques, the first man replied, "They won't run."

"One officer came up to me and put a shotgun at the back of my head," said Jacques. " 'Nigger, how fast can you run the fifty-yard dash?' "

"I said, 'I can't run it at all.' He kicked me in the side two times, and the other officer put his foot on the back of my head."

No officers were convicted for their behavior during the riot.

Yet stories such as Jacques's—even if they might have been complete fabrications—undeniably added fuel to the riot's flames.

"GET WHAT WHITEY HAS"

Looting of liquor, appliance, grocery, and furniture stores cost their own- ers millions of dollars. Most of the looters had never before been known as criminals (75 per cent of the adult rioters did have criminal records, but the typical adolescent looter had never been arrested before).

One unemployed man on welfare explained the motivation of some of the rioters: "They wanted everything the whites had, including color TV. They saw the stores were open. If you are hungry and don't have no money, you want anything and everything. Having no job isn't no fun. With store windows broken and the police doin' other things, what would you do?"

Objective social conditions prompted this desire to "get what whitey has." Not only did Watts have a generally high rate of unemployment, but joblessness was especially acute among young males. In the age group of seventeen to twenty-five—the element most likely to riot—about 41 per cent had not been able to find jobs.

Repeated promises in 1964 and 1965 that War on Poverty funds would soon be forthcoming were not fulfilled. The federal Office of Eco- nomic Opportunity stipulated that representatives from poor areas should participate in handling poverty funds, but city officials refused to change the composition of the responsible boards.

The looters, in other words, saw tempting items spread before them along 103rd Street, but they had no money to purchase them. Not unnatu- rally in a climate of anarchy, they took what they wanted.[7]

THE SEARCH FOR DIGNITY

An intangible but pervasive impulse guided many of the rioters: a simple desire to prove their manhood. Many men viewed the riot as an insurrec- tion against the white establishment, as a way of bringing attention to them and to their area, which had been neglected for so long.

---

[7] Thousands of guns were stolen during the riot. Of these, only some 700 have been recovered by the police—a bad omen for Watts, if rioting occurs again.

Joe, a jobless young Negro interviewed by reporters after the riot, articulated this sentiment.[8] He believed that white policemen were always stopping him during the so-called field investigations:

> It seemed like they always were trying to see if they could make me break, make me do something that would save them time. It seemed like they figured they'd eventually have me in jail and they wanted to save time.

He recalled an incident that had happened long before the riot:

> One night . . . a cop stopped me and said: "I've seen you before. You've been in jail. I'm gonna check on you, punk."
>
> That night I really wanted to do something—something to that white face. But I kept thinking about my mother, how she always had told me to stay out of trouble. I figured I'd gone this far without trouble, so I held back.

When the riot began, Joe interpreted the looting in this fashion:

> I didn't realize what they were doing when the looting began. I didn't understand the object of the looting. At first it just began with people breaking windows and taking nothing. Then I realized the object of the looting: it was to move all the whites out of Watts. We don't want white people in Watts.

Asked if another explosion might occur in Watts, Joe replied:

> Would I riot again? I just don't know. But I know the slightest thing could touch me off.
>
> If it comes again? I guess I will be there. Everybody has to be willing to sacrifice something for what he believes in. I'd be out of place, wouldn't I, if my race was out there fighting and I wasn't?
>
> We really don't live alike, the whites and the Negroes. As long as the whites keep trying to brutalize my people, I'll have to be out there trying to stop them.

Another Negro, a college graduate, summarized the search for dignity in this way:

> You can stand on 103rd Street, on the edge of Will Rogers Park, and look up and see the big silver and gray jetliners pass overhead. Watts is on one of the approach routes to Los Angeles International Airport. If you fly over and look down you cannot tell Watts is there. It does not look any different from any other part of the city. The things that make it Watts are invisible.
>
> Watts is a state of mind as well as a place. Part of what it is is

[8] Cohen and Murphy, pp. 208–209.

symbolized by the low, sweeping passage of planes overhead. Standing in the heart of Watts, you can look up and see the big world,
the expensive and expansive world, but the people in that world
cannot see you. Your existence is not visible to them. You can see
them but they cannot see you. You can never reach them. You can
shout but they won't hear you. Waving or running or jumping will
not make them see you.

There was only one time when the people up in the sky saw
the people down on the ground. . . .

That was when the flames of Watts riots leaped and spiraled
into the air, lighting up the approach route to Los Angeles International Airport. . . .

Since 1965 many agencies have launched serious efforts to transform
Watts into a community like Compton.[9] Federal aid, in the form of anti-
poverty funds, has poured into the area. New programs—credit unions,
"Head Start" training, even an art festival—have been created. Proposition 14, the measure designed to imbed segregation legally in California,
has been declared unconstitutional. The mayor has appointed a city
Human Relations Commission and ordered fuller integration among City
Hall employees. And the American Civil Liberties Union has established
complaint bureaus where citizens may voice their grievances and receive
legal counsel.

Within Watts itself, numerous indigenous organizations have sprung
up. Groups such as "SLANT" and "US" adhere to a black-power ideology
or emphasize the African cultural heritage of American Negroes.

"The Sons of Watts," composed in part of former rioters, attempts to
build community spirit by, among other things, distributing litter cans to
help clean up the debris of Watts. And, in 1966, during the "Watts Festival," this group policed a large parade (regular officers stayed out of the
area) so effectively that Mayor Sam Yorty rode in an open car and the parade was unmarred by any incidents.

Another group, the "Citizen's Alert Patrol" armed itself with tape recorders and cameras and followed police to the scene of every arrest as a
guard against "police brutality."

Still another organization, which cannot be named, claims to have infiltrated all of the others in the hope of guiding black-power energies into
constructive channels. Its young leader believes that the proliferating organizations in Watts can be brought together in a union which will become
a base for Negro economic independence and Negro political power.

All these movements may have wrought a psychological change in
Watts. Indeed, former rioters themselves make up a majority of their

[9] "Proposals for the Improvement of Human Relations in Los Angeles Metropolitan Area," Los Angeles County Commission on Human Relations, November
1965, p. 13.

membership. In 1967 one detected more hope, more dignity, and a greater sense of importance in Watts than before the riot.

But, without denigrating this possible change in spiritual climate of the central district, it must be recognized that the basic problems of Watts remain unsolved.

One barometer of potential trouble is the attitude of the younger, unskilled males. The 120 men interviewed in 1967 as part of our random sample of the Watts population voiced considerable anger about their situation. Fifty per cent believed that the riot had helped Watts; only 20 per cent believed that it had hurt. Eighty-one per cent favored the use of violence in defense of civil rights; only 19 per cent definitely opposed it. Fifty per cent said the police were abusive toward them; only 3 per cent thought the police adhered to "fair" standards of treatment. A very high proportion (78 per cent) admired the concept of black power; only 6 per cent opposed it.

Objective measures of the socioeconomic situation in Watts confirmed that little has changed since 1965:

Unemployment apparently has not been reduced. While conflicting reports exist, the weight of evidence indicates that joblessness has stayed at about the same level as before the 1965 riot. The Chamber of Commerce attempted a crash program to produce more jobs but, according to the County Human Relations Commission, came up with perhaps 200 to 300 jobs and job-training opportunities when at least 5000 were needed to make a serious impact upon the Watts problem.[10]

Further, a phenomenal high of $5,500,000 in welfare aid went into the riot area each month in 1966—a rather sure indication that the conditions of unemployment had not been alleviated. Roughly 60 per cent of Watts residents were on relief that year.

Despite these disillusioning facts, some 2000 Negroes continue to arrive in Los Angeles each month, still lured by the promise of a better life. Almost all of them settle in the central district, and few have the technical qualifications demanded by Los Angeles industry.

The face of Watts has changed little since 1965. The rubble has been cleared and littered parking lots have replaced the burned-out stores. Few businessmen have re-established their enterprises, often because they are unable to secure insurance for their premises. The businesses which have been rebuilt resemble fortresses: massive, windowless, concrete structures.

There are no signs in most of the central district, as there are in Compton, of the emergence of a Negro business class to replace whites. Some groups, such as Westminster House (a Presbyterian organization), encourage Negro "industry," but the products produced by untrained handicraft workers—ashtrays made from discarded Coke bottles, papier-mâché bracelets—could hardly bring prosperity to the region.

[10] "Proposals for the Improvement of Human Relations . . . ," p. 27.

Despite the repeal of Proposition 14, the housing pattern of Los Angeles has showed no evidence of greater integration. The Negro population has been growing at a rate about four times that of the white, and, as we have noted, almost all Negro families are congregated in the central district.

The ultimate effect of this trend has been prophesized for Los Angeles by urban expert Victor Palmieri: "This . . . is the city of the future—the very near future. A black island spreading like a giant ink blot over the heart of a metropolis which is bankrupt financially and paralyzed politically." [11]

Palmieri reasons that three established factors—the rate of population growth of Negroes, the increasing mobility of whites, and the resulting "domino effect" upon schools—guarantees that the core of Los Angeles will be all black by 1980.

He points out that Los Angeles in 1967 can hardly handle her financial problems, since the property tax rate approaches $10 per $100, a level regarded as one of "negative return" by most economists because of its hindrance to local economic growth.

Beyond this, Palmieri argues that Los Angeles County will not manage her political problems. The region is split into more than seventy autonomous cities (and even more independent school districts) which cannot reach a consensus on such issues as urban renewal, open-housing laws, or police-review boards.

Although more optimistic in its conclusions, the McCone Commission considered a similar possibility: a complete breach between whites and blacks which could result only in further violence. The Commission concluded: "So serious and so explosive is the situation that, unless it is checked, the August [1965] riots may seem by comparison to be only a curtain raiser for what could blow up one day in the future."

Yet Los Angeles has still not looked deeply into its future. Although the McCone Commission put forward some constructive ideas, it failed to recommend drastic changes in existing white institutions or to suggest ways of linking the values of the Negro subculture with those of the larger society.

Unless there are radical changes, such objective observers as sociologists Robert Blauner and Victor Palmieri foresee a crippled, festering Los Angeles, increasingly populated with frustrated Negroes. The rioters expressed their unwillingness to continue to accept indignities; until the white community realizes this, Los Angeles can look forward to more holocausts.

[11] Victor H. Palmieri, "Hard Facts About the Future of Our Cities," Los Angeles County Commission on Human Relations, 1967, p. 3.

53 / Rebellion in Newark

TOM HAYDEN

The violence that began in Watts and has continued sporadi-
cally since has highlighted other aspects of minority politics.
In the case of the riot in Newark, New Jersey, on July 12–17,
1967, one aspect of interest is the impact of workers in the
war on poverty. The programs to eliminate poverty in the
United States began with the passage of enabling legislation
by Congress in 1964. A separate organization, the Office of
Economic Opportunity, was created under the leadership of
Sargeant Shriver. Many programs, such as Head Start, Job
Corps, and the education of the children of migrant workers,
were developed. The most promising program, and also the
most controversial, was community development, a concept
based on the theory that the greatest long-run benefit for a
ghettoized group will occur if the people are trained to solve
their own problems. However, to train ghetto people to solve
their problems through the political system creates tension
within the system and is opposed by those in power. In Newark, the sequence of events prior to the actual riot showed
this pattern, and the postriot question to consider is, What will
people who are aware of their potential power and of the violence that the rest of society will unleash against them do
next?

SOURCE: From *Rebellion in Newark,* by Tom Hayden. Copyright © 1967 by
Tom Hayden. Reprinted by permission of Random House, Inc., pp. 5–7, 69, 71–72.

When Newark exploded, *Life* magazine called it "the predictable insurrection" because conditions in Newark were known to be terrible.

Leaders of the business and political communities knew as much long before the violence broke out. Business officials announced in January 1967 that their own studies showed Newark's problems to be "more grave and pressing than those of perhaps any other American city." Political officials described this grim reality in their spring application for planning funds under the Model Cities Act. According to the application, Newark has the nation's highest percentage of bad housing, the most crime per 100,000 people, the heaviest per capita tax burden, the highest rates of venereal disease, maternal mortality and new cases of tuberculosis. The city is listed second in infant mortality, second in birth rate, seventh in the absolute number of drug addicts. Its unemployment rate, more than 15 per cent in the Negro community, has been persistently high enough to qualify Newark as one of the five cities to get special assistance under the Economic Development Act.

But knowledge of the problems was not enough. Important business and political figures were deadlocked with civil rights groups over the proper solutions. The elites tended to propose pouring money into job training and social service programs through the existing agencies of government. Their priority was to restore Newark as a city suitable for business, commerce, and middle-class residents. The Chamber of Commerce newsletter, *Exec,* called for a new convention arena downtown as part of a development plan to "overwhelm the creeps" currently inhabiting Newark. The summer issue of the Chamber of Commerce magazine promised a "new life in Newark" on its cover. The article within complained that the positive features of Newark, especially its closeness to New York City and its rich undeveloped resources, are overlooked too often because of the "partially true" rumors that Newark is "crowded, it has slums, and *the Negro population is growing rapidly."* The city's vast programs for urban renewal, highways, downtown development, and most recently a 150-acre Medical School, in the heart of the ghetto, seemed almost deliberately designed to squeeze out this rapidly growing Negro community that represents a majority of the population.

Civil rights and anti-poverty activists saw the proper solution in terms of power, rather than money, for the black majority. Black people occupied only token positions in city administrative and political life and these positions were more dependent on the Mayor's will than the support of ghetto voters. Negro leaders blamed government and social agencies for fostering and neglecting problems, using federal funds to bolster their patronage rolls rather than meeting the crisis of the city. In the weeks before the riot, tensions between the government and the Negro leadership were never greater. Nearly 1000 Negroes disrupted Board of Education meetings when Mayor Hugh Addonizio tried to appoint a Democratic Party ally to an educational post over a fully-qualified Negro candidate. Another large group carried on a filibuster for weeks at Planning Board hearings on the decision to declare "blighted" the site for the Medical School. Addonizio changed his mind only slightly on the education appointment, leaving the post filled by the man who held it before. The Planning Board ended its hearings without yielding to the protest against the Medical School. Many speakers at the hearings, including leaders of the Negro Democratic "establishment," warned that Newark was on the verge of bloodshed and destruction. . . .

The conditions slowly are being created for an American form of guerrilla warfare based in the slums. The riot represents a signal of this fundamental change.

To the conservative mind the riot is essentially revolution against civilization. To the liberal mind it is an expression of helpless frustration. While the conservative is hostile and the liberal generous toward those who riot, both assume that the riot is a form of lawless, mob behavior. The liberal will turn conservative if polite methods fail to stem disorder. Against these two fundamentally similar concepts, a third one must be asserted, the concept that a riot represents people making history.

The riot is certainly an awkward, even primitive, form of history-making. But if people are barred from using the sophisticated instruments of the established order for their ends, they will find another way. Rocks and bottles are only a beginning, but they cause more attention than all the reports in Washington. To the people involved, the riot is far less lawless and far more representative than the system of arbitrary rules and prescribed channels which they confront every day. . . . [T]actics of disorder will be defined by the authorities as criminal anarchy. But it may be that disruption will create possibilities of meaningful change. This depends on whether the leaders of ghetto struggles can be more successful in building strong organization than they have been so far. Violence can contribute to shattering the status quo, but only politics and organization can transform it. The ghetto still needs the power to decide its destiny on such matters as urban renewal and housing, social services, policing, and taxation. Tenants still need concrete rights against landlords in public and private housing, or a new system of tenant-controlled living conditions. Welfare clients still need a livable income. Consumers still need to control the quality of merchandise and service in the stores where they shop. Citizens still need effective control over those who police their community. Political structures belonging to the community are needed to bargain for, and maintain control over, funds from government or private sources. In order to build a more decent community while resisting racist power, more than violence is required. People need to create self-government. We are at a point where democracy—the idea and practice of people controlling their lives —is a revolutionary issue in the United States.

54 / The Kerner Commission Report

**NATIONAL ADVISORY COMMISSION
ON CIVIL DISORDERS**

As a result of the several long, hot summers of violence in the urban centers of the North and the continuing tension between police and the black ghetto dwellers, President Johnson decided in 1967 to appoint a commission to study the causes of these events and to recommend changes in government policy. The group, called the National Advisory Commission on Civil Disorder, was headed by Governor Otto Kerner of Illinois and came to be known as the Kerner Commission. Its report was issued in the spring of 1967 and caused an immediate sensation because it laid the responsibility for the riots not on the black community alone or even primarily, but on American society, which, it concluded, was racist; therefore the responsibility for correction lay with the white majority. The commission rejection of the theory that a conspiracy of communist militants was causing the riots—a theory popular with the police especially—contributed to the relative lack of support for the report. The recommendations, which included specific proposals for changes in police practices, have been almost entirely disregarded, and the report has had little influence on government policy.

SOURCE: National Advisory Commission on Civil Disorders, *Report* (Washington, D.C.: U.S. Government Printing Office, 1968), pp. 71, 91–93, 265.

Once the series of precipitating incidents culminated in violence, the riot process followed no uniform pattern in the 24 disorders surveyed. However, some similarities emerge.

The final incident before the outbreak of disorder, and the initial violence itself, generally occurred at a time and place in which it was normal for many people to be on the streets. In most of the 24 disorders, groups generally estimated at 50 or more persons were on the street at the time and place of the first outbreak.

In all 24 disturbances, including the three university-related disorders, the initial disturbance area consisted of streets with relatively high concentrations of pedestrian and automobile traffic at the time. In all but two cases—Detroit and Milwaukee—violence started between 7:00 P.M. and 12:30 A.M., when the largest numbers of pedestrians could be expected. Ten of the 24 disorders erupted on Friday night, Saturday or Sunday.

In most instances, the temperature during the day on which violence first erupted was quite high. This contributed to the size of the crowds on the street, particularly in areas of congested housing.

Major violence occurred in all 24 disorders during the evening and night hours, between 6:00 P.M. and 6:00 A.M., and in most cases between 9:00 P.M. and 3:00 A.M. In only a few disorders, including Detroit and Newark, did substantial violence occur or continue during the daytime. Generally, the night-day cycles continued in daily succession through the early period of the disorder.

At the beginning of disorder, violence generally flared almost immediately after the final precipitating incident. It then escalated quickly to its peak level, in the case of one-night disorders, and to the first night peak in the case of continuing disorders. In Detroit and Newark, the first outbreaks began within two hours and reached severe, although not the highest, levels within three hours.

In almost all of the subsequent night-day cycles, the change from relative order to a state of disorder by a number of people typically occurred extremely rapidly—within one or two hours at the most.

Nineteen of the surveyed disorders lasted more than one night. In 10 of these, violence peaked on the first night, and the level of activity on subsequent nights was the same or less. In the other nine disorders, however, the peak was reached on a subsequent night.

Disorder generally began with less serious violence against property, such as rock and bottle throwing and window breaking. These were usually the materials and the targets closest to hand at the place of the initial outbreak.

Once store windows were broken, looting usually followed. Whether fires were set only after looting occurred is unclear. Reported instances of fire-bombing and Molotov cocktails in the 24 disorders appeared to occur as frequently during one cycle of violence as during another in disorders which continued through more than one cycle. However, fires seemed to break out more frequently during the middle cycles of riots lasting several days. Gunfire and sniping were also reported more frequently during the middle cycles.

We have seen what happened. Why did it happen?

In addressing this question we shift our focus from the local to the national scene, from the particular events of the summer of 1967 to the factors within the society at large which have brought about the sudden violent mood of so many urban Negroes.

The record before this Commission reveals that the causes of recent racial disorders are imbedded in a massive tangle of issues and circumstances—social, economic, political, and psychological—which arise out of the historical pattern of Negro-white relations in America.

These factors are both complex and interacting: they vary significantly in their effect from city to city and from year to year; and the consequences of one disorder, generating new grievances and new demands, become the causes of the next. It is this which creates the "thicket of tension, conflicting evidence and extreme opinions" cited by the President.

Despite these complexities, certain fundamental matters are clear. Of these, the most fundamental is the racial attitude and behavior of white Americans toward black Americans. Race prejudice has shaped our history decisively in the past: it now threatens to do so again. White racism is essentially responsible for the explosive mixture which has been accumulating in our cities since the end of World War II. At the base of this mixture are three of the most bitter fruits of white racial attitudes:

PERVASIVE DISCRIMINATION
AND SEGREGATION

The first is surely the continuing exclusion of great numbers of Negroes from the benefits of economic progress through discrimination in employment and education, and their enforced confinement in segregated housing and schools. The corrosive and degrading effects of this condition and the attitudes that underlie it are the source of the deepest bitterness and at the center of the problem of racial disorder.

BLACK MIGRATION AND
WHITE EXODUS

The second is the massive and growing concentration of impoverished Negroes in our major cities resulting from Negro migration from the rural South, rapid population growth and the continuing movement of the white middle-class to the suburbs. The consequence is a greatly increased burden on the already depleted resources of cities, creating a growing crisis of deteriorating facilities and services and unmet human needs.

BLACK GHETTOS

Third, in the teeming racial ghettos, segregation and poverty have intersected to destroy opportunity and hope and to enforce failure. The ghettos too often mean men and women without jobs, families without men, and schools where children are processed instead of educated, until they return to the street—to crime, to narcotics, to dependency on welfare, and to bitterness and resentment against society in general and white society in particular.

These three forces have converged on the inner city in recent years and on the people who inhabit it. At the same time, most whites and many Negroes outside the ghetto have prospered to a degree unparalleled in the history of civilization. Through television—the universal appliance in the ghetto—and the other media of mass communications, this affluence has been endlessly flaunted before the eyes of the Negro poor and the jobless ghetto youth.

As Americans, most Negro citizens carry within themselves two basic aspirations of our society. They seek to share in both the material resources of our system and its intangible benefits—dignity, respect and acceptance. Outside the ghetto many have succeeded in achieving a decent standard of life, and in developing the inner resources which give life meaning and direction. Within the ghetto, however, it is rare that either aspiration is achieved.

Yet these facts alone—fundamental as they are—cannot be said to have caused the disorders. Other and more immediate factors help explain why these events happened now.

Recently, three powerful ingredients have begun to catalyze the mixture.

FRUSTRATED HOPES

The expectations aroused by the great judicial and legislative victories of the civil rights movement have led to frustration, hostility and cyncism in the face of the persistent gap between promise and fulfillment. The dramatic struggle for equal rights in the South has sensitized Northern Negroes to the economic inequalities reflected in the deprivations of ghetto life.

LEGITIMATION OF VIOLENCE

A climate that tends toward the approval and encouragement of violence as a form of protest has been created by white terrorism directed against nonviolent protest, including instances of abuse and even murder of some civil rights workers in the South; by the open defiance of law and federal authority by state and local officials resisting desegregation; and by some protest groups engaging in civil disobedience who turn their backs on non-violence, go beyond the Constitutionally protected rights of petition and free assembly, and resort to violence to attempt to compel alteration of laws and policies with which they disagree. This condition has been rein-forced by a general erosion of respect for authority in American society and reduced effectiveness of social standards and community restraints on violence and crime. This in turn has largely resulted from rapid urbaniza-tion and the dramatic reduction in the average age of the total population.

POWERLESSNESS

Finally, many Negroes have come to believe that they are being exploited politically and economically by the white "power structure." Negroes, like people in poverty everywhere, in fact lack the channels of communication, influence and appeal that traditionally have been available to ethnic minor-ities within the city and which enabled them—unburdened by color—to scale the walls of the white ghettos in an earlier era. The frustrations of powerlessness have led some to the conviction that there is no effective al-ternative to violence as a means of expression and redress, as a way of "moving the system." More generally, the result is alienation and hostility toward the institutions of law and government and the white society which controls them. This is reflected in the reach toward racial consciousness and solidarity reflected in the slogan "Black Power."

These facts have combined to inspire a new mood among Negroes, particularly among the young. Self-esteem and enhanced racial pride are replacing apathy and submission to "the system." Moreover, Negro youth, who make up over half of the ghetto population, share the growing sense of alienation felt by many white youth in our country. Thus, their role in recent civil disorders reflects not only a shared sense of deprivation and victimization by white society but also the rising incidence of disruptive conduct by a segment of American youth throughout the society.

INCITEMENT AND ENCOURAGEMENT
OF VIOLENCE

These conditions have created a volatile mixture of attitudes and beliefs which needs only a spark to ignite mass violence. Strident appeals to vio-lence, first heard from white racists, were echoed and reinforced last summer in the inflammatory rhetoric of black racists and militants. Throughout the year, extremists crisscrossed the country preaching a doctrine of black power and violence. Their rhetoric was widely reported in the mass media; it was echoed by local "militants" and organizations; it became the ugly background noise of the violent summer.

We cannot measure with any precision the influence of these organizations and individuals in the ghetto, but we think it clear that the intolerable and unconscionable encouragement of violence heightened tensions, created a mood of acceptance and an expectation of violence, and thus contributed to the eruption of the disorders last summer.

THE POLICE

It is the convergence of all these factors that makes the role of the police so difficult and so significant. Almost invariably the incident that ignites disorder arises from police action. Harlem, Watts, Newark and Detroit—all the major outbursts of recent years—were precipitated by routine arrests of Negroes for minor offenses by white police.

But the police are not merely the spark. In discharge of their obligation to maintain order and insure public safety in the disruptive conditions of ghetto life, they are inevitably involved in sharper and more frequent conflicts with ghetto residents than with the residents of other areas. Thus, to many Negroes police have come to symbolize white power, white racism and white repression. And the fact is that many police do reflect and express these white attitudes. The atmosphere of hostility and cynicism is reinforced by a widespread perception among Negroes of the existence of police brutality and corruption, and of a "double standard" of justice and protection—one for Negroes and one for whites.

To this point, we have attempted only to identify the prime components of the "explosive mixture." In the chapters that follow we seek to analyze them in the perspective of history. Their meaning, however, is already clear:

In the summer of 1967, we have seen in our cities a chain reaction of racial violence. If we are heedless, we shall none of us escape the consequences. . . .

CONCLUSION

One of the first witnesses to be invited to appear before this Commission was Dr. Kenneth B. Clark, a distinguished and perceptive scholar. Referring to the reports of earlier riot commissions, he said:

> I read that report . . . of the 1919 riot in Chicago, and it is as if I were reading the report of the investigating committee on the Harlem riot of '35, the report of the investigating committee on the Harlem riot of '43, the report of the McCone Commission on the Watts riot.
>
> I must again in candor say to you members of this Commission—it is a kind of Alice in Wonderland—with the same moving picture re-shown over and over again, the same analysis, the same recommendations, and the same inaction.

These words come to our minds as we conclude this Report.

We have provided an honest beginning. We have learned much. But we have uncovered no startling truths, no unique insights, no simple solutions. The destruction and the bitterness of racial disorder, the harsh polemics of black revolt and white repression have been seen and heard before in this country.

It is time now to end the destruction and the violence, not only in the streets of the ghetto but in the lives of people.